Creative Arts Marketing

Books are to be returned on or before
the last date below.

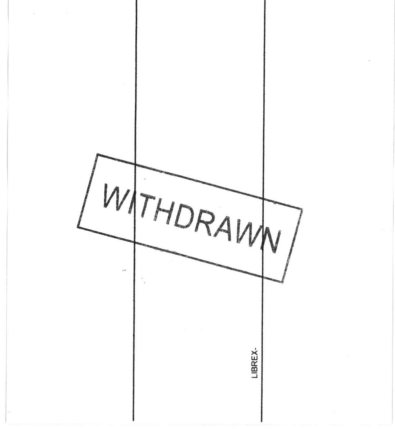

LIBREX-

Creative Arts Marketing

Second edition

Liz Hill, Catherine O'Sullivan and
Terry O'Sullivan

AMSTERDAM BOSTON HEIDELBERG LONDON NEW YORK OXFORD
PARIS SAN DIEGO SAN FRANCISCO SINGAPORE SYDNEY TOKYO

Butterworth-Heinemann is an imprint of Elsevier
Linacre House, Jordan Hill, Oxford OX2 8DP, UK
30 Corporate Drive, Suite 400, Burlington, MA 01803, USA

First edition 1995
Second edition 2003
Reprinted 2004, 2006 (twice), 2007, 2008

Notice
No responsibility is assumed by the publisher for any injury and/or damage to persons
or property as a matter of products liability, negligence or otherwise, or from any use
or operation of any methods, products, instructions or ideas contained in the material
herein. Because of rapid advances in the medical sciences, in particular, independent
verification of diagnoses and drug dosages should be made

British Library Cataloguing in Publication Data
Hill, Elizabeth, 1960 –
  Creative arts marketing. – 2nd ed.
  1. Arts – Marketing. – 2nd ed
  I. Title II. O'Sullivan III. O'Sullivan, Terry, 1957 –
  700.6'88

Library of Congress Cataloging-in-Publication Data
A catalog record for this book is available from the Library of Congress

ISBN: 978-0-7506-5737-2

For information on all Butterworth-Heinemann publications
visit our website at books.elsevier.com

Printed and bound in *Hungary*

08 09 10 10 9 8 7 6

Working together to grow
libraries in developing countries

www.elsevier.com | www.bookaid.org | www.sabre.org

ELSEVIER   BOOK AID
            International   Sabre Foundation

Contents

Foreword

And old Dave, he'd go up to his room, y'understand, put on his green velvet slippers – I'll never forget – and pick up his phone and call the buyers, and without leaving his room, at the age of eighty-four, he made his living. And when I saw that, I realized that selling was the greatest career a man could want. 'Cause what could be more satisfying than to be able to go, at the age of eighty-four, into twenty or thirty different cities, and pick up a phone, and be remembered and loved and helped by so many different people? . . . In those days there was personality in it. There was respect, and comradeship, and gratitude in it. Today, it's all cut and dried, and there's no chance for bringing friendship to bear – or personality.
Arthur Miller, *Death of a Salesman.* Reprinted by permission of International Creative Management, Inc. Copyright © 1961 Arthur Miller

Marketing is still often confused with sales – the two terms become interchangeable. And in popular terms, both become less than honourable professions with less than honourable intentions – selling us something we do not want to buy. It's all cut and dried.

I hope I am just being over sensitive.

As the introduction to this book explains, marketing has come a long way in a relatively short time. Arts marketing as a discipline has had to cover the same ground in an even shorter period of time. So still, in the arts as in business, it is often maligned and often misunderstood. Definitions of marketing are plentiful and various. It does not help the cause that at any one time marketing can be a business philosophy, an organizational function and a process with a toolkit of techniques and tactics. So is it surprising that within arts organizations it is frequently interpreted narrowly and applied narrowly? Consequently, rather than a management function it becomes the work of one department working in isolation, rather than a planned and strategic process it becomes a reactive exercise, rather than understood and embraced by all it becomes the province of the specialist.

There are elements of arts marketing which should always remain the province of the 'specialist', but the underlying principles of marketing in all/any of its guises must be understood by those leading, managing and funding the organization. Equally it must be acknowledged that marketing is there to enable the organization to achieve all its objectives: financial, social and artistic. There can be inherent tensions in the latter but if the organization is clear about its objectives and is honest about its reasons for pursuing them, these tensions can be understood, incorporated and even used creatively.

Creativity is at the heart of arts marketing – and not simply because what is being marketed is the product of an individual or group creative act. Arts marketing needs to communicate an experience; and an experience that can be elusive, indescribable, transformative, or simply bloody good fun. To create effective, persuasive communication for a variety of audiences – almost certainly with limited resources – requires imaginative solutions. As with any creative act the rewards for carrying this off successfully are huge.

If you are reading this book as someone who is working in arts marketing or interested in doing so, make sure this book is not far from your desk. Your task will be to marry the theory, knowledge and good practice contained within with your individual situation – and probably on that limited budget. Good luck!

If you are a policy-maker, producer or manager, I hope that this book serves to deepen understanding of how marketing can serve arts organizations. If you do not already embrace an integrated approach with a central focus on the audience, I hope you will be persuaded otherwise by what you read here.

Finally if you ever doubt the true value or real purpose of arts marketing, I would urge you simply to remember the first time you yourself were taken to a gallery, theatre or concert and were moved or inspired. The 'product' we have can be unbeatable. The marketing of it requires patience, dedication, enthusiasm, imagination and passion. In return there may not be gratitude at every step but there is community, satisfaction, respect, friendship. What could be more satisfying?

Ivan Wadeson
Chair, Arts Marketing Association

The Arts Marketing Association, in existence in the UK since 1993, aims to support the personal and professional development of its members through a range of services, events, training and advice. If *Creative Arts Marketing* has whetted your appetite and you would like to join a thriving community of arts professionals interested in bringing audiences into contact with the arts, find out more at www.a-m-a.co.uk

Acknowledgements

In the first edition of this book the Acknowledgements section named the friends and colleagues who had helped us on the book with their ideas, experience, example and inspiration. For the second edition those thanks still stand – but the list of people to whom we owe profound gratitude has grown to the point where we feel uncomfortable about naming names in case somebody gets left out. So, to all of you who have offered advice, answered questions, read and commented on sections, and demonstrated how to combine creativity, artistry and marketing – thanks for your patience and generosity.

We would also like to take this opportunity to thank those individuals and organizations who have given use permission to use and adapt material for this book. Every effort has been made to trace the owners of copyright material, though in a few cases this has proved impossible and we apologize to any copyright holders whose rights may have been unwittingly infringed. We trust that in the event of any accidental infringement, the owners of the material will contact us directly.

Introduction

A (very) brief history of marketing

This book is aimed at people who are working in the arts (as practitioners, policy-makers, producers or managers), or studying arts marketing, management or policy, or even just studying marketing and looking for a fresh perspective. You may be part of a professional or voluntary organization, or you may be in the commercial or public sector. As authors we cannot take too much for granted about how much you know about marketing or even what you feel about marketing. Perhaps you have picked up this book gingerly, dubious of the desirability of applying tacky marketing techniques to something as important as the arts. Or perhaps you are happy about marketing in general, but sceptical about the difference it can make to the success of your organization or project.

This introduction is here to help you. We hope that, whatever your background, reading it will put you in a better position to understand and apply the ideas we cover in more detail in the rest of the book. It may answer some of the doubts or uncertainties you have about the appropriateness of marketing to arts organizations, and it may help clarify your expectations of the kind of contribution marketing can make. In it we intend to trace a brief (and necessarily oversimplified) history of marketing itself – and how it has grown from its origins in commercial organizations to applications in a variety of other situations. This will clarify how it differs from less effective approaches to running an organization which are often confused with it (namely, product orientation and sales orientation). Such clarification is important, particularly when defending the marketing concept in the face of criticism which may be laid more appropriately at the door of one or other rival approach.

In the beginning . . .

Marketing, whether in the arts or in any other field of human enterprise, is simply the active recognition by organizations that without customers they have nothing but costs. From that point of view, you could argue that the history of marketing is merely the history of common sense. But marketing as a recognized management discipline tends to trace its origins to the mid-twentieth century. It first emerged in post-war America, when, spurred by technological progress, industry found itself capable of producing consumer goods on an unprecedented scale for a newly-prosperous workforce. Manufacturers discovered that in the face of increased competition they had to rethink their attitudes to business. The old ways of operating, which had concentrated on the organization's view of its own products as good enough in themselves (product orientation), or on its need to sell products which its customers might not necessarily choose for themselves (sales orientation), were no longer working (Keith, 1960).

Product-led businesses maintained that if a product was of sufficiently high quality people would flock to buy it on its own merits. It is an attitude rather like that attributed to Ralph Waldo Emerson in the famous dictum that 'If a man . . . make a better mouse-trap than his neighbour, tho' he build his house in the woods, the world will make a beaten path to his door' (*Oxford Dictionary of Quotations*, 1953: 201). Certainly, as we shall stress in this book, quality is essential to marketing success. In the arts a central part of a customer's experience is the sense of excellence itself – the deftness of a painter, the grace of a dancer, the 'rightness' of a theatrical moment, the welcome extended by a venue. But in an environment where there are so many other claims on people's attention and energies, the arts cannot afford to hide their light, however bright, under a bushel. Excellent work needs energetic marketing, or it runs the risk of not being noticed.

Sales-led businesses maintained that the key to success lay in an organization's ability to sell its goods to customers. High-pressure sales techniques appeared to offer a way for businesses to browbeat their way to prosperity. It is probably true that, given energy and application, you can sell anything. But you will probably only be able to sell it once unless it satisfies a genuine need in your customer. The principles of selling, as we shall see, have an essential role in the way that arts organizations service their customers. Certainly arts marketers need to be as evangelistic about their product as the most fervent 'foot in the door' sales representative. But genuine success in the arts, as elsewhere, lies in seeing customers as partners rather than targets. Long-term relationships based on mutual benefit are the key to this.

The marketing approach facilitates such relationships. The UK industry's lead body, the Chartered Institute of Marketing, defines it as 'the management process which identifies, anticipates, and supplies customer requirements profitably'. By moving the focus of an organization's planning and decision-making on to a consideration of its customers' requirements, what the organization produces can be made more appropriate to their needs. This in turn should lead to their choice of it above the alternatives available in the marketplace, guaranteeing an organization's success and growth. As we have already observed, this may sound like nothing more than common sense. But by their very nature organizations have a tendency to drift away from external focus to considering their own interests and convenience first, even to the point where they lose touch with their customers (Levitt, 1960).

Marketing, then, is a total approach to the way an organization operates. It is, to quote the definition, a 'management process'. This has two implications. The first is that it should imbue every aspect of the way an organization is run. Marketing is too important to be left to the marketing department alone. It will not work unless the organization as a whole adopts it. The second implication, stemming from the fact that it is a 'process', means that the job of marketing never ends. It needs to be finding new ways of improvement, new areas where an organization can develop its approach to customers to the long-term benefit of each party. The corollary of this is that marketing itself is in a process of development, as it responds dynamically to the challenges offered by a changing environment.

Marketing moves on

A large number of manufacturing firms on both sides of the Atlantic adopted the marketing approach in the late 1950s and 1960s, and the influence of American business thought in post-war reconstruction guaranteed its diffusion further afield, particularly to Japan. The geographical spread was paralleled by a spread in application. From its origins in manufacturing industries producing products for ordinary consumers, marketing found new realms to conquer, such as services (like banking or accountancy) and industrial goods (such as capital equipment). These developments were spurred by writers such as the American Philip Kotler, who maintained that 'marketing is a relevant discipline for all organizations insofar as all organizations can be said to have customers and products' (Kotler and Levy, 1969).

A particularly important development was the spread of marketing into the service sector from the early 1970s. Industries in this sector, which includes the arts alongside medicine, tourism, transport, professional and financial services, are now worth more in most developed economies than the manufacturing industries from which marketing principles originally developed. Unlike manufacturing industries, service organizations offer their customers an intangible service rather than a product which can be handled and examined. As we shall see in Chapter 4, this presents particular problems and opportunities for marketing which result in a distinctive approach to how services are marketed. An important point to note is that this distinctiveness is typical of the way in which marketing thinking and practice adapt to new areas of application, even though the core idea of the central importance of customers remains unchanged.

Even the concept of customers, however, is a problematic one for some of the organizations into which marketing has spread since the 1980s. Talking about customers carries connotations of simple commercial exchanges which are inappropriate in areas such as healthcare, education and the arts, where organizations often prefer to describe their customers as clients or service users. In such organizations the imperative to make a profit (which is the rationale for marketing in the commercial sector) often exists alongside, or is replaced completely by, other organizational objectives. Furthermore, the nature of the exchange between such organizations and the people they serve may not involve any immediate financial consideration (as in free admission to

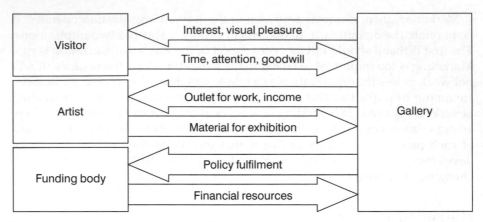

Figure 1 Exchange relationships for a gallery

an art gallery), nor even a clearly identifiable single customer on which to concentrate. For example, the art gallery's customer could be argued to be the visitor, the artist or, for a public sector gallery, the funding body. All three bring resources without which the gallery could not survive (namely, attendance and patronage, contemporary works of art, and funding) but all three want different things from their exchange with the gallery (Figure 1).

Non-profit and public-sector organizations are well represented in the arts sector. Such organizations present a further tier of complexity to marketing because of their diversity of purpose. According to a classic article by Hofstede (1981), non-profits often have ambiguous goals and objectives and there is frequently internal disagreement on how these are to be achieved most effectively. The situation is further complicated by the difficulty of measuring outputs meaningfully. At least profit-oriented companies have a clear criterion for success – the return they offer on investment. As we shall see, the bottom line in the arts is smudged not only by the varying objectives of different organizations, but by the difficulty of measuring the impact and value of the activities they generate. Marketing's role in such organizations is to offer a route to effectiveness: the achievement of organizational objectives which will include, but not be limited to, financial ones. Marketing has therefore moved on from an automatic association with big business – its analytical models and techniques are relevant to a much wider field.

Contemporary marketing: stakeholders and relationships

Its application in non-profit contexts is one of the factors driving developments in the way marketing is carried out more generally. A perennial issue for non-profits, many of which receive subsidy from national or local government, is to be able to manage the political environment. By political here we mean not just the narrow sense of who is in government, but the wider field of opinions and interests which affect an organization. The concept of stakeholders is a central one in this regard, and has long been of importance in non-profit and arts marketing. It is a concept to which we will return in Chapter 2. Put simply, a

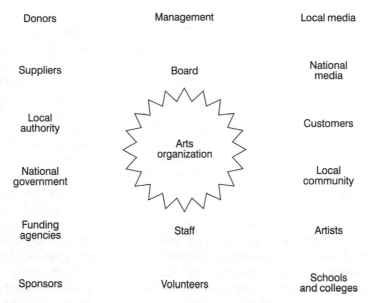

Donors   Management   Local media

Suppliers   Board   National media

Local authority   Customers

                  Arts organization

National government   Local community

Funding agencies Staff   Artists

Sponsors   Volunteers   Schools and colleges

Figure 2 Stakeholders for an arts organization

stakeholder is any group or individual who has an interest (a 'stake') in the success of an organization. Stakeholders may not even be direct customers of the organization in question but they affect its access to resources and support. For an arts organization such groups might include funding bodies, local and national government, the media, the local community, the professional community and so on. Because of their lack of material resources, much of the marketing effort of non-profit organizations has traditionally focused on establishing and maintaining a good reputation with a wide variety of influential publics. Arts organizations have a public relations advantage here, because the news media tend to be interested in their output, and even dedicate specialist correspondents to their coverage.

Following its recognition of the importance of stakeholders, a second major change affecting marketing thinking in the last few decades has been the environment in which it takes place. As we have seen, the marketing concept dates from the mid-twentieth century. In those days, many of the industries which embraced marketing had plenty of potential to grow. The emphasis was, therefore, on finding new customers. Towards the beginning of the twenty-first century, however, growth slowed down or stopped in most of the traditional marketing-led industries. With a few exceptions, the developed economies of the West now feature static or declining markets. The need to seek new customers is still there, but the emphasis in most industries has moved to retaining existing ones.

This newly-defensive environment for marketing has led to a rethink about its direction and purpose. The emphasis in many businesses has moved from recruiting new customers and hoping they will stay, to analysing and managing long-term relationships with existing customers to try and make sure of keeping them. Marketing theorists call the first kind of marketing 'transaction based' because of its concern to facilitate exchanges (rather like single-ticket purchases in a theatre). The second kind, with its emphasis on a continuing relationship (rather like subscription-based marketing in the performing arts) is known as relationship marketing. While relationship marketing is not appropriate for every kind of product or service, the traditional transaction-based conception of marketing has given way to a relational one in much marketing theory and practice since the 1990s. The scarcity of new customers has led to a concentration on building and maintaining links with existing customers – and the decreasing cost of computer technology has meant that marketers have been able to gather and use information about customers which helps them to do this. Furthermore, the emergence of powerful new technologies such as the internet has made it easier than ever before to maintain an informed relationship with customers.

Relationship-marketing theorists go so far as to stress the need to create a relationship before exchanges can take place, rather than seeing a relationship as the result of such transactions (Grönroos, 1994). Thus charities will invest money and resources in what they call 'donor acquisition', running events or mailings in order to attract supporters. The initial outlay means that the charity will only see a return on the investment months, or perhaps years, into the relationship. It encourages them to think of their donors, or customers, as assets. Rather than thinking about the value of individual sales or donations made by a customer, such organizations focus on the value of a customer throughout his or her lifetime. The attraction of such an approach to marketing the arts, where a long-term relationship with an audience is often an essential strand of artistic policy, is clear. At the same time, much arts marketing is driven by a missionary zeal to reach out to new audiences – making transaction-based marketing (with an eye to the longer term) of continuing relevance as an essential audience development strategy. The tensions between the two varieties of approach have been the source of some stimulating controversy, particularly in the UK arts marketing community – although, in the long term, the rival schools of thought may have more in common than their advocates care to admit.

From consumers to stakeholders

Faced with a 40 per cent decrease in audiences over two years in the mid-1990s, Coventry's famous Belgrade Theatre changed its approach to marketing. In classic 'relationship-marketing' style, it reframed its marketing efforts on its existing customers, talking to them and learning from them rather than just selling to them. From its research, the theatre came to the conclusion that the decline in audiences had happened because it had taken their loyalty for granted, in a relationship which only went one way. In much the same way as a football club expects to count on a local following, the Belgrade had made the assumption that local theatregoers would gravitate towards it as of right. In fact the dwindling audience figures provided evidence that it was losing touch with its natural constituency.

In a radical shift of policy it began to change its relationship with the audience. In the words of the Belgrade's head of marketing at the time: 'The Belgrade has formed a much closer partnership with its customers, involving them in the strategic processes of the organization, seeing them as stakeholders rather than end-consumers. The marketing activities of the theatre centre around talking to and learning from its audiences, which influences decision-making. The venue's work has now been recognized as striking a balance between innovation and populism, steering a course of non-cynical customer focus. The Belgrade has learned that loyalty as a concept is no longer valid and focuses on alliance or, more exactly, equity.'

Source: Daykin, 1998, reproduced by kind permission.

Summary

We have briefly reviewed what differentiates marketing from other ways of managing organizations which are sometimes confused with it (i.e. product orientation and sales orientation). What distinguishes marketing is its orientation towards the customer, moving the focus of an organization's planning and decision-making on to a consideration of its customers' requirements. In the long term, such orientation produces organizations that are more profitable or more effective (depending on their objectives) than their rivals.

Marketing as a named management approach has its roots in 1940s' American consumer-goods businesses. Since that time its application has spread to business-to-business contexts, service markets and non-profit markets including the arts. New areas of application, and changes in the environment for existing markets, have revealed a focus on two linked themes in contemporary marketing: stakeholders and relationship marketing. Stakeholder marketing addresses a wider range of publics than an organization's immediate customers. It takes into account all the different groups who have an interest in the organization, and who can affect its access to resources. Relationship marketing emphasizes the long-term value of customers rather than concentrating exclusively on isolated transactions with anonymous buyers. Both of these ways of thinking about marketing owe a good deal to the experience of applying marketing outside the commercial sector. They are particularly relevant to arts marketing – which needs to consider a wide range of important and influential publics, and has a mission to develop life-long relationships with them.

References

Daykin, S. (1998) 'Why audiences love being sent to Coventry', *ArtsBusiness*, 7 December, 11.

Grönroos, C. (1994) 'From marketing mix to relationship marketing', *Management Decision*, Vol. 32, No. 2, 4–20.

Hofstede, G. (1981) 'Management control of public and not-for-profit activities', *Accounting, Organisations and Society, Vol. 6, No. 3, 193–211.*

Keith, R.J. (1960) 'The marketing revolution', Journal of Marketing, January, 35–8.

Kotler, P. and Levy, S. (1969) 'Broadening the concept of marketing', *Journal of Marketing*, Vol. 33, January, 10–15.

Levitt, T. (1960) 'Marketing myopia', *Harvard Business Review,* 38, July–August, 24–47.

Oxford Dictionary of Quotations (1953) 2nd ed. Oxford University Press.

1

The evolution and context of arts marketing

This chapter sets the context for the chapters which follow. In it we will examine the nature and environment of arts marketing, and flag up some key issues facing arts marketers. Marketing the arts involves not only the day-to-day work of attracting audiences to events and activities, but also the need to understand and promote more widely the value of an organization's work. Arts marketers are arts advocates. They need to take an active interest in cultural policy and the political environment if their work is to be solidly based. Arts marketers are also marketing advocates. They need to understand what marketing is (and what it is not) in order to enthuse their colleagues towards achieving their shared objectives. This chapter seeks to sketch out in broad strokes some of the most important of these issues as a foundation for thinking about arts marketing practice.

The issues we will address are as follows:

- the evolution of arts marketing theory and practice
- the arts marketing environment
- key issues and problems for arts marketers: the arguments about arts subsidy, the peculiarities of the sector, the arm's-length principle, excellence vs. accessibility, professional and amateur arts, traditional vs. new art forms, special constituencies, and internal resistance to marketing in arts organizations.

Definition: Arts marketing is an integrated management process which sees mutually satisfying exchange relationships with customers as the route to achieving organizational and artistic objectives.

This definition sums up the understanding of arts marketing that we are trying to convey throughout this book. It is integrated because it needs to harmonize all of the activities of the organization around the customer. It is a management process because it needs to reflect vision and commitment at the most senior level, and we use the word 'process' because creative marketing is constantly learning about what it is doing, in order to do it better throughout the scope of an organization's activities. Creative arts marketing works through mutually satisfying exchange because it values reciprocity – indeed, it sees the essence of arts experience as an active, participative process. It focuses on relationships because it is interested in growing both the organization and the customer over a meaningful period of time rather than seeing the encounter as an isolated transaction. It focuses on customers because their needs define the relevance of an organization's work, and their resources empower it. Finally, it claims for marketing not only a key role in promoting organizational survival, but also in advancing the artistic mission of an arts organization. By integrating a marketing perspective into the artistic planning process, it seeks to bring the audience into the beginning stage of the process, as well as its culmination stage of performance, exhibition or event.

The evolution of arts marketing: theory

Philip Kotler, whose work we have cited in the Introduction, was one of the first advocates of marketing's relevance to the arts – arguing that arts organizations produce 'cultural goods', and in doing so compete with each other for consumers' attention and for a share of national resources (Kotler, 1975). Later marketing authors have explored the tensions implicit in marketing cultural goods, in an attempt to reconcile giving customers what they want with the artist's need to find an outlet for creative expression independent of market forces. The quality and value of cultural goods frequently depend on their originality or radical nature. Features such as familiarity, which might increase appeal to consumers, or political expediency, which might help access external resources, are not necessarily to be found in good art.

One of the first books to concern itself with arts marketing specifically (Mokwa *et al.*, 1980) acknowledges this tension as a point of difference between arts marketing and commercial marketing. In its commercial incarnation (at least as commonly understood), marketing dictates the nature of a product or service through conforming it to the requirements of the customer. The artist, on the other hand, needs to create independently of such conformance, because of the special nature of cultural goods. Marketing's role is, therefore, not to influence the kind of art produced but solely 'to match the artist's creations and interpretations with an appropriate audience' (Mokwa *et al.*, 1980). This matching, rather than shaping, role is echoed by another early writer whose definition of arts marketing stresses its role in bringing 'an appropriate number of people into an appropriate form of contact with the artist' (Diggle, 1984). Melillo (1983) sees marketing as tainted by its association with commerce, arguing that the arts require marketing principles and practices to be 'transformed before they are integrated into the creative process'. More recently, Hirschman (1993) and Colbert *et al.* (1994; 2001), have developed the notion of the independence of the arts 'product' from the dictates of market forces as a distinguishing feature of arts marketing. Arts marketing is a special case, they argue, because it needs to start with the product and find customers for it, rather than react to market demand.

Does the central importance of artistic product mean that marketing orientation in the arts is really only what we have called product orientation under a different name? Another recent writer (Butler, 2000) suggests that it may. He argues that arts marketing actually has strong overtones not only of product orientation but also of sales orientation – the other heresy we outlined in the Introduction. According to him, arts marketing presents a challenge to marketing orientation in its accepted sense.

Certainly the extension of marketing to areas like the arts has led to developments in theory and practice (such as the importance of networks and relationships mentioned earlier). But there is no fundamental contradiction between emphasis of the arts on product quality and our earlier idea of marketing as beginning with the customer. Customer focus in orthodox marketing has always involved harmonizing internal capacity with external opportunity. One of the UK's most influential writers on strategic marketing identifies the central idea of marketing as 'a matching between a company's capabilities and the wants of customers in order to achieve the objectives of both parties' (McDonald, 1999). While the customer is the critical factor in the equation (because he or she brings resources to the organization), the nature of the product and the organization's objectives also need careful consideration in the exchange – whether commercial or non-profit. Thus, while artistic planning cannot be dominated by market forces, marketing needs to be an integral part of the process of artistic planning. That is one of the reasons why we argue that marketing is a creative process.

Furthermore, marketing's role, even in the commercial sector, is not simply to relay what customers say they want to the production department, stand back and wait for the money to roll in. Quite apart from the difficulty of interpreting research and market trends, just asking customers what they want is unlikely to yield genuinely innovative ideas. The Sony Walkman is only one example of a new and unfamiliar product idea to be misunderstood or even resisted in research, before going on to become a spectacular success when eventually brought to market (Du Gay *et al.*, 1997). Ironically, products which appear racing certainties when researched, only to flop in the real market, are even more common. So, even organizations with an eye on profit through mass appeal cannot afford to rely on a simple process of reaction to customers in their search for new opportunities. The search has to be informed by a vision which rises above immediate ideas of demand to a sense of the long-term relevance of a product. In this sense, commercial marketing can take on a missionary aspect not dissimilar from that of the most visionary arts organization. Mercer (1996) describes the evangelizing zeal of companies like McDonald's and Coca-Cola as 'commitment' marketing. Such companies have found unlikely success in exporting an unfamiliar model of business around the world, but with such fervent belief in its rightness that customers are carried along with the flow.

To sum up thus far, much of what has been written in the past about arts marketing has tended to contrast it with orthodox marketing by limiting its role to something more like selling – a tactical process limited to finding audiences for existing work. The argument of this chapter is that contemporary understandings of marketing reveal more similarities than differences between commercial and arts marketing. Both need to balance organizational and customer needs, both need to take into account a wide range of stakeholders alongside the immediate customer, and both are focused on creating and maintaining long-term relationships of mutual value. Instead of dismissing marketing as a shallow concession to popularism or fashion, arts organizations can benefit from its creative value as a strategic perspective on planning and operations.

The evolution of arts marketing: practice

The practice of marketing in arts organizations has developed alongside this growing understanding of its scope. Traditionally, because of the natural newsworthiness of much of the output of arts and entertainment, marketing activity for most arts organizations concentrated on media relations. Depending on resources, the 'press' officer who handled this side of operations might work alongside the 'publicity' officer who looked after the production and distribution of printed publicity materials. In smaller organizations the role might be combined in one very busy individual. Tickets were sold by a box office or admissions counter, or by ticket agents remote from the organization itself. Little information was exchanged as each functional department – usually overstretched – got on with the job. The process was overseen by an administrative director who worried about the sales figures while an artistic director exercised final editorial control over press releases and publicity material as the guardian of the organization's public image. Whatever the merits of such a way of running an organization, customer focus was not one of them, and marketing – if the term was used at all – was seen as a tactical function.

In the 1970s in the UK, inspired by tales of American success (Newman, 1977), but also building on traditional ways of selling concert tickets dating back to the eighteenth century, subscription-based marketing became the focus of much of the activity of performing arts organizations hoping to convert their single-ticket buyers into loyal regular patrons. Price discounting on a series of tickets was the central tool – but while box office, marketing staff and artistic directors had well-developed theories on the characteristics of the audience, there was little systematic information on which to base decisions. It was as if the marketing department were flying blind – guided by their theory of who the audience was, but still seeing the ticket buyer in the organization's image. While they were moving closer to customer focus, the prospects were limited by a lack of strategic information.

By the mid to late 1980s computers were available to many marketing departments. Targeted direct mail became the focus of much activity, driven by database systems (whose sophistication was rapidly increasing for those who could keep pace with the necessary expenditure). Not only could mailing lists be stored in a flexible medium, but the more advanced organizations could analyse and manipulate their customer records. Arts marketing was moving from the transaction-based thinking of earlier years towards a more relational approach to the customer – in a way which anticipated developments in mainstream marketing as noted in the Introduction. However, the uneven adoption of new technology meant that computer systems tended to be incompatible with each other, preventing the building of strategic information resources. Even within individual organizations computers would not talk to each other – which clearly limited the prospects of attempts at co-operation on regional or national levels. We could give the name 'database marketing' to this evolutionary stage of arts marketing practice as arts marketers began to realize the possibilities of understanding their audiences differently (for example through postcode profiling). Yet, while individual organizations and departments had significant information resources, there was little hope of using them proactively or co-operatively in a way which reflected true customer focus. Like transaction-based marketing, the database marketing stage was still a one-way process.

The great step forward for arts organizations in the UK came, as it had for their US counterparts some years earlier, with the advent of integrated computerized ticketing systems in the 1990s and beyond – working internationally across the arts, sports and the entertainment industries, and offering ticket buyers the option of purchasing on the internet if desired. These sophisticated tools have presented arts marketers with a comprehensive single source of data which relates ticket sales immediately to customer databases. As a result, the whole organization can achieve an integrated view of the customer which feeds into accounting, marketing, operations and development – literally customer centred. The danger of such a comprehensive system is, of course, information overload and the temptation to interact with computers rather than people. But, appropriately applied, the exciting result is that the rhetoric of relationship marketing becomes achievable. Technological sophistication paradoxically enables the personal touch, and allows marketers a direct sense of what they are achieving against their objectives. Ideas like segmentation (to be examined in Chapter 2), which involves aiming at particular sections of the market rather than taking a scattergun approach, or tracking individual customers in order to understand their needs better, are now part of the arts marketer's toolbox.

25 years of change

Peter Bellingham, Executive Director at Welsh National Opera (WNO), is a witness to the evolution of arts marketing: 'The industry has changed since I started 25 years ago. There were no computers, no real databases and certainly no targeting, tracking or segmentation. It makes you realize just how much things have moved on, with several special projects [aimed at specific audience segments] conducted by the WNO every year, to boost our audiences.'

Source: Precision Marketing, 2002.

This development, from transaction, through database, to relationship marketing, is commented on by the Harvard-based management experts Prahalad and Ramaswamy (2000) as the trajectory on which marketing in general is set for the twenty-first century. While they do not mention the arts specifically, their view of the shift from passivity to collaboration on the part of customers is one which arts marketing can identify with wholeheartedly.

Parallel to this developing understanding of the scope of arts marketing has been the growth of a professional infrastructure for workers in the field. As is often the case in things marketing, American initiatives have led the way. One such initiative, the Arts and Business Council, dates back to 1965 in establishing formal links between commercial and arts marketers to exchange ideas and know-how. Originally confined to New York, the Council now has a national presence – and is behind a number of training and partnering schemes, including the Artsmarketing.org website. The UK has seen similar kinds of co-operation develop. For example, the Association for Business Sponsorship of the Arts was set up in the early 1980s to administer a UK government-funded scheme aimed at encouraging commercial sponsorship of the arts. In 1999 it became Arts & Business, reflecting a broader mission and a more even-handed idea of partnership between the arts and commercial organizations.

Such initiatives are a response to an industry conscious of its own developing professionalism. At the beginning of the 1990s a representative selection of UK arts marketers identified a number of performance goals through consultations leading to the then Arts Council of Great Britain's 'A National Strategy for the Arts' (ACGB, 1992). The areas covered are relevant to arts marketing world-wide:

1 To become more scientific: 'We need to improve our understanding of marketing tools; to prove what works and what doesn't.'
2 To develop a more consistent approach to market intelligence: 'To improve our knowledge of audiences, current and potential.'
3 To rethink the way audiences are seen and addressed: 'Arts organizations really need to focus on the customer in: (i) communications (print, copy, our whole attitude); (ii) customer care.'
4 To see an improvement in the infrastructure and resources for marketing – financial, human and technical.

Some of these aspirations have seen progress towards their fulfilment. As we have seen, the falling cost of computing power and the increasing sophistication with which box office information can be used, is leading to a growth in accountability and confidence in marketing activity. Furthermore, many arts venues have invested substantially in customer-care programmes and extended the ways in which they relate to their audiences. On the other hand, the availability and reliability of market intelligence beyond a venue's internal data remains problematic, while marketing infrastructure and resources continue to be under pressure.

The UK has at least seen the development of a national cross-art form trade association of arts marketers, the Arts Marketing Association, set up in 1993 from the merger of two existing, but geographically distinct, organizations. Membership had trebled by 2001 to 1200. Services offered include conferences, seminars, and a marketing qualification developed in partnership with the UK marketing industry lead body, the Chartered Institute of Marketing. Parallel to this, marketing training in the UK continues to be provided by groups specific to a particular art form (such as the Theatrical Management Association) or as ad hoc events organized by funding bodies or other facilitating organizations.

Academically-based programmes in arts management, with a considerable focus on marketing, have also grown in number. In the UK, the pioneering example of the Department of Arts Policy and Management at London's City University, which started offering qualifications in arts management in the 1970s, has been followed by institutions across the regions. The academic apparatus of conferences and journals has also grown – as indicated by the list of resources at the end of this chapter.

All of these developments contribute to the strong impression that arts marketing is showing signs of a new maturity and critical mass after a period of existence on the margins of arts administration and marketing management. This is not to deny that there continue to be problems in either its practical or theoretical aspects. Arts marketers still tend to have less managerial status than their fellow administrators in most arts organizations. Poor pay and conditions still tend to be the rule rather than the exception. And, while academic interest in arts marketing is growing, arts organizations tend not to be able to offer the kind of research funding that has led to rapid theory-building activity in more commercial sectors. However, both as a professional practice and as an academic discipline, the evidence is that arts marketing is growing in practical confidence and theoretical sophistication.

There's a beauty in candlelight

Jude Kelly, former Artistic Director of the West Yorkshire Playhouse, put her vision of marketing as follows:

'The arts release things in people: like courage, flair, skills. It's like finding your own personality. And the kind of people who work in the arts have a sense of Utopia. They are ambitious to share what they have got with others, but there is often a kind of fear that holds them back. It's as if you have a secret knowledge that what you actually need to do is grapple with humanity at the most ordinary level – but don't because there is a kind of marketing "industry" approach backing up reasons for not doing it. Arts marketing is about loving people. You have this sense that you've got something that matters and you want them to have it too. Real evangelists get a lot back from dealing directly with customers. But that kind of marketing is called nonsense because it's not sufficiently "technical". Yet repeat bookings come from customer loyalty. People respond to the place because they like the people there.

'Word-of-mouth is the best kind of marketing because it's leading to a personal encounter with the art. But there's the temptation never to leave the office, never to cut yourself free from the computer or the telephone, never to get out and see the public, but take refuge in talking about C1s and C2s, instead of human beings. Or worse still, calling customers "punters", as if they were being conned into parting with their money on a gamble. We do a lot of mouthing off about "communities", but we lack the courage to go out and meet them as we should. Arts marketers need to believe in their own power as people. Even something as simple as giving out leaflets, talking to people, telling them direct that they'll love it when they come: they'll remember you, and you build up a greater "evangelism" yourself through it.

'For a while the vocabulary of arts marketing was redolent with the kind of language you would expect from Littlewoods catalogues. It didn't contain the generosity of the language of art itself. You almost need an "event" culture – a sense that every performance, every encounter with art, is unique and special. But being open 52 weeks of the year means you fall into thinking of it not as one event, even though that is how the customer sees it. There needs to be a phenomenal amount of attention to the personal; but unless you take that attitude as your ideal in all your marketing you are not reflecting the character of what you are talking about. You need to harness the technology, but you must get the balance right. Nobody is saying electricity should never have been invented, but there is a beauty in candlelight.'

Source: Personal interview.

The arts marketing environment

One of the difficulties of analysing the environment for arts marketing is the diversity of activity covered by the arts. A popular and inclusive definition was provided by the 89th US Congress, and later endorsed by what was then the Education, Science and Art Committee of the House of Commons:

> The term 'the arts' includes, but is not limited to, music (instrumental and vocal), dance, drama, folk art, creative writing, architecture and allied fields, painting, sculpture, photography, graphic and craft arts, industrial design, costume and fashion design, motion pictures, television, radio, tape and sound recording, the arts related to the presentation, performance, execution and exhibition of such major arts forms, and the study and application of the arts to the human environment. (ACGB, 1993)

Since the 1990s a whole category of computer-based art has been added to this list with the proliferation of digital technology. Definitions such as this are not just a case of hair-splitting pedantry. Arguments about how much we should spend on the arts, as individual customers or as taxpayers, often depend on comparisons with other countries. Definitions of culture, art forms, or the boundaries of expenditure, can vary significantly from country to country and even, within countries, between organizations. For example, a 1998 Arts

Council of England study into comparative arts funding between countries excluded libraries, historical buildings, education and public service broadcasting from its calculations, but included film production, community arts, museums and galleries, and festivals. The message from this is that statistics in the arts, where they are available at all, need to be used with care.

In this section of the chapter we will follow the 'STEP' model of Sociocultural, Technological, Economic and Political environmental factors in analysing the peculiarities of the arts marketing environment. This is widely accepted as a framework for analysis of the wider environment of any organization, and we will return to it in Chapter 8 as a starting point for the marketing planning process. In particular, STEP factor analysis reveals long-term trends and forces which help explain the opportunities and threats facing arts organizations. Of course, like any model, it is meant to be a framework rather than a straitjacket. There are, for example, elements which cross over from one category of factor to another. This is particularly the case in the Economic and Political categories, where government policy can have a very close bearing on economic conditions. Furthermore, the sheer number of trends and factors that may have an impact on arts marketing means that we can only offer a very brief selection here to illustrate the scope of each domain. Finally, while the trends chronicled here are centred on the UK, many of them are replicated elsewhere in the developed world.

Socio-cultural factors

Leisure trends

Arts customers and their motivations, consumption occasions, and art forms themselves are almost infinitely variable. The arts tend to spread outwards and, as with many activities with a strong social dimension, they cross-fertilize with other areas and programmes. This was well illustrated in the UK's Voluntary Arts Network (VAN) report *Strengthening Foundations* (1994), which emphasized individual motivations for arts participation or arts attendance: 'People go out "to sing", "to paint" or "to play football". They do not go out "to participate in local cultural activity".'

The complex question of audience motivation is addressed more fully in Chapter 2 but, as Table 1.1 suggests, the arts are just one part of a wider portfolio of leisure choices in people's lives. In addition to the more active pursuits listed, we watch, on average, about 25 hours of television a week in the UK (Euromonitor, 2000). Perhaps arts marketers can take heart from the fact that drama is the single most popular genre. A taste for fiction, which might also indicate a susceptibility to other forms of artistic expression, is evident from the fact that 58 per cent of men and 71 per cent of women read at least one book a month (Office for National Statistics, 1997).

The popular stereotype of socially egalitarian 'sport' set against the elitist 'arts' is laid to rest by figures which suggest that participation rates for music, painting and drawing are as high as, or even exceed, those for pursuits such as darts or golf (VAN, 1994). Indeed, the UK's Theatrical Management Association claims that live theatre is more popular than soccer as a live spectacle, claiming 30 million attendances in 1998 in comparison with professional

Table 1.1 Leisure activities in the UK

Activity	Percentage of population (16+)
1 Visiting a public house	73
2 Meal in a restaurant (not fast food)	68
3 Meal in a fast-food restaurant	47
4 Library	39
5 Cinema	33
6 Historic building	31
7 Short holiday break	30
8 Disco or nightclub	26
9 Museum or art gallery	24
10 Funfair	21
11 Theatre	18
12 Theme park	16
13 Camping/caravanning	16
14 Bingo	10
15 Betting	8

Source: National Statistics/Euromonitor, 2000.

football's 26 million. At an average ticket price of £11.80 rather than the £14.60 paid by the average football fan, theatre claims to offer better value for money (*ArtsBusiness*, 1998).

Market potential?

Survey research in 2000/1 revealed that 15 per cent of the adult population in the UK described themselves as attending plays or art exhibitions 'these days', while 8 per cent admitted to going to classical music concerts. This proportion has remained relatively stable for over a decade. That there is potential in the market for the performing arts, however, can be argued from the experience of cinema attendances. These reached 137 million in the UK at the millennium, a figure more than double that of 15 years earlier. A number of factors may be related to this: the development of multiscreen cinemas around the country (which has accompanied a decline in traditional cinemas), and the increased number of films with a PG rating (which clearly increases the available audience). Having said that, however, cinema attendance in the UK is still a far cry from its peak of over 1 billion in the early 1950s.

Other recent UK marketing success stories in the arts include the British Museum and the National Gallery, both of which practically doubled their admission numbers in the two decades to the millennium. And, in spite of a persistent cloud of negative publicity hanging over it, the infamous Millennium Dome in London's Greenwich set new standards for an exhibition by attracting more than 6.5 million paying visitors in its one year of being open. This suggests that there is potential in the visual arts and exhibitions market just as there is in the performing arts.

Source: TGI/BMRB International, cited in Social Trends 32, 2002.

Shifting demographics: age, gender and ethnicity

Age is a factor in what people choose to do. Because of a steady decline in birth rate, the developed world has an ageing population – and the age profile of arts attenders is a source of concern to many organizations.

Age shall not wither them . . .

'I never lay awake nights worrying about the age of the audience – I just wanted to get an audience . . . I figured some would be young, some middle-aged, some old. People have been worrying about the ageing of the audience for 40 years – and it's still about the same age it always was.'

Source: Danny Newman, author of Subscribe Now (1977) quoted by Scher, 2002 in the San Diego Union-Tribune.

However, people do not define themselves by their chronological age, but as belonging to a particular cohort with shared experiences. In general, activities such as listening to recorded music are more popular with younger people, gardening more popular with older people. Weather and the number of daylight hours affect the attractiveness of leisure alternatives, introducing a note of seasonality to people's availability as attenders. This is particularly the case with older people. Improved levels of health in many developed countries have led to increased expectations of longer active lives for retired people. This has created a number of opportunities for arts organizations.

Case 1.1 Making Hey

The West Yorkshire Playhouse opened in 1990 with an artistic policy aimed at a wide spectrum of audiences. One example of this in practice is Heydays, its innovative programme for people aged 55 and over. Devised in consultation with Age Concern and the University of the Third Age (UK organizations which campaign for older people), Heydays meets every Wednesday at the Playhouse and offers its 600 subscribing members a wide selection of activities connected with the theatre. The activities – such as talks, practical sessions and courses – offer the participants a stimulating social space where they can meet and share their interests in a relaxed social atmosphere. Members get discount on tickets, as well as reduced prices for food and refreshments at the venue.

The programme of activities is planned and presented by the Playhouse using a wide team of artists, tutors and Playhouse staff, as well as some of the Heydays members themselves. The whole project is overseen by a steering group of 14 members. It is widely admired as an example of the proactive involvement of older people with an arts organization, and in 1999 it was chosen to launch the Yorkshire celebration of the International Year of the Older Person.

Source: Meeks, 2000.

Gender roles and the family

Gender roles are another area where long-term trends are having a significant effect on marketing in general and the arts in particular because of their impact on family life and discretionary time. The number of UK women in paid work has increased from 10.0 million in 1971 to 13.2 million in 2001, even though much of this increase has been in the part-time sector (*Social Trends 32*, 2002). However, taking on the new role of paid worker has not led to an immediate relinquishing of other roles as mother or housekeeper for the majority of women. Men's roles are changing too. Permanent work, which used to be an important source of male identity, is now less reliable with the growth of 'portfolio careers'. As with changes in women's roles, this has had a liberating effect for those in a position to benefit from the flexibility it brings, but it has also helped erode traditional institutions. Marriage, for example, has become more fluid. While there were 159 000 divorces in the UK in 1999, there were also 110 000 remarriages (*Social Trends 32*, 2002). This suggests that people still have faith in the institution of marriage – but not in its permanence. The complications this causes for family life are considerable, with well over a million children living in stepfamilies in the UK alone.

Again, this creates opportunities for arts organizations. Family time together, whatever the precise details of the affiliations involved, is increasingly precious. The arts can provide quality time, allowing family members to have memorable experiences with one another and to develop their relationships. On the other hand, traditional venues may have to work hard to adapt themselves successfully to the requirements of the family market, particularly in developing their portfolio of activity to include participatory events (O'Sullivan, 1999).

Ethnicity

Britain has always been the product of a mixture of cultures, but the explicitly multicultural nature of contemporary society in the UK has been something which commercial marketers have been slow to pick up on. This is an area where arts and non-profit marketing have made significant inroads, but there is still a long way to go. The UK's 3 million-plus 'ethnic minority' community is young, urban, well educated and has an estimated disposable income of £12 billion (Khan, 2001). Yet Asian and Black audiences continue to be under-represented in arts venues – in spite of the fact that one in five is a university graduate (compared to one in four of the white population). There is evidence that marketing approaches which may have worked well in the past for traditional theatre audiences are ineffective, or even counter-productive, when targeting the Asian community (Bhuchar, 1999; Wilson, 2001). Word-of-mouth, personal recommendation and informality of presentation are key to reaching this growing segment. Marketing to ethnic-minority audiences involves building and accessing networks, and showing consistency of purpose in programming and outreach work. While these observations are specific to the UK, the principle can be extended elsewhere.

Alien nation

'If you manage to get Asian audiences into the theatre, they discover British theatre conventions are alien to many of them. For instance, the idea that a performance will start at the time stated on the tickets needs to be constantly drummed home. They can cope with that idea when going to the cinema, but no Asian has ever seen a "live" event start on time. Asian audiences are also noisy ... they like to express themselves when they are enjoying themselves ... This is, of course, anathema to the British way of enjoying entertainment. Asians are more into the free-flowing spontaneous methods of having a good time. Maybe British audiences should be less po-faced and become more involved with productions.'

Source: Bhuchar, 1999

Technological environment

While the arts themselves will always be a heavily people-dependent business, with limited opportunity to substitute capital equipment for human labour, developments in information and communication technology have caused a revolution in arts marketing in the years around the millennium. Computers and telephones, including mobiles with text-messaging facilities, have opened up new forms of audience contact and sales channels. The rapid diffusion of the internet has presented arts organizations with a powerful new tool, the website – as shop window, selling tool and delivery platform. As we will see in Chapters 2 and 3, computers have given even small arts organizations the power to process and manipulate data about their customers in a way which has made their marketing more focused and productive. Virtual reality (the creation of vivid three-dimensional renderings of buildings and environments in a digital format) offers venues the possibility of showing ticket purchasers the different view of the auditorium available from different seats. Sophisticated telephone management systems can inform callers of the length of the queue they are in – and perhaps convey promotional messages about future events and attractions. Furthermore, digital technology is also making an impact in areas such as photography, reprographics, print production and news coverage – all of which are key to the work of arts marketers. The nature of technological change makes any attempt to write about particular technologies or applications liable to rapid dating.

We have already seen how the wider availability of computers has driven the evolution of arts marketing through the stages of direct mail and database marketing to more sophisticated conceptions of relationship marketing. We will examine some more of the opportunities it presents arts marketing in different functional areas in the following chapters. Overall, what technological change means for arts marketers is a new imperative to keep in touch with a shifting landscape, plan for the acquisition of new skills on a regular basis, and explore collaboration with other organizations in order to minimize the drain on resources, and maximize the potential benefits, of emerging technologies. It also introduces new responsibilities, in particular compliance with legislation aimed at protecting the privacy of data on customers (a theme to which we will return in Chapter 8).

Technology also gives arts customers the opportunity to experience the performing arts via broadcast and packaged media such as CD and DVD. The advent of subscription-funded specialist TV channels has provided those who can afford it with continuous access to opera, concerts and specialist arts programming. One effect of this is to leave some customers very well informed and with extremely high expectations of live performance. A less desirable outcome is that the place of the arts in general broadcast programming becomes more vulnerable, as schedulers can point to their availability on minority channels. The challenge for arts marketers is to stress the unique advantages of live performance in terms of warmth, immediacy and social benefits.

Love music, hate concerts

The majority of American adults are interested in classical music, a third listen to it regularly, yet only 5 per cent go to concerts. A study of 13 500 respondents by the US research group Audience Insight revealed that 18 per cent listen to classical music on the radio several times a week, and 14 per cent regularly listen to recorded music at home. The survey also revealed that, in spite of the popularity of subscription marketing as a way of developing regular audiences for classical music on both sides of the Atlantic, potential concert-goers prefer buying single tickets rather than subscriptions.

Source: Mattison, 2002.

Economic environment

The arts are a mixed economy. In the UK, for example, there is a strong commercial sector concentrated in London. This is complemented by a large subsidized sector with a predominantly regional presence, but with national flagship organizations housed both in the capital and in larger regional centres. There is considerable mobility between the subsidized and commercial sectors and other media (for example, broadcasting, advertising and film work). This is not just a case of the individual career trajectories of artists, managers and marketers. It also concerns the flow of investment. The arts are closely allied to some of the larger industries of modern Britain: the broadcast media, publishing and recording, sport and leisure, and tourism. Commercial productions play in subsidized venues, work which is developed in the subsidized sector is taken up by commercial producers, there are co-productions and joint projects – many of them international. The performing arts themselves employ something like 75 000 people in the UK. Less than half are directly employed by organizations, with the others self-employed. Generating ticket sales and sponsorship income of £662 million in 1999, the performing arts are a significant economic force in the UK (DCMS, 2001).

General economic conditions affect both production and consumption in the arts. For commercial theatre producers, for example, the importance of creating a spectacular experience which offers audiences something unique to the live event has meant an increased reliance on special-effects technology or big-name stars. Neither comes cheap, making the industry highly capital-intensive. Fluctuations in interest rates, which effectively dictate the 'price' of money, are therefore an important constraint on commercial producers. Another effect of the spiralling cost of productions is the trend towards maximizing financial return on existing creative assets. Stage adaptations of novels or film stories are a familiar staple of theatrical programming, but a more recent international trend has seen the Disney Corporation diversifying into musical theatre productions which play in major cities around the world, extending the profitable life of its animated films. The internationalization of commercial productions, and the importance of the arts to international tourism, makes the sector vulnerable to fluctuations in exchange rates – the relative values of different national currencies. The advent of a single currency in Europe should have a stabilizing effect at least within the member states of the EU but, with the number of North American visitors to many European destinations depending on the strength of the dollar, the single currency may well amplify tourist attendance trends across the continent as a whole.

Inflation is another important part of the economic environment for arts marketing. The question of cost inflation in the arts was examined in the late 1960s in a pioneering article by the American economist W.J. Baumol. He argued that production costs for performing-arts organizations inevitably rise faster than those for the economy as a whole, because the arts do not have access to the benefits of scale economies in the way that other industries do (Baumol, 1967). Labour costs, usually the largest single item of expenditure for arts organizations, cannot be reduced beyond the minimum necessary to mount a play or a concert. A symphony orchestra, for example, needs a specified minimum number of players beneath which it cannot perform a particular work. In practice this means that, while the rest of the economy becomes more efficient through mechanization, the arts are limited in their access to productivity gains. Costs therefore rise faster in the arts than in the rest of the economy – and the more efficient the rest of the economy becomes, the wider yawns the gap. Baumol concluded that in order to pay wages that matched those outside the sector, arts organizations would have to increase their incomes (for example, by raising the price of tickets) at more than the average level of inflation. Of course his argument, based on US data, does not take into account the effect of public subsidies, or the technological advances which have reduced costs in some elements of artistic production (for example, computerized stage lighting systems). However, it does provide clues as to why wages in the arts inevitably lag behind those elsewhere, and perhaps gives an economic reason for the increased presentation of smaller-scale performances, for example pared-down ensembles presenting authentic baroque music or small-cast plays.

While costs (as we will see in Chapter 5) are one influence on ticket prices, the most important influence is the customer's willingness to pay. The arts fall into the category of discretionary purchases – what people spend their leftover money on. This is a highly subjective category, hence the importance to the arts of consumer confidence or the 'feel-good factor' beloved of politicians. Some studies argue that, while lowering price has little effect on increasing attendance, raising it beyond an upper threshold becomes a deterrent (Ford Foundation, 1974). Talking to arts managers suggests that when mortgage interest rates increase, or people are worried about job security, one of the first casualties is paid attendance at arts events. Keeping an eye on consumer confidence is, therefore, important for arts marketers as it affects not only conditions for ticket sales, but also the willingness of commercial organizations to enter into sponsorship arrangements. Committing money such as sponsorship or programme advertising to promote goods and services makes more sense when customers are relaxed about spending than when they are watching every penny.

There's money in creativity . . .

The British, Americans and Japanese spend more on entertainment than they do on clothing or healthcare. The Creative Economy (a term which draws together the arts, publishing, advertising, broadcasting, software, fashion and design) grew four times faster than manufacturing in OECD countries during the last decade of the twentieth century.

Source: Howkins, 2001.

Political environment

The political environment for arts marketing exists at three levels: local, national and international. Local authorities are a very important source of support for the subsidized arts – sometimes running venues directly, but often providing the principal source of finance and having significant representation on management boards. In 1999 they provided over half of the public funding for the performing arts in the UK (DCMS, 2001). One of the most significant achievements of what was then called the Arts Council of Great Britain from the 1980s onwards was to leverage increased arts funding from local authorities in the UK. It did this by making its own central grant aid conditional on increased support at the local level. The priorities, perspectives and even political affiliation of a local authority may differ markedly from those of national government, and certainly its arts funding agenda is likely to place civic amenity and local identity at the top of the list. It is important for arts organizations to understand the resulting expectations. As a key stakeholder, a local authority has the advantage of being accessible. Keeping in touch with individuals and policy developments is an important part of any arts marketer's task of environmental management.

On a national level most political administrations value the arts as something worth promoting. They are seen as what economists call a 'merit good' – in other words, something of social value (like preventive healthcare and education) but which people might not be prepared to pay for if left to themselves. As a result, governments tend to see supporting the arts as part of their remit (although the priority given to this is variable). In the UK and much of Europe such support is through direct funding mediated selectively through a mixture of national and local agencies and local authorities. In the USA the emphasis is on forgoing tax revenues to encourage private and corporate giving to the arts by offering tax incentives to donors. The different forms of support make like-with-like comparisons between nations very difficult. Thus, while US government spending on the arts worked out at £3.63 per person in the population in 1997, a paltry sum compared to the equivalent figure in Germany (£56.50 in 1993), the US statistic ignores the loss in tax revenues suffered by the government in order to make giving by individuals, foundations and businesses as attractive as possible (International Arts Bureau, 2000).

While politicians tend to agree that the arts are a good thing, the question of subsidizing them remains controversial (a subject to which we will return in the next section). Interestingly, all political parties debate the issue with equal ferocity, and find little consensus within party ranks. Alongside the 'merit good' argument are cases made on philosophical, aesthetic and economic grounds. The cultural economists Sir Alan Peacock and Dr Samuel Cameron demonstrated some scepticism about the latter sort of argument in their report to the Arts Council of Great Britain in the early 1990s:

> A number of our comments concern overestimation of beneficial effects. This should not be misconstrued as meaning that the arts are not important in economic terms. One of the main drawbacks of impact studies is their focus on measurement in terms of money without reference to value. The sums which have been computed fail to put a value on many of the socio-economic effects of the arts which are not directly registered in the marketplace. (ACGB, 1992)

Nevertheless, political attitudes to the arts based on economic arguments have gained precedence over more value-laden ones in recent years (see Table 1.2). Perhaps this is because of a fear of appearing elitist or paternalistic in advocating the improving effect of the arts on the electorate. In 1998 Chris Smith, MP, the then Culture Secretary, articulated a typically modern justification for state funding for the arts on five fronts, most of them connected with economic benefits: '. . . to ensure excellence; to protect innovation; to assist access for as many people as possible, both to create and to appreciate; to help provide the seedbed for the creative economy; and to assist in the regeneration of areas of deprivation' (Smith, 1998: 19).

This is essentially a utilitarian valuation of the arts, with its hard-headedly democratic themes of social inclusion, economic benefit and active participation. The emphases on excellence and innovation underline the link with industry which is an important part of Smith's perspective. However, his

Table 1.2 Public attitudes to the arts

In November 2000, the Arts Council of England commissioned the Social Survey Division of the Office for National Statistics (ONS) to survey attendance, participation and attitude to the arts in a sample of UK citizens:

- 97% thought that all schoolchildren should have the chance to participate actively in the arts.
- 74% agreed that there should be public funding of the arts.
- 73% said that the arts play a valuable role in the life of the country.
- 72% said that arts from other cultures made a significant contribution to this country.
- 75% claimed they would not feel out of place in an art gallery, museum or theatre.

Source: Skelton et al., 2002.

defence of subsidy only goes as far as protecting excellence and innovation which might not survive in the open market because it is new, difficult or esoteric. He points to the popular music industry as a fine example of unassisted excellence. We might well disagree with him on that front, but the advantage of his argument in general is that it gets away from the kind of paternalistic elitism which has been used in the past to defend public subsidy, and which cuts little ice in these less deferential times.

Strangely enough, Smith elsewhere cites just such an argument from the economist John Maynard Keynes in a 1945 radio talk on the role of the fledgling Arts Council (founded a year later):

> ... to create an environment, to breathe a spirit, to cultivate an opinion, to offer stimulus to such a purpose that the Artist and the public can sustain and live on each other in that union which has occasionally existed in the past at the great ages of communal civilized life. (Keynes, 1945, cited Smith, 1998: 17)

Here the artist sustains and is sustained by an appreciative, but respectfully passive public. Gritty economics is replaced by a vision of civilized community abstracted from history. Such political idealism can be understood given the fact that Keynes, and J.B. Priestley (whose arguments in favour of subsidizing the arts are quoted in Table 1.3), were writing at a time of national reconstruction following the Second World War. However, contemporary political attitudes to the arts tend to be based on practicalities rather than idealism.

Alongside economic effects, a second fundamental strand in contemporary political attitudes to the arts has been their social impact. This is an area which has attracted considerable interest in recent policy documents on the role of the arts in combating social exclusion – a condition of being cut off from normal opportunities by a complex mixture of low income, poor health and housing, and vulnerability to crime (Jermyn, 2001). It builds on long-standing themes: 'expanding access has always been an important part of the funding system ... Advocating the role the arts can play in addressing social exclusion is,

Table 1.3 Artist opinions on subsidy

'The function of the arts is to bring order out of chaos, coherence out of the endless static, the gibberish of the stars, and to render people capable of thinking metaphorically. The arts are an essential part of public education.' Edward Albee (1988)

For the motion: J.B. Priestley	*Against the motion: Kingsley Amis*
People in general should have the opportunity to experience good art . . . the more people have this chance, the more natural understanders and appreciators we shall discover	The trouble with bringing art to the people is that it tends to become fatally damaged in transit
art is like yeast in the doughy stuff of life . . . life without art is life already turning sour. Something must take the place of that leaven	if you really are interested in quality, one way of allowing it to improve would be to withdraw public money from the arts
I do not believe the state should maintain its artists so long as they are able to work and maintain themselves. All that the state should do is to create the conditions most favourable for the self-maintenance of artists	If you're paid in advance or have your losses underwritten, the temptation to self-indulgence is extreme. If you have to please to live, you'll do your best to please
Good taste and judgement in these matters of fine art will not be miraculously bestowed on the leaders of collectivist society	We'll supply the finance, you'd better supply the interest; a very clear example of the Socialists' habit of giving the public not what it wants but what they think it ought to want
We English are beginning to cry in the darkness for the colour and grace and glory of the arts	The Victorians bought a pre-Raphaelite picture because they liked it, not because some interfering git called Ruskin said they should
Source: Priestley, 1947.	*Source: Amis, 1979 – Conservative Party Conference, 1979.*

however, a new departure' (ACE, 1999). It is a sobering thought that in the UK at the end of the twentieth century over a quarter of the population were living in poverty, defined as not being able to afford what the majority of their fellow citizens would see as conventional necessities (Joseph Rowntree Foundation, 2000). The arts were represented in one of 18 Policy Action Teams (PATs) mandated by government in 1998 to examine the contribution they could make to action on the problem. PAT 10 – the relevant team – reported that the arts had a significant role to play, but that there was a lack of 'hard evidence' to support good practice in future interventions. Certainly, as is the case with economic effects of the arts, social effects are difficult to track with certainty because of their long-term nature. There is also, as we have seen, a considerable amount of controversy over how and what to evaluate in a way which does the arts justice in this kind of context.

This has not prevented some ground-breaking and influential research, much of it from the UK arts policy think-tank Comedia. Their publications (for example, Landry *et al.* 1995; Matarasso, 1997) have established that there are genuine, if complex, social benefits to be had from participation in the arts – and that these can be planned for. Also, the difficulty of measurement in the area has not prevented funding bodies from including exacting social impact criteria as part of their funding agreements with arts organizations as a matter of course in the early twenty-first century.

The implications for marketers are that they must be clear about how national arts policies fit into wider policy frameworks, and manage their organizations' relationships with key stakeholders accordingly.

Case 1.2 Everybody needs good neighbours

The West Yorkshire Playhouse had been open for ten years, with a thriving programme of community activities, when it realized that it had hardly any contact with its nearest local community – the Ebor Gardens Housing Estate. Separated from the Playhouse's flagship Quarry Hill site by the thundering divide of the A64 trunk road, Ebor Gardens has 3000 residents – but only a handful were on the theatre's database in July 1999.

The Playhouse devised the 'In Our Neighbourhood' project to make itself more accessible to the local residents. Initially it expected that the process would involve adjusting the mix of product and services offered by the theatre in order to attract a bigger audience from Ebor Gardens. An introductory event was organized by the Playhouse which appeared to go off well. However, the project hit a snag with the second specially-organized event – which was poorly attended and left both partners feeling rather embarrassed. The intention had been to organize it in partnership, but the precedent set by the project launch had left the Ebor Gardens side of the relationship feeling that they had a very hard act to follow, and so they had lacked the self-confidence to get properly involved in making it happen.

The Playhouse rethought its approach. Instead of its customary, but in this case slightly intimidating, dynamism, it became a lot more laid back. This gave the Ebor Gardens partners more space to come forward – and a significant number of residents started venturing out to attend mainstream theatre events. In fact they proved considerably more popular than the 'community-oriented' performances that the project's planners had envisaged as the focus of this new audience's attendance.

What emerged was that the residents were just as interested in mainstream theatrical fare as any other theatregoers – only a lack of confidence that the theatre was 'their sort of place' had kept them away. This impression was in danger of being compounded by the theatre's assumption, sincere if possibly misguided, that the new audience would only come if specially invited to specially-developed provision.

Most literature on the social impact of the arts focuses on the benefits (in terms of self-esteem and skills development) of participatory arts activities. The 'In Our Neighbourhood' project suggests that arts attendance itself, with its accompanying activities of organizing friends and family to come along, and summoning the courage to go in the first place, may have a significant contribution to make as well.

Source: Downing, 2001.

The international political environment is clearly important to touring companies, and exhibition organizers, but is becoming more relevant to the sector as a whole. In spite of the complexity of application and reporting procedures, a growing number of arts organizations are looking to European sources of funding for projects involving collaboration between organizations in different member states. Such sources are managed by the EU in the form of named initiatives with specific social and cultural goals. They either operate vertically (i.e. looking at a particular art form or sector in several countries) or horizontally (bringing together organizations from different sectors). International political groupings see the arts as an essential tool in cultural development, and it is likely that this trend will continue to offer increasing opportunities for arts marketers to extend their audience reach.

Key issues and problems for arts marketers

This chapter has considered the arts marketing environment, focusing on the UK, and the multiplicity of forms of arts activities carried out within the public and the private sector. It has looked at some issues of cultural policy, including in particular the case of political expectations of the arts. The mixed economy model gives rise to some dynamic tensions which can act as a constraint or as an opportunity for the marketing teams of arts organizations. A general awareness of some of the principal areas of tension will facilitate an understanding of how marketing techniques and general principles are specifically applied within the arts sector.

Arguments for and against a subsidized arts sector

Practitioners in the subsidized sector, particularly in the marketing department, are often asked to justify the use of public funding in the arts. The arguments split broadly between the belief that market forces alone should determine the product and level of funds needed to support the arts (i.e. through entrance fees and ticket prices); and the counter-argument that the arts are a fundamental right of the individual, akin to education or health, and are therefore too important to leave to the marketplace. This latter argument is strengthened by socio-economic arguments that the sector is a major employer and provides wealth to the nation through direct and indirect taxation. This argument was cogently put forward by Myerscough (1988) in one of the first studies of the value of the subsidized sector as a means of wealth generation. However, as we have seen, the statistics underlying such arguments are often controversial.

The market forces line can be summed up in what Sir Alan Peacock (ACGB, 1992) described as the doctrine of 'consumer sovereignty':

● The individual should be free to buy whatever services he or she wants at a competitive market price, which implies no subsidy.
● The individual is the best judge of what he or she wants, and there is no hierarchy of tastes or preferences. This argument 'explicitly rejects the idea

that the creative artist, the performing artist, or the informed aesthetes can have . . . any special status in the community when it comes to the allocation of resources to the arts'.

● Even if the individual is not a good judge, no one else is necessarily better. People should be allowed to make up their own minds.

Sir Alan Peacock acknowledges that this 'free market' attitude does not allow for inequalities in the distribution of provision hence restricting choice; inequalities in income; and inequalities in education in the broadest sense. At the same time it chimes with a postmodern sense of replacing official highbrow taste with more authentic and pluralist values in the arts.

On the other hand, powerful arguments for subsidy of the arts stem from the belief that they are life-enhancing and that therefore nobody should, because of inequalities in provision or income, be refused access to them. To the fact that they add meaning and colour to life, arts advocates would also adduce the following benefits (and there are many powerful and persuasive advocates to do so, as the quotes taken from the Americans for the Arts website (http://www.americansforthearts.org/artsexchange/quotes.asp, accessed 18 January 2003) demonstrate):

● Education
  'Recent research documents that the arts stimulate learning, improve overall academic performance, teach discipline, promote teamwork, and help children develop problem-solving skills.' Karen Evans, Director of Education, Arena Stage (1998).

● Inspiration
  'Music can give you your dreams. It will teach you hard work, it will break your heart and make you so happy you can't stand it . . . I don't think I'd have been president if it hadn't been for music.' Former President Bill Clinton (2001) at an event celebrating the restoration of music programmes to the Newark Public Schools.

● Urban regeneration, employment and community growth
  'When we're out recruiting businesses, they look at the whole city. They do, in fact, want to know if we've got a symphony, an opera, a ballet. It's just good business for the city to have alternatives to sports.' Hugh L. McColl Jr, Chairman of the Board and CEO of NationsBank Corporation (1997).

● The hallmark of a civilized nation
  'Our place in the community of nations is enhanced by permitting the creative energies of our artists to touch the lives of people throughout the world.' American Council for the Arts (1989).

The main problem with arguments both for and against public subsidy of the arts (as we have seen) is finding reliable data to substantiate either case. The exact boundaries of the subsidized part of the sector are far from clear. Furthermore, statistical evidence can always be criticized on the grounds of methodology of collection or the validity of interpretation, but never more so than when the arena of interest is so hard to define.

The arm's-length principle

The arm's-length principle is fundamental to the funding of the arts by political bodies. It holds that the organizations which distribute the funds remain independent of local or central government and do not seek to bend creativity or artistic interpretation to party politics.

It has its roots in the creation of the Arts Council in the UK in 1946, after the end of the Second World War. At that time, the horrors perpetuated by fascism were starting to emerge, and the effects of communist ideology on freedom of expression were beginning to be manifested. Later governments, more removed from ideological conflict, have strained the arm's-length principle by their power to grant or withhold funds. Nevertheless, it remains a touchstone of arts support policy, as indicated by the Arts Council of England's description of itself as 'an independent, non-political body working at arm's length from the Government' (ACE, 2002).

Central to the operation of the arm's-length philosophy is the use of peer appraisal in funding allocations. Groups of practitioners and specialists in an art form assess the work of their fellow artists and this is fed, over time, into the decision-making process. Arising from this is the freedom of the funding bodies to take on new clients and to recognize new forms of expression. Finally, and most importantly, freedom of expression is assured to clients while the funding body assumes the burden of financial accountability to central government.

All countries which operate a system of arm's-length funding find the principle can become severely strained on occasions by political pressure. In Australia, for example, serious political concern about the inequalities in distribution of opportunities throughout the regions has caused enormous pressure on the Australian Arts Council's independence in their distribution of arts funds.

For marketing staff, the arm's-length principle has implications about the quality of the product and the positioning of the organization. Peer appraisal is based first and foremost on the quality of artistic product – but the artistic product does not exist in isolation. The image of the organization, particularly its standing with critics and its media profile, makes a crucial contribution to the perception of quality. For an organization which truly integrates its marketing, artistic quality will be reflected in all aspects of its performance.

It could be argued that the arm's-length principle will become less important as the economy continues to become more mixed, with arts organizations diversifying their sources of income and becoming more commercially autonomous. Funding structures are not fixed in stone, as demonstrated by the number of reorganizations the Arts Council has been through in the UK since its foundation. Devolution, changing priorities, the relationship between central and regional decision-making, and the search for economies of scale have been some of the most important influences on this process. From their post-war beginnings as a single Arts Council of Great Britain, the separate Arts

Councils of England, Scotland, Wales and Northern Ireland have developed roles in co-ordinating, advocacy and planning alongside or instead of direct funding. On the other hand, the diversification of funding sources is likely to present arts organizations with a number of possible agendas. Careful assessment of stakeholder values, with a mission to manage funders' expectations, will be a priority for arts marketing in the twenty-first century.

Excellence vs. accessibility

As outlined above, peer-group appraisal places a high value on excellence. This involves both innovation in new forms, and the preservation and renewal of art forms from either minority cultures or the past. An equally important imperative is 'access' – the sector-wide commitment to increase the number and range of people who enjoy and participate in the arts. More difficult or unusual expressions of artistic creativity may prove a barrier to building big audiences or increasing the number of visitors to an attraction, particularly to those sectors of the community who traditionally are non-attenders. As we have suggested earlier in the chapter, presentation strategies which work well for existing audiences may actually deter newcomers from the theatre, concert hall or gallery.

Modern technology is shaping audiences' expectations of a live performance. For example, the widespread ownership of video recorders and DVD players, which allow the viewer to go forwards, backwards and to pause, may have an increasing impact on the attention span of audiences. In museums, traditional display methods which depend on written explanations may be seen as too inaccessible, both in terms of difficulties in understanding and also problems with getting close enough to read the text. The ways in which we access entertainment media have become increasingly individualized, as opposed to the communal experience of being part of an audience for a live event:

> The shift towards greater spending on cultural hardware . . . as opposed to services has also meant that entertainment is increasingly located in the home . . . The privatization of pleasure – driven by basic economics – has become a fundamental issue, whilst traditions of civic, municipal, and public cultures are being swept away. (Mulgan and Worpole, 1986)

It is the role of marketing staff to be aware of, and responsive to, the changing needs of customers in this social and technological context. The artistic director or exhibition curator and their teams will tend to be production-centred in that they will always hope to challenge and stimulate their audience by giving them something beyond their expectations. At its best, this tension is dynamic and challenging. Often in practice it is difficult to achieve the correct balance between 'excellence and access'. The tension between being at the cutting edge of an art form and the need to be inclusive of a wide audience is a long-running issue in the arts. Sir Kenneth Clark, Chair of ACGB in 1958, summarized this debate as 'raise or spread'. It is a theme that runs throughout the following chapters, impacting all areas of marketing planning and practice.

Professional vs. amateur arts

The dichotomy between performance standards of professional orchestras, companies and performers and those of amateur groups is another manifestation of the 'excellence vs. access' debate. It stems in part from the highly unionized musicians and actors workforce, and from the limited resources available to producers, which may tempt them to use non-union or untrained staff. In part, too, it has its roots in a belief that perhaps stems from Matthew Arnold and other Victorian thinkers: that there is a divide between 'high' art and 'popular' culture, and that the first is preferable to the second. This suggests that professional practitioners have a mission to educate and enlighten the non-professional: 'The men of culture are the true apostles of equality' (Arnold, 1869).

The growing and powerful community arts movement seeks to break down this divide by fusing the trained skills of professional workers with the commitment of local and community groups to produce, often large-scale, works whose value lies as much in the process of developing the piece as in its final performance. There has also been, particularly in the wake of the National Lottery, a growth in emphasis on participatory arts as a funding target. However, there are certain restraining forces on the growth of the community arts movement.

The first of these is finance – and, in particular, a hostility among some community arts workers to the whole funding system. Community arts work tends to be fairly small, informally organized and fast changing. This makes systematic funding more difficult than the funding of comparatively stable building-based or larger companies. Perhaps as a result of this, community arts workers often believe that historically they have been underfunded for the value of the contribution their work makes. If salaries are an indication of the funding coming into arts companies, there certainly appears to be truth in this claim. An examination of the salaries offered in community arts work as opposed to larger building-based companies does show a significant differential.

> The community arts movement has let the elitist aesthetics of the dominant subsidized culture off the hook. Most community artists [are] opposed to this cultural elitism, and yet, by forming a separate entity, 'community arts', they allow themselves to be appropriated by it. (Lewis, 1990)

The tendency of art workers in the community is to perceive these larger organizations as highly bureaucratic. This perception extends inevitably to the even more remote funding organizations:

> European arts bureaucrats have never lived so high on the hog. Community arts organizations have never been so bureaucratically harassed, nor so starved of money. Is it not time to organize an Underground Arts Resistance movement, with the aim of destroying the Flying Circus of European Freeloaders and all their supporting bureaucrats? (Pick, 1993)

A second, related area is political activity. The nature of community-based arts work lends itself to work with the socially disadvantaged, in order to develop individual potential, revitalize local communities and encourage urban regeneration. Often the projects take place in areas of particular political tension, poverty, unemployment or high crime.

> It is in precisely those areas that community-based arts activities are flourishing. Most especially drama, the art form that tackles human conflicts, human dilemmas, human emotions, head on. Community drama groups are offering local people an opportunity to reassert and redefine their personal and cultural identity, to tell their own stories in their own way ... (Moriarty, 1993)

Out of this type of work can arise a strong articulation of injustice, division and lack of opportunities in certain sectors of society. This type of message is unpalatable for some.

The third area is that of control. Community arts work is structured and is targeted at particular sections of the community, or may be funded to have a particular geographical focus. Some critics feel that this should exclude the traditional arts attender, i.e. the white middle-class pottery-maker who has other opportunities to enjoy arts activity. The counter-argument is that community arts offer a unique chance to participate and should be open to all enthusiasts. Debates over control also concern the role of paid professional leader/facilitators; the community remit of building-based companies who are funded by the whole community, not just the attender at their building; and the lack of structured follow-up activity.

All these problems lead to a perceived gap in provision filled by the continued flourishing existence of amateur arts. An amateur group will usually be self-financing, have no paid workers (though frequently amateur companies consist in part of people who have worked or trained professionally) and no restrictions on membership, other than group consensus. They may not seek to broaden their member base, or to strengthen their skills in areas of weakness. Their primary motive for coming together is to have fun, and this may lead to an avoidance of issue-based material. Audience motivation to attend amateur arts events may also be different from audience motivation at professional events. Amateur arts generate an enviable sense of network, drawing on family and social affiliations to build strong, loyal and well-informed audiences. A second motivational factor may be repertoire. Amateur productions, because of the obvious economies available on labour costs, are becoming almost the only provider of affordable large-scale musical theatre (particularly of specific repertoire such as Gilbert and Sullivan opera) to large numbers of attenders not catered for even within the subsidized sector.

The Voluntary Arts Network (1994) has argued that amateur arts have suffered at the hands of the Arts Councils and other funders who chose to concentrate on professional work and therefore left the funding of amateur activity to the Department for Education. This led to the anomalous situation of the English Folk Dance and Song Society receiving its only public support from the Sports Council, who inherited them as a client. They go on to discuss the particular disdain for amateur dramatics, which is the dominant art form in the public sector. This can be epitomized in the comment of Lord Goodman in the House of Lords: 'My Lords, I speak for the Arts, not for amateur theatricals.'

VAN contrast this attitude with:

- amateur choirs, or amateur lacemakers, who have a far more positive image
- the attitude in other countries, including Wales, Scotland and Ireland
- other cultures, such as the place of carnival in some communities
- the positive image of amateurs in sport, all the way to the Olympics

Their examination of the distinctions our cultural tradition imposes on arts activity paves the way for a re-examination of national preconceptions. Such preconceptions form an important part of the background against which arts marketing activity takes place.

Although there are some conflicts between professional/community/ amateur groups, the strengths and cross-fertilizations outweigh these. The variety of the types of organization is a sign of the continued interest in the arts in Britain and arts funders are recognizing this by ensuring that all three types of company are eligible for funding. All three sectors have marketing needs. Community groups will perhaps have a particular focus on 'place' – that element of the marketing mix which considers in particular how a product is made available/accessible to its customers. Amateur groups in contrast may find their hardest decision is 'product' – they know their audiences and the best way to reach them, the difficulty is to choose a piece that the group wishes to perform and that family, friends and the local community will want to attend.

Traditional vs. new art forms

This is the area which most feels the impact of new technology. Audiences' expectations are changing as a result of improvements in telecommunications and the mass media. We live in the age of the 'sound bite' and this may alter the attention span of a captive audience. Digital home entertainment may increase expectations from live PA systems, for example of a rock concert audience, and enormous video screens are now commonplace at stadium performances. The technology is available for this, blurring the distinction between audiences watching videos of the band and attending live performances.

There are considerable opportunities for cross-fertilization across art forms arising from new developments in technology. Some of these are incorporated into the production values of a performed piece of work, and others might arise in ancillary activity around the main performance. Examples of these might be lighting and sound technology, the use of music, video links, photography and audio recordings. New art forms are being recognized in their own right, involving new technology, or multimedia cross-fertilizations integrated through digital environments. New times can lead to new ways of working; our current concern with the environment has developed a new interest in public art and site-specific artwork, and pieces of work in which decay is part of the lifecycle of the artwork.

Participative theatre is also breaking down barriers between art forms and, in particular, is fusing minority and folk art with the mainstream European arts tradition. Particularly successful examples of this might include reggae musicals, dance drama and the use of 'artists-in-residence', such as sculptors working for a period with dance groups. Commercial considerations may encourage companies to mount co-productions of large-scale or touring work which might otherwise not get an airing.

New work is often exciting and highly visible, and thus can present a great opportunity for marketing staff. On the other hand, the unfamiliar can challenge or threaten core audiences and thus offer particular problems with promotional or pricing decisions.

Refreshing the parts others don't reach . . .

As we have seen, marketing needs to be integrated into all levels of an organization's work – nowhere more so than in the area of new audience development. For those organizations who most believe in equality of opportunity for all, a market-centred philosophy must be developed in the culture of the whole company so that particular groups can be identified at a strategic level and a systematic approach taken to encouraging their attendance.

While this is an organization-wide responsibility, in reality the marketing and education departments will often carry out much of the day-to-day work of audience development with targeted groups: women, ethnic-minority groups, gay men and lesbians, and the physically and mentally challenged. In these areas, market research will play a significant part to avoid the charge of tokenism or patronage.

> Nor is it about making mainstream arts – the ones which use spoken language – accessible to deaf people. I'm not knocking interpreted performance . . . [but] for many deaf people the initial impulse is to create art which makes a statement about the integrity of the deaf community . . . an exploration and celebration of difference. (Wilson, 1993)

It is a very difficult task to offer the appropriate opportunities and experiences to such varied and disparate groups. In some cases, there are increasingly radical and politicized organizations with whom a dialogue can be established, if the initial approach is correctly handled. In these cases, it is important to recognize that these groups may be justifiably angry because of the lack of understanding of their needs that they have experienced from the wider community. In other cases, one of the first difficulties can be to identify a way of reaching the particular targeted group. All too often, marketing to Asian women can begin and end with leaflets sent in Urdu to community groups.

Marketing practitioners in arts organizations will want to build new audiences to create new markets for their product. However, as we have seen, alongside this missionary role marketing nurtures relationships with existing audiences to widen and deepen their engagement with the organization. The strategic objectives of the organization, which might include addressing particular publics, need to be held in balance with the general objective of maximizing attendance.

Overcoming internal resistance to marketing

Selling our souls?

'Many artists think that "marketing" has nothing to do with them or isn't something they want to get involved with. For some, the word conjures fast-talking city types or megabuck artists who have sold their work and their souls to some sort of promotions devil.

'Of course there is a mercenary side to marketing, there has to be – selling is big business. But there's marketing and there's marketing. Being clever about how you "sell" your work, yourself, your exhibitions and projects, etc., doesn't have to mean selling your soul ... or your valuables to finance it, for that matter.'

Source: Extract from material originally published on www.anweb.co.uk,
© Jennifer Shaw 2002.

Championing marketing in the arts can mean overcoming a considerable amount of internal resistance from colleagues (and superiors) who see it as an exploitative and unethical process serving materialist ends. As we have argued, it is often misconstrued as sales orientation rather than a strategic discipline: 'It's the marketing department's job to sell what the artistic director decides' (Drummond, cited in Tusa, 1999). An antipathy to commercial culture as epitomized by marketing can often be part of the motivation which attracts people to work in the arts in the first place – a career choice which is rarely materially rewarding and which challenges what it sees as passive consumerism. Kotler and Andreasen (1991) relate this negative perception of marketing to the non-profit sector in general:

> Over the years, marketing has had difficulty in gaining acceptance in a number of non-profit organizations. One hindrance was the view that marketing really wasn't necessary. It was argued, for example, that good health does not need to be sold, that hospitals don't need to be marketed . . .

They further identify that non-profit organizations may see marketing as a waste of public money, an unnecessary overhead; that market research may be perceived as intrusive; and that marketing is seen as manipulative. In the arts there is the further perception that marketing can lead to a 'lowest common denominator' approach, i.e. by promoting only that which the marketplace demands rather than seeking to develop new taste, or to raise standards: 'There is certainly nothing in economic theory which tells us that a competitive market will bring about an optimal level of investment in the formation of tastes' (Blaug, 1976).

However, the argument of this first chapter has been that such objections to marketing are frequently based on a misunderstanding of the nature and scope of marketing in general, and of its role in arts organizations in particular. Marketing thinking has an important contribution to make to the success of arts organizations, not only in the area of improving their use of resources and helping them to operate more efficiently and accountably, but also in helping them think strategically about how they engage with their audiences.

Peter Drucker, perhaps the twentieth century's most influential management writer, described the purpose of any business as 'to create a customer' (Drucker, 1964). This way of seeing a firm's only genuine assets as its customers (without whom its products or services would not be worth producing) offers a challenge to any organization to redefine what it is doing. The challenge is particularly relevant to organizations in the arts sector. Instead of thinking of themselves as producing theatre or exhibitions or concerts, it invites them to see their mission as winning the attendance and engagement of audiences: creating arts customers. Given the strong social commitment that many arts organizations embody, this measure of success has a lot going for it.

Marketing: the big picture . . .

Mary McMenamin, former Artistic Director of Mainstreet, South Australia's professional regional theatre company based in Mount Gambier: 'Marketing works with the big picture. It's holistic. It's the conduit of information about the art, who creates it, why, and who will be interested. It's understanding the heat of the work and its relationship with audiences. It's the network of blood vessels that provides the two-way communication between arts practice and the public.'

Source: Hodge et al., 1998. © Australia Council for the Arts, Commonwealth of Australia.

Marketing in its authentic sense is not some kind of confidence trick aimed at beguiling unsuspecting consumers. Instead it is an overall orientation which requires organizations to be externally focused, adapting what they offer to the developing needs of customers. Successful arts organizations have been doing so for years. Instead of maintaining a frozen, reverential approach to their work, their creative efforts achieve a dynamic, flexible relationship with their customers. Whether reinterpreting a classic stage work for a contemporary audience, or presenting an unfamiliar painter or musician in a way which allows audiences new insights, their approach recognizes and satisfies the changing needs of customers. They might not call it 'marketing', they might even have misgivings about the word, but essentially that is what they are doing.

Putting this vision into practice involves the application of techniques which we will be examining in depth in the following chapters. Together they provide the route by which an organization 'identifies, anticipates and supplies' what its customers need and want. In this process, the hidden areas of research and planning are every bit as important as the more visible ones of promotion or distribution as marketing functions. For example, the serious adoption of marketing research by an arts organization does not mean that it abdicates its responsibility for programming choice. Marketing research helps you find out about your customers' needs, and can help you manage risk, but it does not make decisions for you. Similarly, being customer centred does not necessarily mean what is sometimes called 'populism', or dumbing down. Marketing input needs to be at a senior, strategic level. It is not a veneer that can be applied to existing decisions to make them successful. It needs to be involved from the earliest stages of planning to connect the organization with its customers.

Summary

This chapter has traced the evolution of the concept of arts marketing, both in theory and practice, and looked at the environment for arts marketing, before examining some of the key issues and problems facing arts marketers at the beginning of the twenty-first century. Having defined arts marketing as an integrated management process which sees mutually satisfying exchange relationships with customers as the route to achieving organizational and artistic objectives, we followed its development as an idea through some of the marketing literature from the 1970s onwards, as well as indicating the growth of a body of practice and an industry infrastructure which has helped to give it a distinctive, critical mass as a professional activity. We then surveyed some important aspects of the socio-cultural, technological, economic and political environment for arts marketing. Our analysis focused on the UK although we would expect it to have parallels elsewhere in the developed world. Fundamental trends include an ageing population, changing gender roles, increased diversity in society; the rapid adoption of digital technology; the effects of changing rates of interest, currency exchange, and inflation, the peculiarities of cost inflation in the performing arts; and the pressures on arts marketing from local, national and international government. We concluded with a brief examination of some of the issues which arts marketers have to face: the arguments for and against subsidizing the arts, the meaning of the 'arm's-length principle', tensions between access and excellence, relationships with the amateur sector and community arts, competing art forms, addressing particular publics in the arts and, finally, the need to champion the marketing function and philosophy within arts organizations themselves.

Key concepts

accessibility
arm's-length principle
arts funding system
community arts
cultural goods
customers
database marketing
marketing orientation
merit goods

product orientation
public subsidy
relationship marketing
sales orientation
social exclusion
STEP factors
subsidy
transaction-based marketing

Discussion questions

1 Should the goal of arts subsidy be to create art or to create access to the arts? To what extent are these two compatible?
2 In what ways might the roles of marketers involved in community arts and building-based arts differ?
3 List the objections that an artistic director or curator might put forward to having a marketer involved in programming decisions. How would you reply to each of the points raised?
4 What do you predict will be the most significant changes in the environment to affect the practice of marketing in the arts over the next ten years?
5 What types of evidence reveal the extent to which an arts organization is 'customer oriented' as opposed to 'product oriented'? And what would characterize a 'sales oriented' arts organization?

Case study: Going Dutch

Birmingham's ArtsFest started in 1998 as a collaboration between Birmingham City Council and the local arts marketing agency, Birmingham Arts Marketing. For three days, the city showcased a dazzling variety of performances and art forms, using outdoor stages and venues throughout the city centre. Over 100 arts organizations participated, contributing free performances which lasted no more than 30 minutes. The aim was two-fold: to develop audiences by giving people who might not otherwise attend an arts event a free taster of something new, and to provide a showcase (both national and international) for the cultural strength and diversity of both city and region.

Research suggested that of the estimated 75 000 people who attended an event, a third were either new to the arts or very infrequent attenders (defined as people who had not been to an arts event at all, or only once in the past two years). The survey revealed that ArtsFest had succeeded in drawing a much younger audience than the population as a whole, and that the majority were from the local area. A follow-up telephone research poll some months afterwards attested to the success of the strategy in creating paying arts customers for the future. Eighty per cent of respondents had attended at least one arts event since the festival, and of those, almost half had done so as a consequence of seeing the particular performers or art form at the festival.

In subsequent years the event has grown. 1999 saw 150 organizations participating, and a big screen city-centre singalong finale featuring a live link-up to London's Last Night of the Proms. 2001 saw the establishment of an Art Village in the city centre's Centenary Square which acted as a focus for a succession of short performances, multiple exhibitions, a shop and an information centre. The festival has continued its tradition of bringing arts into the most unlikely places, with activities in the train station, supermarket and hospital. The 2001 weekend featured over 400 performances, with 250 participating groups. The programme extended to events for the under-5s, DJ-ing and comedy. Follow-up research suggested that 70 per cent of respondents would be more likely to attend an arts event as a result of ArtsFest.

Birmingham ArtsFest is based on the model provided by Amsterdam's Uitmarkt – an enormous free festival which takes place at the end of August. Uitmarkt has been going since 1978 and, with an average attendance in recent years of 500 000 people, is designed to offer the opportunity for all the organizations involved to launch their new seasons. It is billed on its website (www.uitmarkt.nl) as the national opening of the cultural year. The 2001 festival attracted major sponsorship from Heineken and Barclays, with a number of local media partners. The festival offers a one-stop preview of what is on offer from Holland's theatre, cabaret, dance, music and film – and makes good use of a wide variety of venues as Amsterdam becomes one enormous street party. Alongside the celebrations, an Information Market gives 250 cultural institutions direct access to their potential audiences, and the Amsterdam Book Market provides a platform for the nation's publishers to air their new lists.

Questions

1 Argue the case for and against ArtsFest being a free event.
2 How might the organizers of an event like ArtsFest or Uitmarkt take account of trends in the social environment when planning a programme of activities?
3 List and discuss some of the challenges involved in evaluating the success of ArtsFest (you may find it useful to refer to Chapter 3 on marketing research in the context of answering this question).

Source: http://www.uitmarkt.nl/home.cfm; http://www.artsfest.org.uk/,
accessed 18 January 2003.

References

ACE (Arts Council of England) (1999) *Addressing Social Exclusion: A framework for action.* ACE.

ACE (Arts Council of England) (2002) 'Introduction' (available at: http://www.arts-council.org.uk/ace/index.html).

ACGB (Arts Council of Great Britain) (1992) *45 Consultation Papers and Draft Towards a National Arts and Media Strategy.* ACGB.

ACGB (Arts Council of Great Britain) (1993) *A Creative Future: The way forward for the arts, crafts and media in England.* HMSO.

Albee, E. (ed. Kolin, P.C.) (1988) *Conversations with Edward Albee.* University of Mississippi Press.

Amis, K. (1979) *An Arts Policy?* (Pamphlet based on a lecture given at Blackpool during the Conservative Party Conference, October 1979.) Centre for Policy Studies.

American Council for the Arts (1989) *Why We Need the Arts.* ACA Books.

Arnold, M. (1869) 'Culture and anarchy'. In Collins, S. (ed.) (1993) *Culture and Anarchy and Other Writings by Matthew Arnold.* Cambridge University Press.

ArtsBusiness (1998) 'TMA reports theatre more popular than football league', *ArtsBusiness,* Issue 28, 7 June, 1.

Baumol, W.J. (1967) 'Performing arts: the permanent crisis', *Business Horizons,* Autumn, 47–50.

Bhuchar, S. (1999) 'What's different about Asian audiences?', *ArtsBusiness*, 32, 2 August, 5–6.

Blaug, M. (1976) *The Economics of the Arts*. Martin Robertson.

Butler, P. (2000) 'By popular demand: marketing the arts', *Journal of Marketing Management*, Vol. 16, No. 4, May, 343–64.

Colbert, F., Nantel, J. and Bilodeau, S. (1994; 2nd ed. 2001) *Marketing Culture and the Arts*. Morin.

DCMS (Department for Culture, Media and Sport) (2001) 'Creative Industries Mapping Document 2001' (available at http://www.culture.gov.uk/creative/mapp_foreword.htm).

Diggle, K. (1984) *Guide to Arts Marketing*. Rhinegold.

Downing, D. (2001) *In Our Neighbourhood: A regional theatre and its local community*. Joseph Rowntree Foundation.

Drucker, P. (1964) *Managing for Results*. Macmillan.

du Gay, P., Hall, S., Janes, L., Mackay, H. and Negus, K. (1997) *Doing Cultural Studies: The story of the Sony Walkman*. Sage.

Euromonitor (2000) *Consumer Lifestyles in the UK, November*. Euromonitor.

The Ford Foundation (1974) *The Finances of the Performing Arts: Volume 2*. Ford Foundation.

Hirschman, E.C. (1993) 'Aesthetics, ideologies and the limits of the marketing concept', *Journal of Marketing*, Vol. 47, Summer, 49–55.

Hodge, S., James, J. and Lawson, A. (1998) 'Miles ahead: arts marketing that works in regional Australia', Australia Council (available at www.ozco.gov.au. Accessed 15 May 2002).

Howkins, J. (2001) 'Money for new rope', *Independent on Sunday*, 10 June, 11–16.

International Arts Bureau (2000) *A Comparative Study of Levels of Arts Expenditure in Selected Countries and Regions*. Arts Council/An Chomhairle Ealaíón.

Jermyn, H. (2001) *The Arts and Social Exclusion: A review prepared for the Arts Council of England*. ACE.

Joseph Rowntree Foundation (2000) *Findings: Poverty and social exclusion in Britain*. Joseph Rowntree Foundation.

Khan, Y. (2001) 'Marketing to multicultural Britain', *The Guardian*, Pulse Section, 26 June.

Kotler, P. (1975) *Marketing Management: Analysis, planning and control*, 3rd ed. Prentice-Hall.

Kotler, P. and Andreasen, A. (1991) *Strategic Marketing for Non-Profit Organisations*. Prentice-Hall.

Landry, L., Greene, L., Matarasso, F. and Bianchini, F. (1995) *The Art of Regeneration: Urban renewal through cultural activity*. Comedia.

Lewis, J. (1990) *Art, Culture and Enterprise*. Routledge.

Matarasso, F. (1997) *Use or Ornament? The social impact of participation in the arts*. Comedia.

Mattison, B. (2002) 'Americans like classical music but don't go to concerts, study says', andante website (http://www.andante.com. Accessed 18 April 2002).

McDonald, M. (1999) *Marketing Plans: How to prepare them, how to use them*, 4th ed. Butterworth-Heinemann.

Meeks, P. (2000) 'Heydays: creative opportunities for the over 55s in Leeds', *ArtsBusiness*, 22 May, 9.

Mercer, D. (1996) *Marketing*, 2nd ed. Blackwell Business.

Melillo, J.V. (1983) *Market the Arts!* Foundation for the Extension and Development of the American Professional Theater.

Mokwa, M.P., Dawson, W.M. and Prieve, E.A. (1980) *Marketing the Arts*. New York: Praeger.

Moriarty, G. (1993) A safe place to dream, *Mailout*. June/July, 10–11.

Mulgan, G. and Worpole, K. (1986) *Saturday Night and Sunday Morning*. Routledge.

Myerscough, J. (1988) *The Economic Importance of the Arts in Britain*. Policy Studies Institute.

Newman, D. (1977) *Subscribe Now! Building arts audiences through dynamic subscription promotion*. Theater Communications Group.

Office of National Statistics (1997) *General Household Survey*. HMSO.

O'Sullivan, T. (1999) 'Meet the family', *ArtsBusiness*, 13 September, 5–6.

Pick, J. (1993) 'A pick up the arts', *Mailout*, June/July, 5.

Prahalad, C.K. and Ramaswamy, V. (2000) 'Co-opting consumer competence', *Harvard Business Review*, Vol. 78, Part 1, (January–February), 79–80.

Precision Marketing (2002) 'Arts marketing raises curtain on new stage', *Precision Marketing*, 8 March, 11.

Priestley, J.B. (1947) *The Arts under Socialism . . . Being a lecture given to the Fabian Society, with a postscript on what the Government should do for the arts here and now*. Turnstile Press.

Scher, V. (2002) 'Arts "salesman" follows own advice: make 'em subscribe', *The San Diego Union-Tribune*, 21 April, 8.

Shaw, J. (2002) 'Introduction, Section 8 of Artists Stories: Marketing and Promotion', Artic Producers Publishing Co. (available at: http://www.anweb.co.uk).

Skelton, A., Bridgwood, A., Duckworth, K., Hutton, L., Fenn, C., Creaser, C. and Babbidge, A. (2002) *Arts in England: Attendance, participation and attitudes*, Research report 27. Arts Council of England.

Smith, C. (1998) *Creative Britain*. Faber.

Social Trends 32 (2002) The Stationery Office.

Sullivan, M. (1988) *Arts Councils in Conflict*. The Canada Council.

Tusa, J. (1999) *Art Matters: Reflecting on culture*. Methuen.

VAN (The Voluntary Arts Network). (1994) *Strengthening Foundations*. VAN.

Wilson, J. (1993) 'Signs of definitions', *Mailout*, August/September, 6–8.

Wilson, J. (2001) 'Challenging the Asian equation', *ArtsBusiness*, 12 February, 8.

2

Audiences

For most artists the audience is an integral part of an artistic experience. Only when the public experiences what the artist wishes to communicate is the creative process complete. The audience is vital for more practical purposes too. Art which does not generate audiences will seldom generate revenues, whether from box office receipts or funding bodies and sponsors. The development of audiences is therefore a fundamental responsibility of the marketing function. In practice, this means that the main task of arts marketing is to motivate people to attend performances and exhibitions or purchase art works or crafts, encouraging them to share in the artistic experience being provided.

To do this effectively, arts organizations must understand the needs, desires and motivations of all those people who are, or could be, attenders at their events or venues. This chapter aims to shed some light on the characteristics of audiences, and then goes on to look at how this information can be used and applied in practice. The chapter includes sections on:

● the nature of audiences
● how audiences engage with new artistic experiences
● the decision to attend
● target marketing

What is an audience?

The term 'audience' can take on a variety of meanings in a variety of contexts:

Audiences as 'arts receptors'

Lamos and Stewart (1983) see the audience as 'a sounding board for the artistic impulse . . . The artist is the communicator, the audience is his other self.' They imply that an audience consists simply of those who experience art.

From a marketing point of view, this definition is of limited value as it excludes the notion of intention. It may, though, be useful in considering the audience for, say, public art. Public art, such as sculpture in a city centre, may or may not be actively sought by those who see it. It may simply be an expression by the artist which exists in people's lives, thereby making them members of its audience even in the absence of any intention on their part to view it.

Audiences as stakeholders

An audience can also be thought of as comprising all those with whom an individual or organization has some form of communication. For an arts organization, this may include all those who support the arts in any way, or who have an interest in their development. Attenders of arts events are obviously central to this, but the definition also refers to those with less direct contact with the organization, such as:

- central government funding bodies
- regional arts funding agencies
- local authorities
- charitable trusts
- primary, secondary and tertiary educational establishments
- the local/national/regional press and media
- potential customers for ancillary services, such as catering, space hire or costumes
- local, regional or national business sponsors
- other artists or arts organizations
- friends or members, trustees or governors of arts organizations

Audiences as customers

This approach views the audience as being involved in a transaction with an artist or arts organization. 'The theatre invests money, time and artistic commitment to give the audience pleasure. The audience invests money and time in support of the theatre. It also invests emotional commitment' (Schlosser, 1983).

This definition sees audiences as being those with whom the arts organization is trying to exchange something of value. For marketers it is the most useful definition, as it implies that people make choices about the art forms or events that they wish to be involved with and are willing to offer something in return for that participation. Marketing activity can be undertaken in an attempt to enhance the value of the exchange process to both parties. Schlosser sees it as activity which '. . . directs the traffic on this two-way street that connects theatre and audience, and keeps the movement going in both directions'.

This definition sees primary audiences as those who do (or could) attend or participate in arts events, including audiences at a play or concert, customers at a gallery looking at pictures, children participating in drama workshops and even collectors buying pictures from a selling exhibition. It is this concept of an audience that will be the emphasis of the rest of this chapter.

The idea of audiences as customers performing transactions is also of relevance to secondary audiences such as funding bodies, sponsors and members, who are also looking to exchange value with arts organizations. Marketing activity can also be used effectively in developing these relationships.

Audience development

If we view the objective of marketing activity as enhancing the value of exchange processes between arts organizations and audiences, we can view the task of building audiences as being more than just increasing the numbers of attenders (though this is often a priority in the short term, usually for financial reasons). Total value can certainly be enhanced if the same people enjoy the arts more often, but equally this goal can be achieved by enabling people who do not usually attend to enjoy the experience. Audience development is as much about increasing the range of audiences as it is about the size of audiences.

Maitland (2000a) defines audience development as: 'a planned process which involves building a relationship between an individual and the arts'. Rick Rogers (1998) gives a more specific definition which indicates the breadth of objectives that audience development activity may include: 'sustaining and expanding existing or regular audiences or visitors, creating new attenders and participants and enhancing their enjoyment, understanding, skills and confidence across the art forms'.

In the long term, the task of audience development is one of improving access to the arts for a wide range of people, not just those who are already committed attenders. It requires that the arts are made more accessible in variety of ways – physically and geographically, but also socially and psychologically, breaking down traditional elitism which threatens to devalue the arts for sizeable proportions of the population.

To achieve this, arts organizations need to understand people's relationships with the arts and to identify the range of influences on the decision to participate. Only then can the needs of potential audiences be identified and catered for and techniques designed to help them to get the most out of the arts.

Developing respect

Not everyone agrees that it is appropriate to try to develop audiences, including Dave O'Donnell of Community Music:

'The basic premise of audience development, or access, or community outreach, or whatever we want to call it, is patronizing and corrupt. It is predicated on the assumption that the public has got it wrong; that if only we could throw enough Lottery money at enough orchestras to put enough players into enough inner-city primary schools to play to enough Black kids, or even worse, get enough Black kids to copy classical composers and call it creativity – if only we could overcome the young people's stubborn refusal to go to concert halls – then we would save them from a life of cultural poverty and justify our salaries.

'Surely we must get more sophisticated in our thinking. Surely we have to realize that we, the white, university-educated, salaried autocrats, the cultural power brokers, the decision-makers, are the ones who need to change. We need to develop some respect for what young people want, some respect for their music.

'Then, if we are lucky, they will reach out to us, and do us the honour of enriching our lives and involving us in all that power and fun, and perhaps we would see the wonderful sight of teams of working-class youths being funded by the Lottery to run outreach programmes for middle-aged arts managers to encourage them to lighten up a bit and join the party.'

Source: O'Donnell, 1999. Reproduced with kind permission.

As the task of audience development is so broad, marketing is but one of three approaches that arts organizations adopt to develop their audiences. Education work is widely practised, tending to focus on the long-term development of an individual's appreciation of the arts and usually aiming to create an 'audience of tomorrow' rather than active arts attenders today. Participatory activity with small groups is commonly used with a view to providing an experience that will help change attitudes to and understanding of artistic work. Artists also take part in audience development activity, by creating work that can be accessed by target audience segments. 'Concerts for Children', for example, is a concept adopted by some orchestras, with a view to presenting musical programmes which can be appreciated by those with little or no musical knowledge or background. Collaboration between the marketing, education and artistic functions can create the most effective audience development activity of all.

Case 2.1 Galleries go for new audiences

When the opening of the Tate Modern in London proved to be a catalyst to changing attitudes towards contemporary art, a three-year initiative involving five contemporary art galleries in Hampshire set out to attract a group of potential attenders described as 'the interested but wary'.

The 'Gallery GO' initiative involved Aspex Gallery in Portsmouth, John Hansard Gallery, Millais Gallery, Southampton City Art Gallery and the Winchester Art Gallery. The group identified its core target audiences using the Mosaic's geodemographic profiling system (see Chapter 3), which splits the population into 12 main lifestyle groups. Stylish Singles, described as people for whom 'self-expression is more important than conformity', were deemed the lifestyle group most likely to participate in the programme. A combination of complete newcomers, lapsed gallery attenders and occasional gallery visitors were targeted with regular mailshots inviting them to attend specific events.

The programme consisted of an introductory session and more advanced events that were designed to build interest and confidence in the subject. At the introductory level the intention was to capture interest with talks linked to exhibitions. These lay the groundwork for attenders to begin to form their own judgements. Research into the project confirmed the advisability of this 'softly softly' approach. As one early attender put it, her initial reaction was 'Good grief! Am I going to have to express an opinion on it?', but by the time these people were ready to attend the more advanced 'Critical Circle' discussions dealing with more complex issues surrounding contemporary art, they were armed with enough knowledge to contribute confidently to discussions.

Source: Simmonds, 2001.

The adoption of the arts

Given that audience development is about extending the experience of existing customers into new areas, and trying to get potential customers to try something new, an understanding of the way that new ideas spread in society provides arts marketers with some valuable insights. Everett M. Rogers (1962) concluded that society can be divided into five groups according to their propensity to espouse new ideas or new products (see Figure 2.1).

Innovators

These experimenters make up less than 3 per cent of the population. They tend to be younger than average, financially stable, well educated and confident. Their affluence means they can afford to be first on the block with new products, although their strong drives lead them to be selective and image

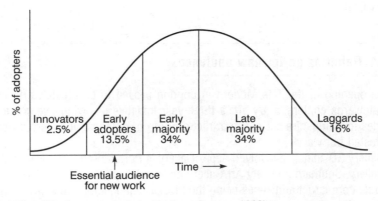

Figure 2.1 The diffusion process (adapted from Rogers, 1962)

conscious. They can be observed at first nights and private views. They are excited rather than disturbed at the prospect of the unfamiliar.

Early adopters

Following the Innovators into the market are the Early Adopters, a larger but less adventurous group. Their receptiveness to new ideas is reflected in high readership of magazines. They are educated and confident. They are usually already keen on the area in which the innovation is being made. So, for example, early adopters of contemporary dance forms will tend to come from within existing dance audiences. Winning early adopters is crucial. If they do not try out an experience there is no chance of it spreading further by word-of-mouth. Rogers found that there was a close correlation between this group and 'opinion leaders', people whose attitudes and behaviours influence members of their social and family groups (as discussed in Chapter 6).

Managing the risk

The type of people who normally buy original, innovative artworks are described by Morris (1991) as opinion leaders with the confidence 'to spend money on items purely for their own sake rather than as a way of conforming with the values of a majority group'. To appeal to a slightly wider group, marketing activity has somehow to remove the risk attached to such a purchase. The online gallery at www.britart.co.uk attempts to do this in a number of ways. Its home page encourages the nervous by saying 'buying online . . . it's not scary, really!' A quality assurance statement is made: 'All of the art represented by Britart is carefully chosen by our panel of art specialists. The selection committee comprises of artists, art critics and art lovers as well as senior members of the Britart team . . . Only when the team agrees the art is of the appropriate quality and value will we represent it on the site.' And finally, a no-questions-asked money back guarantee is offered for 14 days after purchase.

Sources: Morris, 1991; Maitland, 2000(b); and http://www.britart.co.uk 16 May 2002

Early and late majority

Encouraged by the example of the early adopters, the majority of customers then become willing to take an idea on board. Together these groups constitute more than two-thirds of the total market. The early majority tend to be solid and middle class. Late majority members are older and more traditional in their values, making them naturally conservative. They are reluctant about innovation, but finally come round to it once everyone else has done so.

Laggards

These are the arts marketer's greatest triumph: the people who are on the far reaches of the arts universe but are eventually led to realize that arts experience has something special to offer them, and climb on board.

Non-adopters

No matter what the product or service under consideration, there will still be a group of people whom it will never reach. In the arts the 'hostile' segment of society is the resolute non-adopters. They may have tried the arts and found them wanting, or their self-image or personal culture has inured them against the prospect. For the subsidized sector, in particular, arts non-adopters pose a dilemma as they have already contributed to the arts through national and local taxes. It may be, for example, that a theatre's open day attracts people who will never return as audience, but have had their experience enriched by that much contact with arts activity. Similarly the bar or catering facilities may attract non-arts clientele, again justifying their investment in the organization.

The diffusion model of how audiences respond to innovation suggests that it is a gradual and risky process. It confirms that, if you can identify it, there is always a market for new work. But it also predicts that at first, at least, it is a very restricted market. Even though the innovation-friendly part of your audience know what they like, the majority like what they know. The importance of a patient approach is underlined by the model's prediction that the total market for any offering will contain less than 20 per cent of people who responded readily to it in the first place.

As we have seen, this scant 20 per cent will tend to be established regular attenders. The figure brings to mind what is known as the 'Pareto effect', a phenomenon first noted around 1900 by the Italian sociologist Vilfredo Pareto, who observed that 20 per cent of the people held 80 per cent of the wealth. In many markets, 20 per cent of consumers are responsible for 80 per cent of the business. These heavy users need to be jealously maintained, but they are also the best prospects for innovation. What is true for the arts is true for the fashion industry, like the arts a production-led business. It manages to take the mass of clothes buyers with it by concentrating at first on a very small but significant section of its market by presenting the collections of the big designers. Six to nine months later, colours and styles in the high-street shops start to reflect the look that has been unveiled on the catwalk and the ordinary clothes buyer catches up with his or her moneyed counterpart. Your existing users are the best prospects for innovation, and innovations will not stick if your existing heavy users do not take them up.

Lawrence Till, former Chief Executive of the Bolton Octagon, saw a balanced programme as the key to sustaining audiences for his theatre:

> You don't provide a diet of what they know they like to eat; you ask them to taste some new flavours as well. It's important you don't pander to the lowest common denominator but try and present work that will challenge people.

Sometimes you experiment. Sometimes you hope that the beetroot doesn't bleed on the lettuce: or sometimes that's useful . . . a lot of buildings are either doing fewer plays or turning into arts centres and presenting touring work. Everyone could make their job easier sometimes by presenting tours but the people I work with are incredibly creative and they have to have an outlet. (Murdin, 1994)

So new and unfamiliar work is essential. It provides staff and performers with new opportunities to develop, and it provides audiences with fresh experiences. However difficult it may be to attract viable audiences for new work, this is a vital part of the marketing task. An arts organization that fails to innovate will gradually lose touch with its market.

The decision to attend

Patterns of arts attendance are not uniform throughout the population. The wide variety of definitions of arts activities makes measures of participation in the arts problematic, but the general conclusion that emerges is that although attendance patterns vary across art form, arts audiences are most likely to emerge from particular age groups, social classes and educational backgrounds (Jermyn *et al.*, 2001). The overall profile of UK arts attendance can be drawn from the data gathered in the Target Group Index, discussed further in Chapter 3, and national statistics such as those cited in Chapter 1.

The reason arts attendance is not uniformly spread throughout the population is because, as in most buying decisions, people are influenced by a wide variety of social, personal and psychological factors which either predispose them towards the arts or serve to alienate them. The better arts organizations understand these factors, the better placed they are to find ways of breaking down the physical and mental barriers which restrict access to the arts and hinder the development of wide-ranging audiences.

Influences on arts attendance: social factors

Social factors, especially the influence of culture, reference groups and social class, can affect patterns of arts attendance considerably.

Cultural factors

A culture comprises everything in society, both tangible and intangible, that is created by its people. This includes the values and behaviours which are acceptable, and these values and behaviours are learned and passed on from one generation to the next. Societies which value cultural features such as education, creativity and leisure are the ones most likely to support a strong arts infrastructure and place importance on the development of the arts and audiences.

Subcultures can be found within cultures, where there are groups of people displaying even closer similarities of attitudes, actions and values than in the culture as a whole. These subcultural groups are usually separated by geographical regions or ethnic background. Culture-specific events may be appropriate if subcultural groups are sizeable, but other factors may be influential in encouraging or discouraging arts attendance. For example, Marplan (1988) found that 'the welcoming atmosphere and entertaining nature of the performance were much more important than other factors' for Asian, African and Caribbean live arts attenders in the UK; and Desai and Thomas (1998) found that a significant barrier to ethnic-minority communities visiting museums is the perception that the selection of exhibits and their presentation fails to reflect the contributions of Black and South Asian people to British society.

Reference groups

A reference group is any group, including family, friends and work associates, with whom an individual identifies so closely that he or she adopts many of their values, attitudes and behaviour patterns. Parental influences are particularly strong, more so than the influences of school. Children whose parents actively support the arts, particularly those involved at the amateur level, are more likely to participate and to continue to do so as adults, than those from homes with little interest in the arts (Waters, 1989).

Parent power

Research in the US has found that 60 per cent of those who buy tickets for classical music concerts started attending aged 17 or younger, and for over 40 per cent of these, their attendance was influenced by their parents – significantly more than the number who were influenced by their schools.

Age started attending classical concerts	Percentage of group	Motivating factor	
<18	60	42% family (parents)	26% school
18–24	23	30% like music	23% friends
25–34	11	29% friends	25% family (partner)
35–54	6	33% unique	25% curious

Source: Kolb, 2001. © International Journal of Arts Management.

Reference groups encourage individuals to build up pictures of themselves which include 'what people like me do in their spare time' or 'how people like me behave'. If arts attendance is seen as irrelevant or alien to a person's reference group, it is likely to be rejected. This is particularly so in the case of the performing arts, where only a small proportion of attenders are likely to be alone and having a companion will be a deciding factor in participation for most people. Arts organizations can turn this situation to their advantage by making special efforts to target the social secretaries of clubs and organizations, who can be relied upon to make party bookings and bring in groups of individuals who might not otherwise have been interested in attending.

Social class

A social class is a group of individuals who are seen to have a similar rank in society. Class membership has traditionally been based on the occupation of the head of the household (see Table 2.1), although there are many other factors (such as education and habits of consumption or taste) which have an influence.

Those within the same social class tend to develop similar attitudes, values and behaviour patterns, and this is evident in arts participation. Audience surveys from across the UK continue to demonstrate that members of the ABC1 social grades are more active in almost all types of arts participation than those in the C2DE grades. Jermyn *et al.* (2001) reported the proportions attending at least one arts event in the previous year as ranging from 88 per cent of ABC1s to only 61 per cent of C2DEs. The professional and administrative classes were also more likely to have bought or read a novel, written stories or poetry; played a musical instrument for their own pleasure; painted, drawn or sculpted; done photography; and used computers to generate art. Some argue that practical difficulties, such as low income levels and lower car ownership among the lower grades, are responsible for the disparities, but evidence suggests that psychological barriers are more influential than these. The gap

Table 2.1 Social grade as defined by the National Readership Survey.

The National Readership Survey (NRS), a regular survey of UK reading habits, divides the population into social grades according to occupation (http://www.nrs.org.uk) – a system widely adopted by marketers in the UK. The most recent guide to which occupations denote which grades is published by the Market Research Society (2003).

Category	Social class	Occupation of chief income earner in the household
A	Upper middle class	Higher managerial, administrative or professional
B	Middle class	Intermediate managerial, administrative or professional
C1	Lower middle class	Supervisor or clerical and junior managerial, administrative or professional
C2	Skilled working class	Skilled manual workers
D	Working class	Semi and unskilled manual workers
E	Those at the lowest levels of subsistence	State pensioners etc. with no other earnings

Source: http://www.mrs.co.uk, accessed 18 January 2003.

between the classes becomes even more apparent when different art forms are considered, with opera and ballet being almost exclusively the domain of the higher social groups. This in itself is likely to alienate those who are not familiar with the established social conventions.

Influences on arts attendance: personal factors

Personal factors, including age, gender, income and education levels, appear to influence an individual's predisposition towards the arts, though the last two factors are the strongest predictors of arts attendance.

Sex makes a difference

Gender differences are more apparent in arts participation than they are in arts attendance. Similar proportions of men and women are found to attend most art forms, with the exception of pantomime and dance, which are more likely to be attended by women, and jazz, which is more likely to be attended by men. However, women are more likely than men to have

- read or bought a novel, work of fiction, play or poetry
- done textile crafts or bought a craft object, and
- danced, other than clubbing or ballet

and men are more likely than women to have

- used computers to generate artworks
- played a musical instrument either to an audience or for their own pleasure
- done wood crafts, and
- done photography

Source: Jermyn et al., 2001.

Age

As a rule, arts attendance is greatest in the 35–54 age band, but there are notable departures from this across the different art forms, and different patterns emerge within certain ethnic-minority groups, so generalizations are difficult and can be unhelpful. Audiences for contemporary dance, for example, are far younger than audiences for ballet: typically, around 45 per cent of contemporary dance attenders are aged 25–44, and a further 14 per cent aged 15–19 (Talking About Dance, 1998). A survey of Asian, African and Caribbean live arts attenders (Marplan, 1988) recorded 85 per cent of attenders as under 35, whereas the average for the UK population as a whole was only 33 per cent. Age differences are particularly marked for those who access digital art through the internet. Jermyn *et al.* (2001) found that one in four of those aged under 35 had done so in the previous 12 months, but only one in 50 of the over 64s. Even within an art form, the age of attenders will vary. An audience survey for English National Opera at the Coliseum showed that over half the audience for Philip Glass's contemporary opera *Akhnaten* were under 35 whilst 60 per cent of the audience for Smetana's nineteenth-century classic *The Bartered Bride* were over 45.

Gender

Patterns of arts attendance are related to gender, but this varies widely across art forms. Women buy more theatre tickets than men and dance audiences record very high proportions of females, but more men than women attend jazz.

Income

A close relationship can be demonstrated between income levels and attendance at arts events though it is not clear whether this relationship is primarily due to social class, as the higher social groups tend to earn higher incomes. If income is a strong influence on attendance, then ticket prices or admission fees could be expected to have a major impact on attendance, though there is conflicting evidence on this point. For example, a survey of London concert audiences revealed that the proportion of C2DE social groups was much larger for light music than for symphony concerts, though ticket prices were comparable. On the other hand, the introduction of even voluntary admission charges at national museums in the UK was found to reduce attendance, and when entrance charges to national museums were abolished towards the end of 2001, on average visitor numbers in the first month doubled in comparison with the same period the previous year. Undoubtedly there is a relationship between arts attendance and income levels, particularly among the unwaged and those on the lowest income levels, but the picture becomes less clear at the higher income levels.

Education

There is consistent evidence to show that attendance at an arts event is closely related to the age at which full-time education was completed. The 2000/2001 TGI survey showed that 72.5 per cent of those who took their education to 19 or over were currently attending arts activities as opposed to 52.6 per cent and 34.1 per cent of those who left education at 17/18 and 16 respectively (Verwey, 2002). Differences can be seen, though, between different types of performance and/or venue. For example, about half the visitors to the Victoria and Albert Museum had been in full-time education until at least 20 years of age but six out of ten visitors to the National Railway Museum had completed their full-time education by the age of 16. The importance, therefore, of including cultural education in the National Curriculum cannot be underestimated. Attempts by marketers to create appeal are likely to fail if their target audiences have insufficient basic understanding of an art form to enable them to appreciate it. Jenny Haughton, the director of Artworking, a Dublin-based visual arts agency, in a personal interview said: 'We need to develop the way the visual arts are in Germany. They are a compulsory element of the curriculum throughout the education system. As a result the Germans are serious purchasers. They see pictures as important in the home.'

Influences on arts attendance: psychological factors

Psychological factors, especially perception, beliefs and attitudes, personality and motivation are also influences on the decision to attend arts events.

Perception

This is the process by which people make sense of the world. Each of us selects, organizes and interprets information to produce meaning. Because we are unable to be conscious of all the messages which surround us every day, we select information that will help us to satisfy our needs, and screen out messages which are of no use to us (known as selective perception). Then we interpret that information based on the attitudes and beliefs we have stored in our memories (which may or may not be accurate), and only if the information is deemed important will we remember it (selective retention).

This explains why arts organizations find it difficult to attract groups who have traditionally shown little interest in the arts. First of all, these groups ignore the messages about the arts – they are unlikely to notice the advertisements or critical reviews. If they do notice them, they may interpret them negatively if they hold negative attitudes towards the arts. Promotional activity has to break through selective perception before it can communicate its messages, and the messages must attempt to break down any negative attitudes or override any previous experiences before they will be retained and interest generated.

This may mean that sizeable proportions of the total potential market for the arts are effectively unavailable to individual arts organizations (Diggle, 1994). The process of breaking through selective perception, distortion and retention is likely to be one that takes time as well as money, and education rather than promotion is the most likely means of achieving this breakthrough. The emergence of audience development agencies which run projects designed to reach out to the 'unavailable audience' is one way in which this problem is being tackled.

The marketing challenge

The process for developing audiences will depend on a target audience's predisposition towards arts participation:

Segment	Task	Challenges	Tactics
Disinclined	Engage	Perceptual	Change perceptions/ deconstruct myths
Inclined	Involve	Practical/logistical	Remove barriers
Participating	Deepen	Experiential	Create meaning

Source: Yoshitomo, 2000.

Beliefs and attitudes

A belief is a descriptive thought that a person holds about something, which may be based on knowledge, but also on faith or opinion. Beliefs lead to the formation of attitudes, which are an emotionally charged reaction to a set of beliefs, and lead to behaviour patterns which are very slow to change. For example, if a person believes that 'only intellectuals and tourists go to art galleries' then they may conclude that they would feel uncomfortable in such an environment and form negative attitudes which will deter them from attending.

Personality

This includes all the internal traits and behaviours that make a person unique and arises from both heredity and personal experiences. Personalities are described by characteristics such as compulsiveness, gregariousness, author-itarianism, extroversion, introversion, aggressiveness and dogmatism. Because these traits are generally difficult to measure, links between personality and arts attendance are also difficult to measure, though stereotypical images exist as to the types of people who, for example, are most likely to participate in amateur productions or to frequent museums. These images may need to be dispelled to avoid other personality types being alienated.

Motivation

Reasons for involvement with the arts are wide-ranging, but people can be seen as satisfying needs at all levels. People with similar motivations can be identified and grouped together. They will often need to be offered different types of arts experience, services and facilities to satisfy their wide-ranging needs. In the performing arts, these groups have been characterized as follows (NOP, 1991), and it is interesting to note that several of the motivations identified have little, if anything, to do with the arts event itself (Figure 2.2).

- Entertainment seekers: motivated by the need for amusement and the arousal of curiosity.
- Self-improvers: driven by a need for personal development.
- Trend-setters: wishing to be identified with an elite intellectual minority.
- Status seekers: wishing to be identified with a socially superior minority.
- Lonely escapists: motivated by an opportunity to be in the company of others.
- Inspiration/sensation seekers: looking for sensory and emotional stimulation.
- Extroverts/performers: motivated by a forum for self-expression.
- Social attenders: anticipating that a social setting will add to their enjoyment of the arts.

How is choice made?

If arts organizations are to develop audiences, they need not only to understand the factors that influence the decision to attend, but also the way in which people make choices and come to decisions about attending arts events.

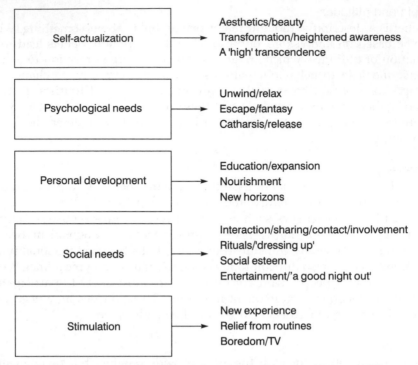

Figure 2.2 Motivations for arts attendance (adapted from Cooper and Tower, 1992)

Arts organizations face competition from a wide range of sources (discussed further in Chapters 5 and 8). Potential audiences start off with the choice as to whether to attend an arts event at all (maybe they could choose a sports event, a shopping expedition or an evening in front of the TV instead), and those who decide in favour of the arts will be faced with the dilemma of choosing between a wide range of both similar and different artistic experiences.

Audiences generally pass through five distinct stages in making these choices, as shown in Figure 2.3.

Problem recognition

This can occur when individuals become aware of a desire or need. Sometimes it is a stimulus from the environment which can prompt the desire. A person may read a critical review in the newspaper which sparks an interest, or receive a leaflet which announces the tour of a famous artist or favourite play. On other occasions, the awareness of a need stems from unrelated factors. For example:

- 'It's Saturday afternoon and I haven't got anything to do.'
- 'It's my birthday and I want to mark the occasion.'
- 'I want to have a good time with my friends.'
- 'I need some ideas for my English homework.'

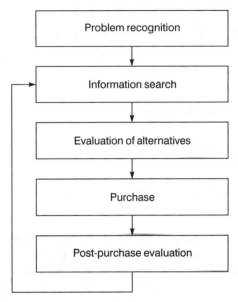

Figure 2.3 The audience decision-making process

Although the needs expressed here are wide-ranging (in these cases for pastime, celebration, entertainment and education) each of them could potentially be satisfied by attending an arts event. It is problem recognition which turns the public into potential attenders.

Information search

Next, a search is undertaken for information to help these potential attenders solve their problems and satisfy their desires. They will first of all search their memories for previous experience of solving similar problems (e.g. 'Did I enjoy my last visit to an art gallery?' or 'Was my last theatre trip good value for money?'), but if this is insufficient to convince them as to a course of action, they will look externally. Common sources of information include the opinions of friends and relatives, advertisements and leaflets and editorial comment.

As a result of this information search, potential attenders focus on a much narrower group of alternative ways to satisfy the problem identified – known as the 'evoked set' (Rice, 1999).

Evaluation of alternatives

Each potential attender will then identify criteria for comparing the options in the evoked set. For an arts event, the comparisons will be made more between expectations of the event than any tangible features. Expectations have to be the basis for the evaluation of aspects such as the quality of performance, or the ambience, as it is not until the show or exhibition is actually produced that such features are realized. Thus the prices of events can be compared at this stage, but their value for money cannot.

Purchase

When the alternatives have been evaluated, choices are made as to

- what to attend
- when to attend

and the transaction is made when

- the tickets are purchased
- the event is attended

The potential attenders are converted into members of the audience.

Post-purchase evaluation

After the event, members of the audience will evaluate the experience to see if it met expectations. This evaluation will be used in the information search for the next arts-related decision process. If expectations are not met, the disappointment is likely to lead to considerable negative word-of-mouth publicity. 'Whereas, on average, a satisfied customer tells three people about a good product experience, a dissatisfied customer gripes to eleven people' (Kotler and Armstrong, 1991).

This process of choice has some important implications for arts organizations, who must ask themselves a number of questions:

- *What problems are we solving for our audiences?*
  Identifying why people attend is fundamental to satisfying their needs and attracting others with similar needs. It is the underlying principle behind the whole concept of target marketing, discussed later in this chapter.
- *Where do our audiences find their information?*
  Efforts must be made to ensure that audiences store positive impressions in their memories, and research must also be done to identify the most effective form of publicity materials.
- *Which are the most influential evaluative criteria?*
  Organizations need to identify the most important factors that potential attenders take into consideration in deciding between alternatives. The knowledge of this should influence a whole range of factors, from pricing policy to programming schedules. They can also be highlighted in promotional materials to attract audiences.
- *How easy is it for potential customers to complete the transaction?*
  If galleries have limited opening hours or box offices have continually busy telephone lines, unhelpful staff or limited payment options, a decision to attend or purchase can be reversed even at a very late stage.
- *Are expectations met and exceeded?*
  Customer satisfaction needs to be continually assessed, as the consequences of dissatisfaction for the reputation of the organization can be very serious. The causes must be identified as soon as possible. They may be quite easy to remedy, for example in the case of misleading promotional material, but there may be fundamental problems related to corporate image, customer

care or target markets which need to be addressed to bring the arts experience in line with expectations; either this or the customers must be educated into appropriate levels of expectation (discussed in Chapter 4).

The process of marketing research is the means by which answers to these questions can be revealed. This is covered in the next chapter.

Who makes the choice?

Not every member of an arts audience will have played the same role in the decision to attend. Indeed, the whole decision-making process may have been divided up between a group of individuals, who collectively are known as the decision-making unit.

- The initiator is the one who first suggests a visit to a gallery or museum, or a trip to the theatre (e.g. a friend suggests you go to a particular concert on Wednesday).
- The influencer's advice carries weight in the evaluation of alternatives and his or her opinion is valued by other members of the group (e.g. a colleague of yours went to the previous night's performance but wasn't very impressed, and recommends an alternative).
- The decider makes the final choice as to where and/or when to go (e.g. you decide that you'd like to go to this recommended concert on Tuesday, rather than the one your friend suggested).
- The buyer performs the transaction (e.g. your friend agrees with you and buys the tickets).
- The attender experiences the event (e.g. you both go to the concert).

If a person chooses to attend an arts event alone, he or she may take all of these roles and be responsible for all the stages of the choice process. Normally though, a range of people are involved, so the arts organization needs to be aware of all who participate in the decision process and the ways in which they affect the choice. Influencers are particularly important, and the importance of critics as opinion leaders should not be underestimated.

Target marketing

The study of audience behaviour leads us to the conclusion that potential audiences consist of sub-groups of individuals with similar needs, characteristics, motivations and buying practices. For arts organizations to attempt to attract members of all of these groups at the same time for the same events is unrealistic. Target marketing is the process by which the specific needs of different parts of the total potential audience are matched with the artistic product being produced. This process has two distinct steps: firstly market segmentation, whereby marketers identify the nature of the relevant sub-groups for their organizations, and secondly market targeting, when different activities are aimed at different groups using different marketing techniques.

Market segmentation

A market segment simply consists of buyers with similar needs and wants, and markets can be usefully divided up according to those buyer needs. Different groupings will be appropriate in different markets and one of the most important tasks of the marketing function in an arts organization is to identify the most appropriate ways to divide up their potential audience. In dividing up a potential audience, two important constraints have to be borne in mind.

Size
Is the group big enough to be worth treating it separately? The ultimate form of market segmentation is customization, whereby each person's differences are recognized and each individual is offered something different to match their needs exactly. Clearly this is unrealistic and unnecessary for arts organizations operating with scarce resources. One of the key criteria for dividing up potential audiences has to be the size of the group identified. The numbers of people in each group have to be quantified so that decisions can be made as to whether the effort of reaching them can be cost-effective (or at least justifiable in educational or social terms).

Accessibility
How easy is it to communicate with this group? As the purpose of market segmentation is to enable potential audiences to be targeted more appropriately, unless the sub-groups in that potential audience can be extracted from the overall market and exposed to separate marketing offers the segment is of no practical use.

Case 2.2 Pink dilemmas

Lesbian and gay arts organizations face two fundamental marketing issues every time they present their work: what is 'lesbian and gay artwork?' and 'how do you target a lesbian and gay audience?' These are issues faced by David Leddy, Festival Producer for the UK's largest and most diverse lesbian and gay arts festival, Glasgay, every time he makes a programming decision. The Festival includes theatre, music, comedy, visual arts, community events, film, literature and clubs, and finding a gay link to all these genres can be problematic. Theatre, for example, is fairly simple, as gay-themed plays are of particular relevance to gay audiences; but what counts as 'gay art' when it comes to music is more tenuous and potentially much more limiting, often based purely on the sexuality of the performers rather than the work itself.

At first glance, the notion of a gay audience is an easier one, but on closer inspection, this is clearly not the case. David Leddy says: '. . . we see a disparate audience ranging through all class, race and age brackets. Does a 50-year-old lesbian professional have the same artistic tastes as a 20-year-old gay man working in a shop? Probably not. Predicting quite what they do want is a tricky business. Should a promoter play it safe and book a Shirley Bassey-style torch-song singer for the boys and a tree-sister Tracy Chapman lookey-likey for the girls? Would audiences dismiss it as old hat? The difference between "new" and "old" gay tastes is a vague area. Is your audience open to gay work which does not fit the mould? Many lesbians and gay men harbour prejudice towards their bisexual and transsexual peers. Does a promoter take the moral high ground by programming events for these communities only to find that they are poorly attended? Who knows. So, it seems that not only is "gay art" a misnomer, so is the idea of a single unified "gay audience".'

The problems for promoters of lesbian and gay work do not end there. Having characterized potential attenders, they are faced with the problems of actually finding them. The commercial gay scene revolves around nightclubs and bars, but these may not be the type of people who are also likely to attend an exhibition by a lesbian artist or a film about same-gender marriage. Publicity materials distributed there could fall on deaf ears. Indeed, arts events can provide an excellent alternative for the many lesbians and gay men who do not go out 'on the scene', and feel marginalized in such venues. Getting in touch with these people is most often done through direct mailing and posters, each with its drawbacks. Developing a good mailing list is tricky, but they are invaluable when they exist; and posters are expensive, given that only a tiny proportion of the people who see them will be interested. Press coverage, on the other hand, can be easier to obtain. Magazines and newspapers are keen to cover events which are unusual enough to warrant a story, and gay events can often fit the bill. The downside is that the desire for a story can go in quite the opposite direction, with the wrong kind of media attention ruining events and even jeopardizing public funding and private sponsorship.

Source: Leddy, 2002; www.glasgay.co.uk. Reproduced with kind permission.

The bases for market segmentation

With these constraints in mind, there are four broad bases from which to start the process of market segmentation.

Geographic segmentation

Audiences can be divided up according to where they live. First of all, arts organizations have to identify their geographical catchment area, which will normally consist of those living within a certain drivetime of a venue. Within this catchment area, certain postcodes are more likely than others to be the homes of arts attenders (for more information, see the discussion of Mosaic in Chapter 3). In targeting these homes, for example with direct mail or leaflets, arts organizations can be more certain of appealing to those who are positively disposed towards the arts and who are more likely to at least evaluate the possibility of attending rather than rejecting it outright.

Certain postcodes are also more likely than others to house young people, families, the elderly, the unemployed, students or the ethnic minorities. This is useful if a production or exhibition is of special interest to one or more of these groups; by using direct mail or a leaflet drop they can be reached with relative accuracy and a minimum of waste of promotional expenditure.

Tourists may form another discrete geographic segment. Their needs may be quite different from local people. They may, for example, be available for matinée performances at a theatre or concert and may require language translations at galleries and museums. They are more likely to be attracted through posters and literature in hotels and tourist offices than direct mail or newspaper advertising.

A computerized box office system (explained in Chapter 3) is an invaluable geographic segmentation tool. Arts organizations which capture name and address details at the point when their customers purchase tickets have the ability to segment their audiences by postcode. They will know the geographical composition of their audiences, and are in a position to target their marketing activity at the areas where their attenders are most likely to live.

Demographic segmentation

As we have seen when looking at influences on arts attendance, some demographic factors are good predictors of audience preferences. The benefits sought by attenders in different age, sex, income, education and racial groups may vary widely and different productions and approaches may be required to attract them and satisfy their needs. Demographic segmentation can be useful, but it is often an incomplete means of segmenting arts audiences. Closer and more effective target marketing can sometimes be undertaken if the attitudes and behaviour of audiences are considered alongside their demographic characteristics.

> All we know about non-goers is who they are rather than why they never visit galleries and what it might take to induce them to do so. Even so, this offers a starting point for future policy direction. Non-goers tend to be disproportionately concentrated among . . . the elderly, children, homemakers, tourists, rural dwellers, men, members of low-income households, non-English speakers, and those with only primary or secondary education. (Bennett and Frow, 1992)

Case 2.3 Family friendly

Farnham Maltings is committed to targeting the family audience, and goes to great lengths to provide a warm welcome for parents and children alike. Ticket prices are low, with a further 25 per cent discount for groups of four or more, to encourage several parents to book and pay together. Parking is free for cars, and buggies can be left in the theatre's front lobby. As well as adult meals, children's meals, such as burgers and nuggets with beans and chips, are served in the café prior to a performance, and birthday celebrations can be accommodated – anything from an elaborate party to simply juice and cake.

The performances themselves are generally held at 10 a.m. or 2 p.m. and last only about an hour – short enough to keep most children's attention. In the performance hall, children receive priority seating, with a special mat placed at the front near the stage, giving the children more chance to interact with the actors and puppets. Parents can sit further back, with less confident children and babies in prams. Clowning, clay modelling and drama workshops take place during school holidays and half terms, including all-day events for older children, so that parents can drop them off in the morning and collect them later in the afternoon.

Source: Westbrook, 2002.

Psychographic segmentation

Audiences can be segmented according to their psychological characteristics, as discussed earlier. Perhaps the most important of these psychographic segments are attitude groupings.

Diggle (1994) suggests that potential audiences comprise:

- **Attenders**: those with very positive attitudes towards the arts and whose attitudes are translated into attendance, either just from time-to-time or on a regular basis.
- **Intenders**: those who think the arts are a 'good thing' and like the idea of attending, but never seem to get around to it.
- **The Indifferent**: those who have no strong opinions on the arts and no strong desire to attend either.
- **The Hostile**: those who dislike the idea of the arts altogether and have no intention of participating.

The extent of marketing activity (and resources) required to encourage arts participation by attenders at the top of the attitudinal ladder (Figure 2.4) is far lower than that required to change the attitudes and motivate behaviour among the indifferent and the hostile. The further down the scale people are, the greater the efforts required to get them to attend. Indeed, Diggle refers to the indifferent and the hostile as the 'unavailable audience', as the extent of marketing activity (and resources) required to encourage arts participation by these groups is beyond the scope of most arts marketing budgets. Consequently, segmentation on the basis of attitudes towards the arts creates a dilemma. Attenders and intenders are undoubtedly the most cost-effective groups to target if an organization's objectives are simply to increase audience numbers. But, as attenders and intenders normally come

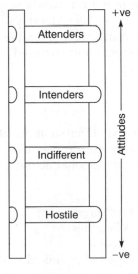

Figure 2.4 The attitude ladder

from similar social and educational backgrounds, to expend effort solely in this way is likely to mean ignoring those from other socio-economic groups, ethnic minorities and other sectors who have traditionally eschewed any involvement with certain art forms. This may not sit very comfortably with a prevailing mission statement which espouses access for all, but may be the only practical solution to audience development for arts organizations under severe financial constraints, for whom 'bums on seats' makes the difference between survival and extinction. Funding bodies, however, may take a different view.

Attitude change is a process which often takes years, or even generations. Education and public relations through appropriate media can speed up the process, but for most arts organizations this will not take place quickly enough to stimulate seat sales and admissions among those who are less well disposed to the arts. The attitudinal segments most important and accessible to arts organizations are likely to remain the attenders and intenders, at least in the medium term. The task of converting the indifferent and the hostile is likely to require the resources of the funding bodies and a positive attitude from both government and the media.

Behavioural segmentation

This involves dividing buyers into groups based on their responses to the arts product, and for arts organizations can be usefully examined in the following five ways:

When do they attend?

Audiences can be grouped according to those who prefer to attend matinées as opposed to evening performances, and weekends as opposed to weekdays. A number of galleries are finding that there is a sizeable segment wishing to attend on Sundays and are moving towards seven-day opening or shifting their weekly closing day to either Mondays or Tuesdays. Here again, computerized box office systems are a valuable tool, as information about attenders' behaviour can be stored and analysed to draw conclusions as to the popularity of different timings.

Why do they attend?

We have already looked at the different motivations people may have for attending the arts, and these groupings can be useful when planning programmes and designing promotional activity. People may attend because they want to:

- celebrate (events such as birthdays)
- socialize (with friends or colleagues)
- do business (entertaining clients)
- learn (either for self-development or linked with formal education)
- purchase (artwork for their own collection or for a present, for example)

Under what circumstances do they attend?

Some people will attend when there is nothing good on television; others will combine a theatre or gallery visit with a shopping trip, or only attend when they are on holiday. If an associated activity can be identified, then this may be used as a basis for the promotional message and in particular influence the distribution of literature.

Profiting from groups

Group bookers can prove to be a very lucrative market segment. When the direct marketing agency The Phone Room ran a campaign for The Empire Theatre, Sunderland, calling group bookers and schools from their mailing lists to promote their pantomime, 5177 seats were reserved at a value of £49 878. Twenty-four per cent of all the groups called actually booked.

Source: Phillips, 2002.

How knowledgeable are they?

Different programmes will attract those with different levels of expertise, or indeed confidence, in the art form being presented. Classical music programmes, for example, can be broadly divided into the popular and the highbrow, with certain works being accessible to relatively wide audiences with little or no music education, while others are enjoyed more by those who are able to appreciate the subtleties of technique and form. Failing to segment the market in this way can lead to disappointments for both groups and may alienate them from future events. For some there is nothing worse than the embarrassment of clapping in the wrong place among an audience who knows the music better than they do; others may be equally horrified at the rustling of sweet wrappers in the midst of a piano recital!

How often do they attend?

This is another factor that can be investigated easily with a computerized box office system. Frequent and committed attenders can be identified and approached in a different way from those who attend occasionally. Season tickets, subscription schemes, friends and members clubs and similar activities may be appropriate for those who see the arts as a central part of their lives and who are looking for involvement as well as the pleasures of attendance. Little inducement is required to encourage them to attend, so the marketing emphasis to this group should be on providing information to make it easy to plan ahead and book tickets. The irregular attenders are far more challenging as a promotional target. The promotional campaigns need to be more intrusive, as this group is not actively seeking information about arts events.

Case 2.4 Symphonic segments

During the 1990s, sales trends at the City of Birmingham Symphony Orchestra (CBSO) showed a decline in numbers of tickets purchased, which was affecting the financial stability of the orchestra. Preliminary sales analysis identified that the fall in sales was not in single tickets, which were holding up well, but in subscription, traditionally a strong area for CBSO. The orchestra had for decades been running a traditional subscription scheme which offered patrons whole seasons of concerts on specific days of the week or combinations of seasons, encouraging people to book for as many as 20 or 30 concerts in one booking. It had also introduced a 'General Selection' scheme which offered a choice from a limited range of often less popular concerts with a small discount off top prices.

Analysis found that while retention of existing subscribers was generally good (86 per cent each year), there were some hidden problems:

- A long-term decline in the number of subscribers willing to commit to multi-series bookings.
- An increasing volatility in the behaviour of less-committed subscribers. These people were very repertoire-sensitive and their volatility was increased by some of the CBSO's more adventurous programming.
- Many new subscribers had attended only very infrequently – and some not at all.

The CBSO had to find a way to maintain subscriber retention, while at the same time increasing the loyalty of existing single-ticket buyers. Since present subscribers were generally resistant to change, this meant introducing a new package which would appeal to a broad range of potential bulk purchasers, without damaging the loyal and valuable relationship that CBSO had with existing subscribers.

Reactions to developments in package design demonstrated that full-series subscribers were very sensitive to change of any kind. Each time an innovation was made, subscription levels dipped, so as few changes as possible were made to full-series subscription in terms of balance of repertoire and artists and numbers of concerts. Existing die-hard subscribers were also found to be strongly attached to the benefits of the 'Full Series' package and all such benefits were exclusively maintained.

However, the General Selection package was failing to have the broad appeal that CBSO wanted. It appeared to be neither comprehensive nor flexible enough to build loyalty. It was recommended that this scheme be replaced with a 'Flexible Discount Scheme' offering a comprehensive choice of repertoire, ticket exchange and accumulating discounts, which would have broad appeal for all tastes, typologies and frequency of attendance. The 'Symphonic Selection' was created, offering a generous expansion of the former General Selection subscription. This did not, however, offer some key benefits provided by the Full Series subscription, which existing subscribers valued so highly, so it would be unlikely to encourage these attenders to defect from full-series subscription.

The subscription brochure was redesigned with simplified text content and composed from a potential subscriber's point of view. Experimentation elsewhere had demonstrated that summaries of information produced in-house in letter form worked as well as, and in some cases better than, full-colour designed print for re-subscribers and it was therefore possible to tailor subscription print for individual market segments.

Finally, a programme of active customer care was recommended to 'ease' existing subscribers into the new structure, including an enhanced and more heavily promoted customer enquiry telephone line and outbound calls to the most valuable individual subscribers.

Source: Baker, 2002.

Market targeting

Market segmentation is a critical step in the matching process between the arts product and its potential audience. Market targeting is the process by which those sub-groups are approached with appropriate offers. Most arts organizations are faced with a choice between a concentration strategy and a multi-segment marketing strategy.

The young ones

Anyone who is planning to target young people must be prepared to start breaking down a whole range of attitudinal barriers to involvement with the arts.

Type of barrier	Arts involvement is hindered by . . .
General attitude	. . . the view that it's 'boring rubbish'
Talent	. . . perceived lack of talent ('I can't draw', 'I'm tone deaf')
Discomfort	. . . unfamiliarity and perceptions of irrelevance ('theatre is for snobs', 'dance is for girls')
Non-stimulus	. . . failing to engage (it doesn't deliver a 'buzz')
Unease	. . . a sense of embarrassment (becoming the centre of attention through participation)
Situation specific	. . . a particular person or place (e.g. a disliked teacher)
Group image	. . . it not being 'the done thing' (especially among peers)
Self-image	. . . an alternative self-image ('I'm more into sports')

Source: Harland et al., 1995.

Concentration strategy

Some arts organizations have a specific mission which requires them to focus their activities on a single market segment, such as young people, disabled people, an ethnic-minority group, inner-city communities. These organizations will follow what is known as a concentration strategy, whereby they target their product and promotional efforts at just one fairly homogeneous group, and will attempt to build an audience by putting out a single clear message to this target audience. Credibility needs to be built up within the target market so that all members of that market know that 'people like me attend this arts organization'. In many ways, this is quite a straightforward task. The organization is in a good position to build its reputation as it will have a good understanding of the needs of its audiences – vital if the matching process is to be effective.

Multi-segment marketing

Other arts organizations need to attract a diverse audience and typically their task is more difficult. Local authority venues, for example, which may be attempting to serve a wide range of people within their boundaries, will need to put out diverse messages about their activities and aim these messages at different parts of their total potential primary audience. This is known as a multi-segment marketing strategy. Organizations following this strategy often find it difficult to position themselves in the minds of their potential audiences. People can be unsure as to whether that organization is 'for them' as they may, on occasions, investigate what is on offer and find that it does not appeal to them at all. They may then exclude that organization from consideration in the future.

Communicating with a number of different segments can be costly and is likely to require considerable marketing expertise. Computerized box office systems which enable arts organizations to use a direct marketing approach make the task easier and more cost-effective. Public relations is also a useful tool for addressing a number of segments.

Summary

Audiences are an important element of the artistic experience. They are the customers for the art form and the *raison d'être* of the arts organization. But audiences are not homogeneous. They comprise sub-groups of individuals who display similar characteristics, behaviour, motivations and attitudes. To satisfy the different sub-groups, the marketing function in an arts organization must know their composition and their needs, so that the art being produced can be targeted most appropriately at those who will appreciate the experience on offer and return for more as a result. The mechanism for gathering such information is known as marketing research, which is the subject of the next chapter.

Key concepts

age
audience development
beliefs and attitudes
concentration strategy
culture
decision-making process
decision-making unit
demographics
education
gender

income
market segmentation
motivation
multi-segment strategy
perception
personality
psychographics
reference groups
social class
target marketing

Discussion questions

1 Imagine that you are a visitor from the planet Mars and you have been invited to attend a production of *Aida* at the Royal Opera House. What social conventions might you be in danger of breaking?
2 Is there anything that a mixed programme venue could do to increase the number of men who attend their ballet performances? Should they bother to try? If so, why?
3 What type of negative attitudes do you think people hold about art galleries? Are they justified? What could be done to correct any distortions?
4 Do tourists form a single market segment, or are they simply parts of other geographic, demographic, psychographic or behavioural segments?
5 'Elitism in the arts is perpetuated by the need to break even.' Discuss.

Case study: Let the good times roll!

When London's South Bank Centre (SBC) decided to learn more about the range of attitudes held by its classical music attenders, a research exercise was conducted which enabled its audience to be classified into four imaginatively-named typologies:

- *Conservative fanatics*: 4 per cent of SBC attenders fell into this group. These very frequent attenders of classical music tended to be males, aged 50 and over. They were found to be self-confessed connoisseurs, who were pursing an ongoing quest for a peak music experience. The nature of the venue was very much a secondary consideration for them, and concerts were carefully chosen for a specific programme, conductor, soloist or orchestra. Authenticity and purity in classical music were key concerns.
- *Mainstream stalwarts*: 35 per cent of SBC attenders fell into this group. Also frequent concert-goers, the group comprised a broader age range, though members were generally over 30. Classical music was important to them, but they had relatively narrow and very specific tastes, and were clear about what they did and did not enjoy.

They tended to seek the familiar and were wary of experimentation, with new works being experienced through their inclusion in a mixed programme rather than by choice. Although a primary motivator for attending classical music was the programme – with a programme that included a known and loved work being key – the whole experience of concert-going, including the venue, was found to be important.

- *Good-time novices*: 60 per cent of SBC attenders fell into this group, which comprised occasional concert-goers of both sexes, and tended to be younger. Their primary motivation for attending was the opportunity to share a social experience through concert-going, which included the atmosphere, drinks, music, and even people-watching. The venue was critical to the enjoyment of the event. The music programme was usually little known, and concerts were chosen because of big-name performers or popular composers.

- *New modernists*: 1 per cent of SBC attenders fell into this young, mixed gender group. These people were found to have an intense involvement with classical music, but were only interested in concerts of twentieth-century music. Open-minded, experimental and willing to take risks, they were interested in contemporary art as a whole, enjoying its freshness and the sense of discovery associated with it. A mix of artists and repertoire were enjoyed, and the presence of a composer at a concert was a major draw.

Having revealed the typologies present among the SBC audience, further work was done to assess the appropriateness of the promotional materials and communications methods that were being used to target those who attended. It was concluded that the vast majority of promotional print was appropriate for the group that was formerly considered to be the core audience, namely the 'Conservative fanatics' who in fact accounted for only 4 per cent of SBC attenders. They contained features such as histories of the orchestras, ensembles, and artists performing, and details of works to be performed, but included little that would break down barriers for newcomers.

To redress the balance, a campaign known as 'VITAL' was launched, aimed at the 'Good-time novices'. Six concerts were selected for their accessibility for new audiences, and two-for-one deals were offered for the events. A leaflet was designed to include a selection of quotes about the emotional responses to live music, and a reply-paid postcard was included to capture information. The design was also used on poster sites across London, with the posters making reference to the leaflets and encouraging telephone response, too. Some 20 000 infrequent attenders from SBC's database were mailed; 850 postcards were returned requesting information and all the 1200 seats made available under the special offer were sold, generating some £11 000 in income.

Questions

1 What initiatives might you implement to appeal to the 'Mainstream stalwarts' and the 'New modernists'?
2 How might ACORN or Mosaic data be used to identify more potential 'Good-time novices'?

3 SBC created a 'two-for-one' offer for Good-time novices. For which of the other typologies might special offers (known as 'sales promotions') be effective? Design appropriate offers for the group(s) you identify, and propose an offer that will encourage Good-time novices who have just attended for the first time to come again.

Sources: Baker, 2000; Denton, 1999.

References

Baker, T. (2000) *Stop Re-inventing the Wheel*, Association of British Orchestras.

Baker, T. (2002) 'Researching the right package', *ArtsProfessional*, Issue 18, 26 January.

Bennett, A. and Frow, J. (1992) 'Art galleries: who goes?' In *Marketing the Arts* (S. Blackall and J. Meek, eds), pp. 137–51. The International Council of Museums.

Bhuchar, S. (1999) 'What's different about Asian audiences?' *ArtsBusiness*, Issue 32, 2 August.

Cooper, P. and Tower, R. (1992) 'Inside the consumer mind: consumer attitudes to the arts'. *Journal of the Market Research Society*, Vol. 34, No. 4, 299–311.

Denton, C. (1999) 'Retaining audiences for classical music', Revolving Doors: Arts Marketing Association Awayday, Warwick.

Desai, P. and Thomas, A. (1998) *Cultural Diversity: Attitudes of ethnic minority populations towards museums and galleries*. BMRB, commissioned by Museums and Galleries Commission.

Diggle, K. (1994) *Arts Marketing*. Rhinegold.

Harland, J., Kinder, K. and Hartley, K. (1995) *Arts in their View: A study of youth participation in the arts*. National Foundation for Educational Research.

Hill, E. (2002) 'Sadler's Wells pioneers SMS ticketing', *ArtsProfessional*, Issue 25, 6 May, 3.

Hill, E. (2002) 'A stomping success', *ArtsProfessional*, Issue 26, 20 May, 4.

Jermyn, H., Skelton, A. and Bridgwood, A. (2001) *Arts in England: Attendance, participation and attitudes*. Arts Council of England

Kolb, B. (2001) 'A study of the Philharmonia Orchestra audience', *International Journal of Arts Management*, Vol. 3, No. 2, Winter.

Kotler, P. and Armstrong, G. (1991) *Principles of Marketing*. Prentice-Hall.

Lamos, M. and Stewart, S. (1983) 'Theater: the vital relationship'. In *Market the Arts!* (J.V. Melillo, ed.), pp. 17–21. Foundation for the Extension and Development of the American Professional Theater.

Leddy, D. (2002) 'Queer and pleasant danger', *ArtsProfessional*, Issue 21, 11 March.

Maitland, H. (2000a) *A Guide to Audience Development*, 2nd ed. Arts Council of England.

Maitland, H. (2000b) *Is it Time for Plan B?* Arts Marketing Association.

Market Research Society (2003) *Occupation Groupings: A job dictionary*, 5th edn. Market Research Society.

Marplan (1988) *Survey of Asian, African and Caribbean Live Arts Attenders.* Marplan Ltd.

Morris, G. (1991) *Selling the Contemporary Visual Arts.* Arts Council of Great Britain.

Murdin, L. (1994) 'It's important you don't pander to the lowest common denominator'. *Arts Management Weekly,* 1 December, 2–3.

NOP (1991) *Report on Qualitative Research into the Public's Attitudes to the Arts.* Commissioned by the Arts Council of Great Britain.

O'Donnell, D. (1999) 'Reaching the audience of the future: Paul Hamlyn Foundation June Conference'. In *Stop Re-inventing the Wheel* (Baker, T. (2000), ed.) Association of British Orchestras.

Phillips, A. (2002) The Phone Room. www.phoneroom.co.uk

Rice, C. (1999) *Understanding Customers,* 2nd ed. Butterworth-Heinemann.

Rogers, E. (1962) *Diffusion of Innovations.* Free Press.

Rogers, R. (1998) *Audience Development: Collaborations between education and marketing.* Arts Council of England.

Schlosser, R.J. (1983) 'Audiences'. In *Market the Arts!* (J.V. Melillo, ed.), pp. 87–98. Foundation for the Extension and Development of the American Professional Theater.

Simmonds, E. (2001) 'Gallery *Go*: Winning new friends', *ArtsBusiness,* Issue 70, 12 March.

Stark, P. (1985) 'Can the arts do anything about unemployment'. In *Arts and Unemployment* (A. Battram and C. Segal, eds), p. 24. Research Training Initiatives Talking about Dance (1998) Conference Report.

Verwey, P. (2002) *Target Group Index 1999/2000 and 2000/2001: Summary of results.* The Arts Council of England.

Waters, I. (1989) *Entertainment, Arts and Cultural Services.* Longman.

Westbrook, C. (2002) *Future Dream Media,* www.theatreforfamilies.net

Yoshitomo, J. (2000) 'New fundamental and practices to increase cultural participation and develop arts audiences'. *Grantsmakers for the Arts Reader,* Vol. II, No. 1, Summer.

3

Marketing research

Marketing research[1] can be defined as the process of collecting, analysing and interpreting information to help managers make better marketing decisions. This chapter will introduce a number of techniques of marketing research which can help arts organizations to gather and use information more efficiently and effectively. This will include sections on:

- the benefits and scope of marketing research
- setting research objectives
- research methodologies
- sources of secondary data
- methods for collecting primary data
- conducting a survey

This chapter is more than just a step-by-step guide to the process of research. It encourages the consideration of both the information needs of an organization and the way in which information can be used, as well as examining the variety of techniques for gathering that information.

1 The term 'marketing' research is often shortened to 'market' research, though strictly speaking this is incorrect. Marketing research is a wide-ranging discipline which seeks to gather information about any aspect of an organization and its environment, while market research is concerned only with trends in customer or audience behaviour, and is usually known as 'audience research' in an arts context.

The benefits of marketing research

Organizations that have taken marketing research seriously report significant benefits. At the South Bank Centre in London (which includes both visual and performing arts venues), marketing research has long been at the heart of their planning and has driven the Centre's development over the years. Programming and marketing decisions, merchandising policy, advance booking systems and sponsorship strategy have all been influenced by the results of numerous marketing research projects (McCart, 1992).

Objections to marketing research

Arts organizations which choose not to undertake marketing research may give a number of reasons, but the following are perhaps the most common:

'. . . it's too expensive'

A popular misconception is that marketing research is a highly technical discipline which can be successfully pursued only by experts (and normally at great expense). Certainly it is a systematic and orderly process, and it is possible to use sophisticated information technology to interpret large quantities of data. There are some industries and organizations for which vast consumer surveys and detailed statistical analysis can be extremely cost-effective; but there are many more organizations that reap significant rewards from a whole host of far less expensive methods for gathering the information that they need to help them better serve their customers. Even the smallest arts organization can benefit from a more rigorous analysis of its box office data, informal discussions with its regular attenders and a closer examination of the impact of press comment and publicity material, all of which can be done at very little cost.

To say that marketing research is too expensive implies that an organization may not have fully considered the range of marketing data available and the very limited costs involved in the majority of data collection. Perhaps also it has not considered the cost of poor decision-making which could lead to marketing mistakes and consequently lost audiences.

Marketing research is certainly not the exclusive property of large, wealthy private-sector commercial organizations; neither is it such a complex discipline that it must be left to professional marketing research agencies, whose fees may be beyond the reach of all but the central arts funding bodies.

'. . . we don't want to be popular'

It is sometimes feared that marketing research will identify demand for a programme of events which would be popular but not worthy. The research may be resisted on the grounds that its findings would not be implemented for cultural or artistic reasons. Trevor Nunn, as Artistic Director of the South Bank Centre, came under fire for his production of *My Fair Lady*, which was accused of being populist and inappropriate for an organization supported by public subsidy (Moss, 2001). While accessible programming such as this is supported in some circles, and seen as a commitment by more progressive directors to reaching as wide an audience as possible, by others it is condemned as an insult to the serious performers and a betrayal of the classical culture that the funding bodies intend to be served. Again this is a flimsy reason for ignoring marketing research, which can be a very useful tool for identifying the most appropriate programmes, facilities and services within the ruling artistic policy, and without alienating existing interest groups and audiences. At the end of the day, marketing research cannot make decisions for you, but it can help you to make better decisions yourself.

Measuring the immeasurable

'Social inclusion' is high on governments' agendas, and arts funders and policy-makers are keen to be able to demonstrate to their paymasters that the arts can, for example, help individuals to develop self-esteem and contribute to the development of community identity. However, arts organizations can be hesitant when asked to evaluate the social impact of their work, expressing fears that the essence of what they achieve is immeasurable. Morlarty (1997) summed up the wariness arts workers have towards evaluation as: '. . . the anxiety that something very precious may be lost, that the complexity of an experience which includes relationship, enjoyment, learning, exploration, expression will be destroyed, diluted or reduced . . .'.

Sources: Jermyn, 2001; Moriarty, 1997.

'. . . we know what our audiences want'
Service providers in the not-for-profit sector are renowned for their over-confidence in knowing instinctively what their customers want. On the other hand, faced with an overriding profit motive, commercial arts are keenly aware of their customers' opinions, which are critical to their survival. In the subsidized sector, marketing research is often the only tool available to arts organizations to assess the extent to which their own non-profit objectives are being met. To ignore it is to ignore the core of the marketing concept, which places the needs of the customer at the heart of the organization.

The scope of marketing research

The definition given of marketing research is deliberately broad in scope. It refers to any attempt to gather information from the environment which may be useful in the planning of marketing activity. However, marketing research can be subdivided into a number of categories, according to its purpose:

Audience research

In the arts, this is primarily concerned with profiling, that is, identifying the nature, composition and preferences of current and potential audiences. It is commonly used to help organizations identify audience groupings (or market segments) with similar characteristics and arts preferences, enabling visitor or audience profiles to be constructed for different types of exhibitions or performances. An audience survey will typically ask for details of demographic characteristics including age and sex, but also income, occupation, education, and perhaps means of transport and distance travelled to the venue. This type of information helps galleries and theatres to target their future programmes, events, promotional literature, fund-raising and advertising more precisely, and it can provide useful quantified information when negotiating sponsorship.

Customer satisfaction research

This aims to measure the extent to which an arts event has met its audiences' expectations. Word-of-mouth recommendation has been found to be the most influential factor in the choice of leisure services, so it is important for organizations to understand and respond to their customers' perceptions of both the artistic product and the environment in which it is produced.

Case 3.1 Mystery benchmarks

For many years, executives in some high-profile German museums had supported only inwardly-directed scholarly museum functions, and disregarded visitor perceptions when evaluating their institutions' performance. They had assumed that everything was satisfactory; but a brief analysis of attendance figures suggested that this may not have been the case. The annual number of visits to the more than 53 300 registered museums in Germany had reached a plateau in the late 1980s at around 95 million visits, despite a boom in new museum buildings and extensions. Local and state authorities were starting to question the rationale for providing financial support.

Twenty-one museums volunteered to take part in a research programme to evaluate service and six 'mystery shoppers' were deployed to the various participating institutions. Their brief was to asses four major areas of the museums' services:

- arrival and welcoming
- availability and quality of peripheral services, such as cloakrooms and cafés
- scope and quality of communications with staff, and
- impact of the exhibitions

The mystery shoppers, all professional market researchers, completed a 50-point questionnaire, rating services on a scale form 1 (very positive) to 6 (very negative). The testers gave the highest overall score to the friendliness and politeness of museum staff, followed by the quality of the cloakroom, shops and cafés. Significantly lower scores were given to the process of ticket buying and the information booklets available in the foyers. Further analysis of the figures was conducted to identify the importance of the different service elements, and this revealed that only three items had a major impact on overall perceptions of a museum visit, these being the contact with staff, initial impression in the entrance area, and the availability of a useful booklet.

Service component	Average score (all museums) 1 = very good; 6 = very poor
Friendliness and politeness of personnel	1.78
Coat check (cloakroom)	2.04
Museum shop	2.19
Museum café (environment)	2.20
Staff reactions to flash camera use in exhibition area	2.22
Environment of exhibition area	2.24
Museum café (service)	2.26
Toilets	2.27
Entrance area and orientation	2.37
Advice about personal guided tours	2.42
Positive overall experience in the museum	2.43
Staff reactions to coat/bag carrying in the exhibition area	2.56
Accessibility and surroundings of museum	2.72
Advice about renting audio guide	2.77
Information booklet	3.57
Process of ticket buying	4.42

The figures collected from the whole group of museums were subsequently used as benchmarks by individual museums, which were able to compare their own performances with that of the whole group. Those with below-average evaluations knew where improvements had to be made, and those with above-average evaluations were able to boast about them in their promotional campaigns.

Source: Kirchberg, 2000.

Motivation research

This attempts to get to the bottom of audiences' reasons for attending a particular event or venue, again to enable better market segmentation and improved targeting of potential audiences. It has also been successfully used in developing an understanding of reasons for non-attendance and hostility towards the arts. At its simplest, motivation research involves asking direct questions of visitors as to why they chose a particular event in a particular venue on a particular day and time. But as many people are unable to describe exactly why they act as they do, some motivation research involves a variety of less conventional techniques in seeking a deeper understanding of the more covert or even unconscious reasons for attendance.

Competitor research

It is often argued that arts events do not face direct competition, as it is difficult to imagine two venues within close geographical proximity of each other offering identical programmes at the same time. Nonetheless, audiences do have choices as to how, when and where to spend their money, and different venues and programmes will be competing for a share of that money over a longer period of time. For this reason it is important for arts organizations to understand how their audiences perceive them in comparison with other similar organizations. Competitor research can help organizations to understand these perceptions and then to differentiate themselves positively from other providers of similar arts services. Failing to do so can lead to an ill-defined image and consequent rejection by key target audiences.

Product research

This is quite a difficult area in the arts. Commercial and industrial organizations conduct product research to help them improve the products and services they offer to their customers and to identify demand for new developments. This reflects the overall objectives of most firms in the private sector, which are related to profitable trading activity. If demand exists which can be supplied, then there is an opportunity to make money. Perhaps the nearest the arts come to this kind of research is when cinema producers try out different endings on preview audiences, or television companies research the popularity of particular characters in long-running soap operas. Quite apart from the question of aesthetic integrity, the expense and complexity of such a procedure renders it out of the question for the vast majority of arts organizations.

Product research in the more tangible areas of facilities, such as retailing and catering, is more viable, of course. This type of research can help to identify both inadequacies in existing provision and demand for new facilities and services which may improve audience perceptions of a venue, encourage new attenders and consolidate customer loyalty.

Pricing research

For commercial arts organizations, this can help in the setting of entrance fees or ticket prices. Revenue from the box office or entrance fees can be maximized if the organization has done some pricing research to help it understand the monetary value that audiences will place on the experience they are expecting to enjoy (there is more discussion on this point in Chapter 5). In the non-profit sector, pricing research can also be used to help the formulation of pricing policies that will promote wider access to the arts. An understanding of the key influences on audience price sensitivity can be gained by experimenting with different price levels and monitoring the associated attendance figures.

Promotional research

This is normally undertaken to assess the effectiveness of different media, messages and promotional techniques in attracting audiences. It is generally retrospective. If money has been spent on promoting an event, it is important to be able to gauge the cost-effectiveness of the chosen methods and media of promotion. Promotional research attempts to gather information which will identify the most persuasive promotional techniques by linking them to attendance figures. Under some circumstances it may also be of use to pre-test advertising campaigns, to identify the most effective visual or verbal creative concept, and to identify the target audiences to whom a particular campaign appeals.

Policy research

National organizations such as the UK's arts councils use marketing research to help them make recommendations about the levels of arts provision and the allocation of resources. Information about national and regional public attitudes towards the arts, as well as attendance and participation figures, is invaluable in creating a strong case for public funding of the arts. Research can demonstrate economic benefits from the arts, such as spending in restaurants or attraction of tourists. It could indicate the effect of arts facilities on the image of a town, or on local or national pride. Marketing research can also be used to detect audience trends and attitudes in other countries which may have domestic implications or simply provide early warning of likely developments at home.

Conducting marketing research

If marketing research is to be an effective tool for improving the quality of marketing decisions, it needs to address three key questions systematically:

What do we want to know?

The first stage of marketing research should be to examine the marketing problem or opportunity which requires further investigation and this should lead to a set of specific objectives for the research. Having set clear, unambiguous objectives it is possible to pinpoint the nature of the information that must be obtained to help solve the problem or develop the opportunity.

Where can the information be obtained?

Secondly, it is essential to identify who can provide the information and the best method for collecting it. The most visible aspect of marketing research is the collecting of information using surveys. While surveys are very important, they are but one mechanism for finding out about people, and may be neither the most appropriate nor the most cost-effective method of data collection.

How do we use the findings?

Marketing research provides facts, but information is created when the facts are interpreted in the context of the original problem. The final stage, therefore, is for managers to make sense of the findings and ensure that they influence decision-making in the organization. Without intelligent interpretation, research is at best worthless and at worst can be misleading and dangerous.

The rest of this chapter explores the techniques and research methods which will help managers to answer these three questions for themselves in their own organizations.

Research objectives

Why set objectives?

Research objectives are explicit statements of what the organization wants to know. They are important for two main reasons. Firstly, they are a constant reminder to managers of what they are trying to find out. This can prevent time and energy being wasted on the collection of information which will not ultimately be of use in solving the marketing problem facing the organization. Secondly, they can provide a benchmark or target against which the results of the research can be measured. This enables managers to assess whether the research was effective, which can be a crucial activity for arts organizations, particularly in the subsidized sector. If money is scarce, marketing research may be viewed as a luxury and marketing managers are likely to be required to justify their expenditure in this area.

Categories of objectives

Broadly speaking, research objectives can be divided into three categories:

Exploratory objectives tend to be quite broad in scope and are normally specified when an organization feels that it needs a better insight into the nature of certain marketing issues. For example, a lot of exploratory research is conducted by funding bodies to help them make policy decisions and set planning priorities, as well as to give guidance to those they subsidize.

Descriptive objectives are usually set when an organization needs more concrete evidence to support specific marketing decisions. Audience research reports are normally descriptive. In other words, they describe an audience or potential audience by their characteristics and preferences, so that the relationships between different characteristics and preferences can be examined. For example, it would be possible to design a survey which investigates the age, gender and socio-economic profile of a regional opera audience, as well as their musical preferences. It could then be determined whether opera-goers are also interested in orchestral concerts, pop concerts or ballet, and whether any particular age group, social class or gender is more likely to prefer one of those art forms to another. This type of information could be very helpful in promotional campaigns.

Causal objectives are set with a view to identifying cause-and-effect relationships, in an attempt to explain why things happen. Experiments are widely conducted to test alternative prices or concessions by monitoring their impact on audience size and composition. This type of research could be used for developing access policies, or simply for assessing audience price sensitivity. Similar exercises can be performed to assess the impact of different advertising media, programme design or even interval length, thus providing information to help with promotion and programming decisions.

In practice, a major marketing research project may require all three types of objectives to be set. Exploratory research could lead to the design of a survey which would enable an audience to be defined and described. The significant relationships between the different characteristics and preferences of this audience could then be further investigated in a causal study. Nonetheless, the distinction between these types of objectives is very useful in helping managers to focus systematically on the purposes of the research.

Research methodologies

Process of research

Objectives determine the *process* by which marketing data should be collected. Generating marketing information requires the collection of marketing data, the term 'data' referring to the facts and figures that must be gathered to achieve the research objectives.

Secondary research, also known as desk research, involves the gathering together of relevant data that exist prior to the start of a marketing research programme. The researcher is a secondary user of already existing data, hence the name. Internal secondary data already exist within the organization conducting the research; external data have been collected outside the organization, for example by the government, by funding bodies or by commercial marketing research houses. It is possible that both these types of data were originally collected for a purpose other than marketing research, but nonetheless they can be valuable to the researcher. If secondary data are adequate to achieve the objectives of the research, then the more costly processes of primary research can be avoided.

Primary research involves the generation and collection of original data. The organization determines exactly what information is necessary and from whom, and then sets about acquiring it. The data are thus specific to the purpose for which they have been acquired. It is quite likely that primary research will be undertaken after secondary research, to provide a more complete set of answers to the researcher's questions.

Style of research

Having set research objectives, it is also possible to identify the *style* of research which should be undertaken.

Qualitative research is undertaken if research objectives require information to be generated about why people act as they do, or how they think and feel about the experiences that the arts are offering them. Qualitative research usually requires interviews to be conducted with small numbers of people, though other techniques such as observation and experimentation may also be useful in getting to the root of audience behaviour. In the arts, qualitative research is particularly useful as it is able to explore the subtleties of people's reactions to the aesthetic experience. It may seek to explore issues such as:

- motivations and inhibitions for participating in the arts
- what people are looking for from the arts
- perceptions of different art forms
- reactions to specific productions, titles and artists
- reasons for success or failure of productions or events
- appropriate types of promotion
- sources of influence over audiences (reviews, advertising, word-of-mouth)
- the perceptions of sponsoring organizations

Quantitative research is undertaken if the research objectives require information to be generated about how many people hold certain views or fit into certain categories. Conducting quantitative research usually requires a survey to be undertaken among a sample of the population of interest to the researcher. The findings can then be interpreted with the help of statistical techniques, and assumptions can be made about the whole population from the information generated among the sample. This is a very common form of research in the arts, and is a popular method for investigating the nature of audiences.

Duration of research

The necessary *duration* of research is also implied by the research objectives.

Continuous research examines an issue or problem on a regular basis in order to monitor changes that are occurring over a period of time. For example, funding bodies are interested in changes in arts attendance patterns, hence their use of TGI data (discussed later in this chapter).

Ad hoc research is the term used to describe a one-off piece of research undertaken to obtain information relating to a particular issue or problem. The findings of this type of research are reported in such a way as to help a specific marketing decision to be made.

Sources of secondary data

Internal sources

Internal data already exist within an organization. Arts organizations frequently own a lot of data which can potentially be used for marketing research: the accounting system, for example, may be able to identify the relative popularity of catering and retail outlets during specific exhibitions or performance programmes; staff may be able to report on customer reactions to ticket prices at the box office; but the most important sources of internal data for arts organizations are invariably their databases storing details of attenders.

Performing arts organizations which use computerized box office systems are best placed to make the most of this type of data.

Box office systems

Tomlinson (1993) describes box office systems as '. . . systems which integrate ticketing and marketing functions, compile a patron or customer database as a central function, and offer additional opportunities to record information'. Any organization which maintains a comprehensive database through its box office system has immediate access to information which can help answer both strategic and tactical questions. For example:

- At whom should we direct mailshots for contemporary dance productions?
- What price concessions should be offered on which days of the week?
- At what point should action be taken to improve ticket sales for a low-selling event?
- Who should I include in a sample for conducting primary research into attendance at productions of Shakespeare?
- What type of person prefers to attend exhibitions on a Sunday as opposed to a weekday?

Compared to their manual predecessors, computerized box office systems have vastly extended the range of transaction data and details of attenders that can be gathered and processed. Indeed, the researching and analysis of potential audiences, and information retrieval and statistical analysis related to these audiences, may only be possible with help from the computer.

Data can be recorded as part of processing the ticket sale – name and address, ticket prices and concessions, details of event attended, time of performance or exhibition etc. (see Table 3.1). Valuable additional data can be added to this by simple questioning – for example: How did the customer hear of the event? What was the main influence on attending?

For research purposes, there are many uses of box office data. Historic booking patterns can be analysed to inform forecasts (e.g. how far in advance did people book? did they come in groups or alone? which were the most popular seats? what was the average ticket price?). Current patterns which depart significantly from forecast patterns can be flagged up and remedial action taken (e.g. if advance ticket sales are very slow, more effort can be put into promotion or price promotions introduced; if an event is quickly sold out, efforts can be made to switch-sell the disappointed customers). A box office system can also provide a statistical overview of the audience for a particular venue. This information is particularly useful for touring companies trying to include towns and cities where the profile of local attenders is similar to the profile of attenders for their own art form. Catchment areas, demographic customer profiles and attendance patterns can all be collected and stored.

Drye (1998) discusses a segmentation system developed by Heather Maitland on the basis of box office information about the intervals between ticket purchase. She discerned a sizeable number of what she termed 'Bouncing balls' – people who enjoyed going out for an evening at regular intervals, but were happy to consider a broad range of entertainment options.

Table 3.1 Useful data for customer records

In addition to basic customer information relating to names and home addresses which are quite easily obtained (particularly from those who pay by credit card), arts organizations may attempt to include the following data on their customer records:

- title
- gender
- initials, first name and familiar name (if different)
- qualification (as a suffix)
- employment
- posts in voluntary organizations
- business address
- temporary address (such as holiday homes)
- telephone number(s)
- date of birth/age
- socio-economic group
- ethnic origin
- geodemographic classification (based on ACORN or other coding)
- performance(s) attended
- source(s) of information about the performance
- other links with the organization (e.g. member, sponsor)
- number and types of tickets bought
- prices paid
- payment methods
- time of booking

In theory these data should be quite easy to obtain, but new procedures may have to be set up and rehearsed by the box office staff who will be required to input this accurately and consistently into the system.

Source: Tomlinson, 1993.

By contrast she called another segment 'Festival attenders' – people loyal to a particular art form who were prepared to attend arts events in concentrated bursts of frequency rather than at regular intervals.

This kind of perspective on an audience allows marketing resources to be targeted more effectively. For example, if you recognize a patron on the box office database as a 'Bouncing ball', regular contact via direct mail or e-marketing would be appropriate to try and match this regular attendance pattern. Conversely, the 'Festival attender' is likely to respond better to more closely targeted mailings about visiting companies and events which are more specific to a particular art form. Box office information of this kind allows marketers to confirm the intuitive pictures they form about audience motivations and experiment with their approaches accordingly. When merged with external data it can add powerful insights to guide marketing activity.

External sources

Published data are widely available for use by arts organizations, through universities, libraries, through arts marketing agencies and through regional and national arts funding bodies.

Published surveys

The Arts Council of England carries a database of surveys carried out both by itself and by a wide range of arts organizations; and the journal *Arts Research Digest* lists a wide range of published research reports and gives details of work in progress. These can be of considerable help in the investigation of similar problems in different organizations, or simply in planning a methodology for the implementation of a piece of primary research. Care must be taken in their use, though. It is important, for example, to check who the original client was and their reasons for conducting the research. This will indicate whether a particular slant has been taken in the interpretation of the findings. The nature and size of the sample is also relevant. Findings should be treated with caution if the number of respondents in any sub-group is small, particularly if comparisons are made between different groups of people.

Geodemographic profiling systems

These are consumer classification systems which have been created by combining geographic and demographic information gathered from a diverse range of sources, including the census, the electoral roll and the Royal Mail postal address file. The systems work on the assumption that people living in similar neighbourhoods (defined by postcodes) are likely to have similar interests, incomes and purchasing habits. Two of these systems, ACORN and Mosaic, are commonly used by UK arts organizations to help them understand more about the types of potential audiences within their catchment areas.

Matching audiences to sponsors

One innovative use of Mosaic profiling for the arts is to attract sponsorship. Manchester's Bridgewater Hall promotes itself to potential sponsors with the following copy on its website:

'The Bridgewater Hall attracts a substantial, sought-after audience and offers unique, tailor-made opportunities, like associations with international concerts and prestigious festivals, for you to raise your company's profile within this desirable market. Mosaic profiling of The Bridgewater Hall's audience for International Season concerts reveals high proportions of Chattering Classes, Clever Capitalists, High Spending Greys, Ageing Professionals, Gentrified Villages, Rural Retirement mix and Studio Singles. The audience covers a wide geographical spread, with 84 per cent of attenders based within a 45 minute off-peak travel time of The Bridgewater Hall. Benefits include your company profile against international quality events in a variety of publications, complimentary tickets, and the chance to entertain your clients and guests in the spectacular surroundings of Manchester's high quality international concert and conference venue.'

Source: www.bridgewater-hall.co.uk, 20 May 2002.

Table 3.2 Mosaic classifications and groups

Mosaic types	Mosaic classifications	Mosaic groups	Mosaic types	Mosaic classifications	Mosaic groups
A1	Clever Capitalists	A	G30	Bijou Homemakers	G
A2	Rising Materialists		G31	Market Town Mixture	
A3	Corporate Careerists		G32	Town Centre Singles	
A4	Ageing Professionals		H33	Bedsits and Shop Flats	H
A5	Small Time Business		H34	Studio Singles	
B6	Green Belt Expansion	B	H35	College and Communal	
B7	Suburban Mock Tudor		H36	Chattering Classes	
B8	Pebble Dash Subtopia		I37	Solo Pensioners	I
C9	Affluent Blue Collar	C	I38	High Spending Greys	
C10	30s Industrial Spec		I39	Aged Owner Occupiers	
C11	Lo-Rise Right to Buy		I40	Elderly in own Flats	
C12	Smokestack Shiftwork		J41	Brand New Areas	J
D13	Coalfield Legacy	D	J42	Pre-nuptial Owners	
D14	Better-off Council		J43	Nestmaking Families	
D15	Low Rise Pensioners		J44	Maturing Mortgages	
D16	Low Rise Subsistence		K45	Gentrified Villages	K
D17	Peripheral Poverty		K46	Rural Retirement Mix	
E18	Families in the Sky	E	K47	Lowland Agribusiness	
E19	Victims of Clearance		K48	Rural Disadvantage	
E20	Small Town Industry		K49	Tied/Tenant Farmers	
E21	Mid Rise Overspill		K50	Upland and Small Farms	
E22	Flats for the Aged		L51	Military Bases	L
E23	Inner City Towers		L52	Non-private Housing	
F24	Bohemian Melting Pot	F			
F25	Smartened Tenements				
F26	Rootless Renters				
F27	Asian Heartlands				
F28	Depopulated Terraces				
F29	Rejuvenated Terraces				

Source: www.micromarketing-online.com, 16 January 2003.

Mosaic

The Mosaic system allocates every postcode in the UK to one of 12 predicted lifestyle groups and one of 52 personality types (see Table 3.2). For example, those living in postcodes classified as Group 4 are predicted to be 'High Income Families', but within this group there are a number of categories, including 'Clever Capitalists' and 'Ageing Professionals'.

Clever Capitalists are described as

> ... wealthy people involved in business, particularly in the setting up and financial management of companies and in commercial trading, importing and exporting. The areas are characterized by company directors living in large detached houses though not necessarily with extensive grounds, in well-established residential areas within reasonable reach of city centres.

The demographic profiles suggest that these people have a more than average likelihood of having children, though not very young children. They will probably be outright owners of their homes and will be professionals or managers working in service industries. Descriptions are given of all people in all 12 groups and 52 types, along with a prediction of their demographic profiles and financial status.

ACORN

The ACORN system (an acronym for A Classification of Residential Neighbourhoods) divides the UK population into primary categories according to lifestyle (see Table 3.3). For example, category A consists of those described as 'Thriving' – people who are established at the top of the social ladder, who tend to be healthy, wealthy and confident consumers. Each category is then broken down into groups, with category A, for example, being subdivided into three groups: 'Wealthy achievers in suburban areas', 'Affluent greys in rural communities' and 'Prosperous pensioners in retirement areas'. Finally, each of these groups is broken down further into types, according to any distinctive differences within the group. In total there are six primary categories, 17 groups and a total of 54 types, all of which can be identified by postcode.

Nationally, certain groups are more likely to be the most frequent arts attenders. Group 8, for example, comprises 'Better-off executives, inner city areas', who are well-qualified people, over a third of whom are single with no dependants. The age profile of this group is relatively young and there is a high proportion of students, professionals and executives. They tend to read quality newspapers, in particular *The Guardian*, eat out regularly, and are much more likely than average to attend theatres, cinemas and art galleries. Another group which tends to support the arts more than average is group 1. The majority of people in this group live in large detached houses and have access to two or more cars. They are typically well-educated professional people with the money to enjoy very comfortable lifestyles.

In general, groups 1, 3, 6, 7 and 8 tend to be the most frequent arts attenders while groups 11, 14, 15 and 16 attend at a rate below average. However, there are clear differences in attendance pattern according to art form. For example, group 2, the 'Affluent greys in rural communities', are above average attenders at the opera but below average at contemporary dance. Group 15 attend jazz concerts with average frequency but are well below average attenders at classical music concerts.

For marketing purposes, geodemographic information can be very valuable. Arts organizations can have their own database postcodes compared with the Mosaic groups to help them identify the profile of their current audiences. This enables them to identify all postcodes in their catchment area where similar types of people are likely to live and target their promotional campaigns accordingly.

Table 3.3 The ACORN system

ACORN categories	ACORN groups	ACORN types
A : THRIVING	1. Wealthy achievers, suburban areas	1.1 Wealthy suburbs, large detached houses 1.2 Villages with wealthy commuters 1.3 Mature affluent home-owning areas 1.4 Affluent suburbs, older families 1.5 Mature, well-off suburbs
	2. Affluent greys, rural communities	2.6 Agricultural villages, home-based workers 2.7 Holiday retreats, older people, home-based workers
	3. Prosperous pensioners, retirement areas	3.8 Home-owning areas, well-off older residents 3.9 Private flats, elderly people
B : EXPANDING	4. Affluent executives, family areas	4.10 Affluent working families with mortgages 4.11 Affluent working couples with mortgages, new homes 4.12 Transient workforces, living at their place of work
	5. Well-off workers, family areas	5.13 Home-owning family areas 5.14 Home-owning family areas, older children 5.15 Families with mortgages, younger children
C : RISING	6. Affluent urbanites, town and city areas	6.16 Well-off town and city areas 6.17 Flats and mortgages, singles and young working couples 6.18 Furnished flats and bedsits, younger single people
	7. Prosperous professionals, metropolitan areas	7.19 Apartments, young professional singles and couples 7.20 Gentrified multi-ethnic areas
	8. Better-off executives, inner city areas	8.21 Prosperous enclaves, highly qualified executives 8.22 Academic centres, students and young professionals 8.23 Affluent city-centre areas, tenements and flats 8.24 Partially gentrified multi-ethnic areas 8.25 Converted flats and bedsits, single people

D: SETTLING

9. Comfortable middle agers, mature home-owning areas

   9.26 Mature established home-owning area
   9.27 Rural areas, mixed occupations
   9.28 Established home-owning areas
   9.29 Home-owning areas, council tenants, retired people

10. Skilled workers, home-owning areas

   10.30 Established home-owning areas, skilled workers
   10.31 Home owners in older properties, younger workers
   10.32 Home-owning areas with skilled workers

E : ASPIRING

11. New home owners, mature communities

   11.33 Council areas, some new home owners
   11.34 Mature home-owning areas, skilled workers
   11.35 Low rise estates, older workers, new home owners

12. White collar workers, better-off multi-ethnic areas

   12.36 Home-owning multi-ethnic areas, young families
   12.37 Multi-occupied town centres, mixed occupations
   12.38 Multi-ethnic areas, white collar workers

F : STRIVING

13. Older people, less prosperous areas

   13.39 Home owners, small council flats, single pensioners
   13.40 Council areas, older people, health problems

14. Council estate residents, better-off houses

   14.41 Better-off council areas, new home owners
   14.42 Council areas, young families, some new home owners
   14.43 Council areas, young families, many lone parents
   14.44 Multi-occupied terraces, multic-ethnic areas
   14.45 Low rise council housing, less well-off families
   14.46 Council areas, residents with health problems

15. Council estate residents, high unemployment

   15.47 Estates with high unemployment
   15.48 Council flats, elderly people, health problems
   15.49 Council flats, very high unemployment, singles

16. Council estate residents, greatest hardship

   16.50 Council areas, high unemployment, lone parents
   16.51 Council flats, greatest hardship, many lone parents

17. People in multi-ethnic, low income areas

   17.52 Multi-ethnic, large families, overcrowding
   17.53 Multi-ethnic, severe unemployment, lone parents
   17.54 Multi-ethnic, high unemployment, overcrowding

Source: CACI Information Services.

Stoking up an audience

The Regent Theatre is a 615-seat receiving house, part of the Ambassadors group of theatres. It opened in 1999 following a Lottery-funded refurbishment, and its programme consists primarily of opera, ballet, larger-scale musicals, drama and dance.

Approximately 1 million people live within a 45 minute drivetime of the theatre, but the immediate catchment of Stoke-on-Trent is largely low income and low propensity to attend arts events, and those living further away do not historically perceive Stoke as an entertainment destination – instead looking to Birmingham or Manchester. These factors have made attracting audiences to the Regent Theatre a challenge.

The theatre approached the agency Marketing:Arts to conduct a campaign to help them identify potential attenders for a production of *Jesus Christ Superstar*. The short-term aim was to increase audience numbers for *Jesus Christ Superstar*, but the longer-term aim was to work towards developing audiences where a gap had been identified. This involved using Mosaic to profile current ticket purchasers for the show and then finding similar types of people within target postcode sectors in the city. A mailing list of 3000 names matching the profile of existing attenders was purchased and de-duplicated against the theatre's own database to ensure the targeted mailing for the show was only reaching new audiences. Two thousand prospects were eventually mailed with a show leaflet, personalized letter and ticket discount offer.

The mailing resulted in approximately 150 responses generating 346 ticket sales and a gross income of £3460. The response rate was approximately 7.5 per cent from a cold list of people with whom the Regent had had no contact before. Normal levels of response from a cold list were around 2–3 per cent.

Source: Marketing:Arts, 19 April 2002.

The TGI

This is a continuous survey conducted by BMRB International, which asks questions about consumer habits and attitudes. Based on an annual sample of around 24 000 adults, data are gathered weekly through a detailed self-completion questionnaire. The extensive survey includes three questions on nine types of art forms, namely plays, opera, ballet, contemporary dance, classical music, jazz, art galleries or exhibitions, cinema and popular or rock concerts (see Table 3.4).

Annual summaries of national findings are available, and regional findings, broken down by age group, sex, social class, and ACORN group or type, can be compared with national averages.

An interesting feature of the TGI data is its scope. It is possible to relate theatre attendance to all other consumer information contained in the survey, including information about the products people buy, the newspapers they read and their exposure to different media. For the art forms covered, this can help in planning marketing activities to reach potential audiences.

Table 3.4 Arts questions on the TGI survey

	Any performance in theatre	Plays	Opera	Ballet	Contemporary dance	Classical music concerts	Jazz concerts	Popular or rock concerts	Art galleries or exhibitions
1. About how often these days do you go to the following?									
Once a month or more often									
Once every 2 or 3 months									
Once a year									
Less often									
Never go these days									
2. How long ago was the last occasion you went to the following?									
Within the last 4 weeks									
Over 4 weeks ago (up to and including 3 months ago)									
Over 3 months ago (up to and including 6 months ago)									
Over 6 months ago (up to and including 12 months ago)									
Over 12 months ago/can't remember									
3. Which of these do you like to watch on TV if it's shown or like to read about in the papers or magazines if it's reported?									
Watch on TV									
Read about in the papers/magazines									

Source: Verney, 2000.

Case 3.2 A model audience

For many years, UK arts organizations have used a model known as 'TGI/ACORN' to calculate the number of potential arts attenders living in their catchment areas. Created by the Arts Council of England, this 'propensity to attend' model is based on information generated from the UK-wide Target Group Index, a continuous survey conducted by research agency BMRB which asks over 25 000 people each year about their buying habits and attitudes. Information relating to arts attendance at eight different art forms is then combined with the census-based ACORN data, generated by research agency CACI, which predicts the 'type' of person likely to live in the UK's different postcode sectors. The result is a set of figures which estimate the number of people living in each of the UK's postcode sectors who are likely to attend any of the eight art forms.

Arts organizations have tended to use these figures to evaluate their own performance against these estimates of the total size of the market. But invariably they have found that whilst TGI/ACORN data can predict the postcodes where their audiences are most likely to live with reasonable accuracy, the numbers of actual bookers they attract from those areas can be a far cry from those predicted. The problems of using the TGI/ACORN predictions as a benchmark for a venue's potential audiences stem from a few key issues. Firstly, the figures have not been calculated to take account of 'decay' (people who have to travel further are less likely to attend) or competition (there may be half a dozen arts organizations trying to tempt the same few thousand people to attend). Furthermore, many of the estimates are based on relatively small sample sizes, which, statistically, means that there is wide margin for error.

Source: Hill and Whitehead, 2001b.

Collecting primary data

Audience or visitor surveys are very useful and effective ways of collecting certain types of primary data and the final part of this chapter is dedicated to the planning and implementation of such surveys. However, they are not the only methods of collecting primary data. Neither are they necessarily the best methods for collecting certain types of data, in particular qualitative data. Decisions about the best method or methods to use for collecting primary data should always be made by considering first of all the objectives of the research.

There are four methods commonly used to collect primary data:

- observation
- experimentation
- interviews
- survey

Observation

Quite simply, this is a technique which involves watching people, their behaviour and their actions. It is particularly useful when people are unable to give accurate verbal accounts of their behaviour, perhaps because they cannot remember sufficient details of it: for example, if you wished to know what path an individual had taken around an exhibition, which exhibits he or she stopped to look at and for how long. Observation may be overt, whereby the subject of research is aware of the observation taking place, but commonly the observation is covert, so that the true relationship between the audience and an art form can be studied without interference from the researcher. Galleries and museums have benefited greatly from this type of research.

> The real issue is understanding audiences and their experiences. I think closeness of staff to visitors is key. They should sit where they can actually see people, and be encouraged to spend more time in the gallery to observe the nature of participation. This applies to curators, exhibition and education staff as well as to marketing staff. (Macgregor, 1991)

Experimentation

Primary data can be gathered by experimentation, which is a particularly useful technique when some decision is under consideration and the results cannot be predicted from existing experience either of the organization itself, or from the experience of other organizations. In an experiment, the researcher tries out some marketing activity on a small scale, observing and measuring the results, while controlling as far as possible the effects of factors other than the marketing action being taken. The key advantage of experimentation is that the researcher chooses which factors (or variables) are going to be tested. This enables conclusions to be drawn as to the nature of causal relationships between variables.

Suppose, for example, a theatre wished to assess the price sensitivity of audiences for Shakespearean productions. Assuming that attendance profiles at previous productions have been compiled, they can be used as a benchmark (or control) for assessing the impact of a different pricing structure on attendance profiles. Statistics can be compiled to indicate any significant differences in attendance profiles between the production in which the experiment is taking place and previous productions, and these differences can be attributed to the pricing structure. It is important that extraneous variables (i.e. those factors which are not the subject of the research) are as similar to the control situation as possible. One disadvantage of experimentation stems from the extent to which the extraneous factors can be controlled. Factors such as the weather, the economic climate, the promotional campaign, critics' reviews and the style of production may have an equal, if not stronger, impact on audience profiles than the price of a ticket, and if these vary greatly between the experiment and the control situation, it will not be possible to identify the true cause of changing attendance patterns.

Interviews

A high proportion of qualitative data is collected using the technique of loosely structured interviews. Qualitative research does not demand that a formal structure is imposed on the data collected. Indeed, a formal structure may so constrain responses to questions which require the articulation of attitudes and motivations that the findings may be of little real value. The interview is an approach to data collection which is highly sensitive to the views of the individual being questioned. It attempts to probe beneath the surface of the responses which can be obtained to a formal question, the like of which are normally included in survey questionnaires. Two specific techniques are commonly used, namely depth interviews and focus groups.

Depth interviews are usually prolonged one-to-one interviews, during which the interviewer will ask questions on a series of topics, but has the freedom to phrase the questions as seems most appropriate and to order them and probe them according to the responses. The interviewer has only a checklist of points to cover and will be using mainly open questions to encourage full and explanatory responses from the interviewee. The interviewer will attempt to move from the general to the specific and from topic to topic in a logical manner and will also try to monitor the non-verbal behaviour of the respondent. The abilities of the interviewer are of paramount importance in gaining the deepest insight into the behaviour, attitudes and motivations of the research subject.

Focus groups (also known as group discussions) are interviews in which an interviewer, known as a moderator, asks questions of a group of respondents, usually six to eight persons. The essence of a focus group is that group dynamics are used to draw out individual beliefs which might not be so freely expressed in a one-to-one interview situation. The role of the moderator is simply to act as a catalyst to the generation of appropriate conversation between members of the group, intervening as little as possible except to keep the conversation on the right lines and to ensure that all the required topics are covered. The discussion is tape-recorded and can be transcribed. Quotations should be used to support the interpretation.

Conducting a group discussion requires that due consideration is given to the ambience of the occasion and the dynamics of the interaction between group members. The less assertive individuals may feel group pressure to conform to the norms of attitudes expressed in the group and dominant individuals can discourage a full discussion of topics about which they feel strongly. Again, it is the role of the moderator to attempt to control excessive behaviours within the group: '. . . shy members will have to be encouraged to speak out, the "angry silent" types to abandon their self-imposed Siberia and the dominators to keep quiet for a while to give others a chance to voice their views!' (Webb, 1993).

A successful focus group has three major advantages:

- it is quicker and cheaper than interviewing respondents individually
- groups can provide a social background which reflects the fact that many of the decisions made by an individual are taken in a group context, particularly decisions on participation in leisure activities such as the arts – depth interviews do not provide the restraining influence of others' opinions

- the range of opinions being expressed in a group discussion helps to stimulate an individual to articulate his or her own beliefs, attitudes, opinions and feelings – this stimulus is absent from other forms of research.

As a research approach the interview can stand alone, although it must be recognized that, as the size of the sample is generally small and no explicit attempts are made to ensure that the sample is representative, difficulties may arise if the findings from the research are used to generalize about whole audiences or segments. Such information does not provide the statistically significant data created by the larger samples used in surveys. The interpretation of the data, as well as the conducting of the interviews and discussions themselves, is usually the responsibility of the interviewer or moderator, who has observed the data collection first-hand and is therefore in the best position to interpret its meaning. The role of the moderator needs tact and detachment. A good moderator can make all the difference to the success of a piece of research, so it may be worth the investment to hire an experienced agency to do the job for you rather than attempting it yourself.

Used in conjunction with quantitative surveys though, this method has few drawbacks. Interviews can be of immense value in exploratory research or to illuminate further the results of a survey.

Survey

If the objectives of the research require that quantitative data are generated, then a survey must be undertaken. A survey is a method of data collection which involves identical questions being asked of a large number of individuals and a systematic record being made of their responses. This process is usually conducted by means of a questionnaire. The rest of this chapter will take a closer look at the whole issue of survey design, implementation, analysis and interpretation and the way in which surveys should be conducted.

Case 3.3 Finding the hotspots

The M6 Group of galleries is a consortium of visual arts venues in the West Midlands with a mutual interest in developing visual arts audiences in the region and beyond.

In total, visual arts venues and attractions within the region attract 1.8 million visitors per year, but there is still potential to reach new audiences, as the total target catchment area for the M6 Galleries comprises almost 10 per cent of the UK population.

Since the group's inception in 1996 various joint projects have been undertaken to assess current attendance and to develop the first-time visitor market. One of the most influential of these was an audience mapping research exercise undertaken in 1998. This simple research project aimed to provide participating members with a detailed profile of visitors to their galleries.

The postcodes of all visitors to each gallery within a specified timescale were collected to enable a map of the distribution of visitors to be drawn up. A comprehensive Mosaic profile of the likely characteristics of the visitors was then created, and a catchment area was defined for each gallery and presented on the map. These findings were then used to target non-attenders living in geographic hotspots, which contained few gallery attenders but, according to Mosaic, had high potential for arts attendance. A taster event was organized at each of the eight participating galleries, and promotional campaigns were conducted to encourage attendance at these events from the target groups. As the audience mapping exercise had identified potential audience and catchment area overlaps between certain venues, some galleries collaborated in clusters and pooled resources.

Source: Yates, 2001.

Conducting a survey

Arts organizations most commonly use surveys in ad hoc research relating to specific marketing decisions, and in particular to find out more about audiences. If you wish to conduct an ad hoc survey there are a number of stages to consider, as shown in Figure 3.1. These stages will now be examined in more detail.

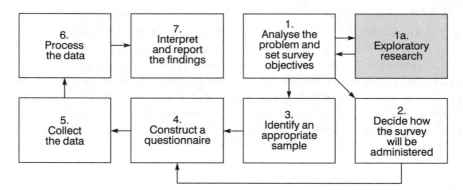

Figure 3.1 The stages of ad hoc survey research

Stage 1: Identify the precise nature of the problem to be solved and set specific objectives for the survey

The researcher should begin by analysing the problem or problems that the research is to address. It is not enough to have a vague notion that you would like to know more about your audience or believe that you could attract more visitors if you changed your promotions. Since the purpose of a survey is to get answers to important questions, a crucial first step must be to state those questions very explicitly in the form of objectives for the survey – when the survey has been completed, precisely what do you want to know the answer to? It may be wise, if not essential, to undertake some exploratory research at this stage to help define the questions more clearly.

The next two stages need to be considered in tandem. Decisions have to be made as to who should be asked to respond to a survey and this may affect the way in which it is administered.

Stage 2: Identify an appropriate sample

The individuals chosen to respond to a survey dictate its findings, so it is important for the target audience for the survey to be clearly defined so that the questions can be asked of appropriate individuals.

Surveys rely upon the mathematical fact that the views expressed by a relatively small number of individuals, known as the sample, will be representative of the views of a much larger group, known as the population, if that sample is chosen in a particular way and is of a particular size. These laws of probability mean that the larger the sample, the more representative it will be of the population from which it was drawn. A random[2] sample will be most representative of all and you can be far more confident in assuming that the views of the sample reflect the views of the whole population than with any other method. In practice, of course, it costs far more to interview and interpret the findings from large samples than it does from small samples. Also, the logistics of identifying each member of your population and ensuring that those you select to be in the sample do in fact respond to your survey can be too time-consuming for most arts organizations. As a result, rules of thumb may be more appropriate to guide the process of sampling in arts organizations than pure statistical techniques.

A number of questions commonly arise in sampling, and the answers to these are useful in designing a sampling mechanism.

1. When should I take my sample?

If the research objectives relate to a specific play or exhibition, the sample needs to take into account the variations in audience profile caused by season (e.g. school holidays), day of the week, time of day and perhaps weather conditions. A gallery or museum may have access to historical data relating to attendance figures. In this case it is possible for a weighting to be calculated and applied so that more respondents are questioned during busier times. If this information is not available, as is usually the case for a specific theatrical programme, the best method is simply to make an estimate of when the busier periods will occur, plan the data collection accordingly but then, before analysing the survey, weight the results to reflect the actual variations in audience profile recorded during the period of the survey.

In the performing arts, unless a single long-running play is the focus for the research, the sample will have to recognize the effects of variations in programme, as well as time of day, day of week and time of year. In this case,

2 Random does not mean haphazard. In survey terminology it means that each person in the population studied has the same chance of being chosen as any other member, and that this probability can be numerically calculated.

the sampling procedure will depend upon the objectives of the survey. If the objective is to compare audience profiles of different plays, all the other factors, such as day of the week, should initially be held constant to allow as direct a comparison as possible to take place. This comparison can be repeated under different levels of the factors concerned (e.g. different days of the week) to be more representative of the total audience.

Sampling England

In order to find out what the population in general thinks about the arts, the Arts Council of England commissioned the research agency MORI to include questions on its omnibus survey exploring people's awareness of and attitudes to the arts. The survey was conducted in 175 parliamentary constituencies across Great Britain. Within each sampling point, 12 respondents were interviewed, selected by means of a ten-cell quota comprising the groups shown in the table.

Quota type	Category 1	Category 2	Category 3
Gender	Male	Female	n/a
Household tenure	Owner occupied	Council/Housing Association	Other
Age	15–24	25–44	45+
Working status	Full time	Part time/not working	n/a

These quotas were based on census and other data about the nature of the population, and in each constituency the quotas were applied to represent the make-up of that area. The final sample size was 12 respondents × 175 sample points (total 2100) across Great Britian, but as only people living in England were asked the Arts Council's questions, the total number of respondents was 1801.

Source: MORI for the Arts Council of England, 2000.

---

2. Who should be in my sample?

The important issue here is how to obtain a good cross-section of responses which will be representative of most of the audience. In some cases it is possible for an exhaustive survey (known as a census) to be undertaken, whereby all visitors or audience members at a venue at the selected time are asked to complete the questionnaire. The mechanism used for this is usually a self-completion questionnaire, discussed further at Stage 3, either left on the seats in an auditorium or available to be picked up. The latter will almost always lead to serious bias in the survey results as the visitors themselves select whether to take the questionnaire and frequently only those with a higher than average interest in the event will take the trouble to complete them. Similar problems can arise with questionnaires left on seats or placed in programmes, though for practical reasons these may be the best methods to use.

A smaller, but carefully controlled sample can produce more accurate results than an uncontrolled attempt at a census, so it may be worth devoting time and money to ensuring that questionnaires are handed out individually, rather than left for collection. This enables the potential respondent to be reassured as to the purpose of the survey and encouraged to take part (most people enjoy having their opinions sought and will generally be happy to co-operate provided they know what you are trying to do).

To approach a representative sample, an objective selection rule is needed to protect the survey from the bias which can arise if interviewers are allowed to choose whom they approach. Inexperienced researchers may unwittingly favour those who make themselves more accessible and avoid those who are less forthcoming. One method would be to approach, say, every tenth person through the door, or to use a quota system, whereby the interviewer or questionnaire distributor is asked to approach a target number of males and females within certain age ranges (though this may have to be based on a judgement which may ultimately prove to be incorrect!). However, as most people attend arts events in groups a good method is to give out one questionnaire to each group of people and one to each person who comes alone. In the case of the group, one person in a party is more likely to fill in a questionnaire than every person in a party. All entrances to the building need to be covered to ensure that all visitors have an equal chance of participating.

3. How many people should be in my sample?

The more questionnaires that are completed, the more confident you can be that the responses obtained are representative of the whole population and not just the individuals who answered the questions (see Table 3.5). In total, a figure of 500 completed questionnaires should be plenty to provide results which are statistically useful, though a minimum of 300 is acceptable under severe resource constraints. (If the sample is any smaller than this, valid comparisons cannot be made between subsections within the population, such as differences between responses by males and females, different age groups, those attending on different days of the week or those who are regular as opposed to infrequent attenders.)

These 500, however, should be spread across the whole time period of the research, and in the case of performances, at least three performances should be sampled to improve the cross-section, even if it is possible to obtain all 500 responses at one performance. Response rates vary according to the way that the questionnaire is administered (see Stage 3), but will be significantly reduced if the survey is not well explained, the questionnaire is poorly laid out or worded, or if there is nowhere obvious to return it.

Stage 3: Decide how the survey will be implemented

Methods of questionnaire administration fall into four main categories.

Table 3.5 Sample sizes

'You don't have to eat the whole cake to know what it tastes like!' Market researchers use this analogy to explain the use of samples to represent the views of a whole population. Statistical techniques enable us to predict just how similar to the population a sample will be. The size of the sample is critical to accuracy. An estimate of the population's response can be calculated from the sample's response by adding or subtracting the percentages given in the table below. So, from a random sample of 1000, if 30 per cent of the respondents give a particular answer to a question, the percentage agreeing with that response in the whole population would fall somewhere between 27.2 per cent and 32.8 per cent (e.g. if 30 per cent of the sample say they have been to an art gallery in the past 12 months, the percentage of the whole population for whom this would be true would be between 27.2 per cent and 32.8 per cent). But if the sample size was only 100, then the response for the whole population could fall anywhere between 21 per cent and 39 per cent.

	Response frequency (%)				
Sample size	10 or 90	20 or 80	30 or 70	40 or 60	50
100	5.9	7.8	9.0	9.6	9.8
500	2.6	3.5	4.0	4.2	4.4
1000	1.9	2.5	2.8	3.0	3.1
2000	1.3	1.8	2.0	2.1	2.2

The table shows how the responses given by the sample more accurately reflect the views of the population as sample sizes increase. Note that a sample of 500 can reflect the views of the whole population with at least twice the accuracy of a sample of 100, but a sample of 1000 does not predict twice as accurately as one of 500. There are diminishing returns to ever larger sample sizes.

Interview surveys

These are conducted face to face with respondents and have several advantages:

● interviewers can be involved in the sampling process by selecting an appropriate range of respondents using a quota system, described above, and eliminating those who are not in the target audience for the research
● the interviewer can encourage respondents to answer as fully as possible and check, where appropriate, that the question has been fully understood
● any materials, such as publicity items, that need to be shown to the respondents can be properly presented
● interviewers can usually persuade respondents to complete the interview and response rates are consistently higher than for other types of questionnaire administration

These advantages mean that the quality of the data derived from interview surveys is generally superior to other methods, but to some extent this depends upon the skill of the interviewer. As Kent (1993) explains,

The interviewer is, on the one hand, trying to be 'standard' in all his or her approaches to respondents, but, on the other hand, may need to react to individual circumstances for the successful completion of the interview – in short, the interviewer needs to act like a robot but retain the appearance of a human being.

The interview itself is a highly artificial process of social interaction and there are dangers of bias arising simply due to the age, sex, social class, dress, accent and personality of both the interviewer and the respondent. The key to removing interviewer bias is good training. For this reason, most commercial organizations rely on market research agencies to supply well-trained interviewers, though this is too costly for many arts organizations. If this is the case, organizations should ensure that they arrange some form of interview training for their own (usually volunteer) researchers, and ensure that they are thoroughly briefed as to the objectives of the survey and the instructions for sampling.

Self-completion surveys

These are distributed and collected on site, either by placing questionnaires on seats, in programmes, or in prominent places in the building. As they dispense with the need for an interviewer, both the costs of interviewing and interviewer bias are entirely avoided. However, as respondents are self-selecting, bias is likely to creep in through the nature of the sample. The best way to avoid this is to construct a visually appealing, concise and self-explanatory questionnaire which attracts the attention and appeals even to those with no particular interest in responding (see Table 3.6).

Mail surveys

Postal surveys are extremely cost-effective, requiring neither interviewers nor telephone systems. Their usefulness in marketing research has increased as arts

Table 3.6 How to make sure you get a good response

To get results you can view with confidence and to make sure the survey is cost-effective, you must aim to maximize the return of the questionnaires. Here are the main ways of achieving this aim:

- Make sure the questionnaire looks smart and short.
- Put up large notices drawing attention to the survey and explaining what you are doing.
- Offer a prize draw – it will encourage people to complete a questionnaire. Cash is the best incentive (say five to ten prizes).
- Provide pens for people to write with.
- Have a table near the return boxes in the foyer so people can write easily.
- Have clearly marked large return boxes 'Post your questionnaire here'.
- Have enough boxes to cover all exits, bars and foyers.
- Make sure the people handing out the questionnaires are smart, friendly and polite.

Source: Walshe, 1992.

organizations have improved their databases and more accurate sampling has become possible. A major advantage of mail surveys is that respondents can devote more time to filling in the questionnaire, so longer questionnaires are possible. Respondents can fill them in at a time convenient to them and consult with other members of their household if necessary.

Several disadvantages of postal questionnaires restrict their use, however. Firstly, the person who fills in the questionnaire may not be the one selected in the sample. In addition, there is no interviewer to assist and encourage questionnaire completion, and therefore certain types of questioning techniques cannot be used. It is often argued, though, that the main disadvantage of mail surveys is the very low response rate usually achieved. This can be overcome to a certain extent by well-constructed questionnaires and in particular by the use of a covering letter which 'sells' the value of the research to the respondent and encourages him or her to respond. The letter should at a minimum explain:

● who is carrying out the research
● what is the purpose of the research
● how the respondent was selected
● that responses will be confidential
● how to complete and return the questionnaire

Enclosing an incentive with the letter (such as ticket discounts, or restaurant vouchers) is known to improve response rates slightly, but the cost of this needs to be weighed against the value of extra responses. It is normal to enclose a pre-paid reply envelope.

It can be useful to send out reminders after two to three weeks, encouraging those who have not responded to do so. If this is the intention, it is important that the original questionnaires are numbered and lists maintained relating named respondents to numbered questionnaires, so that those who have replied are excluded from the follow-up letter. The only problem here is that respondents cannot then be assured of the anonymity of their responses, simply the confidentiality with which they will be treated.

Telephone surveys

While this technique is very common in some industries, and particularly in the USA, the major problem for a telephone arts survey is how to get the telephone numbers of members of the arts audience unless these have been gathered on a database. Systematic sampling, therefore, becomes a very difficult task, and there is a serious danger of bias. Those who have volunteered their telephone numbers are likely to be those most supportive of a particular theatre, museum or gallery, and are unlikely to be representative of the whole population. Also, telephone ownership is by no means universal and parts of the audience, including less affluent yet quite sizeable groups such as students, will be under-represented. The situation is further complicated now that mobile numbers are used alongside, and often in preference to, land lines by some market segments.

If a telephone survey is the preferred method, questions must be relatively straightforward because it can be quite difficult to comprehend complex questions heard over the telephone. Interviewers need to be even more skilled than in face-to-face situations, as non-verbal messages can be neither sent nor interpreted by interviewer or respondent. It is not a suitable task for amateurs, so the cost of employing professionals plus the telephone bill are likely to put this method beyond the budget of many arts organizations.

Stage 4: Design the questionnaire

A couple of points need to be taken into account before starting to construct a questionnaire. Firstly, the way in which the data will be collected will affect the questionnaire length and layout, as well as the style of question. Another consideration is the way in which the data will be analysed. There are a number of quite simple and affordable computer packages which are ideal for the analysis of small surveys. The package to be used must be identified at the stage of questionnaire design as each package places different constraints on the way in which questions are worded. These are seldom constraints which will affect the quality of questioning, but they must be recognized if data collected is to be successfully fed into the system.

A questionable question

Leading questions often come about because you are trying to supply a context for the question. For example, consider the question:

'Most people are willing to pay a small entrance fee to a museum.' To what extent do you agree with this statement?

There are three flaws in this:

- The phrase 'most people' makes it difficult for respondents to answer – who knows what the rest of the population thinks?
- What is meant by 'a small entrance fee'? Small is a relative term which different people will interpret in different ways.
- The question itself asks the extent to which the respondent agrees – it does not suggest that people might disagree.

Criteria for effective questions

As each question is written, it should be evaluated against the following criteria:

- *Relevance:* does it help reach the objectives of the survey? If the only questions asked are those of direct relevance to the objectives, the questionnaire length can be kept to a minimum.
- *Clarity:* will respondents understand every word in the question? Complex terminology and ambiguity must be avoided at all costs. If respondents fail

to understand a question, they will either miss it out altogether or, worse still, guess at its meaning and give a response to the question they think you are asking, which may be very different from what you intended.

- *Brevity:* in general, a question should consist of no more than 20 words, otherwise it becomes too difficult to comprehend quickly.
- *Impartiality:* the wording of the question should not influence the respondents' answers. This is more difficult than it sounds. It is quite easy unwittingly to introduce leading questions by failing to recognize the overtones of certain words.
- *Precision:* each question should only deal with one issue at a time. If two issues are introduced, the respondent may have opposing views on different parts of the question and may not be able to express these within the response mechanism provided.
- *Inoffensiveness:* questions relating to sensitive issues, in particular salary, age, ethnicity and social class, can be construed as offensive unless worded very carefully. They should also be placed at the end of the questionnaire so that the respondent has built up a relationship with the interviewer (if any) and committed him- or herself to completing the questionnaire and is less likely to be put off at this stage.

The form of survey questions

There are two basic ways to ask questions in a survey. Open-ended questions allow respondents to provide answers using their own words, while closed questions (also known as closed-ended, fixed-response or forced-choice questions) provide a limited number of possible responses which the respondents must choose between.

Open-ended questions collect information with minimum direction to respondents, and are very useful if the possible range of responses is very broad. Another advantage of this type of question is that it uses the respondents' own words and therefore allows them to vent strong opinions and helps the researcher to understand the way that people really think about an issue. Probing questions and clarifying questions may be used to gain more

Table 3.7 Examples of open-ended questions

Overall, what did you like best about tonight's performance? Please write your answer below.

And what did you like least?

Table 3.8 Examples of closed questions

. . . revealing facts

Is your age . . .? (tick one)

under 18	☐
18–25	☐
26–35	☐
36–45	☐
46–55	☐
56–65	☐
over 65	☐

. . . revealing behaviour

Approximately how much time did you spend in the gallery today? (tick one)

less than an hour	☐
up to two hours	☐
more than two but less than four hours	☐
more than four hours	☐

. . . revealing attitudes

How interested would you be in pursuing any of the following types of activities?

	very interested	quite interested	mildly interested	not at all interested
participating in				
amateur dramatics				
learning to play an instrument				
taking studio art classes				

. . . revealing opinions

Compared with what you expected, how would you rate tonight's performance? (tick one)

much better than I expected	☐
better than I expected	☐
as I expected	☐
not as good as I expected	☐
much worse than I expected	☐

complete answers to open-ended questions, especially if interviewing is being used to collect the data. Interviewers can build upon subjects offered by the respondents, following up any vague or general terms given in their answers, though they should offer no prompts or suggestions for clarification as this will introduce bias. It is important, too, that sufficient space is allowed on the questionnaire for full responses to be filled in as any curtailment or paraphrasing of an answer can also introduce bias. The main disadvantage of open-ended questions arises in their interpretation. All responses have to be read and coded. This means devising a set of categories that covers the range of all open-ended responses. Inevitably some answers will be ambiguous and difficult to code precisely and, even under the best circumstances, coding is a very time-consuming activity. Bias can creep in simply from poor coding.

Closed questions offer more limited scope for response, so respondents tend to find them easier and less time-consuming to complete and most surveys use a high proportion of closed questions to encourage high response rates. Closed questions also avoid the difficulties of coding, as the code is written into the question in the form of a response mechanism which prevents respondents producing ambiguous answers. Despite the limitations on response, closed questions can be used to investigate a range of issues, including facts, behaviour, attitudes and opinions. They tend to be one of three types:

1. Multiple response questions

These offer a series of possible responses and can allow response in just one, or in a number of categories. Sometimes, a category will be included for those who are unable to respond (the 'don't know' box) and if there is some doubt as to whether all possible responses have been identified in advance, space is provided for respondents to write in their own answer (the 'other' box) and the answers are coded when the results are analysed. For example:

> *What type of admission ticket do you have? (tick one)*
> *student* □
> *season subscription* □
> *single performance* □
> *free pass* □
> *group or party* □
> *senior citizen* □
> *don't know* □
> *other (please explain)* □ _____

Dichotomous questions are particular types of multiple response questions, where there are only two possible answers, such as 'true/false', 'yes/no' or 'male/female'. In practice, these questions should be used infrequently, partly because of their very limited scope but also because a 'don't know' or 'other' category is nearly always needed for some respondents.

2. Scaled questions

These provide a scale on which respondents can express the strength of their attitudes or opinions. This enables different attributes of performances, venues and exhibitions to be compared. Bipolar questions put forward widely differing opinions of a particular attribute and ask respondents to place their own opinion somewhere between the polarized views suggested. For example:

> *Compared to what you expected, how would you rate tonight's performance? (tick one)*
>
> | | |
> |---|---|
> | *much better than I expected* | ☐ |
> | *better than I expected* | ☐ |
> | *as I expected* | ☐ |
> | *not as good as I expected* | ☐ |
> | *much worse than I expected* | ☐ |

Agree/disagree questions (known as a Lickert scale) ask people to indicate the extent to which they agree or disagree with a particular statement. They are useful for measuring attitudes. For example:

> *To what extent do you agree or disagree with the following statement (tick one)*
> *'Some people who go to the opera are only there to impress their friends'*
>
> | | |
> |---|---|
> | *agree strongly* | ☐ |
> | *agree slightly* | ☐ |
> | *neither agree nor disagree* | ☐ |
> | *disagree slightly* | ☐ |
> | *disagree strongly* | ☐ |

Semantic differential questions use words of opposite meaning to suggest descriptions of attributes of, for example, a venue or performance. Respondents are asked to indicate their own perceptions along this scale. For example:

> *Compared with other theatres I have been to, the bar here is:*
>
> *very small*   *very large*
>   *1*   *2*   *3*   *4*   *5*   *6*   *7*
>
> *very cheap*   *very expensive*
>   *1*   *2*   *3*   *4*   *5*   *6*   *7*
>
> *very comfortable*   *very uncomfortable*
>   *1*   *2*   *3*   *4*   *5*   *6*   *7*

The only problem with scaled questions is that people are reluctant to express very strong opinions and therefore tend to avoid the first and last categories in any list. This reduces the sensitivity of the question as a tool for capturing true attitudes and opinions, which is why qualitative research is so useful for this task.

3. Ordering questions

These enable respondents to express preferences and, if appropriate, to state these preferences in terms of priorities.

Preference questions will ask for one or more issues or attributes to be identified as being of more importance than others. They are frequently asked as closed questions, whereby respondents will be asked to choose from a list of possible options with an 'other' box for responses which are not identified, and a 'no preference' box for those who are unable or unwilling to make a selection. For example:

> *Which three benefits do you feel are the most important benefits of belonging to the 'Friends of the Theatre' (please tick)*
>
> *regular information about events* ☐
> *cost savings on tickets* ☐
> *cost savings on other purchases* ☐
> *priority booking* ☐
> *attendance at members' activities* ☐
> *involvement with the Theatre* ☐
> *other (please specify)* _____ ☐

The problem with preference questions is that they tend to magnify perceived differences in preference. Just because a respondent has excluded an item from the chosen list does not mean that these items are very unimportant, and the extent to which they are less important is not clear.

Ranking questions take respondents one step further by asking them to prioritize their preferences. The importance of the items in the list given in the example above could have been investigated by asking respondents to rank them in order. This can be a difficult task though, particularly with lists longer than just five or six items.

There is a common misconception, too, that the intervals between ranked items are equal, but in reality this may not be the case (the first feature may be far more important than the second, but the second and third may be seen as having almost equal importance). There is also an in-built assumption that the respondent is equally knowledgeable about all the items on the list and therefore qualified to compare them all with each other. This is unlikely to be the case. Ranking can be useful, but its limitations must be recognized.

Pre-testing questionnaires

This is sometimes known as the pilot stage, when the questionnaire is tested on a very small number of people who are typical of the people to be included in the sample. Every questionnaire should be pre-tested. Questions which seem very straightforward to the researcher may be thoroughly confusing or even offensive to the respondent. It is important to identify questions which are unclear, ambiguous, annoying, difficult to answer or very time-consuming, and to make changes before the full launch of the survey. You will be glad you did – arts audiences usually contain a number of respondents who will make you feel silly if there are ambiguities in the phrasing!

Stage 5: Collect the data

The data collection method has already been identified by this stage, so the survey is ready to be administered. Interviewers need to be briefed and trained for face-to-face and telephone data collection, and administrative systems need to be set up for self-completion and mail surveys. If the preparation work has been competently undertaken, this can be a very straightforward part of the marketing research process.

Stage 6: Process the data

Data processing is the means by which the raw data (i.e. the responses gathered from the sample) are converted into a form which will enable their underlying meaning to be identified. Unless the sample size is so small that the results will hold very little statistical significance, the most efficient way of processing data is by using computer software designed for this purpose. The job can be done by anyone who has a reasonable level of expertise using a spreadsheet, though a more efficient way would be to use a bespoke software package such as SPSS or SNAP. Alternatively, arts organizations may choose to use a marketing agency which specializes in data processing to perform the analysis, particularly if sample sizes are large and the data quite complex.

Data processing has three main stages:

Data input

The responses from each questionnaire returned are typed into the computer. This is a laborious process which requires no great skill and can be learned very quickly. Large and sophisticated surveys can be set up to use Optical Mark Recognition, to avoid the need for typing in data, but this is unusual in the arts, where sample sizes are seldom big enough to warrant this.

Data summary

The computer will take the raw data and summarize the frequency of responses to each of the questions to produce a list of how many people said what. Visual displays of the data (e.g. pie charts, frequency tables and histograms) can then be produced to depict this information more graphically. As the sample has been designed to be representative of the whole population, it can then be stated with some confidence that the frequency of response observed in the sample will apply to the whole population. Indeed, there is a statistical formula which will indicate how confident one can be that the true figure for the whole population falls within a narrow band around the observed figure for the sample. Table 3.5 illustrates how the level of confidence with which the results from a random sample can be treated is related to the size of the sample (though, of course, the quality of the questionnaire, the interviewing, and the coding are all factors which will influence the quality of the results, too).

Where appropriate, the computer will also calculate the mean (or arithmetic average) response to scaled questions, and measure the dispersion (or standard deviation) of the result (see Table 3.9). The mean does not in itself imply that

Table 3.9 Mean and standard deviation

Suppose 20 people were asked the extent to which they agreed or disagreed with the following statements:

Statement 1
'Children under the age of 14 should not be allowed into art galleries unless accompanied by an adult.'

Statement 2
'Museums should never charge entrance fees.'

1 = strongly agree
2 = agree slightly
3 = neither agree nor disagree

4 = disagree slightly
5 = strongly disagree

The different responses of the 20 people to the two statements might be as follows:

Statement 1
1, 1, 5, 4, 5, 2, 2, 5, 5, 3, 3, 1, 1, 4, 4, 1, 2, 4, 5, 2

Statement 2
2, 2, 4, 4, 3, 3, 4, 1, 2, 4, 4, 3, 3, 1, 5, 4, 2, 2, 3, 4

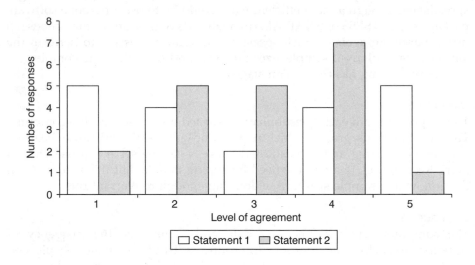

Statistically, these results indicate an identical average response to each statement but different dispersions:

Statement 1
mean = 60/20 = 3
standard deviation = 1.59

Statement 2
mean = 60/20 = 3
standard deviation = 1.13

The relatively high standard deviation in the responses to Statement 1 implies that people have stronger feelings about the admission of lone children to art galleries, either strongly in favour or strongly against. The mean, in this case, does not imply that the majority of people have neutral feelings on the subject, simply that firmly-held attitudes are evenly balanced. There is less divergence in Statement 2, implying that attitudes are more moderate throughout the population.

(Note that this example is given only to illustrate the mean and standard deviation; in reality the sample size would be too small to make judgements about the nature of the population.)

most people thought something. It simply shows the central tendency of the sample. The standard deviation is calculated to indicate whether the mean was generated as a result of most people having very similar views, or people having wide-ranging views on a subject so that the average is simply a half-way position on a very long scale, rather than a representation of popular opinion. The higher the standard deviation figure, the more wide-ranging were the responses from the sample. Sometimes the responses fall into two extremes and, if this is the case, it may be possible to use the findings to identify two discrete market segments within the population.

Data analysis

This is performed to identify interrelationships between the answers to different questions and involves the use of statistical techniques. Cross-tabulation is the form of analysis most commonly undertaken. This enables the responses to any question to be compared with the responses to any other question. For example, it would be possible to identify whether there is any perceived difference in the enjoyment of a performance according to whether a visitor sits in the stalls or in the gods. The expectations of tourists from a visit to a gallery could be compared with the expectations of local people, school groups and art students. Any observed differences could then be investigated more closely using quantitative research.

While cross-tabulation and other even more complex statistical tests can be performed manually, they are such time-consuming and difficult tasks that it is impossible to do a comprehensive analysis. Computer analysis is quick, easy and generates far more valuable information than could be extracted by hand.

Case 3.4 Figuring out the youth market

ROAR ('Right of Admission Reserved') is a programme of continuous research which began in 1995 with the aim of generating a much fuller understanding of the various 'tribes' that comprise the universe of 15–24 year olds. Thus it is of direct relevance to arts organizations attempting to attract those elusive youth audiences.

The research is commissioned by a consortium of six media organizations, comprising an advertising agency, a TV station, a cinema sales house, consumer magazines, national newspapers and a radio station. The co-funding of ROAR is a workable proposition because, although the consortium members have very different commercial aims, they have several common shared goals.

ROAR uses a programme of qualitative and quantitative research to fill in the gaps in the understanding of young people. Its aim is to identify trends, define style leaders and find out what is culturally important to young people.

ROAR uses a panel of 1000 respondents on each wave of research. They are recruited face to face by a research agency, then sent a questionnaire which includes a battery of lifestyle questions which are used to segment the youth population into one of eight ROAR clusters:

- **Casual Geezers** – they go clubbing on a Saturday night, and are definitely going to Ibiza in the summer.

- **Cooling Britannias** – they know how to enjoy themselves, but are not slaves to fashion. They can be found in an All Bar One on a Saturday night.
- **Corporate Clubbers** – the 'live for the weekend' spirit dominates this group, which comprises party animals.
- **Gill and Ted** – this group tend to be at the younger end of the age range, with entertainment focused in their bedrooms: TV, Computers, Hi-fi and Playstations.
- **New Modernists** – often graduates, this group is highly culturally literate, and looks towards creative careers.
- **Modern Moralists** – religious belief plays a large part in the lives of this group, who take their studies seriously and look to settle down with a steady job.
- **Playsafe Careerists** – this group is driven by money and is keen to get into a first job.
- **Style Surfers** – they may not be quite at the cutting edge of contemporary fashion and culture but aren't far behind.

In addition to the quantitative research, ROAR involves qualitative work with a range of methodologies. Focus groups are used to stimulate discussions about topics such as brands and advertising, and in-depth one-to-one interviews are used for discussing personal beliefs. When recruiting qualitative respondents, the same lifestyle questions are used as in the quantitative work so that the findings can be linked to cluster group typologies.

What the research has revealed is that visiting friends is the most regular form of entertainment for young people, and shopping for clothes or music comes next, though book reading features quite highly. As a group they see themselves as being experts in entertainment, with music, television and films topping the list. But they are more confident about their knowledge of narcotics than they are about art or religion. The New Modernists are more than three times more likely to indulge themselves in some culture than the Casual Geezers and though it may be possible to market Chekhov to New Modernists and even Style Surfers, attracting Casual Geezers would be a serious challenge.

Source: Fowles, 2000.

Stage 7: Interpreting and reporting findings

At this point in the survey, facts and figures relating to the respondents who participated at the data collection stage have been collected. The final step is to interpret the meaning of these facts and figures, translating them into usable information which can help decisions to be made.

Interpretation

The figures do not speak for themselves. It is their interpretation that renders them useful (or useless!). In interpreting data, a number of key points must be constantly borne in mind:

- The interpretation should relate to the problem identified at the very beginning of the survey process, and the only findings which should be highlighted should be those which help to reach the explicit objectives of the research.

- No survey is absolutely definitive and no figure absolutely correct, and this should be recognized by indicating the approximation of figures.
- Findings should not be exaggerated or dramatized to draw attention to them. Fair weight should be given to all the relevant evidence.
- Small sample sizes should be recognized and generalizations should not be made from samples which are too small to give statistically reliable results.
- Averages should be recognized as merely tendencies and not be thought of as representing a 'Mr and Mrs Average'.
- Recognition should be given to infrequent but significant answers, as there may be new trends emerging.
- There should be clear distinction between fact (what people are, what they do, what they own etc.) and opinion (what people think about issues). Opinions and attitudes do not always translate into behaviour.
- There should be clear distinction between cause and effect. Associated factors are not necessarily causal. Surveys are useful for identifying effects, but conclusions about causes must be drawn very tentatively and sometimes need further investigation.

Lies, damned lies and statistics

A statement by the Department for Culture, Media and Sport (DCMS) in 2001 raised more than a few eyebrows in the museums' sector. It announced that an extra 5 million people had visited the 17 English national museums and galleries sponsored by the DCMS in 2000–2001, an increase of 20 per cent compared to the previous year. Culture Secretary Chris Smith was quoted as hailing these new figures as a 'success for art, heritage and education'; but on closer inspection, it turned out that the 5 million 'people' were not people at all – it was an extra 5 million visits that had been reported. Assuming that some people had attended more than once in the year, there were a lot fewer than 5 million extra visitors. Furthermore, the 5 million reported was really only 4.7 million. Visits actually went up from 23.7 million to 28.4 million, so the DCMS had created an extra 300 000 visits just in the roundings. And finally, of the 4.7 million extra visits to the 17 museums and galleries, 4 million were made to Tate Modern, which opened its doors for the first time that year. So when Chris Smith said 'These figures are great news and are further evidence of just how popular our national museums and galleries are with the public', what he really should have said was 'Well done Tate Modern!'

Source: Hill and Whitehead, 2001b.

Reporting

The interpretation is usually presented in the form of a report. If this report is to be used by decision-makers, their needs must be taken into account in its preparation. The four main points to bear in mind are:

1 Present only information which is of relevance to the reader. Too much information is confusing, but there must be enough detail to guide decision that is to be made. For example, it is important to give information on sample sizes and details of the research methodology, to enable the reader to estimate the accuracy of the findings. A copy of the questionnaire should also be included to allow the reader to refer back to questions posed. However, when it comes to reporting the responses, some details can be left out. There is no need, for example, to list all the responses to open questions. Also, if a large number of small frequency responses are given to a closed question, some of the categories may be collapsed into one and reported under the heading 'other responses'.

2 Communicate the findings simply. It is useful to report findings visually, with important findings being highlighted and discussed in text. Results are easily produced in the form of tables, where both the actual frequencies and the frequencies as a percentage of the total sample should be reported. Graphical illustration may also be used to highlight important features or trends. Some people cannot or will not interpret the tables or graphs, so their meanings should be discussed in accompanying text. Technical jargon should be kept to a minimum and simple declarative statements used to put the main points across.

3 Do not imply certainty. No survey is absolutely definitive and no figure in a survey is an entirely correct representation of reality. There should be no pretence that you are reporting absolute fact. Findings should therefore be reported as whole percentages rather than to decimal places, both in the tables and in any explanatory text. Unless the sample size is exceptionally large, sampling error alone will make it impossible to calculate percentages with any great precision. If samples or sub-samples are small, readers should be warned that the findings should be treated with caution.

4 Provide an executive summary. Not every reader will want to read the whole report, so a brief summary of the findings, the main conclusions and recommendations should appear at the beginning. Complicated tables, discussion of methodology and analysis should be kept for other sections of the report.

Summary

Much of the theory of marketing research applies to arts organizations in exactly the same way as it does to commercial organizations. A desire for more information needs to be formalized by the setting of research objectives, and a structured, methodical process must be followed in the gathering of facts and figures and in their interpretation. The financial constraints facing most arts organizations do not preclude their use of marketing research, but simply require them to be focused in the objectives they set and resourceful in the techniques they use. The more focused a survey is, the more likely in reality it will be of value to the organization. Vast, all-embracing mega-research tends to lay itself open to challenges on methodology or interpretation of the data.

Marketing research is like a taxi-cab – it will go anywhere you want (providing you have the fare) but the cab-driver must know how to drive, must have a working knowledge of the Highway Code, and the passenger and the driver must agree at the outset as to the final destination. (Webb, 1993)

Key concepts

ad hoc research
causal objectives
continuous research
data processing
depth interviews
descriptive objectives
experimentation
exploratory objectives
external data
focus groups
geodemographics

internal data
marketing research
observation
population
primary research
qualitative research
quantitative research
questionnaire
sample
secondary research
survey

Discussion questions

1 Distinguish between multiple response questions, scaled questions and ordering questions by writing three different questions, each of which could be used to investigate audience perceptions of ticket prices for a professional performance of a Shakespeare play.
2 How could the ACORN or Mosaic classification systems be used to help a dance company plan a national tour?
3 How might an art gallery conduct some qualitative research to help it improve its access and facilities for the disabled? List the practical difficulties of organizing such research.
4 What type of primary data could feasibly and usefully be collected by an amateur theatre group to help with the planning of its annual pantomime? What are the main constraints it faces in collecting the data?
5 What arguments would you put forward to convince the management of an arts complex that it should agree to the appointment of a marketing research agency to investigate audience reactions to the forthcoming season of events and exhibitions?

Main case study: The Aberdeen audience

One of the main problems faced by researchers trying to quantify the size of the market for the arts in a town or city is that attenders of arts events in the area may attend more than one venue for more than one art form. While the box offices of each venue will capture valuable information about bookers at that venue, very little information exists to help marketers understand the extent to which their audience is shared with other venues. Consequently, marketers are seldom in a position to understand the nature of the real competition they are facing, or the potential for collaborative cross-art form cross-venue marketing campaigns.

To gain more understanding of these issues, the Scottish Arts Council commissioned a research project to quantify the market for the performing arts in Aberdeen. The primary aim of the project was to gain an understanding of the nature and extent of audiences for five key art forms at three major Aberdeen venues over a two-year period, with a view to helping the venues develop collaborative and cross-art form marketing strategies. The participating venues were The Lemon Tree, a multi-art form arts centre situated in a former 1930s YMCA building; His Majesty's Theatre, a traditional multi-art form receiving theatre, originally opened in 1906; and the Music Hall, a concert hall, originally built in 1820.

Methodology

During June to August 2000, box office systems suppliers were retained to extract the names, addresses and performances booked, of all bookers[3] at His Majesty's Theatre (HMT), the Music Hall (MH) and The Lemon Tree (TLT) in Aberdeen for performances occurring between 1 April 1998 and 30 April 2000. The 130 performances that took place during the period under investigation were then coded into one of six types:

- stand-up comedy (the only art form presented at all three venues)
- Scottish Opera and Scottish Ballet (these companies perform at HMT and MH, but not TLT)
- classical music: Royal Scottish National Orchestra, BBC Scottish Symphony Orchestra, and Scottish Chamber Orchestra (presented at TLT and HMT, but not MH)
- contemporary drama (presented at TLT and HMT, but not MH)
- contemporary dance (presented at TLT and HMT, but not MH)
- other art forms (those not within the scope of the investigation)

The first five of these performance types were the subject of the research.

The data was then processed to remove duplicate records within each database, and then de-duplicated once more to leave a single record for every booker who had purchased tickets[4] for any event at any venue during the two-year period. All identifying personal information was removed, except for postcode and a unique reference number.

Key findings

- The number of people who had booked tickets at one or more of the three Aberdeen venues during the two-year period in question was 47 310.

---

3 A booker is defined as the person who undertakes a ticket purchasing transaction with an arts organization (as opposed to an attender, who simply accompanies the booker to a performance).

4 For the purposes of this analysis, tickets purchased include all complimentary tickets, but exclude transactions for which no customer could be identified – i.e. 'door sales'.

- Of the 47 310 bookers, 30 028 (63.5 per cent) had booked for HMT, 14 952 (31.6 per cent) had booked for MH and 14 351 (30.3 per cent) had booked for TLT.
- Of the 47 310 theatre bookers in Aberdeen, 36 527 (77.2 per cent) booked tickets at one of the three venues, 9545 (20.2 per cent) booked tickets at two of the three venues, and 1238 (2.6 per cent) booked tickets at all three venues.
- Of those who booked at MH, 64.7 per cent had also booked at other venues; of those who had booked tickets at HMT, 33.2 per cent had also booked at other venues; and of those who had booked at TLT, 23.0 per cent had also booked at other venues.
- Of the 47 310 bookers, 36 658 (77.5 per cent) live within a notional 60-minute drivetime of the Aberdeen venues, and thus the remaining 10 652 (22.5 per cent) live beyond this.
- If residents of the Aberdeen 'region' are defined as adults living within a 60-minute drivetime of Aberdeen, then 13.6 per cent of all adults in the Aberdeen region book theatre tickets at the three venues under investigation.
- Of those bookers recorded for the three Aberdeen venues, 46.9 per cent came from Aberdeen city postcodes, and 28.0 per cent came from Aberdeenshire postcodes.[5] Sixteen per cent of bookers came from postcode sectors which include residents of both Aberdeen city and Aberdeenshire.[6] Nine per cent of bookers are from postcodes outside Aberdeen city and Aberdeenshire.
- Of the five art forms under investigation, contemporary drama is the best attended, having attracted 12.3 per cent of all bookers, followed by classical music with 8.8 per cent; Scottish Opera and Scottish Ballet with 7.8 per cent; contemporary dance with 6.2 per cent; and stand-up comedy with 6.0 per cent.
- Of those who booked for the art forms under investigation, 75.4 per cent booked for only one of those art forms.
- Of those who booked only one art form, 69.2 per cent booked at one venue only.
- Over half of all bookers for the five art forms booked only one art form at only one venue; and only 18 per cent of bookers booked more than one art form at more than one venue.
- Art-form crossover is highest between Scottish Opera and Scottish Ballet and contemporary drama, and Scottish Opera and Scottish Ballet and classical music.
- Bookers for the three Aberdeen venues come from a total of 924 postcode sectors: 20 per cent ('primary target market') of the theatre audiences live within six postcode sectors; 50 per cent ('core audience') live within 21 postcode sectors; 80 per cent ('main catchment') live within 50 postcode sectors; and 95 per cent ('extended catchment') live within 114 postcode sectors.
- The geographic catchments for HMT and MH are very similar to each other, but TLT bookers come from a somewhat different profile of postcode sectors.

5 A small number of Aberdeenshire postcodes incorporate bookers from counties such as Banffshire, Kincardineshire etc. Since political boundaries are defined by 'wards' and not 'postcodes' it is not possible to identify bookers more accurately by county.

6 As above, due to the way in which political boundaries are defined, and the additional lack of availability of data with regard to postcodes for political boundaries following the wide-scale 1995 postcode changes, there are a number of postcodes which are shared between city and county.

● The geographic catchment for classical music, Scottish Opera and Scottish Ballet and contemporary drama was far wider than for stand-up comedy and contemporary dance.

Questions

1 What conclusions can you draw about the willingness of Aberdeen audiences to experience different venues and different art forms? What might be the reasons for this?
2 Given the understanding now gained about arts attenders in the Aberdeen region, how might a geodemographic profiling system such as Mosaic or ACORN be used for a direct marketing campaign?
3 Propose a collaborative marketing campaign which will encourage those who have attended only one art form at one venue in the past two years to attend a different venue or art form.

Source: Arts Intelligence Ltd, 2002. Arts Intelligence/Aberdeen venues data analysis – project information © 2002 The Scottish Arts Council.

References

Arts Intelligence Ltd (2002) Artform and geographic catchment analysis for His Majesty's Theatre, The Music Hall and The Lemon Tree for the period 1 April 1998 to 31 March 2000, A report for the Scottish Arts Council.

CACI Information Services (1994) *ACORN User Guide*. CACI.

Drye, T. (1998) 'Making your ticketing database work smarter rather than harder', *ArtsBusiness*, 3 August, 7–8.

Fowles, G. (2000) 'ROAR – Understanding Young Consumers', Tearing Down Barriers: Arts Marketing Association Conference, Salford, July.

Hill, E. and Whitehead, B. (2001a) 'TGI/ACORN: a culpable scapegoat', *ArtsBusiness*, Issue 66, 15 January.

Hill, E. and Whitehead, B. (2001b) 'Spinning out of control', *ArtsBusiness*, Issue 73, 23 April.

Jermyn, H. (2001) *The Arts and Social Exclusion*. Arts Council of England.

Kent, R. (1993) *Marketing Research in Action*. Routledge.

Kirchberg, V. (2000) 'Mystery visitors in museums: an underused and underestimated tool for testing visitor services', *International Journal of Arts Management*, No. 1, Fall, 32–8.

Macgregor, L.A. (1991) 'The role of marketing in galleries'. In the report of the Gallery Marketing Symposium, commissioned by The Arts Council of Great Britain.

Marketing:Arts, The Technocentre, Coventry University Technology Park, Puma Way, Coventry CV1 2TW (tel: 02476 236235).

McCart, M. (1992) 'Research at the South Bank Centre'. *Journal of the Market Research Society*, Vol. 34, No. 4, 361–74.

MORI for the Arts Council of England (2000) *Public Attitudes to the Arts*. Arts Council of England.

Moriarty, G. (1997) *Taliruni's Travellers: An arts worker's view of evaluation*. The Social Impact of the Arts Working Paper 7, Comedia.

Moss, S. (2001) 'Should the National stage commercial productions?', *Guardian*, 28 March.

Tomlinson, R. (1993) *Boxing Clever*. Administration Research Training Services, commissioned by The Arts Council of Great Britain.

Verwey, P. (2000) Target Group Index 1998/1999 and 1999/2000 – Summary of Results for England, the English Regions, Scotland and Wales. Arts Council of England, September.

Walshe, P. (1992) Guidance notes on carrying out audience/visitor surveys. Millward Brown, prepared for The Arts Council of Great Britain.

Webb, J.R. (1993) *Understanding and Designing Marketing Research*. Academic Press.

Yates, P. (2001) 'Developing Audiences for the Visual Arts', Made in Heaven: Arts Marketing Association Conference, Birmingham, July.

4

Product

Product is the most fundamental and the most important element of the 'four Ps' of Product, Price, Promotion and Place which constitute the 'marketing mix'. It provides the basic building block of any marketing strategy. The product, or in the case of arts organizations, the service which is provided has the dominant role in determining the nature of the other marketing variables. In the 1980s it became fashionable to talk about artistic 'product' and, as we have seen, the arts industry is 'production led' in a way which differentiates it from commercial marketing practice. But what concerns the arts marketer is not so much what is produced by artists, as what is available to audiences as experience. This chapter will address the nature of the experience of art from a customer perspective, concentrating on those aspects of an organization's total offering which the marketing function can hope to optimize. It includes discussion of:

- the nature of products and services
- levels of product
- product decisions
- quality

Products and services

Marketing theory has been built largely on the experience of companies (mainly American ones) selling packaged goods in the 1950s and beyond. But there is a good deal of difference between the marketing perspective of organizations like concert halls or galleries, and that of the makers of soap powder or instant coffee. Arts organizations (along with organizations such as banks, doctors and hairdressers) are providing a service, not a physical product. Services have characteristics which such products lack. Four widely recognized ones are (Bateson and Hoffman, 1999):

- intangibility
- inseparability of production and consumption
- heterogeneity
- perishability

Intangibility

Unlike products, which can be handled and owned, services are intangible. They are experiences rather than objects. Potential consumers cannot inspect an artistic performance before purchase in the same way as they might, for example, test-drive a car. This means that promotion, communicating the benefits of what is on offer in a way which is accurate and relevant, has a crucial role in service marketing generally and in arts marketing in particular. Another marketing consequence of intangibility, as we shall see in Chapter 5, is that prices are generally more difficult to set and justify than they are in product marketing.

The perceived risk of an intangible purchase is much higher than that involved in buying a product (which can always be returned or modified after purchase). Arts promotion needs, therefore, to reassure the potential customer that he or she is making the right decision by providing as full and explicit a proposition as possible. Similarly, distribution patterns in the arts need to focus on being user-friendly and approachable. There is also a sense in which the problem of intangibility in arts marketing can be made into an opportunity. Retailing potential exists for crystallizing the experience of the arts around ancillary products. 'Ancillary' (from the Latin word meaning 'maidservant') denotes products which derive a value from their relationship to the main offering such as theatre programmes, posters, audio and video recordings, books and memorabilia. In the arts they can also be called 'semi-tangibles' because of the way they link the tangible nature of goods to the intangible values of services. Existing in this hybrid category means that their pricing needs careful consideration (see Chapter 5). Raymond (1999) reports profit margins being achieved by the more successful theatres in the UK on ancillary products, revealing potential earnings of 65 per cent on programmes (including advertising revenue), 25 per cent on show-related merchandise and 40 per cent on venue-related merchandise.

Inseparability of production and consumption

Whereas products are bought and used by consumers some time after manufacture, services are consumed and produced at one and the same time. This is clearly the case in the live performing arts. But even in a gallery or museum, the experience of the artworks or display objects is filtered through a controlled and time-restricted environment. The consumer leaves the gallery enriched, but by an experience rather than by a physical possession.

The customer needs to be addressed as participant rather than passive consumer. Certain modes of presentation make this more obvious than others, such as promenade productions, community arts, dance workshops, or small-scale touring drama in intimate venues. But even in an arena environment, such as a stadium rock concert, what distinguishes the experience of live performance for an attender is his or her active participation in the experience of being part of an audience. Ancillary service offerings, such as friends' organizations or regular attendance schemes, recognize a growing level of involvement in the organization's activities by its customers. Finally, inseparability of production and consumption means that direct forms of distribution tend to be the norm in the arts, although (as we shall see in Chapter 7) there are exceptions to this general principle.

Heterogeneity

No two performances are ever the same. Even art objects which do not involve performance are valued for the variety and depth of experience to which they can give rise in the beholder on different occasions – the archetypal work of art, the *Mona Lisa*, is famous for this quality. The quality and essence of an artistic experience can vary according to who is producing it, and even within the same production. To complicate matters further in the performing arts, there are typically a large number of people involved in the delivery of the experience. Not only the members of the performing company itself, but also each member of the front-of-house staff with whom the consumer comes into contact will contribute in some small but important way to the uniqueness of a theatrical experience. This makes like-with-like comparisons practically impossible (although such comparisons are, paradoxically, an important part of the experience for heavy consumers of frequently-performed works within a narrow repertoire, such as different interpretations of the symphonies of Beethoven or the plays of Shakespeare).

The uniqueness and singularity of the artistic experience is a major selling point in a wider environment where so many processes are being reduced to bland standardization. While we will be arguing in this chapter for a systematic approach to the standards of service surrounding the artistic experience, the individuality of arts experience is itself a core benefit. The service sector is a 'people' business. Just as people are different, so the variety underlying the arts needs to be a constant theme in marketing and promotional strategy.

Because of the importance of a shared understanding of the needs of the customer throughout the organization, arts marketing departments need to take the lead in fostering internal marketing (as discussed in Chapter 9). This involves the promotion of customer-first attitudes among everyone who deals directly, or even indirectly, with customers. It also implies the organization's willingness to adopt systems which empower customer-facing staff to take decisions and sort out problems in meeting customer requirements.

Perishability

Like the issue of intangibility, this is a fundamental source of difference between products (which can be stored) and services (which need immediate consumption). Unsold tickets for a performance on a particular date are lost forever as income opportunities, even though the organization will have borne the full cost of providing the service to which they might have gained admittance. Synchronizing supply and demand in a business where what is manufactured cannot be stored is a perennial dilemma for marketers in any service industry.

It presents itself particularly acutely to arts marketers where the size of the audience needs to achieve a critical mass if the experience is to carry credibility (as in the case of a formal theatrical performance), but (as in the case of blockbuster exhibitions) must not be allowed to exceed the available supply. Sometimes arts organizations, because of the pressure from funding authorities to maximize the use of venue facilities, are forced into a position where they may be tempted to do too much. 'Productivity' in these terms is misleading. A clear sense of the organization's mission and capacity is more important than accumulating performance statistics for their own sake. Expansion is not an end in itself.

Much service marketing effort is devoted to trying to cope with fluctuating demand. It underlies, for example, the kind of differential ticket pricing discussed in Chapter 5, where attendance on less popular nights of the week is encouraged by lower pricing than at weekends in most theatres. But it also affects product planning decisions. Many theatres, for example, vary their programmes with other sorts of activity or go dark (i.e. take a break from presenting work) during the summer months in recognition of the fact that this is a time of the year when attendance patterns are traditionally light. There are, of course, exceptions to this general rule. In certain locations popular with tourists the pattern is reversed, as is the case at the Theatre Royal York, or the Stephen Joseph Theatre in the Round in Scarborough. Yet even these theatres, both of whom enjoy summer trade swelled by visitor traffic, tailor their offerings to suit the seasonal audience. They offer production and performance staff patterns of employment which reflect adjustments between demand and capacity to achieve a closer match between the two over an extended period of time.

A model of service delivery

Bateson and Hoffman (1999) attempt to look at the interface between services and their production in a model known as the 'Servuction' model. This sees services as being produced from a mixture of 'visible' and 'invisible' sources: visibility here meaning what the customer can see, and the invisible sources being the organization's own internal systems and processes. In a theatre, the invisible source might include the backstage operation, the period of rehearsal leading to the play, or the box office staffing rota. These systems are concealed from the customer, and parts of them will probably be concealed from staff not immediately involved in them. They shape and support the visible sources like

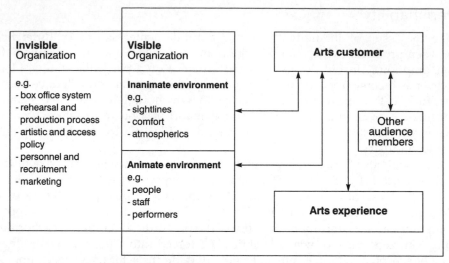

Figure 4.1 The Servuction system model as applied to a theatre performance (adapted from Bateson and Hoffman, 1999)

the unseen mass of an iceberg supporting its visible tip. The visible sources fall into two types. The first is the inanimate environment: the physical surroundings of the theatre, let us say (including aspects like the shape and spacing of the seats, or the sightlines within the auditorium). The other type of visible source, and possibly the more important from the point of view of marketing management, is the group of people who have contact with the customer and provide the service, whether it be the box office worker who confirms the booking, the actor on stage or the person selling coffee at the interval. As can be seen from the Figure 4.1, the model also includes other customers, accurately reflecting how other members of the audience contribute to the experience.

This elegant and inclusive model highlights a number of practical implications:

- *Customer involvement:* Because of the intimate involvement of the customer in the production of the service itself, any changes in how it is produced or mediated will necessitate a change in consumer behaviour. Thus, the introduction of subscription marketing for a concert series or a season of plays will require careful preparation of potential and existing customers so they can adapt to a new way of creating the service.
- *Lack of privacy:* A new production line in a factory can break down without the consumer knowing about it. But a new departure for an arts organization sinks or swims in the full glare of publicity. Mistakes happen at the point of production, and the arts organization has to have systems which can minimize the damage caused.
- *Learning the script:* Customers tend to approach the service experience with a set of expectations. This has been described by some researchers as a 'script'. For example, we all know more or less what is going to happen

when we visit the dentist and we behave accordingly. This internalized customer 'script' is related to externalized roles, where we expect certain types of performance from other people. Customers become uncomfortable and have less satisfactory service experiences if these roles are departed from. In the arts environment this places a great deal of responsibility on everyone involved in customer contact to be competent and comfortable in their roles.

- *The human factor:* Everyone and everything which comes into contact with the consumer is delivering the service. So internal marketing and developing staff is at a premium in the arts. The importance of the human factor explains the focus placed in the present book on managing people (see Chapter 9). People are the organization's most important product manifestation, so it pays the marketing manager to have a full appreciation of human resource issues. This is pointed out by Berry (1981) in connection with a case study on internal marketing at Disneyland, but what he says is true of any arts organization:

> Marketing's scope has traditionally been restricted to the exchange that takes place between customers and organizations. Yet marketing is just as applicable to the exchange that occurs between employees and organizations. Employees are simply internal customers rather than external customers.

- *The growing importance of marketing:* Servuction recognizes the importance of marketing in a competitive environment. Arts consumers arrive to participate in the process with increased expectations nourished by their experience in other aspects of the leisure industry. The marketing function needs to be able to interpret these changing expectations to the organization as a whole, providing its link to the customer.
- *Growth strategies:* Finally, the model suggests that arts organizations, like any other service providers, face particular difficulty in their strategies for growth. Although research in America has demonstrated the success of certain opera audience development programmes in raising the awareness and interest of certain socio-economic groups, it was found that the normal circumstances of its delivery alienated them (Carman and Langeard, 1980). It is difficult, with the emphasis on existing consumers that Servuction implies, to absorb new segments comfortably and permanently.

Levels of product

Kotler and Andreasen (1996) and Levitt (1969) have provided useful conceptual maps which separate the dimensions of product into distinct levels (Figure 4.2), and this type of analysis can easily be transposed to service provision.

Core benefit

At the centre of an organization's offering is the core benefit being purchased. People buying an item of confectionery like a KitKat are not really buying 'four

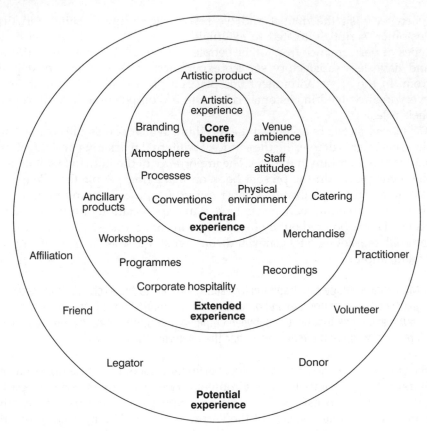

Figure 4.2 Four levels of product in the arts experience

crisp wafer fingers covered in milk chocolate'. As suggested by the advertising slogan 'Have a break', they are buying the pretext for a few moments' relaxation. Similarly, a visitor to an exhibition is less concerned with the precise medium in which the pictures or drawings exist, than with their aesthetic or emotional effect. When we define marketing as activity aimed at 'identifying and satisfying customer requirements' it is important to remember that the customer defines the requirement. The organization aims to satisfy it on the customer's terms. So an appreciation of the core benefit being purchased by the arts consumer in a given situation is essential to a sound marketing strategy. It gives clues to motivation which can then be reflected in promotional copy and imagery, as well as refinements to the presentation of the experience.

The nature of the artistic experience
It is the artistic experience itself that forms the core benefit sought by customers of arts organizations. Reflection on how the artistic experience works, and the kinds of needs it satisfies in its customers, can help identify what is unique about the arts marketing process and separate it from the related areas of leisure and hospitality marketing.

Arts events or objects are essentially acts of communication between artists and audiences, and concepts from communication theory can help clarify our understanding of the benefits which need to be articulated through promotional vehicles, as well as our thinking about product enhancement. They also focus thinking on the relevance of long-term, two-way relationships between artists and audiences, suggesting that the potential contradiction between 'marketing' and 'art' is more apparent than real:

> A customer orientation towards marketing holds that success will come to that organization that best determines the perceptions, needs, and wants of target markets and satisfies them through the design, communication, pricing and delivery of appropriate and competitively viable offerings. (Kotler and Andreasen, 1996)

Different communication theorists emphasize different aspects of the process. Theodore Newcomb (1961), for example, sees communicative acts as bringing people closer together by sharing their understanding of the external world. His approach differs from more linear models because it involves adjustment and consensus on both sides about the subject of the communication. Although his original research emphasized the role of communication in reducing dissonance in personal relationships, his model can be equally applied to the experience of the live performing arts (Figure 4.3).

In the case of this application of the model to a performance (X), it is the dialogue created between the performers (A) and the audience (B) that will each time result in a different X. There is a clear link with the kind of process described in the Servuction model (see p. 117), but Newcomb's model emphasizes the dynamic nature of the relationship between each audience member and the performance. Both parties have an input to make; both are changed by the experience. This could suggest a promotional emphasis on sharing the adventure of art, and a possible 'product' response might be to

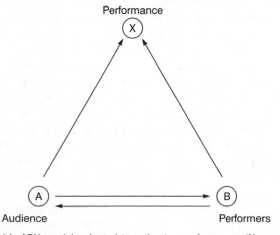

Figure 4.3 Newcomb's ABX model, adapted to a theatre performance (Newcomb, 1961)

increase the frequency of ancillary events which allow the audience to have a voice (such as discussions or question sessions).

Getting Frisky at Walsall

The New Art Gallery Walsall 'aims to increase and broaden audiences for the visual arts (historic, modern and contemporary) in sophisticated ways and to increase opportunities not just for looking at art but also for direct engagement and active participation' (http://www.artatwalsall.org.uk/art/index.html).

Children are a vital part of this vision, although until recently they have been a relatively neglected audience amongst museums and art galleries. The New Art Gallery seeks to redress the balance with a permanent Childrens Discovery Gallery on its ground floor – the first purpose-designed facility to do so in the UK. Here, younger visitors have the opportunity to interact with a number of modern and contemporary artworks, by leading contemporary figures including Damien Hirst and Yinka Shonibare. The exhibition avoids patronising its visitors by presenting high quality art in a genuinely engaging and accessible way – making full use of multimedia technology to help the work speak for itself, and mounting a sustained programme of school and family workshops to extend the process of discovery.

For the payment of a small deposit, young visitors can pick up a 'Frisky Doggy Bag' from reception. This is a backpack containing games and activities to help children explore the rest of the Art Gallery's permanent collection. Lest older visitors feel neglected, the Gallery also runs regular guided visits by a team of Visitor Assistants which provide insights into the works displayed, and the social and historical context behind them.

Source: http://www.artatwalsall.org.uk/art/index.html, accessed 18 January 2003.
Reproduced by kind permission of The New Art Gallery Walsall.

Another influential model of communication, the 'Process' model developed by Shannon and Weaver (1949), was developed in connection with diagnosing problems in telephone systems (Figure 4.4). It sees communication as travelling from the source to the destination, being encoded and decoded on the way. In spite of its mechanical origins, it has been embraced by marketing theorists as a way of separating communication into manageable steps. Many marketing authors use it to explain the basics of promotion, and though in itself the model is not as relevant to the experience of the arts as Newcomb's, it does contain two very useful ideas which are relevant to the arts: noise and redundancy.

'Redundancy' has a specialized meaning when observed in acts of communication. When a message is complex or new there will be a considerable amount of repetition, duplication or unnecessary material, i.e. redundancy. This is because of the high level of rejection or confusion experienced by the receiver. The Shannon and Weaver model shows 'noise' as a disturbance in the channel of communication that distorts or masks the signal, interfering with the receiver's ability to pick up the intended meaning.

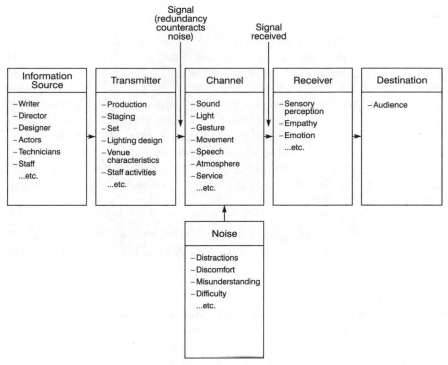

Figure 4.4 Shannon and Weaver's 'Process' model of communication, adapted to a performing arts context (adapted from Shannon and Weaver, 1949)

Redundancy compensates for noise by increasing the predictability of the signal for the receiver. 'Noise', in the context of the arts experience, might be all the internal and external barriers to enjoyment of a performance which a customer may have to encounter. They could include:

● preconceptions of the nature of arts activity
● the difficulty of the piece
● unfamiliarity with a new form or genre
● discomfort with the environment of the activity
● the specialist needs of the audience member him- or herself

The more effort put into strengthening the 'signal' by the performers in rehearsal and production values, and the more the signal is repeated to the audience through their regular attendance, the more clearly it will be received and a longer-term relationship developed. Helpful redundancy comes both from the repeated experience of arts attendance for the audience, and also from programming choice which uses material which in itself has predictable elements. Popular art forms are often criticized precisely for their predictability: stock gags, lots of choruses, stereotypical characters, catchphrases and foreseeable outcomes. But, controversially, communication theory suggests that such work has a role to play in building new audiences more effectively than more challenging, issue-based work.

Posh perceptions

In their research into perceptions of the arts held by African, Caribbean, South Asian and Chinese people, Helen Jermyn and Philly Desai found a number of serious communications barriers: '. . . the dominant images people had of the arts were opera, ballet, Shakespearean theatre, classical music and art in galleries (particularly abstract modern art). Many found this image off-putting and elitist, and assumed that such events were mainly for "posh" people, those over 35, and White people. For some, particularly older people and women, arts relating to their Caribbean, African, Asian or Chinese heritage were also uppermost in their thoughts when asked to define the arts. However, while such arts were central to their definition of the arts, they did not always feel that the dominant definition in society included these activities.'

Source: Jermyn and Desai, 2000. Reproduced with kind permission.

Needs and wants

Communication theory can give us some clues as to what is going on between audience and performers or artists in arts transactions. But our appreciation of the benefits which arts marketing exists to promote can be further enhanced by looking at the basic concepts of needs and wants.

Needs are basic human drives that can be allayed for a while, but never go away completely. Hunger, for example, can be satisfied by an evening meal. But the next morning breakfast is still a welcome sight. Wants are the individual expressions of needs, and are shaped by personal tastes and socio-cultural circumstances. Thus, 'I am hungry' is a need, but 'I want a bowl of cornflakes' is a want. Marketing is often accused of creating needs and wants. But what it really does is to recognize needs and find ways of fulfilling them which consumers find appropriate and attractive. Thus a new brand of breakfast cereal is not creating a 'need', but will hope to establish itself as a possible 'want', among other alternatives, to satisfy the basic need for breakfast.

What kind of needs, then, does the experience of the arts satisfy? Chapter 2 has shown how different needs and wants may be satisfied by the same experience in different market segments. This is known as segmenting by 'benefits sought'. But these needs are clearly not as uncomplicated as hunger or thirst. The American researcher Abraham Maslow came up with a way of analysing needs in 1954 which still has enormous influence on the way marketers think about consumer behaviour: the 'Hierarchy of Needs' (Figure 4.5).

The base of the pyramid represents the needs that human beings must satisfy to maintain themselves: what Maslow called 'homeostatic' needs (from the Greek word for staying in the same place). Without fulfilling hunger, thirst and warmth needs, the physical condition of the individual would swiftly deteriorate. The next level features safety needs. Once the immediate business of keeping alive has been sorted out, the issue of

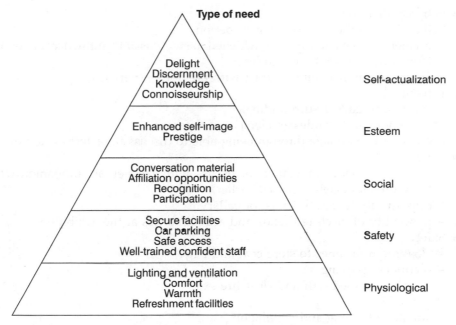

Figure 4.5 Maslow's Hierarchy of Needs, adapted for the arts experience

security from a predatory environment rears its head. As soon as you have more than the basic essentials of life, this suggests, you need to protect them. Social needs then rise to the fore, perhaps to compensate for the alienation which the need for safety implies. Humans need a sense of belonging, and involvement. They also have a competitive streak, and their social needs develop into the next layer of 'esteem needs'. This is the difference, perhaps, between being loved and being seen to be loved. The final level represents 'self-actualization needs'. This level incorporates the ideas of education and self-development. It suggests a need for transformation and transcendence, the need to realize your full potential.

Maslow's ideas offer a way of approaching the question of what kind of needs arts experience satisfies. It is tempting to see them as exclusively, or predominantly, at the 'self-actualization' level. The fact that the arts are 'educational' allows many arts organizations to be registered as charities. Certainly ideas of education and self-improvement are strong motivators for some audience members. But of course, the arts experience hinges on delighting the audience or the beholder rather than educating or improving them. Where does this sense of enjoyment fit into Maslow's hierarchy? Depending on the art form, it might exist across self-actualization, esteem and social needs. Arguably one might find elements of it on the lower levels too. Re-examining the hierarchy of needs in the context of the spread of benefits available to a visitor to an exhibition, suggests that the arts offer satisfactions at all levels rather than just the obvious one of self-actualization:

- Self-actualization:
  - increased knowledge of artist or period
  - greater enjoyment through widened taste (possible influence on own technique if a painter or student)
  - ability to compare and contrast with previous experience
- Esteem:
  - prestige of gallery surroundings
  - customer care includes an element of deference
  - enhanced self-image through being able to discuss the latest exhibition
- Social:
  - pictures provide something to discuss with partner or companion (cf. Newcomb's model discussed earlier)
  - opportunity to join 'Friends' of gallery
  - possibility of meeting friends and acquaintances at the exhibition
- Safety:
  - cloakroom facilities to store coat and bag
  - secure car parking
  - properly trained staff and clear fire exits
- Physiological:
  - adequate lighting and ventilation
  - warmth
  - clean refreshment facilities

The further down the hierarchy we go, the more remote from the actual experience of the art objects themselves the benefits appear to be. But they are all related to the experience of seeing the art objects in a given environment at a particular time, so it is impossible effectively to separate one aspect from any other, although we can recognize that there are priorities at work. For example, the customer might be prepared to put up with inadequate refreshment facilities because of easy parking.

We can conclude that the arts experience offers satisfaction to a complex of needs rather than only one. While this complicates the task of interpreting and communicating the benefits to customers through promotional activity, it means that there is a virtually inexhaustible number of angles from which they can be approached. It also means that there is an inexhaustible number of ways in which managing the product effectively can introduce small but important improvements to satisfy needs more effectively.

The central experience

The tangible aspects of the arts experience surround the core benefit, and mediate it to the customer in an acceptable and appropriate way. This level embraces not only the artistic element itself, but also every aspect of its delivery: venue ambience, staff attitudes, ease of access, and so on. Branding, which we discuss later in the chapter, is also very important at this level for the arts. It is one of the ways in which organizations can respond to the high perceived risk of making an intangible purchase by reassuring their customers with an aura of quality.

As will be clear from the comments about the core benefit above, the features of the central experience are only important insofar as they are the means to the desired end of the benefit being purchased. One of the pitfalls into which organizations of any kind can fall is to confuse features with benefits. In a sense service providers are at an advantage here. Because their offerings have fewer tangible features than those of product marketers, they are more focused on the delivery of the benefits themselves.

Seeing the offering in terms of its benefits rather than its features is the key to putting the consumer at the centre of the marketing process. Cowell (1984) and Lovelock *et al.* (1999) stress the importance of retaining and developing customers in service marketing, and Lovelock *et al.* particularly stress the importance of customer data in this process. New technology is allowing more and more arts organizations to build the kind of knowledge of their customers which enables this 'customer obsession' to be put into practice (see Chapter 3). It recognizes the participative nature of service consumption and focuses our attention on the importance of the customer's point of view.

Location

The artistic 'product' is delivered within an environment the physical characteristics of which have an important effect on the quality of the experience for the consumer. Audience surveys frequently reveal that many attenders at any performance are either first-time or very infrequent theatre-goers. Their unfamiliarity with the conventions associated with theatres and galleries needs to be addressed through high standards of customer care and a welcoming environment featuring elements like clear signage.

There is evidence to suggest that taking theatre and music out of traditional settings can actually reach audiences who would normally feel uncomfortable in the formal surroundings of an established venue. Hesitant theatregoers can be encouraged if the product is taken to them, either in a small venue in their immediate locality, or in a venue which has more comfortable associations like a social club, village hall or public house, or even into the open air. For example, the Promenade productions by the Dukes Theatre in Lancaster's Williamson Park are a regular feature of the theatrical calendar. The productions make use of the remarkable Ashton Memorial as backdrop, but the real star of the show is the park itself, as the audience follow the cast from location to location. Opera in the open air is another way of representing what might be dismissed as an elitist or unsuitably heavy arts experience in a form which will access a larger audience. Of course, an outdoor environment can be difficult to control in many respects, but the popularity of promenade and alfresco productions suggests that this form of delivery offers benefits which outweigh the risks.

Case 4.1 On site

IOU Theatre was formed in 1976 with the idea of combining art forms to make theatre in a variety of contexts. Its work encompasses main stage theatres, studio theatres, small outdoor touring shows, installations, film, video and digital work. The company has been creating site-specific work throughout its history, based on the belief that site-specific shows can produce the most exciting and memorable theatre which offers ready-made advantages over conventional theatre venues, in particular the unique atmosphere generated when a real location is enhanced with the artifice of theatre. The result is stimulating for the artists and thrilling to audiences. Artistic Director David Wheeler describes the show *Cure*, through which the company looked at the nature of illness:

'The development of the show is typical of our approach – devising work through a collaboration between artists working in different art forms. The aim is to extract the central mystery of a theme, fusing fantastic and dream imagery with objects from everyday experiences. All the elements that make up the performance are created by the company: music, songs, text, costumes and mechanical props are brought together to perform shows which have a dreamlike quality, dark and humorous.

'This approach is particularly suited to working in unusual spaces. It is liberating to follow an interesting route to making a show without having to illustrate a particular point or part of a narrative. A real environment with surprising features is a welcome addition to the process. Presented within an office and factory complex, *Cure* used the roofs, buildings and dark underground vaults beneath them. Leading the audience between spaces above and below ground, the underlying "narrative" of the show was expressed through a journey, the audience following a character descending into the trauma of a major illness. Keeping the theme as open as possible for as long as possible in the devising process allowed the artists to respond to the space, and in this way the location helped to lead the development of the show.'

Source: Wheeler, 2002. Reproduced with kind permission.

Atmospherics and design

The physical environment for the building-based arts organization is a highly influential component of the attender's experience, with 'atmosphere' being cited by audiences as one of the most important factors affecting attendance decisions (Figure 4.6). A venue, because of its physical attributes, can build a reputation among its users for quality, comfort and reliability. This is reflected both in the fabric of the building itself and the kinds of systems established by front-of-house staff. The danger is, as is often the case in marketing issues, that the organization misses opportunities to improve matters by being too familiar with the status quo to notice or question it.

A consciousness of design can be of great advantage to organizations wishing to increase earnings from trading. When York City Art Gallery decided to raise the amount of money it earned from trading as an alternative to imposing entrance charges, it remodelled its foyer to accommodate a large area dedicated to fine-art related merchandise – books, guides, postcards and greetings cards, posters and calendars, as well as the standard tourist paraphernalia of branded stationery. Many of these items had been available, in a rather understated way, from the attendants' desk at the back of the foyer before the remodelling. The new design guided visitor traffic through the shop as the obvious way of gaining access to the ground floor galleries. The result was a pleasantly appropriate retail space where visitors could browse in an

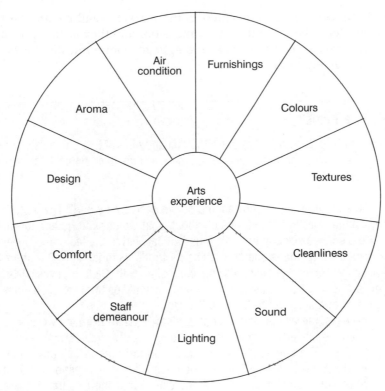

Figure 4.6 The physical environment

unpressured environment, but through which they were guided gently but firmly by the signage and layout of the gallery.

Branding

A successful brand is one that has created, in the minds of the customer, the perception that there is no other product on the market quite like it (Ries and Ries, 1999). It is a 'holistic combination of product and added values' (Randall, 1999) which has several dimensions, and exists at a far deeper level than simply the brand identity – the name, logo and imagery which are the normal outward manifestations of brand. Randall sees the central essence of a brand as being created through four interlocking dimensions relating to an organization and its products and services:

- *functions:* what it does and what it is for
- *personality:* how people feel about it
- *differences:* what makes it better and different
- *source:* what lies behind it, in terms of aims and values

The brand image that forms in the minds of customers will be created from all these, and an organization wishing to change its image cannot hope to do so without a fundamental re-examination of all four dimensions. Brand identity –

the brand message being transmitted to the market – will be strongest when there is consistency between the four dimensions and they are supporting each other. When this is not the case, attempts to communicate the brand to customers are likely to fail.

What's in a name?

Alan Borg, former Director of London's Victoria and Albert Museum, neatly sums up the dilemmas facing organizations which believe that their name confuses their brand identity:

'Is our name an asset or a handicap and do we need a new one? The Victoria and Albert Museum does not tell you much about what we do, and quite a lot of first-time visitors come expecting to find a museum devoted to the life of the Queen and Prince Consort, or perhaps one devoted solely to the Victorian age. Our short form of V&A is even more opaque, risking confusion with C&A or even DNA. The question is whether this matters and whether we should be thinking of changing our name as part of changing the Museum's image.

'In some ways, the lack of any descriptive element, apart from the word Museum, can be seen as an advantage. Many of the world's greatest museums lack descriptive titles. The Louvre, the Hermitage and the Prado are all uncommunicative, while the British Museum does not imply that its collections are mostly archaeological and non-British. Perhaps the clue lies in the fact that the greatest museum in New York is known world-wide as The Met, confirming that descriptive name tag is positively not required if you are well enough known for what you do.

'There is no doubt that the V&A is in the same category, but although our name is widely and generally recognized, we need to convey more clearly what it is we do. The collections are so broad that this is difficult. A cynic might suggest that, in the age of Cool Britannia, we should be The People's Museum, but this says even less than our present title. Is there a neat, snappy name that actually encapsulates all the things we do? . . .

'If there is one word which covers all our activities, it ought to be excellence – in design and in the collections, in their display, in our scholarship and in the service we offer to visitors. As we strive to make the Museum still better, perhaps we need not worry about our name. It's what we do that matters.'

Source: Borg, 1998.

Successful brands combine each dimension into a package which offers customers benefits (both emotional and practical) which they cannot find elsewhere. Branding, therefore, offers organizations the key to differentiating their offerings from alternatives in the market. If done in a relevant and compelling way, this can be a source of long-term advantage as it is very difficult for competitors to copy. For arts organizations this means that the basis of their branding needs to be the thing that makes them uniquely attractive. Theatres need to emphasize the immediacy and spectacle of live entertainment, music venues can point to the direct connection to emotion that their art form offers, galleries and museums need to stress the opportunity for contemplation and reflection. Within these broad categories, each organization will have a local identity, a specialization, or some other kind of personality which can offer a platform for brand development.

Brand management is something that arts organizations tend to be pretty good at, according to Hugh Davidson (2002). His research comparing best practice in companies and non-profit organizations found that non-profits outperform companies in the management of their brands. He attributes this to the fact that the 'source' element of the brand, which includes the commitment and values of the organization's staff, are inevitably stronger in the non-profit sector.

Case 4.2 Reinforcing the brand

Pittsburgh Symphony Orchestra has over 100 years of history, and boasts a formidable line-up of conductors and music directors. It presents a rich array of concerts, educational programmes and summer events, but despite winning accolades in Europe and making a significant impact with its community projects both at home and abroad, the orchestra believed it had lost its profile amongst its home audience, and needed to develop public awareness and greater connection with its local community. In particular, it felt that its efforts were being lost in the flurry of growth and activity of the wider Pittsburgh Cultural District. To address the problem the orchestra appointed a communication, planning and design consultancy to get to the root of the issues, and subsequently launched a three-phase programme to identify new audiences, target market needs and develop more effective communication tools to reach their potential audiences.

Extensive research was undertaken to pin down audience perceptions and needs, which presented the orchestra with some very revealing information both about itself and the nature of the audience. In particular, it revealed that the community was unaware of the high calibre of the Pittsburgh Symphony Orchestra and the range of different programme styles that the orchestra engaged in. The orchestra was simply not getting the credit for the excellent work it was doing. A new brand image was required to convey the true nature of the organization.

A design audit found that printed materials showed no commonality of colour, typeface or design. A bright red was chosen as the corporate colour, to reflect the 'emotion and passion' of the music, but also to complement the interior of the 2661-seat Heinz Hall, the orchestra's Pittsburgh home, which had a gold and red carpeting, seats and curtains. Brand names and logos were streamlined, with over 30 symphony sub-brands consolidated into seven visible marketing brands, which were easier for the public to assimilate as well as easier to administer. The words 'Pittsburgh Symphony' were attached to all of the orchestra's products, such as 'Pittsburgh Symphony Pops', 'Pittsburgh Symphony Bridges' (the education and community outreach programme) and 'Pittsburgh Symphony Curtain Call' (the retailing arm).

At the end of the project, John Sotirakis, the consultant responsible for the re-branding, said of the orchestra 'Their new branding programme allows them to present a new face to Pittsburgh; it allows them to present their image as a vital, growing force in the arts community. For Pittsburgh Symphony, branding meant communicating the emotional benefit of experiencing its brand: "We perform concerts. We provide escape." '

Source: Stone, 2001.

Staff attitudes

Staff attitudes and the systems in place for managing the flow of customers through an arts event are fundamental to the customer's experience of the artistic product. Many large gallery complexes and theatres now number a customer services manager among their key staff. This is not lip-service to a trendy new development in management thinking, but a logical recognition of the importance and diversity of audience needs. As venues are driven by artistic or financial imperatives to make fuller use of their facilities for non-performance activities (day-time events, business and conference hire etc.) the concept of customer service is becoming ever more important. It cannot just be left to the personnel in immediate contact with the customer. A genuinely marketing-oriented organization will imbue all its members with a sense of their contribution to the end-user's experience. The marketing function needs to take the initiative in this process. Tomlinson (1990) observed:

> How often are box office, front-of-house, reception, attendants and other staff seen as separate from the marketing function when in practice they are at the centre of customer relations and customer contact? Spending every working day talking to customers, they probably acquire more marketing intelligence than anyone else – and they may understand what brings customers in best of all!

There is further discussion of customer care in the process of service delivery later in this chapter.

The extended experience

Product aspects at this level tend to merge into other areas of the marketing mix. A credit facility relates to pricing; after-sales service can be considered as promotional activity; and CD recordings can be seen as an aspect of distribution. But they are all directly related to the nature of the product itself, and by enhancing these and other aspects of the customer experience, the organization can extend its offering to specific sectors of the market.

Offering an extended level of experience has a special role in arts marketing. As we have seen, the intangible can be rendered less so by surrounding it with various ancillary products. At most opera houses customers can buy not only tickets to the opera, but also diaries, calendars, recordings and other operatic paraphernalia to make their transient experience of art more memorable. The extended level of experience can also play a part in audience development. Schools workshops are a form of extended experience for a production of a Shakespeare play. Video cassettes are a way of extending the offering of a dance company. What is appropriate or possible will vary from organization to organization, but this aspect of product development is still relatively underexploited in Britain as compared to America.

Programmes and catalogues

Programmes are a service adjunct which should complement the experience of the arts. Apart from their value as souvenirs (research suggests that they are kept well after the performance), they can enrich the experience itself. Normally programmes are produced on a contractual arrangement with publishing companies who sell advertising in them and offer them to the venue at a reduced rate per copy. Predicting likely audience numbers for order quantities thus becomes a very fine art as the relationship between the number of programmes bought and the number sold means profit or loss. Alternatively, organizations can produce their own programmes direct, contracting out advertising sales, or do the whole job themselves (as do amateur companies, to whom income from this part of the operation is crucial).

As we have seen, arts marketing should aim at enriching customers' ability to be better co-operators in the production of the arts experience and in this sense the performing arts can take some inspiration from the visual arts where the concept of a catalogue to accompany and interpret an exhibition is a well-established service adjunct. But in spite of the audience enrichment opportunity presented by programmes, their quality remains a weakness of many arts organizations. Instead of putting the work in context, like an exhibition catalogue, theatre programmes often major on lengthy lists of names of those involved in the production and venue. They seem designed for internal rather than external consumption.

Time and resources may be the reasons for this deficiency. But, given our earlier observations about the nature of the needs which the arts experience addresses, giving programmes a customer focus should be a high priority. What is needed is an acceptable quality level which satisfies customer needs without sacrificing resources from other organizational objectives. Perhaps because of their greater perceived need to interpret their art form, opera companies have led the way in producing programmes which look as if they are really meant for customers.

Catering

Catering offers significant income potential with successful venues achieving profit margins of 55 per cent or so, and 65 per cent on bars (Raymond, 1999), but it is a risky operation. Venues are faced with the decision of whether to run it themselves or to make an agreement with an external contractor who will bring expertise and systems to the opportunity and offer the venue a commission and/or fee for so doing. Whichever route is taken to catering, the image attributes will impact directly on the venue.

Because of this, even venues who contract out their catering spend a good deal of time giving active consideration to bringing operations in house. However, the folk wisdom of performing arts management is replete with anecdotes about how venues have almost been pulled under by disastrous forays into catering. Even when sales are high and customers are apparently happy, unless costs are professionally controlled the effects on turnover can be catastrophic.

Raymond (1999) presents a checklist of arguments for and against in-house catering for theatres which can be extended to any other sort of building-based organization. There is no doubt that in-house operations give the organization more control over the style and quality of what is on offer, and can (if they go well) offer far more profit than what is available (at less risk) from a contractor. The rhythms of a theatre or gallery are peculiar – with patterns of use by patrons which are different from those of other kinds of public buildings. Catering contractors – particularly large firms which operate across a number of sites – may find it difficult to understand and adjust to the specialized conditions of an arts environment. They may be tempted to impose ways of working which, while successful elsewhere, cannot cope with the sudden and short peaks of demand which theatre or concert hall audiences present. Finally, space and staff in many galleries or performing arts venues are a scarce resource. Running catering directly may mean that shared space can be used more flexibly between catering and other operating departments, and that staff can be switched between catering and other types of deployment at different times according to demand.

On the other hand, many of the advantages of a successful catering operation, without the administrative headaches and the financial risk, are available from an arrangement with a contractor. A contractor is more likely to be experienced at controlling costs, and may well have access to discounts and buying arrangements which an individual venue would be denied. Although there are time overheads involved in managing the deal and monitoring performance, contracting out the catering will allow the organization to concentrate on its core activity of arts provision. For some venues there is no choice but to contract out. Theatres, concert halls and galleries run by UK local authorities are obliged to do so, for example. Perhaps the most compelling argument for contracting out is that for minimum risk it offers a modest but reasonably secure source of income (usually based on a flat fee plus a percentage of either profit or turnover).

Even if regular catering, however managed, is not an option because of lack of facilities for food preparation, it can still be added to the overall product on specific occasions. Function catering involves buying in services and ready-prepared food on an ad hoc basis. Such an arrangement can enable a venue to offer a sponsor a full range of entertainment for a particular event, or even offer individual customers and groups the option of a meal before or after a performance if pre-booked. One advantage of this is that there is minimal waste and risk – the quantities are known in advance and profit margins can be established with confidence. A final option for buildings with insufficient space for comfortable dining is to broker deals with premises nearby in order to use their facilities.

Plate night line up

The Class Act Dinner Theatre of Whitby, Ontario, offers patrons the opportunity to dine and enjoy the latest comedies at the same time. Its owners, Rockford and Claudie Varcoe, occasionally appear in the shows, but run their catering service full time. It is available either on their own site, or at the workplaces or homes of customers. Their establishment consists of two banqueting halls, the larger boasting a series of striking murals featuring scenes from Shakespeare. At one end is a flexible stage which for the last five years has presented a series of comedies from authors such as Alan Ayckbourn, Willy Russell and Neil Simon, while diners tucked into their meals on Thursdays to Saturdays, with a Sunday brunch matinée.

Source: http://www.class-act.ca, 15 August 2002.

Merchandise

Like catering, merchandise can offer a useful source of income as well as enhancing the customer experience. The financial risk of the operation has to be considered. Items related to a particular exhibition or production have a shorter life than venue-related branded items. Long-running shows with high predicted seat occupancy (such as pantomimes) are an excellent merchandising opportunity, however. A high proportion of audience members will not be paying full price (children, family ticket holders, parties etc.), yet merchandise allows an organization to recoup at least some of this. Badges, pens, related books, toys and videos are examples of successful Christmas show merchandise, but always read the small print for details of minimum order quantities, lead times and arrangements for re-ordering.

Venue-specific merchandise (T-shirts, china, tote-bags etc.) can provide income if there are retailing facilities in the longer term. But such merchandise is also a useful adjunct to sponsorship deals. If a sponsor is negotiating hospitality as part of the package of benefits available from a venue, it is a good idea to suggest that a gift such as a bag or sweatshirt to each guest can make the evening even more memorable at a very small extra cost. For the right kind of quantities it may be worth conceding a discount on the total price. The quality of the merchandise itself is, of course, paramount. If a sweatshirt is to carry your logo it will be acting as an organizational ambassador. It is no use if it fades or shrinks. Careful selection and testing of items is very important, as is finding out as much as possible about suppliers (see Chapter 9 on negotiation).

Services to business

Sponsorship (dealt with more fully in Chapter 5) is only one way in which business and the arts can exchange benefits. Building-based organizations can offer room hire and conference facilities, although competition in this area tends to be fierce. The kind of standards against which your facilities will be judged will be those of commercial meetings venues such as hotels and conference centres. Nevertheless there may be a segment of the local business market who would respond well to a combination of location and price outweighing four-star comfort. Staging a product launch or a sales conference in a theatre, gallery or historic building, can make a dramatic impact on the memories of the people attending. Membership of local trade bodies such as tourism associations or chambers of commerce can provide avenues to likely customers.

Skills from within an organization can also be offered as services to business. Drama-based training is a technique that can be facilitated by arts venues, and even skills like juggling have been successfully offered to businesspeople to reduce executive stress. The current focus on the value of the creative economy has led many training and development managers to take a fresh look at arts organizations and what they have to offer.

Role play

Business leadership, like other situations in life, often requires a manager to play several roles, and this requires peak performance in areas such as presentation and communication. Leadership situations created by Shakespeare have been used to explore the comparable challenges facing managers today, and senior professionals from companies including Barclaycard, Teletext and the Design Council have attended management development programmes at Shakespeare's Globe in London based around plays such as *Henry V, Julius Caesar* and *The Merchant of Venice*. The programmes combine technical aspects of theatre training, such as making inspiring speeches, with sessions exploring the links between dramatic and managerial performance in order to improve effectiveness. Managers report that the combination of management development with Shakespearean drama produces 'a uniquely rich learning experience – one that is stretching, stimulating and enjoyable, and which inspires creativity and imagination in leading others'.

Source: Clewes, 1999.

Tailor-made entertainment at corporate hospitality events is another possibility, as is a community arts group offering another company banner-making skills. The precise opportunities and resources to match them will vary from organization to organization, but it is worth bearing in mind that services to business can extend far beyond trying to get them to part with money in exchange for publicity benefits. Such relationships can then be built on and developed over time to incorporate other forms of exchange.

The potential experience

This concept results from the way products and services need to change to keep pace with developing needs. Arts organizations need to be focused on the changing external environment in order to keep their provision relevant to new audiences and to refresh it for their existing ones. For an individual arts customer, the potential experience covers a number of forms of deeper involvement: affiliation or membership, becoming a donor or volunteer, or even becoming a more active participant by taking up a particular art form as a practitioner.

Marketing success depends on an organization's ability to add value to its offering. Using a multi-level approach to analysing your product or service allows you to spot opportunities which might otherwise go unconsidered. Like any good model it encourages the marketing strategist to think beyond the immediate situation and anticipate new developments in demand and provision.

Friends

Friends are groups of enthusiasts who actively support their host organization by practical and/or financial means. Often the host organization will assist in starting them up – recognizing the considerable benefits they offer, or prompted by a crisis such as potential closure. From an arts organization's point of view, the prime motivator for setting up a Friends scheme is usually to generate income for the organization, though cultivating long-term loyalty among audiences is also a key driver (Horan, 2001). Friends groups are usually autonomous, however, and power rests with the members. This can lead to tensions between the supporters and the organization being supported. Edwards (2002) reported on Friends organizations for museums and galleries in the Yorkshire region, revealing an ageing (75 per cent retired) and two-thirds female membership. Only 1 per cent reported themselves as having an ethnic minority background. More than half of their practical contribution came in the form of stewarding and assisting the general public when visiting the gallery or museum. Surprisingly, time devoted to fund-raising accounted for only 7 per cent of self-reported practical help. While 88 per cent of respondents reported a cordial relationship with the host organization, at least 10 per cent of the Friends surveyed seemed less friendly. Two quotations from interviews reproduced in the report are telling: 'Friends groups can be helpful, but they can also be the tail wagging the dog ... you can end up with the Friends groups dictating the priorities of service', said one Museum Officer. But, at the same time another admitted: 'Without the Friends to support us we would have great difficulties.'

Clearly there are issues for marketing here – not least in trying to manage the expectations of potential members about what they can expect. Organizations developing Friends groups need to consider very carefully what their objectives are and what kind of benefits they are prepared to offer (and are capable of delivering) to members. Friends of the Royal Opera House, Covent Garden, for example, is one of the largest groups in the UK with nearly 20 000 members. With ticket prices ranging from £5 to £155, the Royal Opera House is adept at segmentation, and its approach to its Friends is no exception. A basic 'Friends' subscription costs £64, which makes it one of the most expensive in the UK. Friends pay as much as anyone else for their tickets – the main benefit in terms of preferential treatment is the opportunity to book tickets before the general public does, thus securing good seats in an auditorium which, while splendid in many respects, offers variable sightlines and levels of comfort. Other benefits include regular mailing with a newsletter and magazine, access to special events, study days and pre-performance talks. As well as the basic subscription, more generously-disposed patrons can increase their annual commitment through a series of Acts of Support – starting at £195 for Act 1 and reaching the grand finale of £1395 for Act 4. Acts of Support are rewarded by respective levels of benefits, ranging from special receptions to the opportunity to book in advance even of advance booking. At the other end of the scale, Friends aged 26 and below are treated to a limited number of discount vouchers, and pay only £25 a year subscription.

While not all arts organizations can muster the level of fanatical following of an international opera house, this approach holds a number of lessons which can be shared by marketers elsewhere. It represents very careful thought about what supporters value and how incentives can be appropriately structured in response.

Given the trend for Friends organizations to get involved in practical help, the whole area of volunteer management needs addressing in this context. Attitudes to volunteering vary among arts organizations. Some fear the danger of projecting an unprofessional image, others (such as festivals) could not survive without a substantial input of free labour from the local community. However, for many arts attenders, volunteering can represent a valued extension to their experience of the organization's work. Successful volunteer schemes should guarantee that both volunteer and organization reap the maximum benefit from the arrangement. This requires good management. Always be clear about what you want volunteers to do, providing written job descriptions, and treat them professionally: they are entitled to the same kind of training and development that your paid staff receive. It is also important to recruit volunteers regularly. The average 'life expectancy' of a volunteer in a charity shop is two years, and although arts organizations might have lower turnovers than this, it is important to allow volunteers to vary their roles by refreshing the pool regularly.

Case 4.3 Being friendly

The Theatre Royal, Newcastle, is a 1300 seat receiving venue in the heart of Newcastle, which presents a mixed programme ranging from classical drama to contemporary dance and large-scale musicals. Offering its audiences the opportunity to 'belong' is something that it sees as fundamental to its audience development strategy.

Its loyalty scheme has three levels. Non-attenders, new attenders and irregular attenders are encouraged by targeted direct mail; but regular attenders are encouraged to take advantage of a scheme known as 'Stage 2', which costs them £5 a year to join, and simply offers them a guaranteed copy of the full season brochure, mailed personally in advance of each season, and priority booking. Becoming a 'Friend' is just one step further and costs £25 a year. The benefits provided are significant. Friends also receive the season brochure and priority booking, but also qualify for 10 per cent discounts on tickets and food and drink. There is a no-quibble ticket exchange process for Friends, who are also entitled to free entry to theatre tours, to receive regular copies of Friends News, and to take part in events known as 'Face to Face' at which Peter Sarah, General Manager of the Theatre, is in conversation with members of the cast over an informal coffee on Saturday mornings. Stage 2 members are encourage to upgrade their membership to become 'Friends' through regular mailings and the promise of a refund of their £5 Stage 2 fee.

The schemes are both closely monitored. In the first nine months after a campaign to recruit new members was launched, Stage 2 membership grew from 1000 to 3500, Friends membership grew by 20 per cent, and there was a 10 per cent conversion rate from Stage 2 to Friends. A fund-raising campaign among the membership achieved the highest yield per contact for any receiving venue in the UK at that time.

Source: Raines, 2002.

Product decisions

Decisions about products and services are invariably complex ones in the arts. They are fundamentally related to the mission of the organization, will significantly influence the nature of the audiences the organization will attract, and will have major implications for the ability of the organization to generate revenues. So an understanding of the nature of product life cycles and the implications of product portfolios can be helpful.

Product life cycle

Like the consumers who use them, products and services have life cycles. In a sense this reflects what has been said earlier about the only relevance of the features of products or services being that they satisfy needs and wants. Because new ways of satisfying needs are constantly emerging, existing ways are superseded. What used to satisfy needs and wants perfectly well a decade ago is now no longer appropriate. These changes are often driven by developments in the external environment, particularly technology. The computer, for example, satisfies a need that used to be satisfied by the typewriter. But because of the superior facilities offered by computers, the new way of answering the need has superseded the old.

Product life cycles also exist in the arts. The advent of television, for example, meant that variety theatres faced closure in the 1950s. Where it exists today, variety entertainment is an acknowledged archaism. It is presented, for example, at the Leeds City Varieties Theatre amid nostalgic circumstances which often include Edwardian dress by the audience themselves.

New forms come to replace the old, however. Their emergence can be led as much by the socio-cultural imperatives of fashion as by the advance of technology. Alternative comedy, for example, has managed to make cult stars out of people who are basically theatrical performers although their following and ethos seems more like that of rock stars. This phenomenon, as has been suggested in Chapter 2, reflects emerging needs and wants from a generation of young people whose tastes have been educated by the electronic media and who find established forms of theatre too much like hard work.

But life cycles in the arts, as in other cultural industries such as fashion or broadcasting, can be short-lived. An Early Music boom provided considerable growth in recording and performing in the 1980s, for example, but the rate of expansion then slowed down considerably, forcing ensembles who were once seen as adventurous into much safer areas of repertoire because of pressures from record companies (Kemp, 1993).

Technology has not only stimulated new forms of artistic expression but introduced new ways of enriching customers' experience of traditional art forms. Music, traditionally an art form concentrating on sound, is broadening into the visual. To some extent this reflects the increasing trend for music to be available on video and DVD as well as CD. In the world of classical music it represents the absorption of product features from live popular music presentation.

The implications for arts marketers are as follows:

- Elements of product need to be constantly reviewed for their relevance to the audience.
- Hard decisions have to be made about dropping initiatives (such as a subscriptions scheme in terminal decline) which have been superseded by needs from new segments. Otherwise they will absorb time and resources uselessly which could be better applied elsewhere (as we shall see in the discussion of product portfolio below).
- The organization must maintain a focus on changes in the external environment (a key feature of marketing orientation).
- In a business that relies so much on its staff to represent the product, their skills and attitudes must be kept relevant to changing circumstances by a genuine commitment to training and development.

Product portfolio management

Few manufacturing organizations can afford to rely on only one product. In spite of the simplicity of such an approach, the risk of having all the organization's eggs in one basket would be too high. Arts organizations are in a similar position. They need to spread the risk involved in producing arts experiences for customers by planning not only a balanced programme of artistic product, but also by maximizing the income they can earn from other activities. For performing arts venues these are often divided into performance-related items like programmes and catering, and non-performance related like room lettings and costume hire. Some aspects of a venue's service portfolio can have a dual identity. Bars and catering are in one sense performance related, insofar as takings go up or down in relation to attendance. But they also play a role in non-performance activities like services to business.

The fact that products and services have life cycles, as we have observed in the previous section, means that at any one time some parts of your total portfolio will be more relevant than others. The need to manage a combination of offerings in a way that optimizes the benefits to the customer as well as the returns to the organization has resulted in the development of a number of product portfolio management models.

The first thing to say about such models is that, even for the packaged goods sector in which they were originally developed, they offer very approximate guides rather than prescriptive rules. With this proviso, however, they can be useful in analysing and planning how a mixture of offerings fits together, and so offer the arts marketer a useful tool. What makes them useful is not their accuracy but their flexibility and the insights they can stimulate.

The most famous example of a portfolio model is the Boston Consulting Group's matrix. The model is based on research into the way that packaged goods behaved across a number of companies in the expanding economy of post-war USA. The researchers found that not only do individual products have life cycles, but the markets in which they exist have life cycles too, expanding and contracting according to broad patterns of demand. They divided markets into those that were growing and those that were declining. Products, on the other hand, were categorized according to whether their share of the market in which they operated was high or low. This led to the picture shown in Figure 4.7.

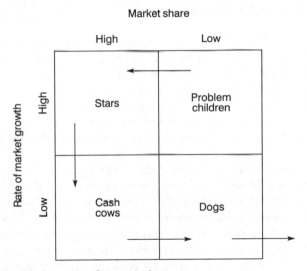

Figure 4.7 The Boston Consulting Group matrix

Relating this model back to the products and services offered by an individual organization led to the following categorizations:

- *High share products in high growth markets: Stars*
  These products are the mainstay of profitability. Their importance to the organization means that they need to be prioritized in terms of management attention and resources. An arts example might be an orchestral 'pop concert' by a big-name orchestra, reflecting the continuing growth in interest for compilation CDs of classical highlights in a programme of extracts from longer works.

- *High share products in low growth markets: Cash Cows*
  These products are the bedrock of many organizations' income, but are not capable of further growth because the market in which they operate is no longer expanding. A municipal choral society's rendition of Handel's *Messiah* will appeal to a predictable but essentially stable audience. Its familiarity as repertoire will, however, provide some kind of guarantee of its commercial success.
- *Low share products in high growth markets: Problem Children*
  These are the possible Stars of the future. Although they need a lot of resources and time, they offer great potential because they provide a foothold in an expanding area. Many arts organizations have identified services to business (conference facilities, promotional services, even training) as ways of accessing a growth area.
- *Low share products in low growth markets: Dogs*
  While still consuming management time and resources, these are products which fail to justify their long-term existence. The markets they are in are not performing as well as others open to the organization, and their share of the available business is low. A theatre group offering community touring productions to a rural area with a declining population might need to reconsider its role, for example.

The Boston Consulting Group saw business strategy as moving resources around an organization so that money and time were not wasted on poorly-performing products. Their advice to managers was to 'polish the Stars, milk the Cows, feed the Problem Children and shoot the Dogs'. In other words, resources should be concentrated on the opportunities most likely to yield returns. Products which are underperforming with no hope of long-term recovery should be jettisoned before they drag the rest of the business under by soaking up its time and money.

Arts organizations need to manage the effective use of time and resources towards their goals through examining their portfolio of offerings. This might involve hard decisions about dropping some aspects of activity in order to be able to concentrate more effectively on others. Especially in a 'people business' such as the arts, these decisions are difficult to implement. The complicated discounting arrangements at some repertory theatres are a case in point. For example, a Friends organization, with its package of discounts and benefits, is often to be found in uneasy co-existence with a more recently introduced subscription scheme, because of the personality and power factors involved.

Case 4.4 Turmoil at the ballet

Canada's oldest dance company, the Royal Winnipeg Ballet (RWB), faced a series of high-profile internal disputes between management and board when its Artistic Director, André Lewis, started to adopt what he described as a 'market-driven' approach to programming. When Lewis was appointed in 1995, RWB had accumulated a financial deficit of C$300 000, and a strategy of cutting expenses was coupled with the introduction of an artistic policy which aimed to boost box office revenues by presenting popular works aimed at 'reconnecting us with our audience'.

RWB had always been known for its populist image, but has also developed a reputation for ingenuity in programming works that have both audience appeal and choreographic integrity. But complaints started to be made that Lewis had pushed the balance too far in the populist direction and allowed overall dancing standards to slip. By the start of the 2000–2001 season the deficit had been eliminated, but the company had suffered badly from highly critical media reviews of its productions of *Beauty and the Beast* and *Butterfly* by choreographer David Nixon. The national daily, the *Globe and Mail*, stated that *Butterfly* '. . . simply isn't of the calibre that audiences expect from RWB'. A number of dancers were also expressing their discontent about the lack of good company teachers and challenging new choreography, and two leading dancers subsequently departed. Lewis defended his policies by saying that he had merely followed the board's instructions. He maintains that he was told very clearly that he could not lose money, and stated that with more money he might have programmed differently.

The whole RWB situation soon came under the scrutiny of the Canadian press. Morley Walker of the *Winnipeg Free Press* wrote that 'Administrative perfection combined with an impossible balancing act of pure art with populist entertainment at bargain-basement prices is just too much to ask', and George Jonas warned in Canada's *National Post* that 'taking the low-road in terms of programming does not always pay . . . you also have to be good'. He remarked that the supposedly high arts are mistaken if they imagine they can appeal to a popular audience without consequences.

Source: Crabb, 2001.

One of the advantages of portfolio models is that they allow simple visual communication of the relationship between a number of complex variables. A modified version of the Boston matrix can be used to model the kind of thinking behind planning a theatre's annual artistic programme (Figure 4.8).

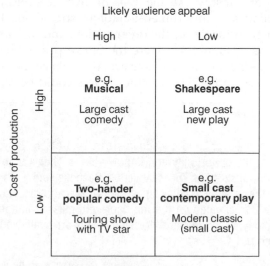

Figure 4.8 A product planning matrix for a theatre season

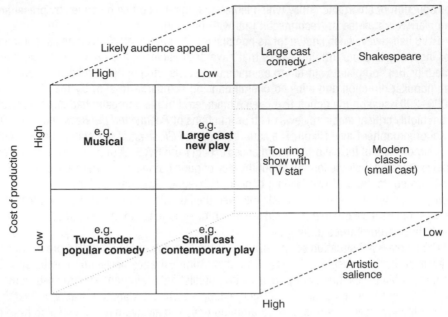

Figure 4.9 A three-dimensional product planning matrix

Replacing the axes of 'market growth' and 'market share' with considerations of 'production costs' and 'likely sales appeal' gives a matrix which can help predict the financial effects of programming choice.

In Figure 4.8 the offerings are divided into four sectors. As with the Boston matrix, there is an implied movement of resources from the Cash Cow two-hander comedy to the other areas. But rather than suggesting that the high cost/low appeal offering be killed off, the illustrative example of a Shakespeare play or large-scale new work signals that this quadrant is the part of the mix most deserving of subsidy. At the risk of over-complicating what is an essentially simple idea, a third dimension (of artistic salience) might be added to reflect the artistic priorities of the organization, and its claim to support by funding bodies, as in Figure 4.9. Here the Shakespeare and large-scale new work are seen in terms of their relative artistic salience, not only to the other quadrants but to each other. Programme choices could be made accordingly.

Taking a vow

When the law changed on where weddings can take place, Bradford's Alhambra took advantage of the opportunity and is now able to offer a whole day's event in the elegant surroundings of its 700-seat venue. Bespoke weddings can be arranged if required, on a theme such as Shakespeare, or opera, and receptions are generally held in the Gods Bar, situated on the top floor with glass frontage and panoramic views across the city. Even the stars' dressing rooms are available for the bride and groom to freshen up!

Source: Renton and Clarke, 2002.

It may be objected that this kind of diagrammatic approach misrepresents the subtleties which should inform a venue's approach to its programming. But the use of portfolio models as a planning aid can be defended on a number of counts:

- it makes assumptions explicit
- it encourages quantification
- it facilitates an appreciation of the way a programme fits together
- it enables the projected work of the organization to be clearly measured against its mission and priorities
- it helps identify gaps in provision

Maintaining quality

The kind of marketing approach championed in this book is centred on creating and keeping arts customers, by thinking about what needs and wants they are seeking to satisfy and reflecting these in the total offering of the organization. Although we have acknowledged that defining customer expectations is a complex task in the arts, the general principle of 'producing output in conformance to customer requirements' underlies this approach. This phrase is also a very basic definition of quality: making sure that the output of an organization is fit for the purpose to which it will be put by the customer (Munro-Faure and Munro-Faure, 1992).

Service quality

The models of service provision we have applied to the experience of the arts emphasize how successful service delivery depends on the interaction of the customer with everyone with whom he or she comes into contact in the organization. Furthermore, the idea of 'invisible' systems, which enable these first-line personnel to perform their roles more effectively, reveals that even those working behind the scenes have a direct impact on the nature of the experience for the customer. The delivery of a quality experience – more commonly known as 'customer care' – is therefore an issue for everyone in the organization, not just the marketing department, and service marketing theory commonly recognizes that a further three 'Ps' can be manipulated by marketers to influence the quality of the customer experience, beyond the '4 Ps' model of the traditional marketing mix (Zikmund and d'Amico, 1993):

- *People:* the importance of the human interface and the co-operative role of the customer are unique to services, and are key aspects of arts experience.
- *Physical evidence:* an appropriate environment for the delivery of the experience is a way of compensating for the intangibility of the artistic product – everything from explicit signage to the dress code of the stewards.
- *Process:* placing the customer at the centre of the sales and marketing systems through which the experience is mediated is essential, particularly in areas such as booking procedures.

Managing customer care is one of the most important contributions marketing can make to the success of an arts organization. Rawlings-Jackson and Shaw (1995) as well as Knight (1999) have written detailed guides to systematic approaches to the issue which specifically consider the circumstances of arts and non-profit organizations. The key to success is in gaining organizational commitment to the priority of keeping customers satisfied, and then the willingness to develop and implement systems (supported by training and development for staff as appropriate).

A good place to start for any organization is with the development of a complaints policy. Instead of seeing complaints as threatening or negative (a temptation for all organizations, especially those with the kind of self-belief that is commonplace in the arts), they should be regarded as an opportunity for learning. Indeed, a leading book on customer care in the commercial sector (Barlow and Moeller, 1996) bears the title *A Complaint is a Gift*. If your customers are not complaining, they may be 100 per cent happy. On the other hand, given the number of potential dissatisfactions available in an experience as complicated as a visit to an arts venue, it is more likely that at least some of them are seething in silence – determined never to darken the door of your venue again, and filled with a missionary zeal to persuade their friends and colleagues not to either. Organizations such as restaurants and hotels actively check on performance, giving customers a direct opportunity to complain. Feedback cards and a waiter returning to your table during the meal to ask 'Is everything satisfactory?' are ways of doing this. Arts organizations might consider the routine use of such cards, and occasionally approaching customers at performance breaks or as they exit galleries to solicit feedback.

A complaints policy allows an organization to accept criticism in a way that makes the complainant feel that they have been properly treated (thus turning a problem into an opportunity) as well as helping the organization to improve its performance. The policy should offer a template to an individual staff member to help him or her resolve a complaint effectively and directly. Here is a five-step approach which can be readily adapted:

1 Thank the customer for the feedback and look positive.
2 If a mistake has been made, clarify the problem with the customer but don't deny it. You don't want to get into an argument, but to resolve a problem.
3 Apologize – once. Too many apologies may sound like words rather than action.
4 Make a personal commitment to the customer to do something about the problem, and then do it. Be specific as to the next step – for example, a telephone call to confirm a course of action.
5 Check back with the customer when you have resolved the issue to make sure your action has been effective.

The prioritization of quality does not mean that the balance between benefits for the customer and costs for the organization should tilt disastrously against the organization's interests. Setting standards such as 'answering every telephone call before the fourth ring' may mean the organization employing extra staff, and the cost/benefit equation may not stack up. Each organization

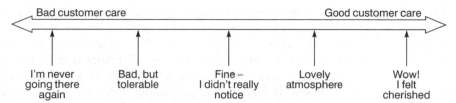

Figure 4.10 The customer care continuum (adapted from Aplin, 2002)

must choose where it wishes to sit on the customer care continuum (Figure 4.10) and strike the balance between investing resources and potentially losing customers who are badly treated.

The customer satisfaction at which marketing aims depends on getting things right. In a service environment such as the arts this means getting it right first time. Getting it right first time means that the organization cuts out waste. You cannot undo mistakes that happen in the service process, as the experience is consumed at the point of its manufacture. The aim should be to prevent problems by anticipating them as far as possible. But by creating reliable systems to deal with problems as they occur, the arts organization not only pacifies the customer more effectively but eliminates a great deal of inconvenience (and expense) for itself. Getting it right first time also focuses the mind on what is essential about the service and what is irrelevant. This can be called 'doing the right things right'. In organizational terms it means a clearer enactment of the mission statement and an increased responsiveness to customers.

The small things count

The Charter Mark is awarded to public organizations that sustain a high quality of service, and Cambridge Corn Exchange was the first concert hall in the UK to achieve the standard three times in a row. Its success reflects its continuing improvements in customer care practice. The organization welcomes feedback through a programme of research, plus a leaflet that actively encourages complaints. Even the smallest issues are dealt with. Cough sweets in rustle-free wrappers were introduced at orchestral concerts at the request of customers who were fed-up with serial coughers, and it was a simple task to satisfy those who wanted coat hooks fitted in the boxes overlooking the stage.

Source: Jones, 2002.

Evaluating service quality

One way to understand how customers perceive quality in service experiences is to establish a list of what they see as the important attributes of quality, and then rate their experiences of the service against their expectations through questionnaire research (although adopting a quantitative approach to an essentially qualitative issue poses a few methodological difficulties).

In its essence this kind of service quality (or 'ServQual') research is a straightforward enough idea. Its original developers (Parasuraman, Zeithaml and Berry, 1985) identified five main areas in which an organization's performance could be measured against expectations. Here we list them as they might be applied to a gallery visit:

- *tangibles:* the physical evidence of a service (e.g. what the catalogue looks like)
- *reliability:* the fact that the service works (e.g. that the pictures are hung in a way that minimizes unwanted reflected light)
- *responsiveness:* the sensitivity of the service to customer approaches (e.g. is there sufficient interpretative material?)
- *assurances:* the degree of confidence the service inspires (e.g. is the exhibition well chosen?)
- *empathy:* the degree of involvement the service allows (e.g. are the staff friendly?)

But applying ServQual in practice as a diagnostic tool is a difficult proposition. While it might reveal some areas for development or improvement, the essential subjectivity of people's responses is always going to be a problem when trying to interpret numerical data based on the difference between an expectation and an actual experience.

Perhaps, too, there may be a clash between the customer's idea of the core benefit and the organization's interpretation of it through the central experience on offer. There is also the danger that people's expectations may themselves be unrealistic. Kotler and Andreasen (1996) suggest that a goal of service providers ought to be to make their users' expectations more reasonable: 'Non-profits should routinely ask themselves: "What are potential customers being led to expect from this organization and what can the organization deliver?" '

This question does not let the organization off the hook of providing the best and most relevant service possible. What it does instead is to encourage marketing planning to focus on what is achievable to a high standard, rather than promising what cannot be delivered. A checklist of attributes important to other service areas may be useful as a template from which to develop research into your own organization's performance. Table 4.1 provides such a checklist, annotated appropriately for the arts industry.

Implementing quality

Having diagnosed the agenda for improvement, with an idea of the gap between the current situation (base line) and the desired result, the organization is faced with having to find ways of implementing changes for greater effectiveness. These need to be tried, checked and then refined. Useful techniques in this process include:

- *brainstorming:* generating ideas in a non-critical environment which are written down and later evaluated

Table 4.1 Determinants of service quality, as applied to a theatre

- **Reliability**
  getting it right first time
  honouring promises
  – charging the correct amount
  – keeping records
  – having tickets ready for collection

- **Responsiveness**
  being ready to perform a service
  – answering questions or enquiries
  – following up contacts

- **Competence**
  the skill and knowledge needed to perform the service
  – being able to advise or explain
  – people skills
  – technical knowledge (e.g. emergency procedures, first aiding etc.)

- **Access**
  approachability
  – telephones not always busy and promptly answered
  – waiting and queuing minimized
  – opening or performance times convenient and consistent

- **Courtesy**
  friendliness and respect from people with whom customers have contact
  – consideration
  – personal appearance
  – willingness to identify oneself on the telephone or by name badge

- **Communication**
  keeping the customer appropriately informed
  – announcements
  – promotional strategy and media chosen
  – clear explanation of options available
  – explicit procedures for handling problems (e.g. lateness, noise, refunds)

- **Credibility**
  honesty and trustworthiness
  – reputation and 'brand image'
  – community involvement

- **Security**
  freedom from danger or risk in the transaction
  – well-lit car parks
  – confidentiality with bank details for patrons paying by standing order/direct debit/
    internet
  – white-lined steps and well-maintained facilities

- **Customer empathy**
  meeting the customer more than half-way
  – flexibility
  – acknowledging the regular customer
  – making the new customer welcome

- **Physical environment**
  the physical evidence accompanying the service
  – facilities
  – uniforms
  – signage
  – other customers

Source: Adapted from Parasuraman et al., 1985.

- *process flowcharting:* mapping out the series of events that constitutes a particular service encounter (e.g. a gallery visit, or arranging a photocall)
- *listing forces 'for' and 'against' a proposed change:* this can aid the choice of the most realistic alternative from a number of possible ways of working
- *diagrams:* like the product portfolio model discussed earlier, diagrams of situations (graphs, charts, tables) can force out assumptions and help share an appreciation of the problem

The process not only has the advantage of improving service to the customer, but the internal communication it generates has an excellent effect on morale and the issues it raises are useful in developing the wider skills of the participants.

Summary

'Product' is the foundation of the rest of the marketing mix. But in service industries in general, and the arts in particular, the product has a number of qualities which distinguish it from the physical products with which much marketing literature is concerned. The intangibility, inseparability, heterogeneity and perishability of the arts experience are all reasons why a further three Ps – people, process and physical evidence – are as important as price, product promotion and place in creating and keeping arts customers. The core benefit offered to arts customers is the artistic experience itself, which is co-produced with the customer, making it akin to an act of communication. Communication models, therefore, have a special role in helping us to think about what we are marketing. Ancillary products have a special importance in the service sector, and (depending on art form) they provide useful commercial opportunities. But they should be conceived in the context of enabling arts customers to enjoy the core experience of the arts more fully, and require careful purchasing and specification. Like any other product, artistic products have life cycles and are subject to technology and fashion. Planning a balanced portfolio is the key to maximizing audience satisfaction and achieving organizational viability. Quality, which begins and ends with the customer, is a marketing issue of direct concern to every member of an arts organization. Each worker is implicated in the customer's experience (directly or indirectly), so practical measures to improve quality need to be as inclusive of the organization as possible. They need, above all else, the commitment not only of marketing but also of the rest of senior management.

Key concepts

ancillary product	Newcomb's ABX model
BCG Matrix	noise
benefits	perishability
brand	process model
customer care	product level

features

friends

heterogeneity

inseparability

intangibles

Maslow's Hierarchy of Needs

needs

product life cycle

product portfolio

quality

redundancy

ServQual

Servuction

wants

Discussion questions

1 Marketing practitioners and theorists make a distinction between physical products and services. How important do you think this distinction is to customers?

2 Discuss three ways in which the perceived risk of attending a new play can be reduced for a prospective customer.

3 Outline some of the practical problems facing a gallery trying to ascertain customer perceptions of the quality of its service.

4 How might the marketing manager of a large touring orchestra approach the issue of quality management in his or her organization?

5 Determine the levels of product offered by an arts organization of your choice and identify any areas which could be improved. What barriers might face a marketing manager wishing to implement any changes?

Case study: Finnishing touch

Based in Finland's second-largest city, Turku, Minna Koivurinta, founder of advertising agency Satumaa ('Fairyland') has a fairy story of her own to tell. Her husband's uncle, a local business magnate, is a keen collector of contemporary art. He had housed his growing collection of over 300 major works in a building on the outskirts of the city. Although his aim was to make the collection accessible to the public, it soon outgrew the original accommodation. The opportunity to purchase a central location, the Rettig Palace in the middle of Turku itself, came up in 1991. Mr Koivurinta had set up a charitable private trust in 1987 to provide finance for the collection's development. He now began planning the move of the collection to its new home.

In the absence of state funding the project plan stipulated that running costs would need to come entirely from earned income. Rather than the 5 or 10 Finnish marks common as an admission charge at the time it opened, the new gallery targeted a standard price of 50 marks (nearly £7). The strategy therefore focused on making the experience as attractive as possible to a wide range of visitors, in order to provide them with value for money as a visitor attraction rather than as a fine-arts museum.

As the building was being converted for its new use, however, the contractors discovered that the palace concealed treasures as yet undreamt of. Below it, to a depth of 7 m, they found the clear remnants of a medieval settlement, which proved to be the lost medieval core of the original township of Turku dating from the fourteenth century. Not only were there substantial vestiges of the original buildings, but also a treasure trove of artefacts – 30 000 in all. The key to the museum's success had been stumbled upon by accident – and the notion of a two-layered experience of Ancient and Contemporary arts replaced the original plan. The museum's eventual name reflected this double experience of archaeology and contemporary art: Aboa Vetus Ars Nova. Aboa is the ancient name for Turku and Aboa Vetus means 'Old Turku'. Ars Nova, on the other hand, means 'New Art'.

The launch campaign sought out a number of different groups:

- Turku residents themselves (Finland's second-largest city with 170 000 inhabitants and a wide catchment area for visitors from the region)
- families and children already attracted to the local area by the lure of nearby Moominworld (a popular theme park devoted to the cartoon creations of Ms Tove Jansson)
- tourists from other Nordic countries, particularly Sweden for whom Turku is the obvious entry port to Finland
- cultural tourists
- the education market (university students and schools)

The launch year, 1995, was, however, a difficult time to attract visitors from the region because of a particularly severe recession which hit Finland. The need to offer value for money in the experience was therefore even more important, as was the need to cut running costs to an absolute minimum. Fortunately, the historical and architectural interest generated by the medieval excavations attracted European Union funding to the project.

An important strategy in the marketing of the museum to international tourists was to feature it in a package of activities over two days, also featuring Moominworld, a steam-ship museum, and accommodation at the Sokos Hotel chain. Thousands of families took up the offer, particularly appreciating the opportunity to let their children participate in a treasure hunt trail round the older part of the museum, while they were free to enjoy it at their own pace.

Originally the museum opened at 8.30 a.m. and closed at 7 p.m. every day of the week. These hours were much longer than the norm for Finnish businesses and visitor attractions. The strategy had been to corner the market in Swedish visitors, large numbers of whom reach Turku in the ferry that arrives at 8 a.m. Unfortunately, after two summers of experimenting with this approach the museum has reverted to the standard visitor attraction opening time of 10 a.m., due to the minimal uptake.

Interpretative signs in three languages, Finnish, Swedish and English, accompany the archaeological exhibits. Sound and lighting effects lead the visitor through an exciting environment. There are human guides who conduct regular tours of both halves of the museum in a number of languages. Alternatively, a number of touch-screen multimedia computers complement the exhibits. These provide on-demand information for visitors about the artworks, as well as computer-generated reconstructions of Turku at various stages of its historical development (matching the different layers of archaeology on display). At the end of the exhibition, visitors can test their knowledge against the computer with a number of multiple-choice quizzes.

Contemporary visual art is not an easy experience to sell, and Minna Koivurinta acknowledges that the archaeological part of the museum, as well as the building's location and mystique, are what attracts the crowds. Separate tickets can be bought to each, but the joint admission price includes a healthy discount to encourage people to experiment. Café and shop are both carefully designed to reflect the museum contents and act as 'tasters' to the casual visitor. The café area offers tantalizing glimpses of the archaeological excavations, and the shop (named 'Laurentius' after Finland's first bookseller) sells modern replicas of some of the finds as well as art books and CD-ROMs. The advertising agency spent a lot of care designing the shop environment and specifying the product range.

The marketing communications campaign which supports the museum is centred on printed material, as might be expected. Having to produce literature in more than one language, while keeping graphics and images standard, adds a further complication to the task. Taking part in trade exhibitions and travel fairs, and carrying out direct marketing to travel operators covers international customers. Direct marketing is also used to promote the museum to businesses in the region as a centre for corporate events and presentations. Carefully targeted advertising in specialist magazines accesses the education market.

Education has proved a key factor in the museum's success. Indeed, students and school students are a key audience. At the very beginning the European Cultural Heritage year supported the development of co-operation with a number of local high schools, planning a three-year study programme of topics raised by the museum's collections (whether contemporary art or archaeological finds). This resulted in a resource book which was published and made available for teachers in advance of a visit in order to aid preparation. Pricing for schools was arranged with a discount but still substantial – at 30 marks a student. Nevertheless the educational material was so good, and so labour-saving for participating teachers, that value for money triumphed over the absolute cost. The museum now has an excellent reputation for school visits, and the schools material has the extra credibility of having been co-ordinated by a peripatetic teacher working full time on a state grant for the project.

Sources: personal interview (1999), Aboa Vetus Ars Nova Magazine 1 (n.d.), Aboa Vetus Ars Nova Teachers' Pack (1997), www.aboavetusarsnova.fi/english/

Questions

1 Draw a product level diagram for Aboa Vetus Ars Nova, indicating the core benefit, central experience, extended experience and potential experience.
2 Draft a 100-word entry for the *Lonely Planet Guide to Finland*'s Turku section, outlining the museum's appeal to English-speaking visitors.
3 As a teacher, write a letter to the museum's management offering advice about its programme of visiting exhibitions and its facilities.

References

Aplin, B. (2002) 'Wearing their skin: the key to customer care', *ArtsProfessional*, Issue 21, 11 March.
Barlow, J. and Moeller, C. (1996) *A Complaint is a Gift*. Berret-Koehler Publishers.

Bateson, John and Hoffman, Douglas (1999) *Managing Services Marketing: Text and readings*. The Dryden Press Series in Marketing, Thomson Learning.

Berry, Leonard (1981) 'The employee as customer', *Journal of Retail Banking*, Vol. III, No. 1, 33–40.

Borg, A. (1998) 'A new name for the Museum', *V&A Magazine*, September–December.

Carman, J.M. and Langeard, E. (1980) 'Growth strategies for service firms'. In *Managing Services Marketing* (J. Bateson, Ed., 1999), pp. 445–59. Dryden Press.

Clewes, P. (1999) 'Exploring leadership through Shakespeare', *ArtsBusiness*, Issue 33, 30 August.

Cowell, D.W. (1984) *Marketing of Services*. Heinemann.

Crabb, M. (2001) 'A matter of principal', *International Arts Manager*, September, 41–2.

Davidson, H. (2002) *The Committed Enterprise – How to make vision and values work*. Butterworth-Heinemann.

Edwards, C. (2002) *Friends Like These: A study of the contribution of friends and support organizations to Yorkshire's museums, archives and libraries*. Re:source, Yorkshire Museums Council and British Association of Friends of Museums.

Horan, K. (2001) 'Knowing who your friends are', *ArtsProfessional*, Issue 15, 3 December, 5–6.

Jermyn, H. and Desai, P. (2000) *Arts – What's in a word? Ethnic minorities and the arts*. Research report 20, Arts Council of England.

Jones, N. (2002) 'Chartered for care', *ArtsProfessional*, Issue 21, 11 March, 9.

Kemp, L. (1993) 'It's the real thing – or is it?' *BBC Music Magazine*, March, 26–30.

Knight, A. (1999) *Effective Customer Care*. Directory of Social Change.

Kotler, P. and Andreasen, A. (1996) *Strategic Marketing for Non-Profit Organizations*, 5th ed. Prentice-Hall.

Levitt, Theodore (1969) *The Marketing Mode*. McGraw Hill.

Lovelock, C., Vandermerwe, S. and Lewis, B. (1999) *Services Marketing: A European perspective*. FT Prentice Hall.

Maslow, A. (1954) *Motivation and Personality*. Harper & Row.

Munro-Faure, L. and Munro-Faure, M. (1992) *Implementing Total Quality Management*. Financial Times/Pitman Publishing.

Newcomb, T. (1961) *The Acquaintance Process*. Holt, Rinehart and Winston Inc.

Parasuraman, A., Zeithaml, V.A. and Berry, L.L. (1985) 'A conceptual model of service quality and its implications for future research', *Journal of Marketing*, Vol. 49, Fall, 41–50.

Raines, K. (2002) 'Getting on the ladder – the DIY approach to quality', *Journal of Arts Marketing*, Issue 04, January, 13–14.

Randall, G. (1999) *Branding: A practical guide to planning your strategy*, 2nd edition. Kogan Page.

Rawlings-Jackson, V. and Shaw, P. (1995) *Paying Attention: A guide to customer care in the arts*. Arts Council of England.

Raymond, C. (1999) *Essential Theatre: The successful management of theatres and venues which present the performing arts*. Arts Council of England.

Renton, A. and Clarke, T. (2002) 'Nuptial brass . . . or take your vows', *Prompt*, Issue 27, 22–3.

Ries, A. and Ries, L. (1999) *The 22 Immutable Laws of Branding*. HarperCollins.

Shannon, C. and Weaver, W. (1949) *The Mathematical Theory of Communication*. University of Illinois Press.

Stone, M. (2001) 'The wonder of branding and the advantage of getting it right', *ArtsReach*, Vol. X, Issue 1, 1, 16–19.

Tomlinson, R. (1990) 'Great show, shame about the staff', *Arts Management Weekly*, 15 November, 2–3.

Wheeler, D. (2002) 'Infinite space', *ArtsProfessional*, Issue 31, 29 July.

Zikmund, W.G. and D'Amico, M. (1993) *Marketing*. West Publishing.

5

Generating income

Generating income is an essential function for all arts organizations, as without revenues they cannot survive. There are several potential sources of income:

- box office sales and entrance fees
- sales revenues from related activities, such as catering and merchandising
- public subsidy
- sponsorship and donations
- trusts and foundations

The first two categories lend themselves most obviously to marketing strategies, and specifically, pricing strategies. But the other income sources, sometimes misleadingly referred to as 'unearned income', also involve customers (be they individual or organizational) exchanging value for benefits of one sort or another, so the arts organization must both examine what is being exchanged and determine the appropriate value of this in the marketplace.

Among the issues examined in this chapter are:

- price setting
- accessing public subsidy
- attracting sponsorship and donations

Pricing

Pricing plays a complex role which links many other marketing mix decisions being made in an organization. In spite of the fact that it is the easiest of the four marketing mix variables with which to tinker in the short term, price should never be dismissed as merely tactical. It is a strategic variable, and getting it wrong not only jeopardizes an organization's income optimization, but also confuses each of the other components of the marketing mix.

Price as a marketing tool

Pricing policies play a major role in determining levels of sales revenue, as they affect demand. Economic theory suggests a simple trade-off: as the price of a product or service increases, demand for it will fall. In practice, however, the relationship between price and demand is much more complex and most arts organizations find themselves having to set a range of prices for the experiences they offer.

Prices imply quality levels. In markets where quality is at a premium such as luxury goods or gifts, the normal relationship between price and demand disappears. Cheap champagnes will not necessarily outsell more expensive alternatives. Similarly, the cheapest seats in a theatre are not always the first to be sold. What matters in both markets is value as perceived by the customer, and price levels may be a way of communicating this.

Pricing policies can also give arts customers a greater sense of control over their purchases and a benchmark for comparison with previous experiences. Research on pricing at arts centres in Wales carried out for the Arts Council of Wales (Marplan, 1988) suggests that arts attenders appreciate a range of prices from which to choose. Respondents indicated that they preferred a choice of prices in order to be able to get the best value seats, usually seen as the second-highest or middle-price bracket. Only 1 per cent of respondents cited high prices as a reason for not attending arts events in this survey, a finding which emerges consistently from virtually all research into the price sensitivity of arts attenders.

A structured approach to pricing

A research programme into ticket buying at the San Francisco Symphony, the San Francisco Opera, the San Francisco Ballet and the American Conservatory Theatre asked single-ticket buyers if, the last time they purchased a ticket for a performance, they obtained their first choice of seat location, date and price, and if not, whether they paid more or less than or the same as, they had originally planned. The survey found that, on average, 77 per cent of single-ticket buyers were able to purchase tickets for the date and price they preferred. For the 23 per cent overall who did not get their first choice of seating location, the great majority moved up in price rather than down, indicating that a good seat location is far more important to them than a lower price. These responses suggest that patrons want the best experience possible and appreciate the value of good seat locations more than a lower priced ticket.

Source: Scheff, 1999.

A further fundamental effect of pricing policy is to split the market into different segments, with the possible consequence of excluding particular groups. For example, if the majority of seats in an auditorium are premium priced because a sell-out performance is anticipated, the arts organization will certainly maximize its revenues, but at the same time effectively deny access to those on lower incomes.

The nature of pricing decisions

Prices should reflect the value that customers place on something offered for sale, so arts organizations usually face a diverse range of pricing decisions which must take into account the value their customers place on the tangible and less tangible aspects of what they offer.

- *pricing intangibles, e.g. a performance*
  Potential audiences are willing to exchange money for tickets in the expectation of a programme of entertainment. They are buying an ephemeral experience the intangible nature of which constitutes a considerable risk. This is discussed at greater length in Chapter 4. The audience will have some preconceived ideas as to the likely nature of the experience but it is not until after the performance that they will be in a position to judge the value they received in exchange for their money.

  In this way arts organizations face the same pricing dilemmas as all service providers who have to price their output to meet customer expectations. Unlike physical products, services cannot prove their quality and reliability to their customers in advance of purchase. Service pricing needs to take into account customers' expectations based on previous experience of similar offerings. This makes pricing new or unfamiliar work particularly challenging.
- *semi-tangibles, e.g. programmes*
  A 'service-adjunct' item such as a programme appears more tangible. It is a piece of print that can be examined by the customer prior to purchase. However, like the performance itself, the quality of the programme cannot be assessed until it has been read and thus here, too, the value will be judged retrospectively. The programme also serves as a souvenir of the performance, and will only have a value in that capacity if the performance itself is judged of merit.
- *pricing tangibles, e.g. ice-creams*
  The pricing of tangibles, such as confectionery and drinks, is in this respect an easier exercise. Customers can gauge value for money with these items before purchase and make direct comparisons with the prices of competing products. However, within the confines of a theatre building, there are not usually opportunities to purchase from competitors. Customers are, in truth, a captive audience. Price setting is a matter of ensuring that the product is seen to represent reasonable value for money in the context of its presentation.

  Premium price can be justified here by the added-value provided by quality, service attributes and convenience. Theatres often provide niche distribution opportunities for small but luxurious ice-cream or confectionery brands which are unavailable elsewhere. This serves to reduce the danger of comparison with much cheaper mass-market brands available in large cinema chains and supermarkets, and heightens the sense of the occasion being an enjoyable treat.

The basic principle of pricing, to reflect the value of a product or service, applies universally. Managers in the arts are faced with the task of creating and implementing pricing policies which will encourage demand for their services, generate revenue to help cover their costs and yet also meet other artistic and social objectives which may not be as explicit in other sectors.

Influences on pricing strategy

In a classic account of theatre pricing, Jules Boardman (1978) categorizes five main influences on pricing, which he identifies as placing significant constraints on pricing decisions:

- the auditorium itself
- the product on stage
- the market (existing and potential customer types)
- the box office (the human element of ticket sales)
- the budget (imposed financial targets)

A more proactive approach focuses not on constraints, but on what an organization wants to achieve (Figure 5.1). Viewed in this light, pricing decisions have to be made at two levels, strategic and tactical. In this section we will concentrate on the strategic level, laying a foundation for implementation and tactics to be discussed later in the chapter.

Arts organizations have to decide upon a general strategic approach to their pricing decisions which is commensurate with their objectives, the position they wish to hold in the market, the composition of that market and the nature and strength of their competitors.

Objectives

Arts organizations are characterized by diverse objectives. While industry and commerce are driven by their requirement to provide financial returns to shareholders, the mission of many arts organizations is broader than this. A number of potentially conflicting financial and marketing objectives needs to be considered in formulating pricing strategies.

Financial objectives

The profit motive may be an influential factor in pricing decisions in some sectors of the arts. In the commercial arts, backers finance performances in anticipation of box office success and financial returns. Therefore West End theatres set prices which are sufficiently high to cover costs and generate a

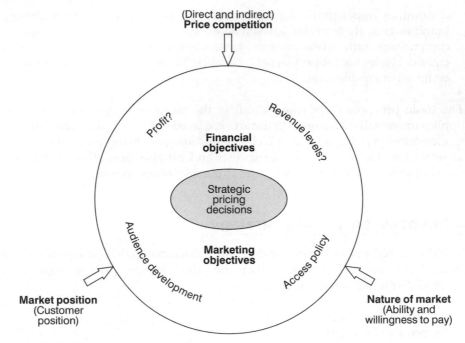

Figure 5.1 Influences on pricing strategy

profit margin. Failing to do so may lead to backers withdrawing their support. However, some commercial venues are indirectly in receipt of subsidy by receiving subsidized productions into their theatres. Similarly, commercial production companies benefit by touring to subsidized venues. Therefore, both of these types of profit-driven organizations have to have regard for wider issues than merely return on investment.

Pricing in the amateur arts may also be guided by the profit motive, in that any profits generated by a production will be used to finance the next. More commonly in amateur arts, the focus is not on profit but simply on covering costs. Internal influences may exert a stronger force here than in professional organizations. All the cast may be involved in democratic decisions, as in a co-operative. This can lead to internal conflict between the desire for short-term returns and the longer-term interests of the company.

The subsidized sector, by its very nature, does not expect earned income to cover all the costs of the company. Financial objectives will be set by the management to ensure that the combination of earned revenue, public funding and other fund-raising activity is sufficient to cover costs. Funding bodies may even set explicit targets. They may require, for example, that a theatre generates 55 per cent of its revenue itself. This means that the theatre must make a judgement as to the price levels and ticket sales which will achieve this.

Marketing objectives

An appropriate pricing strategy is often the key to achieving marketing objectives. The kinds of competitive marketing objectives evident in industry and commerce, such as market share and market leadership, are of limited relevance to the arts. More relevant marketing objectives tend to relate to building a loyal core audience or developing new audiences. A core audience needs to be developed in the hope of gaining repeat business. In order to do this, an arts organization might decide not to maximize profit by charging particularly high prices for a very popular event, for fear of alienating key audiences in the longer term. It may also offer incentives for loyalty by making discounts available to regular attenders, the most prevalent of which is based on the idea of subscription (dealt with later in the chapter). Alongside this core audience focus is the equally urgent need to develop new audiences. This may be to attract new attenders, or to recruit existing attenders to a new art form or performance of minority appeal. Under these circumstances the task of the marketing function is to build audiences rather than maximize revenue. From the customer's viewpoint, buying a ticket is a high-risk purchase as there is relatively little evidence upon which to judge its expected value. Therefore ticket prices will have to be relatively low to attract these audiences, lessen the financial risk for them and encourage potential attenders, regardless of their financial status.

Market position

Market position relates to the perceptions of an organization held by its customers and potential customers. Price can be a determining factor in creating these perceptions and, conversely, the perceptions held about an organization can limit its pricing flexibility.

High-profile, high-status venues and companies are expected to charge high prices. Part of the pleasure experienced by the audience may derive from the exclusivity of the event, and high price is a contributory factor to this exclusivity. To charge lower prices would devalue the experience. To avoid the charge of elitism which might lose them public subsidy, high-cost art forms like opera and dance companies often have access policies and engage in outreach work which, by segmenting their market, allows them to reach the widest possible audience base without sacrificing their premium price position.

On the other hand, if an organization is perceived to be offering lower quality, whether in terms of environment or performance, the opportunities for selling high-price tickets are limited. This is particularly problematic for amateur companies. Regardless of their levels of expertise or the costs they incur in staging a performance, there is a relatively low ceiling on the ticket prices that their audiences will be willing to pay.

Nature of the market

When making pricing decisions managers have to assess the importance of price to their target markets. The nature of the target market will determine not only ability but also willingness to pay certain price levels, as in the following situations:

Commercial venues

The commercial theatre in London, for example, attracts audiences who are relatively price insensitive. Foreign tourists, who may have spent many hundreds of pounds physically getting to the UK, may consider the price of a ticket to be a relatively small outlay in their total purchasing and accept price levels that may be considered quite steep by the average domestic audience. Furthermore, UK ticket prices tend to be considerably less than those in continental Europe or North America, making the arts a bargain for the foreign visitor.

Regional venues

Regional markets may not support the price levels accepted in major cities. Touring companies may provide identical performances in different venues and locations, but pricing will be at different levels to meet the expectations of the local markets.

Amateur events

The market for amateur performances may consist largely of friends and family of the performers. Their primary reason for attending may be quite unrelated to the nature of the performance. They are paying not for the cultural experience but rather to support the cast. Because the performance itself may have limited value to them, the pricing task involves assessing the value placed on giving this support. Price levels which are set too high may restrict audiences to a loyal core, alienating more peripheral supporters.

Educational events

The market for educational art forms tends to be more price sensitive than the market for arts entertainment. The high costs involved, for example, in mounting large-cast Shakespearean productions, might suggest the same price per ticket as a musical. However, experience shows that the market will not bear that price level. The schools market is an important sub-segment with a particular interest in less popular art forms, but they are one of the most price-sensitive segments of all.

Case 5.1 Fees or free?

The introduction of admission charges to England's museums and galleries grew throughout the 1980s as public subsidies were squeezed and additional sources of income were sought. But the wisdom of the practice was widely questioned, particularly when data collected in 1991 by the Policy Studies Institute showed that visits to four non-charging national London museums between 1982 and 1991 increased by 77 per cent, whereas admissions to three charging national London museums during the same period fell by 42 per cent.

However, it has long been felt that the negative impact of admission charges has been exaggerated because attendance figures at the non-charging museums were based on estimates, whereas the charging museums were in a position to supply very accurate admissions records. Also, there is an important distinction to be drawn between the 'number of visits' and 'numbers of visitors'. It is widely believed that regular visitors to museums may visit less often, but stay longer for each visit, when admission charges are imposed. When questioned about reasons for not visiting museums, only 4 per cent of non-visitors in a 1997 survey spontaneously cited admission charges as a barrier to attending, though 55 per cent of adults agreed that entry to all public museums and galleries should be free to everyone.

When the British government announced in March 2001 that it would increase its financial support for England's national museums and galleries to enable them to abolish admission charges, many speculated as to the impact this would have, both on the museums and galleries concerned, but also on other non-national museums and galleries that would have no increase in subsidy and would have to continue charging. Initial figures suggest that the scrapping of charges on 1 December 2001 has given a major boost to the national museums and galleries, though the impact on their competitors will take longer to assess.

	Admissions in December 2000	Admissions in December 2001	Percentage change in admissions figures
Imperial War Museum	31 145	44 046	+41
Natural History Museum	89 650	163 487	+85
National Museum of Science and Industry (Science Museum London and Railway Museum York)	88 603	146 856	+66
Royal Armouries (Leeds and Fort Nelson)	7 365	18 734	+154
National Maritime Museum	33 446	52 714	+58
Museum of London	12 965	24 408	+88
Museums of Science and Industry in Manchester	7 022	12 293	+75
National Museums and Galleries on Merseyside	23 214	36 214	+56

Sources: Glasgow Caledonian University, 1998; Department for Culture, Media and Sport, 2002.

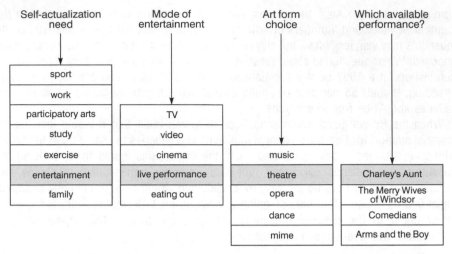

Figure 5.2 Competition facing a performing arts venue (adapted from Kotler and Andreason, 1991)

Competition

In formulating a pricing strategy it is important to be aware of competitive prices. However, for most arts organizations competition is difficult to define, so the influence of competitor prices on pricing strategy will be limited. The situation is complicated by a number of factors. A concert hall, for example, may consider the prices charged by other concert halls within its catchment area. This may be appropriate up to a point, but the quality of the facilities at the different venues will be a factor influencing customer perceptions of value, so this must also be taken into account. Furthermore, on any given night the potential audience may, for example, be choosing between a performance by the Royal Philharmonic Orchestra at one venue and a recital by a well-known pianist at another. Similarly, two adjacent galleries may be showing respectively a multimedia experimental exhibition and a Victorian retrospective. In this respect there is little justification for price comparison. Only if two similar events are simultaneously presented by organizations of similar artistic status at similar venues in the same region are competitor price levels likely to have a major impact on ticket sales. So although general price levels within the sector tend to set a framework for customer price expectations, pricing strategy is often remarkably free from external competitive constraints.

Sometimes, internal competition can be just as significant, if not more so. In venues with more than one auditorium the management may wish to price each performance space equally, if they are considered to be of equal artistic status. However, the public may persist in valuing one space over another (on a 'main house'/'studio' model) which may force the management to differentiate its product (and price) in a way which the audience demands, thus reducing internal competition.

Another form of competition arises from substitute activities such as watching television, going to the cinema or going out for a meal. As the price of these substitutes may range from virtually nothing for watching television, to an indefinable amount for eating out, the practical influence of substitute prices on pricing for arts activities will be limited.

Implementing a pricing strategy

Implementing an overall pricing strategy requires managers to set prices which will meet the objectives of their organizations within the constraints imposed by market and competitive factors. The performing arts environment poses peculiar problems here. A balance has to be struck between internal (cost-based) and external (demand-based) factors in operational pricing decisions for the arts.

Cost-based pricing

Regardless of their specific financial targets, all organizations will set prices sufficient at least to cover costs (Figure 5.3). The extent of the costs covered can vary from one type of business to another. Costs can be classified in two ways. Fixed costs do not vary with the volume of activity, and are made up of central overheads and other indirect expenses of the business. Variable costs, also known as direct costs, relate directly to the activity of the business, and vary according to the volume of sales.

For much activity in the performing arts, there is no correlation between variable revenues and variable costs. A large musical that costs a lot to mount will probably do well at the box office but, as we have seen above, the same will not necessarily be true of a Shakespearean tragedy. Conversely, a three-hander such as Yasmina Reza's *Art* has rescued many a touring venue season by performing well at the box office as well as being relatively cheap to mount.

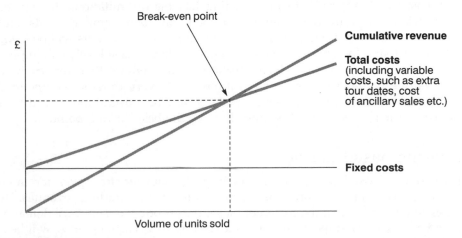

Figure 5.3 Break-even analysis

Table 5.1 Factors in costing repertory productions

Subsidy	Includes all funding from local or regional sources, grants etc.
Fixed costs	Also called overheads, including administration, marketing, premises and equipment
Contribution	Any shortfall between subsidy and fixed costs will have to be funded from net earnings
Variable income:	
Box office	Estimated income per show after allowing for VAT, royalties, discounts and free tickets. Percentage of total available seats
Other income	Income from bar, programmes, ices etc. Moves with box office figure – small audiences will buy fewer programmes
Variable costs:	
Company	Actors, directors, designers
Production	Carpenters, paintshop, wardrobe, wigs, props
Staging	Stage crew, lighting, sound, flying, traps
Other	Musicians, fights, choreography, children

Furthermore, the same play can vary enormously in its costs from one production to another, depending on the artistic concept and the lavishness of the sets. For that reason, different individual productions within a season are rarely priced separately in spite of the fact that one may have cost more than another to mount. Instead, most repertory companies tend to price their seasons at standard ticket prices based on overall costs measured across a whole season (see Table 5.1). Notable exceptions are found with particularly lavish productions the opulence of which is evident to customers, such as musicals or Christmas shows in a season otherwise devoted to drama. Here a premium over the 'normal' production price may be part of the audience's expectations. The same is true of some major opera houses, who price in bands according to the grandeur of the grand opera on offer.

A cost-based approach to price setting has many limitations. It may be appropriate in industries where customers all have similar needs and competitive activity is intense. In these circumstances, customers will be fickle and consistently look for the best deal in the market, so cost levels will impose a floor on the extent to which businesses can reduce their prices in a competitive battle. Most arts organizations face a very different competitive environment, and while break-even analysis may be a useful tool in setting a floor for pricing decisions, it is unlikely to be the best starting point.

Demand-based pricing

Price setting based on customer and market characteristics gives far more scope to managers who are looking to maximize their trading revenues. By assessing the value that the customer places on a product or service, a demand-based approach attempts to set prices according to what the market will bear rather than the costs incurred in providing the product or service.

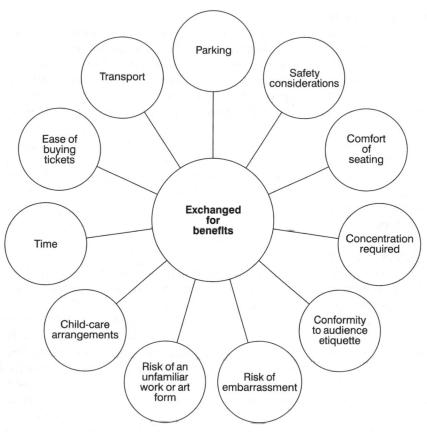

Figure 5.4 Non-financial factors affecting perceptions of price

---

Opera costs

Unlike theatre, where two-handers, or even one-person shows, are perfectly viable, opera is an expensive art form to stage, partly due to the sheer numbers of artists involved. Shostakovich's *Lady Macbeth of Mtsensk*, staged by English National Opera in 2001, required 210 people on stage and in the pit. ENO's key production the following season, *War and Peace*, involved 58 named roles, an 80-strong chorus and 17 actors. Even the very small-scale chamber works staged by Almeida Opera are likely to have between two and 12 singers on stage, an orchestra of up to 13, and a conductor.

Source: Higgins, 2001.

The value audiences place on an exhibition or performance is likely to be a function of the reputation of the artists or performers, expectations of the performance or exhibition itself and the nature of the venue.

Reputation of performers

Popular artists and highly regarded companies or orchestras also offer greater value to audiences, though this may or may not be related to the actual quality of their work. Higher price levels can be achieved simply based on their reputation. It is no coincidence that pantomime producers try to attract stars from the current TV soap operas to perform their Christmas seasons. The appearance of a star name on the billing can mean that tickets prices can be increased by several pounds.

Audiences may consist of people ranging from the highly discerning to those with very little knowledge or understanding of an art form. The former group will be willing to pay for the pleasure of appreciating the quality of experience provided by top-class performers, while the latter may gain value from the fact that others rate that artistic experience. Their own perceived risk is reduced by the endorsement of others.

Expectations of a performance

It is relatively easy for potential audiences to assess how much a ticket for, say, an Oscar Wilde play or a well-known orchestral work is worth to them. It is much less easy for them to judge this if the performance is of a new work by a little-known writer or composer. In this case, prices must be set to overcome the inertia that stems from unfamiliarity. Although some people are highly motivated to attend or participate in new and different arts experiences, they are relatively few and far between. For most people, doubts over whether the performance will actually be enjoyable depress their willingness to part with their cash, and special incentives may be required to generate an audience.

Nature of the venue

Part of the total experience being purchased by audiences is the ambience, location, comfort, prestige and size of the venue. However well respected an orchestra or touring company, the prices it can command in the market will be governed to some extent by the venue it uses for the performance. The venue can either add to or detract from the perceived value of the event and price levels must take this into account.

Pay please

In a public opinion survey investigating reactions to different charging policies by museums and galleries, more support was found for free entry with voluntary donations (71 per cent) than for admission charges with concessions (58 per cent) or free entry with no voluntary donations (51 per cent).

Source: Glasgow Caledonian University, 1998.

Price elasticity of demand

The extent to which raising or lowering prices will affect a potential customer's decision whether or not to buy a ticket is known as price

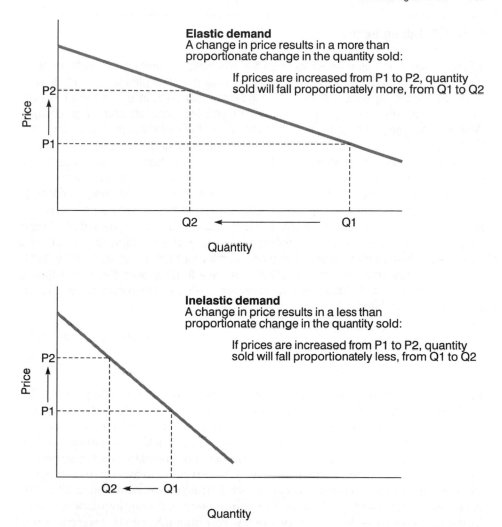

Figure 5.5 Price elasticity of demand

sensitivity. An economic model is useful for quantifying the whole the concept of price sensitivity. The model, known as the 'price elasticity of demand', can be used to estimate the extent by which demand for tickets will fall if prices are raised, and conversely, by how much demand will fall if prices are increased (see Figure 5.5). A market is defined as having elastic demand if a small increase in price leads to a large reduction in sales. This is a characteristic of highly competitive markets, where customers can easily substitute one product for another if they think something is too expensive. As discussed earlier, this is not a market condition facing many arts organizations. Direct comparison with competitive offerings is very difficult in most sectors of the performing arts, so ticket prices are sensitive only to a limited extent. (For further discussion of the relationship between ticket price and demand, see Huntingdon, 1993.)

Case 5.2 Hiking up the price

When cut-backs in public expenditure on the arts placed a squeeze on the finances of theatres across Germany, the Mannheim Nationaltheater attempted to raise its income levels by increasing prices. There were significant increases in prices for all seating categories, together with a more subtly differentiated price structure that charged different prices according to the type, day and time of the performance. At the same time the theatre set about improving the quality of its services, and attempted, by means of an image campaign, to reposition itself in the market to attract new audiences. New innovations included programming enhancement, such as pre- and post-show talks, late-night events aimed at young people, and simplified ticket purchasing procedures, including online reservations. All these changes were accompanied by a new corporate identity. The price and programme changes were met with both curiosity and scepticism on the part of the press and the public alike. The new price structure, which was compared unfavourably with prices at other German theatres, led to particularly harsh criticism; but research into customer reaction showed that, although they were negative about the price rises, the improvements in service levels more than compensated for all the other modifications.

Source: Hermann et al., 1999.

Research consistently finds that price does not have a major impact on the decision to attend an arts event. Research on pricing in the arts (Millward Brown, 1990) revealed that price ranks tenth in a list of 20 factors which people said they took into consideration when deciding whether to attend an arts event. Product-based attributes such as the level of entertainment expected or the subject matter of the performance weighed far more heavily in the equation than the price of the ticket itself. This general attitude was common to all socio-economic groups surveyed, including young people, unemployed people and infrequent attenders. In this study, the few respondents who did see price as a problem tended to be from higher rather than lower income groups. On the other hand, a more recent study by Colbert (1998) found that, among high income groups, it was lack of time, rather than cost, that prevented people from attending the arts more often, though the converse was true of lower income groups.

These findings are backed by economists, who consistently find that ticket prices for the arts are relatively inelastic, and that raising prices has little effect on the number of seats sold. (Income elasticity, however, is generally high: as income levels rise, so does demand for, and willingness to pay higher prices for tickets.) Although this view is often contested by those who work in the arts, who argue that price is a major barrier to access to the arts, Richard Eyre, in his report on the future of the Lyric Theatre in London (1998) conceded that it is not price but perceived value for money that consumers consider when buying tickets.

Price sensitivity is even more limited in the case of peripherals such as catering. As has been suggested earlier, at the point of wanting a drink or a snack customers are faced with no alternative suppliers. During an interval they have a choice between consuming or not consuming, but choosing another provider is not an option. In this respect, the market in which price elasticity operates is unique to the arts organization itself.

A lot can be learned by analysing price/sales relationships in the past, and using the information to predict the price levels that will generate the highest revenues in the future. Hugh Davidson, a leading marketing consultant, reflects that 'Although pricing decisions often have to be taken quickly, the quality of decision-making can be enormously improved by taking a hard look at the price dynamics of a market beforehand' (Davidson, 1984). A scientific approach is the best guarantee of objectivity when setting prices, a process that can frequently involve a highly-charged but not very well-informed debate.

Case 5.3 Mind your step!

Price thresholds are the points on the demand curve (the steps) where an increase in seat prices will lead to an overall decrease in revenues (i.e. where demand is price elastic). Consequently, if venues price close to, but not above their price thresholds, they will maximize their revenues. A consumer surplus exists when individuals pay a price which is lower than they would have been prepared to pay (i.e. below their price threshold). Under these circumstances, the venue has opportunities for premium pricing initiatives, and can attempt to add value to realize these opportunities.

Research at the King's Theatre Glasgow investigated price threshold for performances of two musicals – *Fame* and *Joseph and the Amazing Technicolor Dreamcoat*. The research asked a sample of high-frequency credit-card bookers to musicals at the venue about their expectations of price, and about the highest price they would be prepared to pay for tickets, on the basis of their expectation of the performances. On the basis of the findings, new price breaks were calculated for the auditorium, and it was calculated that thousands of pounds of additional revenues could have been generated from those two performances had prices been set on the price steps – at the maximum price that customers would have been willing to pay. The front stall seats alone could have generated an additional £22 000, though 2690 fewer people would have been attracted to the performance at those higher prices.

	Front stalls, standard ticket prices	
	Fame	*Joseph*
Seats sold under existing price structure	5335	7339
Predicted seat sales under new pricing structure	4268	5719
Predicted increase in revenues	+£5171	+£16 851

Source: Jamieson, 1999.

Tactical pricing decisions

In spite of the relative inelasticity of demand which has been observed in pricing research in the arts, a range of pricing tactics can be effectively used to tempt more people to experience the arts. Much tactical pricing is based on the principle of market segmentation, as discussed in Chapter 2, which asserts that different parts of a market have different needs and expectations from others, and that service providers can meet the needs of their total market best by concentrating on the needs of the individual segments rather than approaching the market as a single entity. Consequently, 'price discrimination' is practised, to recognize that different groups of buyers value products and services differently and that some are willing to pay more than others.

Price structures

Different prices can be charged according to the characteristics of a performance and other aspects of the arts experience. Two criteria are commonly used to determine price structures:

- *Sightlines:* Seats with particularly good visibility are of great value to certain sectors of the audience. Those for whom a visit to a theatre or concert is driven by a need to impress another, such as a corporate client or a new girlfriend or boyfriend, will be happy to pay extra for the privilege, as will those who are highly discerning arts attenders, whose appreciation of an event can be severely undermined by poor acoustics, for example. Conversely, those on low incomes whose motivation for attending is a love of a particular art form may be delighted to find a low-price ticket in the gods, or an affordable restricted view seat. Despite a sometimes impeded view, theatre boxes remain popular and can command relatively high prices as they enable a more communal arts experience for small groups of friends and associates.
- *Time of opening or performance:* People value their leisure time more highly at certain times than others. Weekend evenings are traditionally popular times for entertainment and audiences are generally willing to pay more for the privilege of being able to attend a performance and not have to go to work in the morning. Price setters are faced with a relatively price-insensitive market and are able to charge premium prices at peak times without a significant reduction in demand. This form of price discrimination can be used as a tool for managing demand and encouraging attendance at less popular times. Matinées are a good example of this. Only a limited proportion of the total potential audience is available during the afternoons, so prices are generally set lower than at other times. The aim is to persuade this group to attend at this time, rather than occupy prime-time seats. Some access considerations can be satisfied, without conflict with the organizational aim of maximizing profit.

If an auditorium has a very uniform seating arrangement, and a performance only takes place once (such as a touring comedy show), then a unit pricing approach, which sets prices for all seats in the house at the same level, may be more appropriate. (Price discrimination can only be effective if customers perceive there to be significant differences in the value of different tickets.) An advantage of unit pricing is that it encourages early booking, as the seats that are left towards the end of a booking period, shortly before a performance, will be those which are poorly positioned. The downside is that a late booker may be faced with having to pay more than would normally be the case for seats at some distance from the stage. This may deter those who are not predisposed to book in advance – a growing proportion of all audiences these days.

Concessions

Concession schemes differentiate prices, not on the basis of features of the service but on the basis of the characteristics of the potential customers. They offer cheaper prices to some potential attenders, if they are old, young, poor or unemployed, for example. Inevitably this is bound up with the strategic policy on access and audience development (see Table 5.2).

Table 5.2 Test-drive a theatre ticket

Pressure from politicians and funding bodies to widen access to the arts has led to the proliferation of test-drive schemes at arts organizations across the UK. The theory is that pricing schemes can be used to convert non-attenders into attenders by offering potential attenders incentives to introduce them to the arts for the first time, and subsequent incentives to build their loyalty to the organization. The initial incentives are often free tickets, but might instead be discounted tickets, money-back guarantees or 'value-added' benefits like a free programme, drinks or a CD. So what is the difference between a test-drive scheme and papering, the age-old technique of distributing tickets-for-free to ensure that the auditorium looks at least respectable when the curtain goes up?

Papering	Test-drive
Tactical 'I've got spare seats and I must make the house look good for the producer'	**Strategic** 'How can I use spare capacity to achieve my audience development objectives?'
Last minute panic 'Waah! How can I find 100 people who'd be mug enough to attend tomorrow night for free?'	**Planned well in advance** 'I'd like to use 100 seats from May's children's show to target families who haven't been to our theatre before'
Negative message 'It can't be very good if they're desperate enough to be giving tickets away'	**Positive message** 'How nice, they're wanting us to try out the theatre for the first time'
Short-term benefits Bums on seats	**Long-term benefits** Life-time value
Monologue Persuading customers to get tickets	**Dialogue** Using feedback to create the most enjoyable experience

Source: Roberts, 1998.

Concession structures tend to provide reductions for the elderly, for the unwaged, for students and for children. If standard price levels were charged, these groups might be unable to afford tickets, so this practice fits in with a corporate access policy as well as generating income from otherwise empty seats. Concession schemes are not, however, universally popular. It is argued that pricing policy should not be based on the assumption that everyone is hard up: 'The mistake which is sometimes made is to behave as though the whole community cannot afford to pay our prices and so to keep prices far below the level of general public acceptance' (Diggle, 1984).

In practice, however, it tends to be the case that some of the typical concessionary groups, such as unemployed people or frail elderly people, are less inclined to arts attendance than others such as students. This disinclination may have more to do with social class and physical mobility than with price resistance. If this were so, then the seeming cost of having a thriving access policy expressed in generous concessions might in reality prove an investment. It suggests that the conflict between access objectives and income maximization is less real than apparent. One might even argue that the treatment of students and young people, one of the largest concessionary groups in most theatres' experience, is akin to the use of loss leaders in a supermarket. Present revenue is sacrificed in the expectation of future returns, as they develop a theatregoing habit. In this respect their treatment is more to do with 'discounting' (see below) than with concessions.

Discounting

Concessionary pricing is dictated by strategic considerations of access and equality of opportunity. Discounts, on the other hand, are a mechanism for improving perceived value to potential customers. Discounts can be used tactically to achieve a number of objectives. They are particularly well suited to service providers whose products are perishable. In the case of the theatre, if the curtain goes up and a seat is not filled, the opportunity for income from that seat for that performance is lost forever. If a discount can encourage someone to take that seat, then revenue which would otherwise have been lost can be generated. Popular methods of discounting in the arts are through subscription schemes, group bookings, late availability bargains and previews.

Subscription

Subscription (discussed further in Chapter 6) works on the principle that the most difficult task for an arts organization is to make an initial contact with a potential buyer. Having made that contact, it is no more difficult to sell a package of tickets for a series of plays or concerts than it is to sell a single ticket. The cash-flow benefits of selling a series of tickets at the start of a season are quite significant but, perhaps more importantly, these schemes encourage attendance at less popular events and can dramatically improve box office takings for lesser-known performances.

Discounting is an integral part of a subscription scheme. By offering reduced price tickets for a season arts organizations are providing a financial incentive for potential audiences to commit themselves to attending early on. By attending all the performances they can save amounts of money, so the psychological attractiveness of the discounts are considerable. In practice, should subscribers fail to attend any performance in a given series, the real value of the discount is reduced. Also, if there are only one or two performances in a season which the subscriber really wants to see, he or she would undoubtedly have been better off paying full price for those particular events. This may account in part for the declining popularity of subscription schemes in UK theatre, though they remain popular with orchestras and concert halls.

Group bookings

Arts organizations frequently offer discounts for group bookings in the same way that producers of more tangible products offer discounts for bulk purchases. A theatre or concert seat has no value after the event has taken place, so the prospect of filling a large number of seats at a price which at least contributes to overheads is a very attractive one. The value of a guaranteed audience to the organization is very high, so generous discounts may be offered to groups such as social clubs and school groups. Incentives for the individuals who take responsibility for the booking of the group tickets are particularly important, as they have to invest time and effort in making the arrangements. Further discounts for members of their party will give them an incentive to bring a larger group. In order not to detract from potential full-price revenue, these discounts may apply only to certain performances.

Special promotional discounts

The concept of price bundling can be used to persuade people to buy a package of related services at the same time, for a total price which is less than their prices purchased individually. In arts marketing this often takes the form of a combined theatre/meal ticket, in a package to include overnight accommodation in a nearby hotel. This is especially attractive where groups are involved, and can offer increased promotional opportunities to the enterprising organization.

Price promotion to groups can also involve identifying a speciality interest group and trying to attract them with a specific discount. This can be particularly useful for artistic productions or exhibitions with issue-based content involving social or vocation-specific themes.

For limited seasons of mixed programme activity, cumulative discounts can be offered. These can either be based on simple ticket multiples (for example, a voucher entitling attenders at the current performance to 'two for the price of one' at the next show), or they can be based on stepped percentage discounts. An example of the latter might be a discount offering 10 per cent on tickets for two shows booked at the same time, but 15 per cent discount on tickets for three shows booked at the same time. Vouchers, a flexible if potentially complex promotional medium, can be used to good effect here to target specific market segments.

Alternatively, 'Friends' or 'Membership' schemes can be used to entitle regular attenders to buy discounted tickets on the strength of a yearly subscription. Around a quarter of organizations which run Friends schemes see the chance to ring-fence a market segment for ticket discounts as an objective of their scheme; and special ticket deals and opportunities to 'jump the queue' are key motivations for arts attenders to join Friends associations (Horan, 2001).

Late availability discounts

Given the ephemeral value of a ticket, another form of discount offered by arts organizations is the 'standby' ticket. Heavily discounted tickets may be made available hours before a performance to attract the marginal members of a potential audience who, were it not for the discounted ticket price, may be tempted to go to the cinema or the pub instead. Late availability discounts are a good mechanism for filling spare capacity and generating at least some extra revenue with few associated costs. This should be exploited systematically by linking it deliberately to access and audience development schemes. This avoids the danger that such discounts are seen as a form of dumping unsaleable product, and therefore losing their effectiveness.

Psychological pricing

Consumers' perceptions of value are not developed on entirely rational criteria. While the attributes of a product or service are major factors in evaluation, they do not fully explain price acceptability or sensitivity. A number of other pricing tactics can help to fill the gaps:

Price breaks

Consumer psychology finds that price breaks are very influential in purchase decision-making. A price of £9 is perceived to be considerably cheaper than £10, whereas there is little perceived difference between, say, £11 and £12. Tickets can be priced with this principle in mind, though the extent to which price breaks are significant is at least questionable, since most tickets are sold in multiples of at least two. The mathematics involved in calculating the final price a customer will have to pay will detract from the spontaneity of response to the psychologically acceptable price. By the time the final bill is added up the price of an individual ticket may have lost its impact.

Price/quality associations

The perceived quality of a performance is a benchmark that can be used to help set price levels; but conversely, it is important to consider the effect pricing levels may have in forming new expectations in customers. A tendency to set low prices can lead to a downward spiral in the total quality of an organization's service level, as low prices can lead to low customer expectations. So there exists here an interesting price dilemma. If an arts venue prices too high it will alienate its market by not being seen to give value for money. On the other hand, if it prices too low it may fail to attract the less price-sensitive segments of the market who equate price with quality. And for organizations in receipt of public subsidy, there is also the danger of losing funding from other sources. As we shall see, public subsidy carries with it some inherent contradictions in establishing pricing policies.

Income from other sources

There are a number of different revenue streams available to arts organizations beyond the income they generate from their own sales. In the subsidized sector of the arts a high proportion of the money comes from a diverse range of funding bodies; but businesses, individual donors and trusts and foundations also provide revenues to the sector, and marketing decisions have to be made relating to these sources of income in just the same way as to the more immediately obvious customers of arts organizations, those who buy tickets or pay for admission.

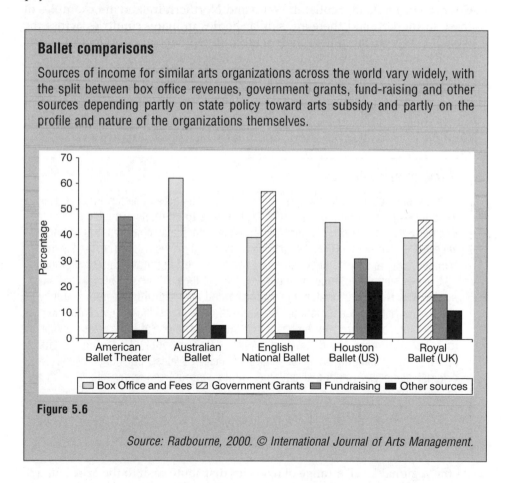

Ballet comparisons

Sources of income for similar arts organizations across the world vary widely, with the split between box office revenues, government grants, fund-raising and other sources depending partly on state policy toward arts subsidy and partly on the profile and nature of the organizations themselves.

Figure 5.6

Source: Radbourne, 2000. © International Journal of Arts Management.

Public funding

A range of public funding bodies exists to support arts activity, and arts organizations can generate income from them if their activity meets the needs of their funders. The marketing issue for an arts organization is how best to market itself to its potential funders – in other words, how best to design a programme of arts activity that satisfies the diverse criteria for allocating subsidy, and how to communicate this to the funders.

The structure of the arts funding system is prone to change with government policy changes but, as we have discussed in Chapter 1, it tends to have several strands:

- At the international level, European funding schemes offer grants to arts institutions and projects which match certain key social criteria. They may, for example, be located in areas of extreme social deprivation, or offer opportunities for collaboration between European countries.
- At the national level, central arts funding bodies tend to allocate government money which is earmarked specifically for the support of the arts. The Arts Councils of England, Scotland, Wales and Northern Ireland are examples of these in the UK, and there are similar bodies in many countries across the world. Governments themselves seldom give financial support to the arts directly, as they tend to operate on the 'arm's-length' principle, with the aim of keeping creativity and artistic interpretation at a distance from party politics. Other national funders of the arts include the Lottery distribution bodies, whose objectives are not artistic but which may fund artistic endeavour if it meets their funding criteria. The Heritage Lottery Fund, for example, will fund the preservation of historic buildings which house arts activity.

A row at arm's length

A high profile row blew up in Wales when Finance Minister Edwina Hart announced that an annual grant of £150 000 was to be made available to fund a Swansea-based chamber orchestra for Wales, to make chamber music more accessible to communities. Allegations of favouritism were flung at the Finance Minister, whose constituency bordered Swansea, and the move was condemned by the arts sector and opposition parties alike, as the cash was to be granted, not by the Arts Council of Wales, the body charged with distributing public money, but by the National Assembly for Wales itself. The grant decision was defended by the Culture Minister on the basis that the Government of Wales Act provides that 'The Assembly may do anything appropriate to support . . . the arts, crafts, sport or other cultural or recreational activities in Wales'; but nonetheless, the original plans were changed and the money was subsequently allocated to a range of projects.

Sources: ArtsProfessional, 2002a; 2002b.

- At the regional level, a range of agencies distribute cash to the arts. Some of these, such as the former English Regional Arts Boards, are exclusively arts funders; but other money is made available by agencies with a wider remit, such as cultural development agencies, regeneration agencies and health authorities.

● At the local level, most local authorities fund arts activity either through direct provision of venues and facilities, or through grant schemes. Local education authorities may also provide some funding for certain types of arts activity. The amount allocated to arts activity will vary tremendously from region to region, as will the criteria for making grants. Local government arts policies vary according both to party politics and to the importance placed locally on arts provision in relation to other leisure funding, such as sport.

Arts practitioners tend to seek out funding from multiple sources to maximize their incomes, but applications to public funding bodies present a series of dilemmas to a marketing department. The price finally paid by a funder (i.e. the grant it gives) in support of arts activity is often negotiable: the arts organization may put in an application for funding to the value of, say, £100 000, but the funder will only allocate £75 000. This may be due to competition from other arts organizations which, where grants are concerned, can be a serious threat because funders can draw comparisons between a range of arts organizations and fund only those that appear to best meet their own funding objectives. Furthermore, an arts organization might become highly effective at marketing to audiences, visitors or attenders and, if evaluated on the basis of performance indicators such as ability to earn income, subsidy per seat and average attendance levels, will be found to be very successful. On the other hand, prices that are so high as to restrict access, and programming decisions that consistently favour a more popular product to a more innovatory one, may jeopardize subsidy, and in practice the ability to generate income from sources other than the public purse can, in a climate of public spending cuts and restricted funds, lead to a cut in subsidy. An arts organization can become a victim of its own marketing success. Indeed, it can also suffer if it becomes more successful at attracting grants from one particular funding body, so that others believe that the levels of grant they have previously allocated are no longer required to ensure the continuation of the arts provision.

Tipping the balance

The relationship between pricing, subsidy and corporate support is a delicate balance. The Royal Opera House (ROH) was subject to much criticism when its prices virtually doubled over a ten-year period in the 1990s. Despite this, demand for tickets remained roughly stable, and accusations of elitism were flung at ROH, which argued that, as production costs had risen and subsidy had fallen as a proportion of income, more reliance than ever had to be placed on attracting sponsorship and audiences which could afford high ticket prices. Objectors said that the price rises created huge barriers to attending for less well-off. More subsidy was provided so that prices could be reduced (£200 top-price seats were reduced to £150) and, supposedly, less well-off people could afford to attend. But commentators were unconvinced that the increased subsidy would do much to open up the world of opera to the masses. They argue that opera auditoria are not

> big enough and opera programming not flexible enough to turn a popular performance into a smash hit, and see broadcasting as the only way by which a significant increase in access to opera can be achieved.
>
> *Source: Towse, 2001.*

The multiple grant applicant also faces the possibility that the grant being targeted is simply not worth the time or resources involved. Applying for grant funding is costly, time-consuming, and can mean that arts organizations take their eyes off the main ball – creating and presenting artistic work. There is always a danger that an organization's policies may begin to be dictated by current funding priorities rather than by its own vision, a sure recipe for eventual disaster.

Trusts and foundations

An important source of unearned income can be found in charitable trusts. The criteria for eligibility for funding are usually clearly laid out in the objectives of the trust, as are the means of application and the timescale for allocation of funds. The particular trust concerned should be researched thoroughly so that the most appropriate application can be made (see Table 5.3). As with all funders, care should be taken to maintain the relationship, particularly by

Table 5.3 Tips for applying to a trust

- Keep your letter clear and concise.
- Describe clearly the cause and the needs which will be met – the people who will benefit from your work, how many and for how long. Pull at heart strings rather than offer a description of your organization.
- Show a conviction about the importance of your work.
- Show that there is something innovative about your work.
- Remember to state the obvious: what your organization does, who the cheque should be made payable to, what the grant is for and how much you are asking for.
- Pitch the size of your grant request to suit each trust (some trusts for example will never be able to make grants of over £500).
- Show that you are responsible and reliable and have thought things through: describe the relevant experience of staff who will work on the project for which you are seeking funds, state what you will do when funding runs out, talk about how you will monitor the work.
- If you want the trust to fund a piece of work which will continue after its grant has run out, try to show how the work will then be funded.
- Maintain contact with the trust during the course of an application. Inform them of any successes, invite them to functions, send newsletters and so on.

Source: Harland, 2000.

supplying information about the progression of the project and the longer-term benefits gained from the funding investment.

The trust sector tends to avoid supporting ongoing activity, preferring a pump-priming approach that gives start-up funding to activities capable of eventually generating sufficient revenue to become self-supporting. There is also a resistance to providing funding to make good a shortfall from the public purse. Successful applicants to trusts will be those who take care to satisfy the trust's own needs in awarding funds.

Individual donations

For UK-based non-arts charities, the majority of income comes from individual donors, and individuals are enormously important to arts funding in North America, where a strong culture of philanthropic giving is backed up by favourable tax policies. The same cannot be said of the UK arts sector. Although there are some good examples of fund-raising campaigns which have generated revenue streams from individual donors, such campaigns must be well-orchestrated as they tend to be costly to set up and administer.

Case 5.4 A very public appeal

The Hallé Orchestra, the UK's oldest professional symphony orchestra, is resident at The Bridgewater Hall, Manchester's newest concert venue. Like all orchestras in the UK it has suffered from a steady erosion of public funding over the last ten years and early in 1998 matters came to a head when a deficit of £3 million made bankruptcy a serious possibility.

An emergency meeting with funders and bankers led to redundancies in the administration staff and cutbacks elsewhere but Manchester City Council and the Arts Council of England, the orchestra's main funders, agreed not to pull the plug if the Hallé could raise £1.5 million in that financial year. So, the Hallé Appeal, which was launched immediately, was a matter of life or death for the orchestra.

The Hallé already had excellent sponsorship relationships with businesses throughout the North West of England, but businesses could not be relied upon to make up the shortfall as this appeal had to raise extra income – it would be no good getting a company donation instead of an existing sponsorship. This left the Hallé relying on a public appeal for most of the money it needed.

Through a fund-raising campaign managed by The Phone Room, over 30 000 people were contacted on behalf of the Hallé using telephone and direct mail, and the appeal received extensive coverage in the local media. The Hallé Development Department concentrated on its existing corporate and foundation contacts. Over £1.5 million was raised and the appeal secured the orchestra's immediate future.

Source: Salmon, 2002.

Individuals may be a more attractive source of support to many arts organizations than either statutory bodies or trusts, because their support is not tied to policy imperatives. They are particularly valuable for capital fund-raising projects, which many trusts and foundations do not fund. Public funders of building work often require matching funding to be found by an arts organization to minimize the pay-out from the public purse and demonstrate the organization's commitment to a project, and recognized giving schemes, such as individual seat covenants, can prove very successful when there is either a building project or a major refurbishment to catch the imagination. Other schemes, such as payroll giving, are proving a lot less popular with individual donors than had originally been envisaged.

One of the most fruitful sources of individual donations can be an arts organization's Friends scheme. Those who join such schemes tend to do so for one of two reasons: either for the benefits they can gain from specials deals and opportunities offered exclusively to those who join the Friends; or to demonstrate active support for the organization and its work. It is this latter group which tends to provide the very fertile ground for donor fund-raising.

Nudes and prudes

Although London's Tate galleries normally top the corporate sponsorship wish-list because of the high profile they offer backers, not a single company came forward to support 'Exposed: The Victorian Nude', the flagship exhibition for the relaunch of Tate Britain. The exhibition, featuring saucy postcards and the naughty, early films made by the Victorians, was felt too risqué by British businesses, which didn't want to want to risk an association with lots of naked bodies. The exhibition was mounted instead with financial support from the 'Friends of the Tate'.

Source: Thorpe, 2001.

Corporate support

Partnership between the public and private sector, to the mutual benefit of both parties, has been a keynote in central government policy in Britain since the mid-1980s. In the arts sector, this has led to some very fruitful relationships, generating benefits that extend far beyond the financial returns; but it can also lead to financial disaster for arts organizations that are overconfident in the targets they set for income generation from businesses. Nevertheless, corporate support is a growing source of arts funding. It takes several forms, including donations, corporate entertainment and in-company training, though the most significant of these is undoubtedly sponsorship.

Sponsorship

Sponsorship occurs when a company provides funds to support a particular arts activity, and in return wants to gain benefits, usually in the form of publicity among its target markets or its stakeholders. This is a straightforward exchange of benefits. The sponsorship money will normally come either out of a company's marketing budget, or from funds it sets aside for community involvement, and the sponsor is likely to want to raise the profile of its company, or its services or products through the arts event. A close connection between the nature of the arts event and the aims of the company is usually vital, but this is not always obvious. Cider-maker H.P. Bulmer, for example, is contacted as a matter of routine every time a regional repertory theatre mounts a production of Laurie Lee's *Cider with Rosie*. The company explains patiently that it positions its cider brands as contemporary beverages, so the nostalgic atmosphere of the play would be entirely unsuitable.

Price can be a key factor in achieving appropriate sponsorship, and setting a price for a sponsorship opportunity is a notoriously difficult exercise. The price/quality/value equation is critical. Sponsorship usually represents a desire on the part of the sponsor to gain value by association with an activity or organization that is perceived as enjoyable, of cultural merit and highly visible. Therefore, if an arts organization prices itself too low, the sponsor will value it accordingly. The association will not feel like a premium product. To ensure that all types of businesses can find a form of sponsorship appropriate both to their objectives and to their budgets, some arts organizations develop 'menus' of opportunities, which might include sponsorship of:

- a building project
- a series or productions or exhibitions
- an individual production or exhibition
- a single night
- an educational project
- a foyer or interval event

Because a number of entry points are offered, each with its specific benefit levels, companies of various sizes can be matched with an appropriate level of sponsorship.

As with all customers, relationships with sponsors should be seen as long term. Research shows that sponsors themselves value relationships over a period longer than that covered by the immediate sponsorship activity. This can be demonstrated by the willingness of many corporate sponsors to trade up or down in their activity in subsequent periods, for example by taking out corporate membership of an arts organization after a successful production sponsorship. Often the sponsorship will be the brainchild of a particular enthusiast within the company, and he or she should gain personal satisfaction from being associated with a successful initiative. Such opinion leaders may advocate the arts organization not only in their employing organizations but also in their own professional or social networks.

As well as being clear about the sponsorship opportunity being offered, it is important to be clear about the benefits that a sponsor is seeking, and see to it that it receives them. The arts organization should ensure that:

- unreal expectations (on, for example, the level of likely press coverage of an event) are flushed out before rather than after the event

- all activity associated with the sponsorship should be of high quality, including catering, printed material and media activity
- senior personnel are in contact with the sponsor throughout
- 'positive stroking', both during and after the sponsorship, is maintained through a systematic process of evaluation and review. Regular contacts can take the shape of a sponsors' newsletter, press releases, and occasional invitations to new events

In a highly sponsored arts organization a variety of different companies can be involved in support of the same event. There may, for example, be a one-night sponsorship during the run of a sponsored concert series. The management concerned, using their knowledge of local competition, can address possible conflicts of interest before they arise. Just as the rules of television airtime sales prevent 'break sharing' (so that two beer brands, for example, could not appear in the same commercial break), so too an arts organization can adopt a policy of not allowing sponsorship by competing organizations, such as two national accountancy firms. When such conflicts of interest arise, an understanding of the different needs of each business can help the arts organization negotiate sponsors into a position where they are prepared to co-operate. If, for example, a concert series sponsor is seeking widespread publicity for a product or service by associating its name and logo with all printed materials and posters throughout the season, but a one-night sponsor mainly wishes to host a prestigious evening for key clients, it should be possible to compromise sufficiently to satisfy both sets of objectives. The series sponsor could decide not to take up seats on the night concerned. Equally, the one-night sponsor could agree to confine publicity requirements to a programme overwrap on the night, and a temporary foyer display about their firm.

Sponsors prefer London

Nearly half of all arts sponsorship in the UK is allocated to London-based activity and institutions. Sixteen of the 23 organizations that raised £1 million or more from business in 1999 were London-based, and the richest 3 per cent of organizations – all of which employ teams of full-time fund-raisers – took more than half of all business sponsorship. Northern Ireland and the north did worst, netting barely £2.5 million between them of the £141 million spent on UK arts sponsorship.

Source: Gibbons, 2000.

Sponsorship in kind

Although sponsorship deals often involve cash, it can be easier to attract sponsorship in kind; in other words, the supply of a product that the arts organization wishes to acquire free of charge, or at a considerably reduced rate. This is more likely to be successful if it is a product that is not usually in demand in the charities sector. It is very difficult to get computers, for example, but would be relatively easy to get trees from a nursery to landscape the venue. So, too, will it be hard to get sponsorship in kind if the arts organization is a primary customer of the sponsoring company (such as theatres for lighting equipment manufacturers) unless it is perceived as a loss-leader as a prelude to a long-term relationship as supplier. The benefit for the sponsor is that the cost of the sponsorship is limited to the cost of the goods. The benefit for the arts organization is the saving on the full price of the equipment.

Employee involvement

One of the hidden benefits of sponsorship is the opportunity it offers for new audience development. A big local corporate sponsor will employ a large number of people living in the local community, who form the potential audience of the arts organization for much of its activity. To generate enthusiasm among sponsors' staff, marketing activities can be specifically targeted at them, including:

- special prices for employees
- a special staff evening, with special activities
- visits to the workplace by actors
- tours of the theatre
- attendance at an open rehearsal

A final note of care needs to be sounded. Many of the people who work in arts organizations have a very different perspective from their counterparts in commercial life. This needs to be recognized at a basic level in the soliciting and servicing of sponsors. The board of governors and staff in an arts organization need to be happy about owning the sponsorship, and there are certain areas of business (tobacco, pharmaceuticals, companies with ethically dubious investments, nuclear power, for example) which may cause difficulties here. Ironically, it is often such companies who are in greatest need of the sort of responsible image which sponsorship can provide. Both sides of the exchange need to be comfortable with the transaction for it to be a success, as in any form of marketing process. If not, the whole arrangement becomes enormously vulnerable, and potentially counter-productive.

Corporate entertainment

Another way in which companies can support arts organizations is by membership of a corporate entertainment scheme. A premium price is paid for a personalized service that might include use of a private bar, priority booking and a free programme. The money paid for this type of activity will usually come out of a business's hospitality budget, and the company will demand a high quality service to impress visiting dignitaries, woo potential customers or show an important supplier how they are valued. Some arts organizations provide different levels of corporate membership, a neat example of segmentation, although in some cases it is hard to distinguish between the benefits offered.

Summary

In this chapter we have considered the main areas where the concept of price is relevant to marketing the arts. Pricing services is difficult; even the apparent simplicity of a cost-plus approach is challenged by the sheer complexity of calculating what the arts actually cost to produce. Not only is accurate costing a problematical issue in the arts, but the other two traditional influences on price setting (competition and market demand) are also atypical in this environment.

Furthermore, the arts have all the usual service-related problems of transience rather than permanence, the need for delivery in person in a specific location, and the subjective values different consumers will recognize in them. Because of the many non-financial costs that customers incur in attending an arts event (difficulty of access, availability of free time, venue comfort) it could be argued that many of the significant pricing issues involved in ticket buying have more to do with product, promotion and place than with price as traditionally understood in marketing terms.

But at the heart of these transactions, as in all marketing processes, is a relationship between buyer and seller which needs to be long term if it is to be successful at all. This is most obviously true in the third area where pricing takes precedence, the long-term relationship which arts bodies need to forge with their funders, be they from the private or public sectors. The mutual benefits involved must be carefully considered, and their longevity guaranteed by a genuine attempt by the arts enterprise to identify, anticipate and satisfy its organizational customers' wants and needs in a way which ensures its own success.

Key concepts

break-even analysis
competition
concessions
discounts
cost-based pricing
demand-based pricing
donations

elasticity of demand
financial returns
market position
price differentiation
price structures
psychological pricing
sponsorship

Discussion questions

1 What are the factors that might influence a customer's perceptions of the value for money offered by a recent visit to the theatre?
2 The director of a community play wishes all tickets to be free. Put the case for a change in policy, and identify the factors to be taken into account in setting the level of prices.

3 Imagine you are the director of an annual puppet festival. List the possible sources of income that you could pursue to generate revenues for your event, including the potential sponsors you might like to approach.
4 How can you evaluate the success of a pricing strategy?
5 How should a gallery determine the most appropriate price levels to set for admission to its special exhibitions?

Case study: Jumping the Q

The first season following the appointment of Artistic Director Bob Carlton at the Queen's Theatre Hornchurch was a critical success. The local press came, saw and praised, and the audiences enjoyed the productions. But there were too few of them to achieve a critical mass, to spread the word. The Queen's audiences had dwindled from 50 per cent in spring 1997 to 25 per cent in spring 1998 and accompanying this was a cumulative deficit of over £250 000.

It was clear that the Queen's had to find a new way to publicize its new and improved wares. To achieve this, a subscription scheme known as 'Jump the Q' (JTQ), was designed to bring in more people, and hopefully, as a by-product, to generate more income. The basic idea was that you could sit anywhere in the house, any night of the week, any show in the season, for just £5 a ticket. The scheme was trialled at the theatre for a month to estimate the audience's response. The previous season's subscriber scheme – a standard two level, two price band deal offering up to 20 per cent savings – had achieved 275 sales. In four weeks the new scheme doubled this number. So the campaign was rolled out with a new piece of print, which was simple and bold, well designed but not showy. The name – Jump the Q – was a clear concept. You could see it and recognize it from across a room, and it went straight to the point – this is a good deal: do not miss it.

The 1998 autumn season attracted 4605 subscribers. Over 40 per cent of seats were sold in advance and 1000 new attenders booked. The theatre achieved an average capacity of 75 per cent across the season.

The following season, the concept of JTQ was extended further. The theatre was in the process of rebuilding its audience's trust and, after years of free ticket offers and substandard work, was presenting a deal which was honest and value for money because what was onstage was good, so it was predicted that 80 per cent of subscribers would renew. No restrictions to the scheme or price changes were imposed, and the number of subscriptions available continued being unlimited. A JTQ2 flyer was printed for general distribution and direct mailing, and an advance newsletter produced offering priority booking to current subscribers. JTQ2 was also marketed as a Christmas present (for which there was a good response).

In total 6156 people subscribed to JTQ2: an increase of 28 per cent from JTQ1. In capacity terms for the spring season, this meant that, two weeks before the season had even opened, each show had booked an average of 61 per cent across each run.

Ninety-two per cent of JTQ2 subscribers were those who had renewed their subscriptions from the previous season. Seventy-seven per cent lived locally, within a 20 miles radius of the venue, and the average number of season tickets purchased per transaction was two. The Queen's achieved 89 per cent capacity, compared to 75 per cent the previous season and 35 per cent the season before that.

When planning began for JTQ3, there were several issues to addressed. Although capacity was exceptionally high, box office income needed to increase to meet revenue targets. Due to the success of JTQ2, the Queen's was increasingly turning away potential full-price ticket bookers on a Friday and Saturday night, because it was sold out with £5 seats, and from a financial point of view it became apparent that JTQ3 had to be limited in some way to avoid being a victim of its own success.

If JTQ was to grow at the rate it had previously, then realistically a heavily-discounted subscriber base of possibly 7500 could be expected the following season which, for a theatre that had to earn 75 per cent of its income, was not financially viable. Options considered were

- holding seats back on peak nights to allow for full-price ticket sales
- introducing supplements for peak-night seats
- increasing the price of JTQ subscriptions
- restricting the booking period
- limiting the number of JTQ3 subscriptions to be sold

To find out what subscribers thought, a series of focus groups were held with both first- and second-time subscribers, to ask them what they thought about JTQ and present suggestions for change.

The research concluded that JTQ was felt to offer excellent value for money. Although there would be some plays in a season that an attender would not be keen on, the low price was found to be a real incentive which encouraged people to take a risk. The simplicity and low price of scheme reduced the intimidation factor massively. One said 'If I don't like it, I leave at the interval: it's only a fiver, anyway.' Another commented 'I wouldn't be here tonight if I hadn't booked this 3 months ago. I'm missing West Ham live on the telly!' It appeared that most people would happily pay up to £7 a ticket, but if prices rose any higher, they would be selective. There was general dislike for the concept of supplements for peak nights of the week, as the scheme would become too complicated.

Questions

1 What might be the impact of each of the proposed options for JTQ3?
2 What other opportunities and threats might arise from the success of the scheme?
3 Devise a marketing strategy for JTQ3, including a pricing structure and a promotional plan.

Source: Duckworth and Wallis, 1999.

References

ArtsProfessional (2002a) 'Assembly faces grants storm', *ArtsProfessional*, 22, 25 March.

ArtsProfessional (2002b) 'Minister on ropes over orchestra grant', *ArtsProfessional*, Issue 23, 8 April.

Boardman, J. (1978) 'Pricing and concessions'. In *The CORT Marketing Manual (Volume 2)* (G.V. Robbins and P. Verwey, eds). TMA/CORT/ATPM with assistance from the Arts Council of Great Britain.

Colbert, F. (1998) 'The importance of ticket prices for theatre patrons', *International Journal of Arts Management*, Vol. 1, No. 1, Fall.

Davidson, H. (1984) *Offensive Marketing*. Penguin.

Department for Culture, Media and Sport (2002) 'Free admission to museums "a spectacular success" says Tessa Jowell', press release, 7 January.

Diggle, K. (1984) *Guide to Arts Marketing*, 2nd ed. Rhinegold.

Duckworth, H. and Wallis, E. (1999) 'Jumping the Q: A tale of subscription', Healthy, Wealthy and Wise: Arts Marketing Association Conference, Cardiff, July.

Eyre, Richard (1998) *The Future of Lyric Theatre in London*. House of Commons.

Gibbons, F. (2000) 'Regions lose out in art's dash for cash', *Guardian*, 18 January.

Glasgow Caledonian University (1998) *To Charge or Not to Charge*. Museums and Galleries Commission.

Harland, S. (2000) 'A trusting hand', *ArtsBusiness*, Issue 58, 11 September.

Hermann, A., Franken, B., Huber, F., Ohlwien, M. and Schellhase, R. (1999) 'The Conjoint Analysis as an instrument for marketing controlling, taking a public theatre as an example', *International Journal of Arts Management*, Vol. 1, No. 3, Spring, 59–69.

Higgins, C. (2001) 'Why is opera so expensive?', *Guardian*, 29 November.

Horan, K. (2001) 'Knowing who your friends are', *ArtsProfessional*, Issue 15, 3 December.

Huntingdon, P. (1993) 'Ticket pricing policy and box office revenue', *Journal of Cultural Economics*, Vol. 17, No. 1, 71–87.

Jamieson, B. (1999) 'The power of pricing', Healthy, Wealthy and Wise: Arts Marketing Association Conference, Cardiff, July.

Marplan (1988) *Pricing at Arts Centres in Wales Report 1988*. Marplan Ltd, 45 Goswell Road, London EC1V 7DN.

Millward Brown (1990) *Pricing in the Arts*. Millward Brown International, Olympus Avenue, Tachbrook Park, Warwick, Warwickshire CV34 6RJ.

Radbourne, J. (2000) 'The Australian ballet – a spirit of its own', *International Journal of Arts Management*, Vol. 2, No. 3, Spring, 62–9.

Roberts, A. (1998) 'Test drive the arts', Building the Future: Arts Marketing Association Conference, July.

Salmon, A. (2002) The Phone Room, tel: 01865 324000.

Scheff, J. (1999) 'Factors influencing subscription and single-ticket purchases at performing arts organizations', *International Journal of Arts Management*, Vol. 1, No. 2, Winter, 16–27.

Thorpe, V. (2001) 'Tate nudes scare away the sponsors', *Observer*, 5 August.

Towse, R. (2001) 'The case of the Royal Opera House, Covent Garden', *International Journal of Arts Management*, Vol. 3, No. 3, Spring, 38–50.

6

Promotion

Promotion is the element of the marketing mix that communicates the benefits of what is on offer to the target audience. By its very nature it is the most visible aspect of marketing activity. It plays an extremely important part in arts marketing strategy, especially where the aim is to reach not only existing arts customers, but also to arouse the interest of new audiences. The costs of such activity need to be carefully weighed. Arts marketing presents them in an especially problematic way because of its frequently 'missionary' intentions on invariably slender resources.

This chapter will look at the following issues in relation to arts organizations:

- promotion in the marketing mix
- advertising
- public relations
- sales promotion
- print
- direct marketing
- e-marketing

Promotion in the marketing mix

Because of its visibility, it is tempting to confuse promotion with marketing itself. Artistic directors and board members without a marketing background can fall into this trap. However, promotion is not some kind of veneer, the application of which to an existing offering can automatically generate high attendances. It can only work as part of a successful marketing mix. If the price is too high, or the product is unattractive, irrelevant or inaccessible, no amount of clever promotion will guarantee success. On the other hand, if promotion is not carefully planned and executed the product will not reach as many customers as it ought. While it is an area that demands flair and imagination, it also demands clear thinking and a highly disciplined approach.

Ads miss the mark

Promotion for arts events often fails to enthuse young people. Comparing theatre advertising with film posters, a 15-year-old boy felt that the theatres did not adequately convey the content of their events, and he felt that arts organizations failed with their media relations. The high profile of films in TV trailers and coverage in youth magazines meant that young people would generally have a good idea of what they were going to see before they got there, and '. . . you're not going to go and watch something that you don't know what it's going to be like'.

Source: Harland and Kinder, 1999.

Most marketing theorists talk about promotion by subdividing it into four main areas of technique: advertising, public relations, sales promotion and personal selling. Some add 'direct marketing' as a fifth element, and it is appropriate that arts marketers adopt this extra element because of the fundamental importance of developing long-term relationships with their customers. Furthermore, as many arts organizations are fortunate enough to possess box office data which provide a wealth of personal details about their attenders, the use of direct marketing techniques can be both straightforward and very effective.

Different industries tend to use different combinations of techniques in their promotional strategies. For example, infrequently-purchased but expensive items like life insurance and holidays have traditionally relied heavily on personal selling, whereas frequently-purchased goods like soap powder or baked beans have tended to rely on advertising and sales promotion. The arts, too, have historically adopted a typical industry mix of promotional activity, tending to rely heavily on public relations and a wide distribution of printed material, including direct mail, supplemented by low-cost advertising and an element of sales promotion. In the UK arts organizations have been slow to embrace personal selling, although a proactive stance in the box office can both improve income and raise levels of customer satisfaction by improving service.

The emphasis on public relations is understandable because of the intrinsic news interest of the arts. Arts events and activities tend to involve 'firsts' of various sorts, and the news media have an insatiable thirst for novelty. Artists and actors are people in the public eye. They make good copy. Furthermore, media critics can be important influencers over a very wide potential audience. Their accolades play a valuable role in attracting people to events in which they might not otherwise have shown any interest. Another reason for the popularity of PR is its perceived value for money. Although larger arts organizations may appoint PR agencies to work on their behalf, for those with smaller promotional budgets costs can be largely internalized if PR activities are initiated in-house.

Advertising, on the other hand, is an extremely expensive business. Its use by arts organizations tends to concentrate on the minimum level of exposure deemed necessary for the purposes of information. However, when used in the right context, advertising can offer significant image benefits, particularly for art forms with a strong visual appeal. Although there is a variety of media in which advertising can be placed, the most popular ones for the arts tend to be print and poster advertising.

Sales promotion activity is designed to increase the amount or speed involved in a transaction. It interfaces with pricing tactics (see Chapter 5) when it offers multiple attendance at a discount through subscription, for example. There is a tendency to regard sales promotion as short term and shrill, but it can be used effectively across a wide range of demographic segments.

Although usually considered to be a 'promotional' technique, direct marketing is in reality much broader, referring to a group of techniques which help organizations create and sustain direct relationship with their customers on a one-to-one basis. The associated philosophy of 'relationship marketing' (see Chapter 1) sees the customer as an appreciating asset with whom the organization has a mutually beneficial connection, or relationship, over a lengthy period of time. This outlook has much to offer arts organizations in terms of developing the tastes of their customers. Because of the uniquely collaborative nature of the arts transaction (see Chapter 4), a continuing and developing relationship with customers is central to the success of arts marketing.

Just as the marketing mix offered by an arts organization needs to be regularly reviewed (because the external environment is always changing), so its promotional mix needs to be constantly checked for its relevance to the audience. The pattern is too often dictated by precedent. There are a number of reasons for this: time, lack of imagination or insufficient experience. Sometimes existing patterns of promotion can be reinforced by arrangements such as standard clauses in contracts between touring companies and managements which will specify responsibility for the cost of printed publicity without questioning whether this is the most appropriate promotional tool in each case. The importance of keeping the balance of promotional activity constantly under review has been drawn into sharp focus by the ever-increasing speed of adoption of new media by the public. Domestic access to e-mail, the internet, mobile-phone technology and digital media continues to grow apace, and arts marketing budgets are now having to embrace the possibilities created by this. SMS text messaging, e-flyers, interactive websites and CD samplers are all promotional techniques that did not exist ten years ago, but now look set to replace – to some extent at least – the techniques on which arts marketers have relied for the last 20 years.

It is important, then, to be prepared to think laterally when planning promotional activity. If, as suggested by advertising research, one of the ways in which marketing communication registers with its recipients is through 'salience' (that is, standing out from the background) then it makes sense to look for different and fresh ways of getting the message across (McDonald, 1992). Placing a new angle on a press story from a theatre or gallery can mean that, instead of being lost on the arts pages, the item may appear in an unusual editorial environment such as the women's page or the sports section. Here it will be seen by a wider audience. Readers who can be counted among existing attenders will see it in a new light. As with public relations, so with advertising. It is worth thinking about different media, or new uses of existing media, in order to reach your audience in as effective and impactful a way as possible.

Planning promotional activity

The three main influences on the shape of a successful promotional mix are:

- the nature of the audience
- the nature of the message
- the size of budget available

The nature of the audience is the most fundamental of these three factors. All effective communication involves speaking the audience's language, not only in the messages sent but how they are conveyed. But managing this without preconceptions can be a difficult process. Research and careful observation are important in order to safeguard your approach. One of the signs of an organization's successful espousal of marketing is the consideration of the customer in each decision. Promotional decisions are particularly important in this respect.

The nature of the message content can also have an important effect on choosing the means for its delivery. In order to communicate the important details about prices, performance times, telephone numbers, and access details, controllable techniques such as advertising, print/websites and e-mailing are appropriate. Public relations can deal with softer information such as personalities or atmosphere.

Promotion is a cost, so the limits imposed by the promotional budget will be a guiding factor as well. Even in profit-driven marketing there is never enough money to mount the ideal campaign. But sometimes resources can be stretched through negotiation, co-operation or collaboration. The role of marketing consortia in planning and executing joint promotional activity (for example, inserting a joint season leaflet in a regional colour supplement on behalf of a group of regional theatres) can make available to arts organizations working together what would be impossible to them on an individual basis.

Budgeting for promotion

How much money should be spent on promotional activity is a hotly-debated issue in any organization. Understandably, the excellence of the artistic product itself will have first call on the scarce resources of arts organizations. Yet, to ensure the success of the product, the marketing department has to be able to justify its claim to an adequate budget. Competing for promotional funds in an atmosphere where marketing itself may be misunderstood or distrusted (see Chapter 1) requires very careful argument and planning:

- *Competitive parity*
  What do other organizations of a similar size and turnover spend? Funding bodies, annual reports and informal contacts with colleagues in other companies can help build a picture of the industry average. Statistics need to be compared on a like-with-like basis (e.g. are salaries included in the figure, or is it a spending-only figure?). Although there are differences between the environments and tasks of different organizations, any large discrepancies may signal the need to question the size (or lack of size) of the budget.
- *Percentage of sales*
  This is another simple, but reductive, technique. Like 'competitive parity' it assumes that there should be an industry average governing the relationship between how much money an organization spends on advertising and promotion, and how much it receives from customers. In most industries the relationship is a stable one, expressed as the advertising-to-sales ratio. Advertising Association figures reveal that 13 per cent of the price of a typical bottle of shampoo goes on advertising, as compared to 8 per cent for coffee and less than 0.5 per cent for petrol (White, 1993). The more important that promotion is in building imagery and communicating benefits to a wide range of audiences, the higher the advertising-to-sales ratio is likely to be. In this sense, the arts resemble shampoo more than petrol. Research suggests that advertising-to-sales ratios for most theatres, for example, are in the region of 12–15 per cent.
- *Objective and task*
  This is the most rational method of budget setting, and (predictably) the most popular with marketing theorists. It operates on the principle that you should first decide what you want to do (the objective) and then cost the necessary action (the task). So, if part of the promotional plan involves reaching 80 000 homes in a particular geodemographic category (see Chapter 2) with a leaflet distribution, then the cost of this will represent an item in the budget. The problem with this technique is that the promotional shopping list can soon exceed the availability of funds. Priorities need to be established, and comprehensive costings should include an allowance for contingency and tactical flexibility.

None of these techniques used on their own offer a watertight solution to the problem of establishing an infallible figure. But used together they can give the marketing department invaluable arguments for defending or developing the promotional budget. It should include not only how much money should be spent on getting the message across in various media like press advertising or mailing, but also how much should be spent on designing and printing the materials themselves: the production figure. Expenditure on the effective delivery of a promotional strategy needs to be planned and controlled like any other form of marketing activity. The techniques outlined in Chapter 9 are particularly relevant to promotion in this respect.

Advertising

Advertising can be defined as paid-for media exposure to inform and/or persuade potential (and existing) customers of the benefits of your offering. The difference between 'inform' and 'persuade' here is an important one. As with the nature of promotion itself, mentioned earlier in this chapter, there is often misunderstanding in the minds of non-marketing managers about how persuasive advertising is. The research suggests that attitude changes as a result of advertising are slight and take effect only in the long term. Nevertheless, the advertising industry has developed a terminology of its own which talks in terms of 'impacts' and 'impressions', as if consumers were easily manipulated into purchase (see Table 6.1).

Providing information about products and services towards which customers are already reasonably well disposed is a far more common function for most forms of advertising. An effective advertisement helps your customer decide in your favour by stressing the advantages of choosing your offering over the alternatives. The lesson to be learnt here by arts marketers is to keep their advertising simple and relevant to the product, and to make sure it is effectively targeted. This applies to writing copy for brochures and leaflets as much as it does to the requirements of mailshots, press or poster advertising.

Media research

Concepts like frequency and coverage are not just abstract ideas. British media research is among the best in the world. Television advertising, for example, relies upon a sophisticated ongoing survey of over 5000 'typical' homes each providing electronically captured viewing data on a daily basis. The resulting information, collected on behalf of the Broadcasters Audience Research Board (BARB), is the currency by which television advertising is traded. Newspaper and magazine readership is calculated by means of the National Readership Survey (NRS) which is one of the longest-established random-sample surveys in the UK. A total of 35 000 respondents are interviewed every year to find out which newspapers or magazines they read. The socio-economic classification of consumers into As, Bs, C1s, C2s etc. (as discussed in Chapter 2) was originally devised by the NRS but has been adopted throughout marketing thinking in the UK.

As we have seen in Chapter 2, consumers' usage of products and services is recorded by a regular survey called the Target Group Index (TGI). It also covers their media usage habits, and (since the late 1980s) their attendance at arts events. This information can be cross-referenced – revealing, for example, that readers of *The Observer* have a higher predisposition to go to the theatre than readers of any other Sunday newspaper. Such surveys can be of great benefit in planning advertising, or even when targeting publications with editorial

Table 6.1 Advertising-speak

Advertising, like any other specialist activity, uses terminology which can bemuse the uninitiated. The jargon conceals what are, invariably, very simple ideas. Here are some particularly useful ones when thinking about the whole area of promotional planning in the arts:

cost per thousand	The cost of reaching 1000 members of your target audience in a particular medium. Although it is a useful statistic when comparing like with like (for example, two free newspapers in a specific circulation area) it is not very helpful in making comparisons between media. For example, the cost per thousand for a poster is many times less than for a television spot but the two forms of communication are very different.
coverage	The number of people which an advertisement or campaign reaches at least once. Within this number (usually expressed as a percentage of the target audience) many will have seen the advertisement more than once in the course of the campaign).
frequency	The number of times an advertisement is seen. Received advertising wisdom is that most advertisements need to be seen more than once in order to communicate effectively. The precise number of times ('effective frequency') will differ from case to case. Exceeding it can be wasteful.
opportunities to see ('OTS')	A similar idea to 'frequency' but used when planning or evaluating advertising to specify the average number of times each member of the audience is exposed to the advertising.
circulation	The number of copies of a publication sold.
rating point	One per cent of the targeted audience viewing or hearing your television or radio advertisement. Called 'gross rating points' because the calculation makes no allowance for the number of times any individual has seen or heard the advertisement. A similar calculation to 'man hours'.
readership	The number of people who read a publication. This varies with the title: it may be from two to four per copy. Total readership rather than circulation is used as the basis of cost per thousand calculations in press advertising.

matter as part of an organization's PR effort. All of these information sources are examples of the kind of secondary research discussed in Chapter 3.

Not every publication is included in the NRS. Many local papers, particularly free newspapers, provide a different statistic for their advertisers – Audit Bureau of Circulation figures (ABC for short) and Verified Free Distribution (VFD). These figures are not the same as readership, and may overstate the actual numbers of papers which reach the consumer (as opposed to reaching newsagents or distributors). But they offer some kind of yardstick of value when comparing rival promotional opportunities.

Two valuable acronyms: AIDA and USP

Simplicity is the key to effective communication. It can be encouraged by the use of two very straightforward templates in the creation of advertising and other promotional activity: AIDA and USP.

The first, AIDA, is attributed to the American advertising guru E.K. Strong in 1925. AIDA is an acronym standing for:

- Attention
- Interest
- Desire
- Action

It can be argued that AIDA is over-simplistic in the way it predicts that advertising draws people through a series of stages to the final goal of purchase. People are not that logical, and they are certainly not as innocent of advertising as the model suggests. But the beauty of a model resides not in its accuracy but in its usefulness and flexibility. From this point of view AIDA is very useful indeed. It can serve as a checklist for message structure, or as a guide to the layout and design of an advertisement or piece of printed publicity. It concentrates the mind on creating communications which are simple and relevant, and can also help in the evaluation of creative work. It is understandably popular – in fact, practically any press advertisement you can find will demonstrate the principle:

- A headline grabs the attention.
- The reader's interest is then captivated by an illustration or a photographic image.
- The words of the advertisement (known as 'body copy') demonstrate how the product or service on offer will provide a sought-after benefit (thus stimulating desire).
- A coupon, telephone number, or list of stockists, will complete the structure, allowing the reader to become a customer by converting interest and desire into the action of purchase.

While AIDA is helpful from the point of view of structuring a piece of communication, what about deciding on its content? Here the ideas of a later American advertising guru, Rosser Reeves, are useful. Reeves coined the phrase 'USP' in the late 1950s, standing for a philosophy of advertising based on what he called the 'Unique Selling Proposition'. This proposes that:

- Every product or service, in order to justify its position in the market place, has to have something unique about it.
- This feature has to be strong enough to persuade customers that the product boasting it is more suited to their needs than rival offerings.
- All promotional activity needs to drive home this unique proposition in a simple and single-minded way.

The idea has influenced some classic advertising campaigns because of its overwhelming simplicity. Lines like 'Persil washes whiter', or 'Guinness is good for you' may no longer be current (indeed, present-day regulations would forbid both of them) but they have become part of advertising mythology because of their compelling single-mindedness. Volvo cars are not the only 'safe' cars on the road, but by using safety as their unique selling proposition in their advertising, they have carved themselves a niche in our perceptions of the car market.

Arts organizations, too, each have a unique selling proposition. As discussed in Chapter 5, funding bodies are not interested in replicating resources. So each arts organization in receipt of public money will need to justify its unique role in the market place. The USP of any product or service needs to be reflected in its performance. It is no use claiming that Fairy Liquid is kind to your hands if it is not. Similarly, the USP you discover for your organization needs to be a recognizable feature of its operation. There may even be more than one feature that is unique to a particular organization in this respect. Possible sources of uniqueness, at least as recognized by funding bodies, are as follows:

- art form
- size
- type of audience served
- geographical location
- physical access

The challenge is to convert these 'features' into 'benefits' which the potential audience will recognize as uniquely suited to their needs. So, if the unique selling proposition of an arts centre is based on its ability to cater for a less formal audience than a more traditional venue, the USP underlying its promotional messages will stress its friendliness and welcoming atmosphere. Similarly, if a craft gallery is the only outlet for regionally-produced ceramics in a particular area, its USP might emphasize the way its exhibitions reflect local interests and tastes.

This principle of establishing what is unique about an organization can be extended to its individual offerings such as plays or exhibitions, in order to facilitate the clear formulation of relevant messages. By operating in a broad direction like this, the total effect of an organization's promotion is strengthened into an overall brand image (see Chapter 4). By establishing a consistent personality for your organization, the kind of long-term relationships with customers that are essential to arts marketing can be made easier to build.

Press advertising

In spite of the steady growth of television advertising since its introduction in 1956, the press still accounts for the lion's share of advertising expenditure in the UK (Advertising Association, 2002). Its ability to reach a well-defined target market, with information which can be checked for details of times, dates, prices and telephone numbers, makes it a popular advertising choice with arts organizations. Like any medium, it has its own special terminology and characteristics. Yet, although the minutiae of the techniques used are different, much of what we can say about the planning, creation and evaluation of press advertising is relevant to the way that other advertising media work.

There is a bewildering variety of press media from which to choose. Newspapers alone include national, regional and local press; evening or morning dailies, weeklies, free newspapers, not to mention trade and consumer magazines which also cover national and regional readerships.

A comprehensive listing of every newspaper and magazine available in the UK (and indeed any other sort of advertising medium) can be found in a publication called BRAD (*British Rate and Data*). It is usually available in the reference section of larger public libraries. While building-based arts organizations will be aware of the relevant media choices available to them in their catchment areas, BRAD can be very useful when planning advertising for touring productions or exhibitions visiting areas with which the marketing department is not familiar. The kind of information provides brief details of circulation, advertising rates, and the mechanical data specifying the form that the advertisement should take when submitted.

The rate card
BRAD information is summarized from media rate cards. Every advertising medium has a rate card which lists the prices for different sizes of advertisement. At first glance newspaper rate cards can look confusing and bewildering. But the seemingly impenetrable jargon explains the requirements of the particular publication with complete, if concise, information. We will briefly examine some different types of advertising space available in newspaper rate cards, before moving to the more technical aspects of the paper's requirements.

Display or classified?
Newspaper advertising, and the relevant rates, falls into three distinct groups: display, semi-display and classified.

- Display advertising is printed from artwork and therefore can feature sophisticated graphics and typefaces. It runs alongside the editorial matter in the paper, the price of the advertisement being relative to its size. The basic unit of display space is called the 'Single Column Centimetre' – or scc for short. Because of the differences in column width from one newspaper to another, the amount of space this actually represents varies among publications. Display advertising space is also offered as full pages, or page fractions such as halves or quarters. National newspapers carry almost four times more display advertising than classified (in terms of value).

- Classified, on the other hand, is more important to the regional press. It features columns of advertisements, made up purely of words, in a series of categories. These advertisements are arranged like a simple directory, in alphabetical order. They are called 'lineage ads' because they are charged for by the line. Classified advertising is set off from the rest of the newspaper in a distinct section, although different papers have different policies on where they position the entertainment section, usually the classification most relevant to arts organizations.

- Semi-display is a compromise category of advertising, offering some of the graphic opportunities of display, but appearing within the relevant classified section rather than among editorial copy elsewhere in the paper. Touring venues often make use of semi-display to create 'ladder ads', featuring a series of boxes showing forthcoming attractions in chronological order.

Classified advertising assumes an active consumer searching through the small advertisements for something he or she already wants. It is naturally of importance to arts organizations who need to keep in regular touch with local or regional audiences looking for entertainment on an ad-hoc basis, a reminder of times, prices or telephone numbers. If we accept this function of classified advertising, basic lineage should be sufficient. However, it is in the newspaper's interests to get its clients to trade up to the more expensive semi-display, using the argument of added impact to justify this expenditure. What dictates the optimum advertising pattern, however, is careful consideration of marketing objectives.

Timing, position and discounts

It may be that the objectives demand display advertising rather than classified, appearing on a particular day or in a particular part of the publication. A new season announcement or an exhibition opening are both examples of situations where this kind of precisely-targeted impact may be appropriate. This will involve a rate-card premium – usually a percentage added onto the standard price to guarantee publication on a Friday, for example, or in the books section. The more specific an advertiser's requirements are, the more the newspaper will charge for meeting them. (It is worth finding out about variations in circulation (the number of copies sold) of daily papers over the different days of the week. It frequently drops on Saturdays, for example, suggesting that the weekend might not offer very good value for the hard-pressed advertiser.) The rate card will often feature special positions inside the paper (for example, the television page, which is likely to receive repeated attention during the life of the newspaper) or on the front or back pages.

- 'Title corners', also known as 'ear-pieces', are available on many newspaper front covers. They are the spaces to either side of the title or 'masthead' of the paper. Some advertisers prize them for their salience, but their ability to carry information is limited by their size.
- A 'solus' position of any type is an advertisement which stands on its own. (The phrase, from the Latin, is used of certain poster sites as well.) Because of the perceived value of having a display advertisement which does not have to compete for the reader's attention with any other advertising in the same field of vision, solus positions are highly sought after and tend to be booked up months in advance. A front-page solus is a particularly vivid way of announcing a new season or a special event such as the launch of

pantomime booking, or the opening of an exhibition. So, assuming the organization's planning schedule is sufficiently long term, it is a good idea to find out from appropriate newspapers when they begin to make such positions available. This enables them to be securely fixed into future advertising plans.

- 'Run of week' and 'run of paper' advertisements give the publisher flexibility as to date of insertion and position in the paper: the advertisement will appear in any issue in a given week or on any page in a particular issue. This flexibility is rewarded by discounts off standard rates. In one sense these discounts represent the laws of supply and demand in the advertising marketplace. However, a canny purchaser of advertising space can use the fact that such discounts are available to negotiate on price even if the advertisement in question does not, strictly speaking, qualify. A salesperson who needs to fill their newspaper may listen sympathetically to an argument along these lines if the alternative is to lose the advertisement to a rival publication.

Arts advertisers who want to use press advertising to maintain regular contact with their audiences may stand to benefit from series discount. This rewards regular advertisers with lower rates. Again, the test of the wisdom of this pattern of advertising is not the size of the discount, but whether it corresponds to marketing objectives. If they change, or if other media become available to achieve the same contact more effectively, the advertising budget needs to be reviewed accordingly.

Case 6.1 The power of the co-op

Small arts organizations are usually at a disadvantage when it comes to buying advertising space in the media. Lacking the buying power to negotiate good deals, they can end up paying list-rate prices for their space, and be overshadowed by larger big-budget organizations which have the budgets and clout to demand the best positions and best prices for their space. This was a major issue for a number of theatre companies in the San Francisco East Bay area – so much so, that the theatre managers got together to investigate the possibilities of replicating the buying power and control of larger organizations by forming a coalition known as the East Bay Theater Coalition, and negotiating as a group.

A pilot co-operative initiative was initially targeted at a group of local daily newspapers – the Contra Costa Newspapers – which had a daily circulation of over 190 000. The tabloid format *Time Out* supplement, inserted on Fridays into all the daily papers, was the primary source of arts and entertainment news for all the residents in the area.

The aims of the collaborative approach were to:

- enable small theatres to benefit from lower advertising rates and better display positions by committing to a long-term schedule
- allow small theatres with insufficient budgets for advertising to do so

- create a specific section for theatre advertising in the same section of the paper every week, to make life easier for potential attenders
- establish a sponsorship arrangement to benefit all companies

The Willows Theater, a medium-scale organization which had a history of advertising with the newspaper group, agreed to negotiate on behalf of the whole consortium, and struck a deal in which both parties agreed to specific undertakings.

The East Bay Theater Coalition agreed to:

- purchase 40 spaces of 2 column by 13 inches in a 12-month period
- nominate the newspaper as its exclusive media sponsor, and give it first refusal the following year
- include the newspaper's logo on all its co-operative advertising
- mention that the newspaper was the group's sponsor in all broadcast interviews
- streamline administration by collecting together all the members' advertising copy and/or artwork each week and forwarding them to the newspaper together
- provide four tickets per member theatre show for the newspaper's own use

Contra Costa Newspapers agreed to:

- sell space to the group at the same rate given to organizations placing twice as much advertising – giving the group an annual saving of $6448
- provide 12 spaces of 2 column by 13 inches free of charge during the sponsorship period
- reserve positioning on regular agreed pages of the Friday *Time Out* supplement
- provide advertising design and layout service free of charge

In total, 15 theatre companies participated in the scheme in its first year, with advertising spends ranging from $320 to $37 000. Such was the success of the arrangement, that the following year the advertisement size was increased to three columns and circulation has been extended to include three more newspapers in the Group. The Willows Theater, which used no other media advertising, saw its audience increase by 25 per cent from 1998 to 1999, at the same time as its print advertising bill fell by 20 per cent.

Source: Holtz, 1999.

Poster advertising

Poster advertising, also known as 'outdoor advertising', is one of the oldest forms of marketing communication. For the fine arts, posters promoting exhibitions can dramatize the benefits of the experience on offer by reproducing art objects with drama and impact (creating merchandise as well as publicity). London blockbuster exhibitions exploit this strength by extensive use of posters on sites on the London Underground. Another aspect of outdoor's long-term association with the arts can be seen in historical 'play bills' – the ornately produced, and extravagantly worded, posters from the eighteenth and nineteenth centuries which are now collectors' items.

Controversy at the V&A

Charles Mills, the Marketing Manager appointed at the V&A in 1987, put the problem of communicating the museum's benefits as follows: 'The V&A once had the slogan, "The Nation's Treasure House", and that is still very accurate. We have so many extraordinarily beautiful things for people to see. Our problem is that it is very hard to sum up and define exactly what we have got here.'

An answer to this complicated positioning problem came in the first year of Mills's appointment with a poster campaign which solved the problem about which art objects to talk about by ignoring them altogether. Instead it featured the proposition: 'V&A. An ace caff with quite a nice museum attached.' One of the posters featured the immortal line 'Where else do they give you £100 000 000 worth of objets d'art free with every egg salad?'

Mills defended the controversial campaign: 'We knew the V&A had a fusty image which was stopping some people visiting us. Trying to shake off this image we produced a campaign that was deliberately controversial. It had to be controversial to get people talking about it. We had a tiny budget.'

The then Arts Minister, David Mellor (himself no stranger to controversy), was impressed. 'It was certainly provocative. While it had some success raising the profile of the museum, and attracting some new visitors, I suspect it alienated those others for whom the museum rather than the support services were a main concern.' Nevertheless, the campaign (as well as a strong exhibition programme for 1988/1989) increased visitor traffic by 10 per cent.

Source: Crofts, 1988; Moyle, 1990.

Billing

Posters have given the theatrical profession the concept of 'billing': the practice of heading the poster with the names of the leading actors. Some theatres avoid it altogether as a matter of democratic policy. Others, particularly touring houses featuring familiar names from television, see it as an essential part of their marketing armoury. A pragmatic approach is to be recommended. Some contracts between a venue and a theatrical or literary management will specify aspects of billing – even down to the relative size and order of the artists' or writers' names compared to the title of the piece. These provisions will tend to apply not only to posters, but to all other forms of printed material including advertising, leaflets and programmes. Clear lines of communication are essential between the marketing department and other areas of the organization in order to avoid misunderstanding.

Economy or effectiveness?

One of the essential attractions of poster advertising to theatrical managements has always been its perceived cheapness. The way that most arts organizations distribute posters has traditionally aimed at maximizing the amount of free display. As well as the essential display work in and near the venue itself, it is common practice to distribute by hand or mail to outlets such as colleges, community centres, doctors' and dentists' waiting rooms, factories, libraries and other arts venues.

Competition in such outlets from other material is fierce. While some venues mobilize staff or volunteers to check and maintain the visibility of displays, there is nevertheless a concern that impact and communication may suffer amid the visual clutter. For example, while audience surveys reveal that students and education workers are an important part of the customer base, colleges and universities are notorious for overcrowded and out-of-date noticeboards. Furthermore, display in many of the outlets listed above may not be reaching other target audiences effectively, or even at all. Their popularity as outlets seems led not by marketing objectives but by their relative lack of resistance to accepting material (particularly as local authorities crack down on the illegal display of posters on walls and street furniture, known as 'fly posting'). While it is important to have a good grass-roots presence for any arts organization with a local constituency, the wisdom of devoting so much time and energy to this kind of activity (together with the substantial mailing and production costs involved) needs to be kept under review.

Poster contractors

The alternative is to consider using paid-for sites, rented from a poster contractor. Although something like three-quarters of all poster sites are owned by the three largest companies, this is still a fragmented industry. Different companies tend to concentrate on particular sizes and types of poster.

As with newspapers, poster contractors each have a rate card. The price will include putting up and taking down the material (which has to be delivered to the contractor) and a period of display. Long-term advertisers are rewarded with better rates than occasional users. The best discounts are to be had if you buy a site on a continuous ('Till Countermanded' or 'TC') basis – usually requiring a period of three months before it can be cancelled. Alternatively, sites can be bought 'Line by Line', which means on an ad-hoc basis. Poster contractors themselves have become adept at packaging their sites in order to offer advertisers greater convenience. Such packages are aimed at the largest users of the medium, however.

Size matters

There is a direct relationship between size and price of a poster site. The traditional building-block of poster display space is the 'sheet' – an area of 30" by 20". These are the dimensions of what used to be a very popular size for theatre posters – the 'Double Crown'. Because of the adoption of international standards in paper size, the Double Crown has been largely superseded by the slightly smaller A2 size posters. But Double Crown ('DC') has been traditionally used by touring managements as the basis for their print orders – with smaller variations known as 'hanging cards'.

The most common commercial-size posters, however, are 6-sheets (1800 mm high by 1200 mm wide) and 48-sheets (the enormous billboards which dominate roadside advertising). Six-sheets are the kind of posters seen at bus shelters or in shopping precincts. Many 6-sheets are backlit, which means they work at night as well as during daylight hours, and are more expensive than unilluminated posters. The better the visibility of a site, the more the poster contractor will expect to charge.

As well as roadside positions, poster sites are widely available at railway stations – a popular choice with arts advertisers targeting a mobile audience. In fact, many larger theatres and galleries will plan posters at railway stations en route to their cities, rather than limiting display to the city itself.

Transport media

Although the majority of the outdoor scene comprises static posters, transport media are developing an important role – from taxi doors to liveried lorries. Tactical use of bus-side advertising is an increasingly popular choice for venues promoting major Christmas shows where high rates of coverage and frequency are required. The sheer size and ubiquity of bus sides guarantees impact, but the cost of producing the advertising material itself is likely to be disproportionately large for small runs.

Different transport advertising contractors will use slightly different terminology, but the kind of opportunities available on most rate cards for bus advertising will include:

- 'T-sides', which run along one side of the bus and have a panel going down to form a 'T'
- 'Supersides', which run along the other side of the bus
- 'End panels', which are good for targeting motorists and business travellers.

Periods of display and discounts are structured in a way similar to other outdoor media.

Using an agency

The scale of operation sometimes suggests the use of an advertising agency rather than negotiating and buying space direct. Advertising agencies can relieve the workload of marketing personnel by reducing the amount of time spent on routine media purchases. They can also provide useful input to planning, as well as offering access to better prices for certain marketing services through their buying power. Services like the preparation of artwork for display advertising, requiring the expertise of a graphic designer and typesetter, are also provided by an agency. This is important, as newspapers can offer to do the artwork for you, but the final results can be unpredictable.

Agency commissions and mark-ups

Advertising agencies traditionally make their money by receiving a commission from media owners (newspapers, radio and television companies etc.) of a percentage of the purchase price of the space they buy. This practice dates back to the early days of advertising agencies, when they sold space on behalf of poster contractors and newspapers. On work such as the preparation of printed materials, for which no commission is payable, agencies mark up their expenditure when billing the client. They justify this on the grounds that their bulk-buying power on services such as printing produces savings which cover the mark-up. For work which involves no purchasing (such as consultancy or conference management) a straight fee is negotiated. Often an agency's remuneration will include all three types of payment: commission, mark-up and fee.

Theoretically, using an agency should cost the client no more than if the client were buying the advertising direct. The commission system means that the larger the client's spend, the more money the agency stands to make. While this does not mean that agencies advise unnecessary expenditure, it does have the effect of making their largest clients the ones on which they lavish most care and attention. Arts organizations with small budgets may find themselves being left behind as a result.

For a variety of reasons, many arts clients have excellent direct relationships with local media which might not be improved by the intervention of an advertising agency. It may even be the case that discounts enjoyed by a long-established venue have a historical or discretionary basis best left unquestioned. Like any aspect of promotional strategy, however, the decision of whether or not to use an agency is best kept under regular review.

Public relations

Well-chosen advertising media are powerful but expensive, so arts organizations have traditionally preferred public relations as a cheaper alternative. PR should not be seen as a way of doing advertising on the cheap. Both advertising and PR need a substantial commitment of time and money, although in differing proportions. In spite of what many journalists seem to think, PR is not a case of applied conviviality to keep bad news out of the press and free advertising in. According to the Institute of Public Relations, it is 'the discipline which looks after reputation, with the aim of earning understanding and support and influencing opinion and behaviour. It is the planned and sustained effort to establish and maintain goodwill and mutual understanding between an organization and its publics.'

Confusing the roles of advertising and public relations can lead to false expectations of what either can do. They are both 'deliberate, planned and sustained'. They operate side by side in the same media. But whereas you can exercise direct control over advertising, public relations relies largely on the goodwill of third parties. Advertising tends to be a one-way process, whereas public relations implies dialogue: what the definition calls 'mutual understanding'. Good public relations involves a lot of listening. Mercer (1996) points to the appropriateness of PR as a promotional technique for non-profit and service organizations: 'PR is often a particularly valuable promotional device for services, since the "authority" offered by independent recommendation in editorial matter can add vital credibility to an intangible service.'

The most important difference between advertising and public relations is choice. An arts organization can choose when and where to advertise – or even choose not to advertise at all. But it has public relations whether it likes it or not. The only choice is whether to manage the process or let things drift along by themselves. Organizations that do not take a proactive approach to PR are still sending out messages about themselves. By their programme choice, pricing, the nature of their buildings or offices, even the way that the telephones are answered (and how long it takes to answer them), they are beaming images to customers, employees, stakeholders, competitors and suppliers.

What can PR do?

Advertising, as has been observed, can be trusted to convey accurate commercial details such as times and prices. Public relations, on the other hand, deals with information which is no less important but is less definite and longer term: atmosphere, excitement, novelty. Furthermore, its advocates claim that public relations, working as it does through editorial, allows your message to reach people who may be averse or desensitized to advertising.

'Word-of-mouth' is the kind of interpersonal publicity at which all promotional activity aims. Public relations recognizes this in the way that it tries to generate two-step communication. This idea, developed as a theory by the American researchers Katz and Lazarsfeld (1955), emphasizes the role played in communication by membership of social groups (including families, organizations, circles of friends and colleagues). By conveying the promotional message to dominant members of such groups (known as opinion leaders) the message is then passed on to the other members with greater conviction and effectiveness.

Case 6.2 Peer promotions

The Cultural Ambassadors' scheme at the City of Birmingham Symphony Orchestra (CBSO) was launched with a view to channelling the enthusiasm and commitment of its most loyal supporters, by using these people's time, energy and experience of concert-going and classical music to encourage new paying audiences who would not otherwise have attended a CBSO concert. The specific objective was to attract 500 new audience members to CBSO concerts in Symphony Hall, Birmingham, by using the concepts of pyramid selling, personal contacts and peer-to-peer selling. This was to be achieved through the creation of a network of well-briefed voluntary supporters who would be willing to evangelize about the orchestra and its work, and who have a sufficiently diverse social network to encourage parties from their friends and acquaintances, or from membership of a club or society. The kind of groups to be targeted were sports clubs,

Women's Institute groups, Rotary clubs, Open University groups, church groups and youth groups, through to musical societies, choirs, music appreciation groups and gramophone societies.

CBSO Society members and patrons who were retired from full-time employment and actively seeking ways to stay involved with their local communities were specifically targeted to become Ambassadors for the Orchestra. They were invited to an introductory evening, which combined a series of presentations about the scheme with advice on how to drum up interest from among colleagues and friends. This included a briefing on how best to respond to some of the questions they might be faced with from people who had very little if any experience of the attending orchestral music events. For example:

- 'Classical music is elitist' – no, it's not. We have mixed audiences of many ages and backgrounds. You don't need to dress up to come along. The reason that the orchestra wear black evening dress is that it is simply a smart uniform and, just like school, a dress code makes life much simpler.
- 'But I'm not a musician' – if your ears work, then open them! You are allowed not to like a piece of music, but just be prepared to give things a go and you might be pleasantly surprised.
- 'But I won't understand what is going on' – you don't need to. It isn't a test. There's a lot to read in your free concert programmes but all you really need to do is listen, relax and watch. Don't worry about trying to 'understand' the music, just enjoy it.

To give them an incentive to undertake the peer-to-peer selling each Ambassador was entitled to a free concert ticket for each group of at least ten new people that they brought, and was responsible for reserving the seats in their preferred price area before going away to get their group of guests together. The Ambassadors' guests bought their tickets for the concert at 25 per cent discount – greater than the usual group-booking rate of 20 per cent.

At the event itself a separate hospitality area was reserved for Ambassadors and their guests, and was available from one hour before the concert with a member of staff ready to welcome them. The Ambassadors were given a drink order form in advance and the drinks were ready for them on arrival, so no one had to queue at the bar. Each member of the party was given a free concert programme and the chance to meet musicians and staff.

Source: Brooker and Silvester, 2001.

This model can be applied to a number of situations to illustrate the way in which an arts organization gets its message across using public relations. In one sense, a features editor on a local newspaper running an interview with a visiting artist is acting as an opinion leader to the readers. In another, people who organize outings for groups of colleagues or associates to the theatre or to exhibitions (the highly-prized party bookers) also justify classification as opinion leaders. Invitations to special presentations, inclusion on mailing lists for press releases and active telephone contact are all ways of nurturing relationships with such key figures in order to reach a wider circle of audience members through this kind of multi-stage contact.

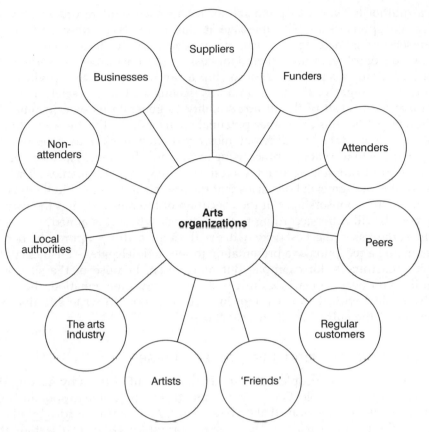

Figure 6.1 Publics of an arts organization

Opinion leaders are one of a number of publics with which an arts organization needs to manage its relations. Figure 6.1 shows how potential audiences can be mapped by dividing them into separate groups or 'publics'.

The importance of internal publics (workforce and colleagues) is easy to underestimate in organizations that operate in a precarious external environment. But keeping staff informed and consulted is a highly cost-effective policy. Their advocacy is far more credible to people outside the organization than the slickest piece of corporate advertising and can create an invaluable promotional resource at minimum cost. Chapter 9 looks at the important but too-often neglected issue of internal marketing in the arts. External suppliers and dealers are also enormously important. Keeping them in the picture means that you are more likely to get the benefit of whatever discretion they can offer in their dealings with your organization.

Having identified the different publics and their value to the organization, it is then important to focus attention on the most important groups and determine the type of messages they are most likely to respond to. Do you, in fact, need to tell two or more different stories? Obviously they must be complementary rather than contradictory, but different emphases may be appropriate for different publics. For example, suppose a theatre funded by a local authority wants to publicize its recent successful record in attracting business sponsorship. The message it directs at its funding body is that sponsorship is helping it reach more people in the local community by attracting employees (and their families) of the businesses concerned. This approach, emphasizing the sponsorship as an outreach activity, will help to avoid the danger of the local authority feeling that it can safely reduce its funding as a result of the theatre's ability to generate its own income. To a different public (this time other potential sponsors), the theatre wants to relay the complementary but different message that here is a new promotional opportunity that competitors are using to gain an advantage. The message here is 'be part of our success like these other leading local companies'. The basic message is the same: in both cases that the organization is now in the business of successful sponsorship. But the execution of the message, and the way it is conveyed, will differ according to the public at which it is aimed.

In some cases the best way will be through a direct approach: perhaps organizing a reception or a presentation to selected delegates – business people or key customers, for example. But more often, because of the size of the publics you need to reach, a third party comes into the equation: the media. How to deal with the media and, in particular, how to write effective press releases, is the subject of the next section.

Media relations and the press release

Journalists are busy people. You can get the best out of them by making their lives as easy as possible. One way of doing this is to be able to spot an 'angle' to a story and, having done that, to be able to communicate the idea briefly and coherently in a press release. The most important knack to acquire, though, is an appreciation of what makes news.

Getting the Info

Ritva Kilpinen of Turku's Kaupunginteateri advocates the 'Info' as a way of maximizing publicity just before the première of a new production. A common practice in Finnish theatre, the Info consists of a press conference about a week before the opening featuring a short extract from the play in costume, interviews and photo opportunities. Because of Finnish rehearsal regulations the actors cannot be called before 11 a.m. or later than 3 p.m. So the Info takes place at 11.30 a.m., giving the actors time enough to get dressed and prepared for the ten minutes or so of performance and photography during or afterwards. The director and other members of the creative team are on hand to talk to journalists, and the whole press conference lasts no more than an hour. It also gives the Finns an opportunity to indulge in one of their favourite social pursuits – coffee drinking. As in other northern European countries, consumption of the invigorating dark brew at frequent intervals is as popular with arts marketers as it is with journalists.

Source: Personal interview.

What makes a story?

If you take a look at your local or national newspaper, you will see that the stories you are reading hang on some particular hook. Journalists are actually trained to look for what is newsworthy. If you want to get them interested in your story, make sure it contains at least one of the following elements:

- action
- arguments and views
- unusualness
- community concerns and local interest
- human interest
- topicality
- relevance to a national issue (e.g. a television soap, political crisis, freak weather, Christmas etc.)

Different papers have different approaches to news. Some are very serious, others mix in the heavyweight stories with quirkier tittle-tattle. The same is true for radio programmes and television. The only way to get a measure of the opportunities facing you as a publicist is to make time to read the papers, listen to the radio and watch television. It is part of the necessary groundwork for success. Journalists themselves are avid consumers of other media. In fact articles in other publications, such as magazines, newspapers, broadcast media and websites, are among the most important sources for their own work (Keeble, 2001). Try and get to know a journalist or two; some arts marketers make a point of attending other people's first nights. Don't be afraid to introduce yourself. Journalists need stories to fill their papers and broadcasts every day of the year. You are doing them a favour, not the other way round (whatever it may feel like).

Another thing to learn, about your local publications in particular, is when deadlines fall. The best story in the world is no good to a journalist if it arrives too late to be used. Do not try ringing a journalist on an evening paper in the morning: you are likely to get very short shrift from someone struggling to get copy sorted out for his or her next edition. Another point to bear in mind is the fact that broadcast media such as television and radio can turn a story round a lot faster than most print media. This means that, if you are not careful about how you release it, you may find that your story is considered old news by a newspaper after it has been run on the local radio.

The good thing about this, however, is that it forces you to look for new angles. A weekly paper cannot hope to compete with a daily paper for news stories. On the other hand it can afford to cover stories in more depth, and run more features and human interest material, which does not need to be quite so up-to-the-minute. A local paper will tend to have one or two people who, as well as doing other things, will specialize in arts coverage. These are, of course, key contacts. But never lose sight of the bigger picture. The business editor, for example, is worth cultivating. Time spent with journalists is a good investment. Staff photographers are another extremely important group whose goodwill and enthusiasm can make all the difference between a routine appearance in the newspaper and a veritable publicity coup. Arts organizations are in the enviable position of being able to offer photographers the opportunity to take pictures which they themselves find interesting and rewarding.

Writing a press release

'Now what I want is Facts . . . Facts alone are wanted in life.'
Mr Gradgrind in *Hard Times* by Charles Dickens.

There are five very important facts any press release should contain, preferably in the first couple of sentences:

- What is happening?
- Who is involved?
- Where is it taking place?
- When is it happening?
- Why is it happening?

The opening sentences, in which these questions should be answered, are crucial to the success or failure of what follows as they will be being scanned by an extremely busy journalist (see Table 6.2). Whether they end up on the desk for further investigation, or in the wastepaper basket, depends on what comes across in the first seconds. Another good reason for getting all the important material into the first paragraph of the release is that sometimes editors print press releases without changing them, only cutting them. Traditionally editors cut from the bottom. So the supporting details should go into later paragraphs. This practice can be verified by reference to any newspaper. Almost invariably the main point of the story (with the essential information) will lie in the first paragraph of each news item.

It is often a good idea to follow up the release by telephone to selected journalists. Persistency pays dividends. Assuming the press are after you for a change, how do you deal with them? First of all, be honest. If you cannot answer a particular question, promise to ring back when you have got the facts. If they are asking questions you would rather not answer, get someone better qualified to deal with them. It helps, if you think you have a crisis on your hands, to get expert advice.

Picture this

There are few things as eloquent as a good photograph. Photocalls are an excellent way of getting to know journalists and giving them a real sense of involvement in what you are doing. Even when there are photographers present from a number of different newspapers, each can go home with a unique interpretation of what you have to offer.

The problem with press releases is that journalists can make of them what they like. This may not always accord with your interests, although it makes a good story. The beauty of pictures is that they are easier to control (in general) and have much more immediate impact than the written word. Best of all, in terms of control, is the ability to supply your own pictures. Here it is worth studying the sort of photographic images that get published in a newspaper. Sometimes what works on stage or in a gallery does not necessarily look good

Table 6.2 Press releases that impress

In writing or approving a press release, check out the following aspects of style and format:

1 Dates should be exact and full: e.g. Tuesday 3 December 2002, not 'this Tuesday'.

2 Addresses, where appropriate, should be given in full. Assume ignorance on the part of the journalist, even if your location is highly familiar.

3 Brevity is the soul of wit, especially in a press release. It's useful to remember that one side of double-spaced A4 fills about 6 column inches in most newspapers.

4 Deal in facts, not opinions. Opinions are for the journalist to form, and you will find that if your press release goes over the top about how wonderful your artistic offering is, it will be dismissed as an attempt to get free advertising.

5 It's often a good idea to include a quote from somebody prominent. This allows the journalist to write as if he or she has interviewed the person concerned, and can inject more life into the final article.

6 Keep it simple and concise. As with any kind of copywriting, complexity puts distance between you and your audience.

7 Check the facts in the release carefully, and get someone else to check them as well. The awful thing about a mistake in a press release is that it is completely impossible to put right. It also makes both you and the journalist look foolish – hardly likely to inspire continuing confidence in your relationship. Now and then ask friendly journalists what they think of your approach to press releases.

8 Ask journalists whether they prefer to receive releases by mail, fax, e-mail, or a combination of these, then supply what they ask for. Don't just post press releases on your website and assume that journalists will be scouring your site to find them. They won't.

9 Make sure it's clear from whom a release is being sent. For releases sent in the mail headed stationery is best. Many arts organizations use a variation on their standard letterheadings to indicate that it is a press release.

10 Make sure there is a contact name on the release for follow-up from the journalist. It is particularly helpful to specify when the person will be available. Many press releases now carry home, office and mobile contact numbers, as well as an e-mail address.

11 Begin the release about a third of the way down the paper, type double spaced and leave wide margins. This leaves plenty of space for journalists to add their own marks and comments to your release.

12 If the release runs to more than one page, type MORE at the bottom right hand corner of each page, and remember to type your company's name or story caption at the top of each new page. At the end of the last page of the release type END.

13 If you have photographs to support your release, include them as colour prints or attach them to e-mails as digital images, and indicate on the release if any images are available in other forms (such as transparencies). Although newspapers will often send their own photographers for newsworthy events, magazines may not. Remember to compress images if the size of a digital file is particularly large – otherwise you are in danger of causing the journalist's computer to grind to a halt!

14 Ensure that captions for the images are included on the release as well as on the images themselves, and always include details of the credit for the photographer if this is appropriate.

in newsprint. Values to aim at in commissioning photography for reproduction in newspapers include:

- close-ups
- upright images rather than sideways ones (i.e. 'portrait' not 'landscape')
- people close together (compact images fit better into newspaper columns)
- people doing something that is easily understood
- tonal variety (large patches of black look dramatic on stage but dull in newspapers)
- upbeat, or unusual, situations (hats, props, costumes, cars and, in spite of W.C. Fields, children and animals . . .)

Organizing photocalls requires a disciplined approach. The objective is to assemble a number of people together for a very short time, often at a stage (because of the proximity of an opening night) when their preoccupations may be very different from your own. The following points are worth following – although every situation can be different:

- Telephone the photographer first to sell the idea if this is to be an exclusive. Listen to whatever suggestions he or she has to make.
- Write down a schedule with timings for arrivals and departures.
- Make sure everyone concerned in the organization knows about the photocall and is fully briefed on their role.
- Be nice to your subjects. The occasional bacon sandwich has been known to melt a heart or two.
- Ring round the photographer(s) on the morning of the photocall to recheck their availability. Their diary appointments are subject to change at the last moment if a news story breaks elsewhere.

Broadcast media

What works for printed media does not always apply to broadcasting, and press releases can be inappropriate when aiming for television or radio coverage. Thinking in pictures is essential when targeting television news or magazine programmes. It pays to think carefully about the visual potential of a news story, and to be able to telephone the producer or editor with a very clear idea of what you have in mind. This will enable them to decide quickly on its merits (and resource implications), and they will often add ideas of their own. It is also worth bearing in mind that performers and artists may expect to be paid union-agreed fees for television appearances in certain circumstances. While this is the responsibility of the broadcasting company, it is a good idea to find out from the relevant union what their requirements are in order to avoid any confusion.

Similarly, radio can provide a useful and effective public relations outlet. Here it is important to think of aural angles, particularly for visual art forms like dance and fine arts which can work surprisingly well in sound only. Radio is very good for personalities and enthusiasm, so select your speakers carefully. Explaining the history of an art object or the soundscape of a dance piece can open up very exciting possibilities.

Table 6.3 Survival guide for broadcast interviews

The following checklist can help focus the mind on the important business of communication by reducing the amount of stress that microphones and cameras can create:

- The object of the presenter is to make entertaining programming and look good. He or she will want to sound in control and confident, so your confidence and positive manner will be a real help.

- Focus on the person who is talking to you. Journalists are practised at putting interviewees at their ease. Be natural.

- Check out in advance whether the interview is to be recorded or is going out live. This may affect what you want to say, especially if it might go out of date quickly.

- Make life easier for your presenter by briefing him or her in advance with some written material. A press release, leaflet or other props can be very helpful. For visual arts marketers, bring along some photographs about your product or company.

- If you find it helps your nerves, jot down the main points you want to make on a postcard and keep it with you.

- The presenter will tend to brief you in advance on the shape of the interview. Don't start answering the questions until you are on air, however.

- Finally, enjoy! It's good fun being on the radio or the television.

When planning for an interview on radio or television, preparation is very important (see Table 6.3). If you are organizing an interview where two people are involved (for example, cast members from a touring production) then think in terms of contrast. A mixture of sexes or ages makes for more interesting listening.

Sales promotion

Sales promotion is something of a catch-all category which encompasses any activity that does not fall into the other areas of the promotional mix, but which increases how much a consumer buys, or how quickly the transaction occurs. Marketing terminology talks about an imaginary line drawn through promotional expenditure. 'Above the line' is expenditure which carries commission (like advertising media as discussed earlier). Consequently, sales promotion activities in their various forms, which do not carry commission, are sometimes also referred to as 'below the line'.

The strength of sales promotion is that it offers something for nothing. This stimulates a positive attitude to the organization's offering among consumers and intermediaries. It tips customers over the edge of the decision to buy, thus leading to immediate sales increases. It is extremely flexible. Used in tandem with advertising, it can be very effective at increasing the impact of your commercial messages. Because of the fact that it needs to offer something over and above the basic proposition, however, it is by nature short-lived. The technique works best with support from elsewhere. Sales promotions are frequently one-offs; only a few are recurring. There is pressure to be original, which means that you lose the economies of scale achieved in a long-running advertising campaign. Because of its tactical nature, it is crucial to plan and pace sales promotion across the range of the organization's offerings to maximize its support for the sales effort. This involves looking a year ahead at timing, techniques, geographical areas, co-ordination, synergy with planned advertising and the need to create selling support material.

Subscription

The type of sales promotion activity in most common use in the arts is known as subscription – a scheme which encourages the advance purchase of tickets for a series of events rather than just a single occasion. As an arts marketing idea its pedigree stretches back to the eighteenth century to the kind of subscription concerts at which the symphonies of Haydn and Mozart were first aired. But like any form of sales promotion, it offers direct inducement (such as extra value) to ginger up the process of a sale.

Subscription selling is a far better established practice in the USA than almost anywhere else in the world, and at many of the major arts institutions, subscribers form by far the largest segment of the audience. That such efforts are made to sell subscriptions there is often attributed to the relatively meagre levels of public funding for the arts; the major benefit of attracting season subscribers rather than single-ticket bookers is that customers make a major financial commitment well in advance of actual events they will be attending. Thus arts organizations are assured of levels of income which would be far less certain if they were dependent on door sales or ad-hoc ticket purchases, and they can draw up their marketing and business plans accordingly.

Subscription schemes can deliver major benefits to customers who are prepared to plan ahead, and are much appreciated by those who say that without their subscription they would not get around to going out! But conversely, they are particularly unattractive to people who like to keep their options open, as well as the ever-increasing number of 'cash rich, time poor' individuals whose working and domestic lives are too busy and unpredictable to enable them to commit to an event at some point in the future. So if subscription schemes are to succeed these days, they need deftly to combine a requirement to plan ahead with the flexibility to change those plans if circumstances change.

Potential subscribers can be offered financial inducements such as discounts, but 'exclusive' opportunities, such as the chance to book tickets for events that are likely to be an immediate sell-out, or to book the best seats in the house, can be equally enticing. The main problem with non-cash incentives is that offering extra benefits exclusively to the 20 per cent or so of the audience that subscribes means offering a lesser experience to the other 80 per cent, and that can seriously undermine any attempts being made to develop new audiences and lead to accusations of elitism. Baker (2002) identifies four different types of scheme that can be offered, depending on the nature of the market:

- *'Take it or leave it'* – an offer of a complete season, likely to attract the most enthusiastic of attenders, but a little daunting for anyone else. Discounts given will have to make up for the fact that not all the events in the package will necessarily appeal to potential customers.
- *'Choose a series'* – a range of different packages requiring different levels and types of commitment. This overcomes some of the problems associated with 'unpopular' parts of a package, but still requires customers to plan ahead.
- *'Pick and Mix'* – a scheme giving maximum flexibility and choice, which helps customers fit events into their lifestyles, but does little to encourage them to attend new or little-known work.
- *Vouchers* – pre-purchase of a package of coupons that can be used at any time during a season. This is the most flexible scheme of all, but can encourage people to leave their booking until the last minute, when ticket availability may be a problem.

Other techniques

Part of the function of sales promotion is to inject short-term interest and generate publicity. So it is worth considering a number of options beside the kind of discount-based technique on which subscription is built.

- *Competitions:* Generally the best response levels are achieved by the simplest ideas. Competitions based largely on luck but usually featuring the words 'Using your skill and judgement' are very popular because entrants accept they are very nearly lotteries (see 'free mail in').
- *Coupons:* Enormously flexible, these offer some kind of saving to consumers when redeemed against the admission price of a particular event. They are widely used in the museum and stately home markets. The possibility of cross-promotion (joining forces with another attraction or venue) can give access to new audiences. Simplicity, which is a feature of all effective promotion, should be paramount when devising coupon offers. They need to be easy to use and easy for your sales staff to handle. Finally, they need to be accurately costed in terms of expected redemption rates.
- *Free gifts/trial:* As the name implies, this involves giving something away with a purchase. In the 1960s plastic daffodils were all the rage with soap powder. In the arts, experience shows that effective offers are limited to ancillary products – such as books, CDs or programmes – which have a direct link to the main experience. For example, CD samplers are valuable devices for helping break down barriers to attending contemporary music performances. By giving potential attenders the chance to listen to a brief extract of the music before a performance, the CD sampler enables people to overcome their fears of being subject to a couple of hours of 'strangled cat' sounds.
- *Free draws/free mail ins:* These are effectively a raffle. The magic words 'no purchase necessary' absolve them from the legal restrictions attached to lotteries where participants pay for a chance of winning. They can be used to create display interest (centring on the entry-form posting box), or to prompt a visit to a gallery or theatre foyer by positioning the posting-box in-house.

Such activity can also result in a list of names and addresses, but only a percentage of these are likely to be good prospects.

Print

Printed publicity is a major item of expenditure for any arts organization. Audience surveys regularly feature the 'season brochure' as the most frequently-indicated method of finding out about the performance on offer. While the design and printing of this will be the province of a graphic designer (either bought in or in-house, depending on the organization) the copywriting will tend to be done by the marketing department. The ability to address the audience directly, in literature which can serve as a sales aid by featuring a postal booking form or telephone sales number, justifies the importance with which this task is viewed.

Copywriting

The position of the arts as a service industry means that the role of printed material in communicating the benefits of a future experience is a crucial one. The time-lapse between preparing promotional material and the delivery of the service itself presents problems. A play, opera or dance event may end up looking very different in performance from the image presented in publicity material designed and written six months beforehand. This is especially a problem with new work as there is no way of telling exactly what will survive in the final version.

One way round this problem is to write brochure and leaflet copy that emphasizes 'benefits' rather than the more literal 'features' of an arts event. At the same time, there is research evidence to suggest that arts attenders expect promotional literature to 'tell us what it is about' in order to help them make an informed decision about what to choose. The acknowledged phenomenon of audiences' preference for familiar repertoire may be less to do with their innate conservatism than with the difficulty that arts consumers face in not getting enough plain information about unfamiliar work.

There is even the perception that copy is sometimes written in a way which deliberately underplays the more challenging aspects of certain sorts of work in order to reduce the risk of potential audiences being scared off. Whatever the truth of this idea, it pays to be explicit about issues like language, nudity and content. Treating potential attenders in any other way is misleading, patronizing and, ultimately, alienating. The philosophy of marketing puts the consumer at the centre of things. This affects copywriting on a fundamental level. The aim should be to talk with, rather than at, the customer.

This approach can be safeguarded by bearing a number of principles in mind when writing promotional copy:

- be specific (what is it about?)
- imagine you are talking to a member of the audience
- use short sentences

- write to predetermined word lengths (this concentrates the mind wonderfully)
- dramatize the benefits in ideas and words that are relevant to the target market
- think visually

Above all: keep it simple.

Commissioning print

Having decided on the role which mailing and print distribution will play in your promotional strategy, the next step is to determine how many items of print you will require in the course of the year. For a theatre needing to promote two seasons of work in a 12-month period, this might entail two season brochures and, say, eight sets of posters and handbills supporting individual shows.

This exercise will indicate what kind of production and design budgets are practicable. They provide a clear idea of financial limits before negotiations with designers or printers take place. An experienced designer will often see ways of saving money on a job. But it is essential to make the size of the budget clear from the outset to avoid the possibility of wasting valuable design time. Although, like any creative service providers, designers find it difficult to predict their costs accurately, a firm quotation should be obtained before any work is started. This is helpful in setting the parameters for both sides in the relationship.

Design, copywriting and print production are enormous thieves of time in arts marketing and so every opportunity to streamline the process should be taken. Consolidating the production of a whole season's print at the start of the season is a ploy which a number of repertory theatres have used successfully to rationalize the time spent on the project while maximizing the buying power available. This may not always be possible. Different organizations have different planning schedules. But the 'opportunity cost' of time taken away from other essential activities by the fascinating process of print production needs to be recognized by a disciplined approach.

Briefing the designer

Good graphic designers are always in short supply. It may be necessary to talk to several before settling on a final choice. There are various ways of finding out about them, including trade directories and Yellow Pages, colleagues in other organizations and local colleges training design graduates.

Briefing the designer should embrace more than just handing them the copy. They need to understand the background to the job. Explaining the organization's mission statement, outlining the audience (with research evidence where appropriate), and involving the designer in the kind of experience on offer, are all essential steps.

Copy needs to be prepared with an idea of how it fits the format of the leaflet. It is useful to bring along to the meeting with the designer a very rough indication of what you have in mind. Visual references are helpful too. Any picture research you can do will save time and ensure you get what you want. A number of arts organizations now commission photography as opposed to illustration in their publicity material. David Ogilvy (1995), an influential advertising thinker, recommends photography over illustration for its selling power. But it also has the advantage over illustration of allowing you to know exactly how the image will look. Many excellent graphic artists are not necessarily very gifted illustrators, and they find it easier to work with photographs or existing images rather than generate original ones.

Print planning schedule

Establishing, agreeing and adhering to a timescale is essential in managing the relationship with designer and printer to achieve the desired outcome (see Table 6.4). It can also be used as the basis for establishing systems and record-keeping which will help streamline print production and maximize the scarce resources of time and money. Problems are much easier avoided than solved, and a schedule helps plan around them. It also imparts a sense of direction to a project. This is crucial when there is a team involved, especially (as is invariably the case with print) if external suppliers are part of the picture.

The schedule for a piece of printed material should include time for conceptualization, copywriting, briefing a designer, commissioning or sourc-ing visuals, gaining necessary approvals, getting printers' quotations, proofing, printing and delivery. Each of these is potentially a time trap. Sometimes the printing and proofing stages get skimped on because of time wasted earlier in the process, with potentially disastrous effects. Approvals, when required, ought to be straightforward. Artistic directors in arts organizations will inevitably (and justifiably) want to be involved. They can be a useful resource, but it is better to manage their involvement at the early, strategic stages. This will save time later on, particularly when it comes to approving proofs.

So anyone involved in approving (or contributing in any other way, with information, material or pictures) must be clear about:

1 The extent of their responsibility.
2 When they need to be available (particularly important for approving copy).
3 Any changes to copy need to be at an early stage in the process. The nearer the project is to completion, the more expensive alterations become in time and money.

Each organization will have its separate scheduling peculiarities. Theatres and galleries presenting touring work, for example, are likely to be working on much shorter notice of what they will be presenting than repertory theatres or opera companies who may have the luxury of long-range programme planning. Having said that, repertory theatres can still be subject to unavoidable changes in plans, resulting in late confirmation of season content. The important thing is to communicate the schedule clearly, and keep in touch with each participant. Managing a major print project like a season leaflet

Table 6.4 A sample print schedule

A reliable first step is to take the date at which the piece of printed material needs to be in circulation, and then work back through each stage to see how much time there is available. Then a detailed schedule can be constructed as follows:

Week 1: Meet to discuss content and format with those involved. Agree procedures and schedule.

Week 2: Gather information and brief designer to prepare a rough version (known as a scamp or rough) for approval of format and overall look. Providing the designer with some kind of model, no matter how rough, can help sort out ambiguities at this stage. A 'flat plan', which gives a page by page idea of what is involved, can be a very helpful reference for longer pieces of print. Especially useful is the way they allow you to see 'facing pages' (i.e. left and right page together) – often known as a double page spread or DPS.

Week 3: Agree content. Begin writing copy.

Week 4: Agree format with approval of designer's rough. Begin sourcing images and visuals.

Week 5: Finalize copy. Discuss it with front-line staff for their comments on comprehensibility and relevance.

Week 6: First draft of copy complete.

Week 7: Deadline for copy and pictures to be assembled.

Week 8: Copy and pictures approved and sent to the designer. Begin getting quotes from printers, who will base their calculations on the size, numbers of pages, how many folds involved for a leaflet (or whether it will be stapled), how many colours and photographs will be involved (see section on Print specification).

Weeks 9–12: The designer creates digital artwork on disk (the time taken for this will depend on the scope and complexity of the job) and produces proofs for checking.

Week 13: Send the final artwork on disk to the printer, where final machine proofs (sometimes called 'Sherpas', depending on the process used) are produced.

Week 14: Approve machine proofs and give OK to printers. Changes made to copy at this stage should be kept to an absolute minimum: some printers charge extra for 'author's corrections'.

Week 15: Await delivery.

Week 16: Receive delivery and commence mailing and distribution.

requires tact, energy and determination to honour deadlines and make things happen.

Print specification

Being a good customer to external suppliers helps an organization serve its own customers more effectively. This is certainly true when buying print, when

Table 6.5 A sample print specification

On your specification (one side of A4) include the following information:

- Your name and contact details and the date.
- The title of the project.
- The format: e.g. A4 landscape.
- Description: e.g. 16 pages of text printed in two colours both sides, self-cover, stapled.
- Materials: the heavier the paper the more expensive the print job, as a rule. Ask for samples. Normal typing paper is about 80 grams per square metre – or 'gsm'. Do you want a matt or shiny finish (also known as 'art' paper)?
- Artwork: what type of software will the designer be using to create the artwork?
- Quantity: e.g. 10 000 and 2000 run-on; run-on meaning how much would a small extra quantity be. It can often be minimal once the job is up and running.
- Proofs: details of how many sets of proofs you require.
- Delivery: more than one point for delivery will increase the cost, but may save you time if you are using a distribution company.

an accurate specification can save a lot of time and energy. A specification is a full technical description of what will be required in the printing job (see Table 6.5). As mentioned in the schedule outline in Table 6.4, some printers will insist that they need to see the artwork before quoting. But a full specification can mean that you are able to access more quotations in advance, and therefore negotiate a better price. By the stage the artwork becomes available, time is likely to be at a premium.

It is a good idea to get at least three quotations. Like the arts, printing is a service business and cannot store capacity. Its machines are either occupied or they lose money. So it may be that, if your print project coincides with a slack period, you get offered very attractive rates. Before making your final decision, it is worth paying the printer a visit. As we shall see in Chapter 9, good supplier relationships are essential to successful marketing, so it pays to find out as much as you can about the printer. Good printers when found are worth cultivating, although the relationship should never become a complacent one.

Direct marketing

The days of the corner shop are long gone where a shopkeeper knew customers by name and could anticipate their needs. Perhaps the last widespread survivor of this kind of 'relationship marketing' is when a publican spots a regular customer coming in and asks 'The usual?'. But technology now puts unprecedented computing power in the hands of organizations which could not have dreamed of such things even ten years ago, and it is now possible for arts marketers to know their customers just as well – in fact, better in terms of

Table 6.6 Parlez-vous printing?

Like advertising, printing has its own specialized jargon. Here are some commonly used terms and their explanations. If ever you are in doubt about the production process, don't hesitate to ask your printers. They like to work with well-informed clients and will be delighted to explain things and make valuable suggestions.

Art paper	Gloss finished paper, coated with china clay.
Bleed	Printing a colour to the edge of the page.
Bromide	A high-definition photographic image on silver-bromide paper.
Colour separation	Process of separating colour artwork into the four process colours (see below) for the production of printing plates for four-colour printing.
Colours	The cheapest form of printing is black on white ('one colour'). Two colours of ink together cost a little more but open up a number of possibilities (including 'duotone' which can look very convincing). If you're strapped for cash, try printing one colour black on a coloured paper. At the other end of the scale, 'four colour' printing, although more expensive, allows you to mix the four 'process' colours to get the full spectrum of effects.
Desk-top publishing (DTP)	The processing of text and images on a computer to create digital artwork. QuarkXpress is a popular software package used for this.
Duotone	A two-colour half-tone (see below) from a single-colour original. Gives an impression of depth and solidity.
Em	A unit of type measurement based on the width of the capital letter 'M'. Unless otherwise specified, an em means a pica (12 point) em. Often called a 'monkey'.
En	Half an em – often called a 'nut'.
Half-tone	A photographic reproduction giving the impression of gradations of colour through tiny dots on the page.
Image manipulation	The process of converting images into a suitable format for a design concept, including the retouching and cropping of photographs. Photoshop is a popular software package used for this.
Justification	Justified type results in lines of equal length, and straight margins left and right. Unjustified type usually has a straight margin on the left and a ragged margin on the right.
Point	A measure of the height of a typeface from the top of the tallest letter to the bottom of the lowest. There are 72 points to an inch.
Process colours	Yellow, magenta, cyan and black – from which colour printing can produce the full spectrum of colours.
Register	In colour printing, the accuracy with which the overlays are superimposed.
Retouching	Correcting or improving a visual image – easy with computer technology.
Reversed out copy	Letters that are white on a coloured background. Impressive, but hard to read in quantity.
Saddle stitched	Stapled, to you and me, but so called because the machine on which the stapling is done looks like a saddle.
Scanning	Making a digital copy of a photograph or illustration.
Tint	A shade of a colour produced, like a half-tone, by tiny dots. For example, a 10% tint means that a pale shade of a colour is printed, whereas a 60% tint is a much stronger colour.
Typeface/font	A style of type. It can impart atmosphere and character to your printed materials.

exact purchasing behaviour, than pub regulars! Box office computers store customers' names, addresses, telephone numbers and e-mail addresses, together with information on their attendance patterns and frequency of ticket purchase. This valuable data is preserved reliably and permanently on a database, and is used extensively by arts organizations which have embraced direct marketing techniques (also known as database marketing) to target potential audiences more effectively and communicate with their customers as individuals.

Despite its obvious attractions, however, direct marketing is not a panacea for all ills. As a technique for audience development it falls short, in that it focuses on known users rather than searching for new converts. Furthermore, badly targeted direct marketing is not only highly wasteful (because of the expense of production and postage), but can also have a negative image, dubbed 'junk mail', or 'spam' in the case of e-mailing. As with any technique associated with high technology, there may be a significant gap between expectations and what is possible. It is a sobering consideration that what really dictates success in direct marketing is not the creative quality of the offer, nor yet the quality or value of the goods being sold, but the quality of the list itself. In the arts this is dependent on the quality of data captured by box office staff during transactions. Out-of-date or poorly maintained lists can undermine even the most imaginative campaigns.

Our examination of direct marketing here will first distinguish between direct marketing and direct response, then at the business of creating a customer database. Finally we will look at the mechanics of communicating with customers on our databases through the main devices open to the direct marketer – mailing, telephone, e-mailing and text messaging.

Direct marketing vs. direct response marketing

The vast majority of direct marketing approaches invite customers to make some kind of response – to buy a ticket, to sign up for a special offer, to attend an event. If the approaches do not then they are missing a trick, as one of the most effective ways in which direct marketing techniques can be used is for a 'call to action', the effectiveness of which can be tested and then evaluated (see below). However, direct marketing is not the only way to solicit a measurable response. Mass media can work too. A poster which emphasizes a telephone number is just as much a direct response medium as a mailshot or e-mail; and television and radio are tried and tested methods of selling products like classical CD compilations which are, famously, 'not available in any shops'. Newspapers and magazines with reply coupons are another popular choice (where the technique is known as 'off the page' selling). This technique has been used with some success by orchestras and theatres promoting subscription series who have taken pages in selected colour supplements. In fact, a response mechanism can be used in any promotional medium to encourage people to act. The key difference between 'direct' marketing and 'direct response' marketing is that with direct marketing, the approach is made to identifiable individuals rather than an unidentifiable mass market.

Database building

Some arts organizations are in the happy position of being able to collect the names and addresses of all existing customers in the course of normal business. This is the case if, as in a theatre box office, the product or service is sold over the telephone to credit card customers, or by post. Capturing personal data face to face at a box office is much trickier. Faced with queues of people wanting to get to their seats in time for the start of a performance, box office staff will be prioritizing customer service rather than collecting personal data, and full details of walk-up customers are notoriously difficult to obtain.

Arts organizations without box offices are forced to take another approach. Prospect names and addresses can be built up from visitor records or mailing list applicants who have responded to an advertisement; or someone else's list can be hired or borrowed. There are a number of companies known as list brokers who can supply the opportunity of mailing different demographic combinations throughout the country. The respondents to the offer are then retained as the basis of a new list.

Whatever the technique chosen, this is the investment stage of the process. Just as a new product will not become profitable until well into its growth phase, so new customers may take a while to repay the expense of their recruitment. However, research shows that the vast majority of all sorts of sales come from repeat business. Store account card customers, for example, tend to spend as much as five times more than non-account customers per year. Getting them to take up an account will have required an outlay. But once acquired they are a business's most valuable asset.

A customer list itself is a valuable source of other customers. Sociologists observe that people tend to behave in similar ways within peer groups. It follows that existing customers' friends may well be potential customers as well. As a result MGM ('Member Get Member') and FGAF ('Friend Get A Friend') schemes are a frequent component of direct marketing customer acquisition campaigns. Any organization's customers exist on a continuum ranging from those who do not know anything about it to those who like its products or services so much that they recommend them to others. This is as true of exhibition and theatregoers as it is of any other group of consumers. MGM and FGAF rely on the fact that most direct marketing operations have extremely well-satisfied customers who have no hesitation in recommending them to their friends. Arts events have the additional advantage that they are often attended in groups. 'Two for the price of one' ticket deals may be a simple way of filling first night seats, but they possibly also represent important sampling opportunities for people who get brought along to the show by a friend.

A related way of prospecting for customers similar to your existing customer base is to identify another group whose members might have similar interests. Care should be taken, however, that your systems are sufficiently sophisticated to detect and eliminate overlap, or you risk creating confusion and resentment among potential and actual customers.

Testing and evaluation

A key characteristic of direct marketing is its capacity to be evaluated. Direct marketers quickly know how successful their marketing activity has been, as they can identify the responses to specific pieces of marketing activity by coding the response mechanisms (e.g. marking reply coupons with an identifier). This kind of accountability helps marketing managers plan and justify their budgets for direct marketing campaigns in a way which gives the marketing function credibility in frequently sceptical arts organizations.

Until recently, direct marketing would never have been considered to be a cheap form of promotional activity. Experience suggests that as a rough guide you might expect a mailshot to yield a response from between 2 per cent and 5 per cent of those who receive it (although the figure will be a great deal higher if you are mailing to the right kind of people). Whereas television advertising is measured in terms of hundreds of people seeing it for every pound spent, a direct mailshot tends to reach between one and two people per pound (depending on the sophistication of the contents). Using the telephone is more expensive still. But it is the rapid spread of access to e-mail that has turned the tables for arts marketers, and reduced the cost of making direct contact with customers to a fraction of what was formerly possible. While sophisticated (and sometimes costly) e-flyers (explained later in this chapter) can be used, a lot can be achieved on tight budgets by arts organizations which are disciplined about collecting e-mail addresses.

Because some forms of direct marketing are expensive, pre-testing of the process and message can be valuable and cost-effective. For example, every part of a mailshot is capable of being experimented with. If you look closely at the next piece of direct mail you receive, you will notice that each item in the envelope will have a unique identifying code. This is because the chances are that each part of that mailing is being experimented with. Letter layout, size and position of suggested price points on the order form, even the colour of the ink, are all variables which can be tested to see which pulls the greatest response. As a result, the creative principles which underlie the following advice about creating and writing a mailshot are actually tested against experience.

The variables in an arts campaign may not be as extensive or as sophisticated as in commercial marketing, but much can be learned from experimentation. For example, printed material can be coded uniquely at very little extra cost by the printer in order to identify response on booking forms from various outlets or mailing activities. Or two different sorts of covering letter can accompany a mailed brochure in a 'split' mailing, and the resulting responses compared. The most important marketing experience you can obtain is that of your own customers.

Direct mail

For arts organizations, sending printed material in the mail is the most popular direct marketing approach. In many ways it is ideal, as it allows a good deal of information and explanation to be conveyed, as well as offering the ability to target an offer precisely to the individual concerned.

What are the essential components of a good mailshot?

The envelope

An envelope can start selling even before it has been opened. Thinking back to the Attention – Interest – Desire – Action model of communication examined earlier in this chapter, the envelope can be used to grab attention. It might be an intriguing line. A famous mailing soliciting subscriptions for the American magazine *Psychology Today* featured the irresistible line 'Do you lock the bathroom door behind you, even when there's no one else in the house?' More elaborate material from companies like Readers Digest, or the Consumers Association promoting *Which?* magazine, often features windows in the envelope through which exciting things like stamps, a 'credit card' or even a key or a coin can be seen. For the arts organization on a limited budget, however, a simple message can be enough. The arts have a positive and cheerful message compared to much of the mundane or tiresome material which usually awaits the householder on the mat in the morning. The cost of having your envelope supplier print it in one colour can be negligible over a large order quantity.

The letter

This is the main selling vehicle. Common sense would suggest that it be kept terse and concise, like a business letter. But, again, research shows that if people are going to read it at all they do not mind length so long as interest is maintained. So the letter should be as long as it needs to be. There seems to be an industry trend towards letters which border on being newsletters, sometimes up to four pages, usually with plenty of verbal and visual variety.

- Keeping paragraphs short is a good idea, as is plenty of white space.
- A useful trick is to end each page with a sentence that runs into the next page, the idea being to keep the reader's attention.
- Letters are a personal form of expression, and even though your letter may be going out to many thousands of prospects, it is well to keep this in mind. Give your letters a personal touch which reflects the USP of your business.
- Many arts organizations boast a charismatic individual as a music director or artistic director. This is an asset to be exploited in direct mail – by scripting a letter as if it came from them.

The response device

A card or envelope which allows the reader to respond to the offer is absolutely vital. If the letter has fulfilled the Interest and Desire part of the AIDA equation, then this fulfils the Action element. Modern print and computer technology means that you can partially fill out this card for the respondent with details of name and address. Just as good press relations make life easier for journalists, so good direct marketing makes life easier for customers (in much the same way as structured telephone call handling does in the box office, as covered earlier). Pre-printing response forms has the additional benefit of making life easier for the response handler as well, as it insures against indecipherable handwriting and incorrect details.

Other mailing components

Received wisdom in the direct mail world holds that the more gimmicks you can cram into the package, the more opportunities you have to sell. If there are eight things in the envelope, the prospect has to say 'no' eight times. Scratch cards, stickers, stamps, envelopes within envelopes, certificates and letters, all promote involvement. The reason they are there in mailings from the Consumers Association, for example, is that research has proved that they boost response. The only unbreakable rule about what to put into a mailing is to be consistent. The whole package must have an internal cohesion. So the message on the outside should be carried forward by the content of the letter. The response device should continue the theme rather than going off on a tangent. Any other components should be flowing the same way, too. Logic should never be sacrificed to creativity, however beguiling the idea might appear in the short term. This is sometimes a difficulty when there are a number of people in an organization whose views contribute to marketing. 'Keep it simple' is a valuable principle.

Always monitor response, as the lessons you learn from your own activity are the most important pieces of marketing information you will be able to bring to bear on your future planning. There is always a temptation to neglect this kind of analysis in the busy world of arts marketing, but as explained above, it is becoming more and more necessary in maximizing the value to be extracted from scarce resources.

Return to sender, address unknown

According to the Direct Marketing Association, poorly addressed items of mail are estimated to cost around £100 million a year to the direct mail industry. Of the 3.7 billion items of direct mail sent out in the UK in 1997 100 million items were sent back, marked 'return to sender' and 80 million were so badly addressed as to be 'undeliverable'.

Tele-sales

Relative to direct mail, the use of tele-sales in the arts is fairly limited. Box offices are fully geared up for 'inbound' sales (see Chapter 7), when customers call them to book tickets; but the proactive use of the telephone as a means of selling individual tickets, subscriptions or group bookings ('outbound sales'), or for fund-raising, is surprisingly uncommon given the potential benefits it offers (see Table 6.7).

At the root of this reluctance lies a widespread deeply-held belief among many arts marketers that the practice of telephoning potential customers to tell them about forthcoming productions or special offers is unethical, a waste of money, and will at best be met with indifference by the customer – and at

Table 6.7 Why use the telephone?

Spectacular results	A well-planned and well-executed tele-marketing campaign can produce better and more immediate results than a comparable direct mail campaign.
Flexibility	When a mailing has been sent, it's too late to change the content; tele-marketing scripts can be changed in response to success rates, and changes in the environment.
Responsive	With mail you know how many people respond, but on the telephone you find out why – and why not.
Interactive	In conversation with potential customers, callers can check understanding, ask questions, make suggestions and listen to reactions to an offer – and change approach if it proves to be unappealing.
Immediate and urgent	Whereas mail packs will only be read by a small percentage of recipients, a telephone is more difficult to ignore and a conversation will always provoke a response of some kind – whether positive or negative.
Personal	Tele-marketing involves people talking to and responding to people – ideal for customer care and relationship building.

Source: Dixon, 2001.

worst, outright hostility. Being tarred with the same brush as cold-calling double-glazing firms is something, understandably, that arts marketers wish to avoid at all costs. It is therefore heartening to discover that, in reality, arts organizations' customers are more than capable of distinguishing between the unwanted intrusion caused by unscrupulous salespeople who openly flout the requirements of the Data Protection Act (see Chapter 7) by picking names at random out of the telephone directory to sell their wares, and arts organizations to whom they have given their contact details calling to ensure that they are fully aware of the forthcoming leisure opportunities available to them. Indeed, research demonstrates that two-thirds of respondents are pleased to be called by their local theatre, and those with the most intensive booking histories are the most enthusiastic of all (Hill and Whitehead, 1997). This applies to fund-raising as well as ticket sales. When 1743 infrequent attenders at the Oxford Playhouse were asked whether they would be happy to receive a call from the Playhouse asking for money, 97 per cent said yes (Dixon, 2001)!

Another objection often raised to the use of tele-sales is the cost of a campaign and, as with direct mail, evaluation is key to determining whether or not a campaign is cost-effective. Generally speaking, the higher the cost of what is being sold, the more likely it is that a tele-sales campaign will produce a positive financial return. This means that season subscriptions and group bookings appear to offer better potential for profitable tele-sales than single ticket booking. However, when the potential 'life-time value' of a customer is taken into account, the costs of using the telephone to kick-start what could be a long-term relationship look far more reasonable.

Case 6.3 Prompting for profit

Buxton Opera House is a 937-seat receiving theatre which hosts a varied programme ranging from drama to brass bands, as well as being a main venue for the Buxton Festival. But in common with many arts organizations, it faced problems in retaining first-time attenders.

A target group was identified from the box office system, comprising patrons who had booked only once, but not in the past 12 months, and had spent less than £60. A tele-marketing campaign known as 'TelePrompt' was launched to encourage these people to return, and then to maintain telephone contact with them every three or four months to keep the relationship going. The aim of the telephone conversation was not to sell tickets, but to act as a 'talking brochure', tailored to a person's area of interest, without any pressure to buy. This was followed up by mail with a personalized letter, booking form, seating plan, brochure and show information sheets.

Following the campaign, an analysis of booking patterns of those in the target group who had received a call were compared with those who had not (the 'control' group). The results are shown in the table:

	Control group	Test group
Number in group	200	200
Booked tickets within 3 months	5%	27%
Value of tickets purchased	£250	£2400
Associated marketing costs	nil	£600
Net income	£250	£1800
Income per patron	£1.25	£9

Seven thousand people on the Buxton Opera House database had the same ticket-buying profile as those contacted in the campaign so, if half of those were contactable on the telephone, it was estimated that a net income of £27 000 could be generated in just 3 months. However, there was one major disincentive to taking this approach further. Contract agreements meant that for every £1 taken at the box office, 80p was paid to touring companies or promoters putting on the shows. If the costs of extending the TelePrompt campaign were to be borne by the Opera House alone, it would not be financially viable.

Source: Dunnett, 1999.

For major campaigns involving hundreds or thousands of calls, most arts organizations will use a specialist tele-marketing agency; but for smaller campaigns, some arts organizations will tackle the task of planning, managing and making calls themselves. Although they are usually quite familiar with the practice of inbound sales described in Chapter 7, the practice of outbound tele-sales raises a number of issues unique to the situation, and these need to be thoroughly planned in advance:

- *Data selection:* Given the relatively high cost of each contact with a potential customer on the telephone, and the potential for a hostile response if you contact inappropriate people, the selection of whom to call (known as 'prospects') is an important one. Choose only those customers whose booking histories suggest that they will be interested in what you want to sell. Customers whose telephone numbers have not already been recorded can be found through a number tracing service, and then all the numbers to be called should be matched against the Telephone Preference Scheme, a national database which records the telephone numbers of households which have specifically requested not to be contacted by organizations for direct marketing purposes.
- *Call scheduling:* A rota of callers, each with responsibility for a certain number of prospects, has to be drawn up to ensure that each prospect is telephoned by only one caller. Inevitably, for every successfully connected call many more will fail because the call reaches the wrong person in the household, or is answered by a voicemail service. It is important to reschedule calls appropriately, and have a policy in place governing the number of attempts that will be made to reach a prospect before giving up.
- *Scripts:* To ensure that all customers are approached in the most consistent and effective way, it is useful for those making the calls to use a script to guide their conversations. A rigid framework might be considered a desirable confidence-booster for inexperienced callers, but in general it is better simply to provide an outline structure for the call, a list of points to be covered in conversation and a set of possible responses to typical questions. Anything more tightly scripted is likely to be noticed by the potential customer, and the sincerity of the message – not to mention the potential for developing a relationship – may be undermined.
- *Call sheets:* Because of the two-way nature of a telephone conversation, every call generates information – much of it very valuable. To ensure that this information is captured effectively, a call sheet should be set up for every prospect to record key elements of the conversation – for example, if a customer wants more information to be sent by post, or asks not to be called again. Of course, if the caller does not have access to a live box office ticketing system, precise notes must also be taken of any tickets required, seating preferences and other details.
- *Fulfilment:* This is about doing what you said you would – putting tickets in the post, sending more information about a show, or even dealing with a complaint. To generate enthusiasm among potential attenders, only then to fail to act so that they can enjoy the experience, renders the entire campaign worthless and creates a very negative impression of the organization. Good administrative follow-up is just as important as a good sales technique.

SMS text messaging

Driven by the exponential growth in ownership of mobile phones in recent years, SMS (which stands for Short Messaging Service) is a newcomer to the portfolio of promotional techniques available to arts marketers. Especially popular among young people, according to Phillips (2002) text messaging offers many and varied advantages over other forms of direct marketing:

- *Urgency:* as mobile phones are carried around by their owners, text messages are usually read immediately by their owners.
- *Popularity:* 80 per cent of the UK population has a mobile phone, and that figure is still growing.
- *Cost:* texting is very cheap in comparison with direct mail and tele-sales.
- *Instant vouchers:* a message can double as a voucher which can be redeemed to claim a discount or a ticket.
- *Easy response:* anyone interested in a promotional offer delivered to their mobile phone can respond by simply dialling a few numbers.

Case 6.4 Testing texting

Much of the pioneering work in SMS text messaging for promoting arts performances in the UK has been undertaken by Sadler's Wells. In March 2002, the venue presented the musical *Stomp*, and used it as an opportunity to test three different approaches to text promotions.

Some 26 000 mobile phone numbers were held on Sadler's Wells's box office database, and in the first campaign 4000 of these, all of whom had 'opted in' to receive marketing information, were sent a single text message to encourage bookings through a targeted offer and provided with an easy opt-out for future messages:

> From Sadlers Wells £15 best tix deal for Stomp: music + dancing with dustbins! 4,5,7,9,10,14 Apr 7.30pm Quote txt on 020 7863 8000. Reply 'Stop' for no more txts

Over 100 tickets were booked and the campaign made a 500 per cent return on investment. Only 8 per cent asked to unsubscribe to future messages, and there were two e-mail complaints.

During the *Stomp* run, two forthcoming shows, *Rome and Jewels* and *Bounce*, which were also aimed at young audiences, carried a message on their posters and in the *Stomp* programme to encourage people to send a text to enter a competition for free tickets:

> Txt 2 win: Text 'Bounce' to 07771 548720 to win tkts for 1st night + show updates

Random winners were chosen and everyone else was sent a text message with a special price ticket deal:

> Sorry u didn't win tix this time. How about a best available for £10 deal? May 28–30. Call 020 7863 8222 Quote 'TxtTix'. 2 unsubscribe text 'stop'

Over 35 tickets were sold and 600 new mobile phone numbers were collected.

The third campaign used a bought-in database of 10 000 names to which a text message was sent and, in addition, 20 000 flyers were distributed around London colleges inviting students to text back for £10 student deals. Respondents were sent a message asking them which date they wanted to book:

> Hi! The 'Stomp' Student specials are for 5,7 and 14 April. Which date would you like? Just reply with the number – e.g.14

Finally, customers were asked to text 'Buy' to proceed. Pre-registered customers had to type in a pin number to purchase, and others were contacted by a call centre to take their credit-card details.

Three hundred responses were generated from the 10 000 messages, and 20 tickets sold; and 690 responses were generated from the flyer, though only five tickets were sold. Feedback suggested that the choice of dates was too limiting for many, and it was discovered that some students were barred from paying by credit card because of the limitations placed on arm's-length transactions by their credit-card suppliers.

Source: De Kretser, 2002.

While text messaging has much in common with other direct marketing techniques, these characteristics mean that it can be particularly useful for time-related promotional purposes, such as special deals on unsold tickets on the day of a performance, a reminder service for friends and members when priority booking opens, or information about last-minute changes to a programme. One difficulty facing arts marketers wanting to launch an SMS service is how to develop a list. While many arts organizations have been collecting land-line telephone numbers for many years, they often have to start almost from scratch with mobile numbers. Capturing the data at the box office, and allowing people to register their interest on a website, are probably the best approaches to this.

E-marketing

As well as creating a new sales channel for tickets (see Chapter 7), the internet and related technologies, especially e-mail, offer arts organizations an invaluable framework for implementing promotional activity (see Table 6.8). Managed properly, they can vastly expand the reach of promotional messages and have an important role to play in attracting new audiences. They also

Table 6.8 E-marketing terminology

Banner ad	A portion of a web page used to carry advertising, often featuring moving images and providing an active link to the advertiser's own website (see 'click-through rate').
Click-through rate	The percentage of people who, seeing an internet banner advertisement, use it as a link to 'click through' to the advertiser's web page.
Cookies	A small text file (think of it as a kind of computerized business card) which is left behind on your hard drive when you visit a website. Some computer users object to cookies on privacy grounds. Your web browser will allow you not to accept them, but many websites rely on cookies to help personalize their content to individual users and so may not work properly if they are disabled.
E-flyer	A virtual leaflet that can be sent either in or attached to an e-mail. Can feature involving content and direct response opportunites. If the e-flyer is sufficiently interesting or amusing, recipients may pass it on to their friends – an example of viral marketing.
Home page	Can have two meanings depending on the context: either (1) the page at which your own web browser first opens (which you can set from the options menu), or (2) the first page of a website owned by an organization or individual. Will carry links to other pages according to how the site is organized. Typing an organization's web address (URL) into your browser will bring you to its home page.
HTML	Hyper Text Mark-up Language – the language in which web pages are written in order to be visible to web browsers.
ISP	Internet Service Provider – an organization which offers space on its server to host your website and offers access to the World Wide Web and other internet services such as e-mail.
Portal	A website that specializes in leading you to other websites, often specific to particular industry, leisure interest or art form.
Search engine	A program that helps users find information on the web through matching the text which they type in (called search terms) with corresponding websites.
Server	A computer which can be accessed by other computers, either on a network, or through the internet. Effectively it 'serves up' web pages to other computers.
Spam	The e-mail version of junk mail – unwanted e-mail which can cause irritation and clog up limited computer space if not deleted.
URL	Uniform Resource Locator. The unique address of any web document, such as a home page. The format of the URL can also reveal what kind of organization a website belongs to, and its geographical location.
WAP	Wireless Application Protocol – a system that allows mobile phones and personal digital assistants (such as palm organizers) to connect to the internet through radio waves rather than cables.
Web browser	A program that makes HTML documents on the web visible (and audible) to users. Common examples are Netscape and Internet Explorer.
World Wide Web	A global network of interlinked servers which share information coded in HTML – in other words, web pages offering direct links to other pages anywhere on the Web. Although the two terms are often used synonymously, the World Wide Web is not the same as the internet – but just one aspect of it. The internet also carries non-HTML information, such as e-mail, newsgroups and direct file transfers between computers.

create cost-effective opportunities for direct marketing among an existing customer base, allowing more personalized and up-to-date messages to be sent to customers and expanding the potential for them to engage in two-way communication, through e-mail dialogue, feedback forms and bulletin boards. But, for all the obvious advantages, e-marketing does not provide a substitute for other promotional activity, rather a complement to it. Although the growth of domestic access to the internet has been meteoric, not all households have, or are likely to have, access to it in the foreseeable future. Furthermore, a website, even if spectacularly designed and offering the ultimate in functionality, is only of any value if customers are drawn to look at it – and other promotional techniques will be needed to lead the way on this. Sustaining quality in e-marketing communications is another issue that has to be faced. According to Smith and Chaffey (2001), ineffective e-marketing is all too commonplace:

> ... broken sites, delayed deliveries, impersonal responses. Whether it's unclear objectives, lack of strategy or simply lousy execution, good e-marketing is relatively rare. Disappointed customers, frustrated customers, angry customers and lawsuit customers are created as a result of sloppy e-marketing.

Websites

An arts organization's website has, in recent years, become its marketing engine room. As well as being the place where customers are increasingly going to buy their tickets (see Chapter 7), it is also the shop window where many now go to browse through and find out what is for sale. A well-designed highly functional website has therefore become a must-have for marketers, which can be a costly business. Initial set-up design costs are only part of the story. For a website to be effective, it must carry up-to-date information, and that means arranging for it to be continually updated. This can be a real headache for small arts organizations without the resources to appoint a dedicated IT professional, as it inevitably involves staff time being diverted from their normal work and will require a level of training.

There are three desirable qualities in any website, according to Julie Aldridge (2002):

- *Magnetism:* the site needs to attract people. The single most important way of achieving this is by including material that people want to know about, interact with and/or respond to, and publicizing this fact. Taking steps to ensure that the site is prominently featured through appropriate keywords on search engines is one important way of doing this.
- *Stickiness:* when people arrive at the site, something has to grab their attention, otherwise they may well surf through without stopping for long enough to take in the marketing messages that you are hoping to convey.
- *Elasticity:* making people want to come back to your site time and time again is a real achievement. There is no greater accolade than to be 'bookmarked' as a site worthy of repeat visits. That is the point at which true relationship-building can really begin.

Even the most basic site – which may be little more than a web-based brochure – can aspire to these three; but more sophisticated sites, which provide additional information not published elsewhere, offer a search facility, provide an insight into the arts experience (such as a video clip or a virtual tour of a venue) and allow two-way communication with customers and potential customers, have a better chance of achieving it. The process of evaluating the volume and nature of web-traffic is a vital one if the effectiveness of a website is to be scrutinized. Anything from simple reports on the total number of 'hits' on a site or an analysis of links (other sites through which people gain access your site), to a route map showing how people feel their way around the site are possible. Outcomes such as tickets sold online, levels of registration, and return of feedback forms are the ultimate measures of the marketing impact of a site.

Classic e-marketing

Classic FM is rigorous in its evaluation of its website, and constantly monitors who visits the site, how often, for how long and at what time of the day or week, keeping track of which web pages have been visited and what merchandise has been purchased. The statistics show that around 10 per cent of the 6.8 million weekly radio listeners now use the site. Primarily people come to listen to the radio online, to find out more about the pieces they have heard and liked, and to enter competitions. The 'home' page and the 'listen' page are therefore the most critical for conveying the organization's messages and drawing people deeper into the site. A significant amount of the station's on-air programming is now driven by the site, including the Classic FM 'Most Wanted', a daily programme where listeners vote for their daily Top 10 from a list of 30 on the site. Popular features such as the annual 'Hall of Fame Top 300', the 'Music Teacher for the Year' award and the 'Classical Brits' award are also voted for online.

Source: Weinberg, 2002.

E-mailing

As a direct marketing technique an e-mail campaign offers a range of clear benefits over direct mail and, if linked to an interactive website, can perform a quite amazing range of functions. The starting point, however, is exactly the same as direct mail: the generation of a list of addresses – e-mail addresses. Lists of e-mail prospects can be created from among an existing customer base by encouraging people to divulge their e-mail addresses at the point of transaction, and further names can be added to the list through print campaigns (such as postcards inviting e-mail registration) or registration forms on a website. There are other major similarities with direct mail, in that messages can be mail-merged and personalized; they can be used to deliver vouchers, coupons or other special offers (sales promotions); and electronic leaflets known as 'e-flyers' can be attached. But e-mails go way beyond this, in that they can include web links to encourage recipients to follow a simple one-step route to vast quantities of further information or, if appropriate, take them direct to a web-based ticket-buying facility. The potential for generating a response of some sort is therefore far greater than with direct mail, as the effort required from the recipient is far less. Furthermore, when someone reads an e-mail and likes what they read, it is not too difficult to persuade them to e-mail it on to other people they know – a technique known as 'viral marketing'. All this, and at a tiny fraction of the cost of printing and distributing direct mail. So what's the catch?

Well, there are very few. Domestic e-mail penetration is still growing, but has some way to go, and the proportion of some sectors of the population, particularly those in older age groups and lower socio-economic groups, having access to e-mail is still relatively low. The penetration of high-grade computer technology – and in particular, computers with fast enough speeds and large enough memories to deal with sophisticated e-flyers – is also uneven. Anyone sending an e-mail with a large attachment is still in danger of incurring the wrath of the intended recipient if it takes them hours to download it or, worse still, causes their system to grind to a halt. Some recipients are highly suspicious of attachments anyway, as their ability to harbour potentially catastrophic viruses is always a cause for concern, and an attachment may be deleted without even being opened. More worrying, perhaps, is the impact of 'spam' – uninvited, intrusive and frequently unsavoury e-mails sent out to mass e-mail lists by unscrupulous organizations – the electronic equivalent of junk mail. Their activities are undoubtedly creating serious reservations among customers about mass e-mailing, dampening their enthusiasm for reading e-mails from little-known sources or signing up to any e-mail list.

Summary

Communicating the benefits of what is on offer from the artistic experience is a fundamentally important part of the activities of the marketing function. While it requires flair and imagination, it also needs determination and a disciplined, evaluative approach. Applying simple structures like AIDA and USP can help reduce the complexity of the task of saying the right things about your offering in the right format.

Arts organizations have a number of promotional techniques at their disposal. Advertising is expensive but can communicate important details to a large number of people very quickly. Print and poster media are traditionally favoured by arts clients, but media possibilities should be subject to constant review. The technique of public relations builds on the strengths of arts organizations and can be used to create background interest in arts activities. It is less good, however, at fulfilling that interest than more specific publicity activity such as direct marketing. Sales promotion is most commonly seen in the form of discounts tied to multiple attendance. But, like advertising and PR, it is capable of a flexible application across a wide range of tactical situations. Printed publicity, in the form of literature like season brochures, spearheads the marketing activity of most performing and visual arts organizations. Writing or editing copy and overseeing design and production involves tact and determination. Developing good systems and working relationships can minimize the risks involved. Direct marketing is among the most popular promotional approaches used by arts organizations, enjoyed for its ability to sustain two-way communications between the organization and its customers, and the potential it holds for developing deeper one-to-one relationships with them. Traditional techniques such as direct mail and tele-marketing are now being joined by those made possible through new technology – namely SMS text messaging and e-mailing. Indeed, e-marketing in general, and in particular the use of websites for marketing purposes, is a discipline in rapid growth, and which appears to unlock the potential for even better two-way communications with customers and potential customers in the future.

Key concepts

advertising
copywriting
coverage
direct mail
direct marketing
e-mail
e-marketing
media
opinion leaders
outdoor advertising
press release
print schedule
print specification

printing terminology
prospect
public relations
rate card
sales promotion
SMS text messaging
solus position
subscription
tele-sales
transport advertising
USP
viral marketing
website

Discussion questions

1 Compare and contrast the roles of printed brochures and websites as vehicles for announcing a new season of productions at a receiving theatre.
2 In what ways might a PR campaign in support of an international touring exhibition differ from a PR campaign for an orchestra embarking on an international tour.
3 To what extent might the launch of a subscription season address an organization's audience development objectives? What features would you design into the campaign to ensure that it could achieve those objectives?
4 If you wanted to use direct marketing to encourage more group bookers to bring parties of friends or colleagues to ballet performances at your venue, how would you identify individuals to target and what would you offer them as an incentive to book?

5 How might you go about evaluating the effectiveness of your organization's advertising expenditure?

Case study: Open all hours

The major promotion aimed at capitalizing on the wave of popularity that the visual arts were enjoying in the wake of the opening of the hugely successful Tate Modern was run by a consortium of eight London galleries between March and May 2002. The galleries shared a set of very specific objectives for the campaign, but all were keen to promote evening attendance:

- to raise awareness of longer evening opening hours
- to increase visitor numbers after 6 p.m.
- to change the perceptions of galleries as boring and stuffy and introduce the concept of galleries as a social venue
- to highlight the full range of activities that visitors could enjoy including special events, lectures, tours, live music, restaurants, bars and shops

Some galleries, such as the V&A, had been doing late-night openings for a couple of years and attracted between 1500 and 2000 visitors a night. Others, such as the National Portrait Gallery, had been doing evening openings two nights a week for less than a year and were attracting between 300 and 400 visitors a night. Others, such as Dulwich Picture Gallery, were not doing evening openings on a regular basis at all and wanted to use the promotion as an opportunity to test out an evening opening policy and see how effective it was.

The target group for the campaign comprised 25–34-year-old culturally aware urban professionals, working or living in London. To attract this market, a very clear central message was developed: 'Love Art? . . . Enjoy it . . . Later.' The message was reinforced with the use of love-heart sweets as the promotional brand. Some 190 000 leaflets promoting each of the galleries, their current exhibitions and their late-night opening were printed, 66 000 of which were distributed around London and the West End by a print distribution agency, with a particular emphasis on bars, restaurants, cafés and clubs. This achieved an 89 per cent pick-up rate. The participating galleries distributed 8000 each, and the remainder were inserted into *Time Out* magazine, from whom sponsorship was secured. Their readership was a good match for the age and lifestyle profile of the target audience.

The leaflet also promoted details of a series of bar nights which were to take place over the course of the three-month campaign at a different gallery each week, giving away free Love Art vodka cocktails sponsored by Absolut vodka. Absolut's brand was also ideal for the age group and profile of visitor that were targeted. The bar nights were advertised in *Time Out* each week who, in return for branding on all publicity associated with the promotion and special ticket offers for their readers, provided editorial support, a launch advertisement, and over the course of eight weeks ran advertisements of where and when the next bar night was taking place. They also printed a special voucher each week that readers could use on an evening visit at the participating galleries to claim a discount off exhibition or gallery entry. Over 1500 of these were collected by the galleries during the promotion. *Time Out* also gave the promotion publicity in a newsletter sent out to their 10 000 subscribers and highlighted listings advertising evening opening hours. In addition to all of this, each of the galleries also did their own publicity to promote their particular bar nights with e-mail bulletins, web links, posters and local press coverage.

The campaign costs were split equally between the participating galleries, with each spending £1400 on the promotion. The bulk of the costs went towards the production and distribution of the leaflet. *Time Out* provided advertising valued at £21 000 and Absolut spent approximately £8000 on the bar nights. It proved to be money well spent.

The first bar night took place at the Hayward Gallery and attracted much higher than average visitor numbers for an evening opening with approximately 300 visitors. A similar experience followed at the National Portrait Gallery, which saw normal evening opening attendance double to around 800. Even Dulwich Picture Gallery, which did not have a regular late-night opening, and therefore no regular audience, with little passing trade, succeeded in attracting nearly 200 visitors. For some, the impact has been sustained. For example, during the campaign visitor numbers at the National Portrait Gallery began to rise and they have since been consistently welcoming over 1000 visitors a night.

Source: Marlow, 2001.

Questions

1 What might be the advantages and disadvantages of working collaboratively on a major promotional campaign with other arts organizations?
2 What sort of data has been gathered during the course of the promotion, and how can it be used after the campaign to build long-term relationships with potential evening attenders?
3 To what extent do promotions such as this run the risk of attracting people to the free drink rather than the free art? What could be done to limit this risk?

References

The Advertising Association (2002) 'UK advertising expenditure down by £263 million in fourth quarter of 2001, compared with a year ago', press release, 8 March.

Aldridge, J. (2002) 'Word of mouse', *Journal of Arts Marketing*, Issue 06, July, 8–9.

Baker, T. (2002) 'Package deals', *ArtsProfessional*, Issue 18, 28 January, 8–9.

Brooker, M. and Silvester, J. (2001) 'CBSO Ambassadors – Making The Most Of Your Supporters' Enthusiasm', Made in Heaven: Arts Marketing Association Conference, Birmingham, July.

Crofts, A. (1988) 'Enhancing the past to secure the future', *Marketing Week*, 11 March, 48–56.

De Kretser, H. (2002) 'U TLKIN 2 ME?' *Journal of Arts Marketing*, Issue 06, July, 18–19.

Dixon, D. (2001) *It's For You: Telemarketing for arts organizations*. Arts Marketing Association.

Dunnett, H. (1999) 'Retaining First Time Attenders', Revolving Doors: Arts Marketing Association Awayday, Warwick, December.

Harland, J. and Kinder, K. (1999) *Crossing the Line*. Calouste Gulbenkian Foundation.

Hill, E. and Whitehead, B. (1997) 'Developing relationship marketing by telephone selling: an empirical study of the impact of telephone selling on the purchase of ballet tickets', AIMAC Conference, San Francisco.

Holtz, A.F. (1999) 'Co-op advertising vastly improves theaters' buying power', *Arts Reach*, Vol. VIII, Issue 1, October, 1, 4, 20, 22.

Katz, E. and Lazarsfeld, P. (1955) *Personal Influence: The part played by people in the flow of mass communications*. Free Press.

Keeble, R. (2001) *The Newspapers Handbook*. Routledge.

Marlow, E. (2001) 'Love Art?', Made in Heaven: Arts Marketing Association Conference, Birmingham, July.

McDonald, C. (1992) *How Advertising Works*. NTC Publications.

Mercer, D. (1996) *Marketing*, 2nd ed. Blackwell.

Moyle, F. (1990) 'Cash cure for art attacks', *Marketing Week*, 30 November, 38–42.

Ogilvy, D. (1995) *Ogilvy on Advertising*. Pan.

Phillips, A. (2002) 'SMS: the benefits', *Journal of Arts Marketing*, Issue 06, July, 17.

Smith, P. and Chaffey, D. (2001) *E-marketing Excellence: The heart of e-business*. Butterworth-Heinemann.

Weinberg, R. (2002) 'E-marketing at Classic FM', *Journal of Arts Marketing*, Issue 06, July, 12–13.

White, Roderick (1993) *Advertising: What it is and how to do it*, 3rd ed. McGraw Hill.

7

Making the arts available

Introduction

The fourth element of the marketing mix – 'Place' – also known as 'distribution', is concerned with making an organization's offering available to the customer when and where it is required. Much of the marketing literature dealing with distribution is about products – moving them about, storing them, displaying them. Yet thinking about ways of improving distribution has much to offer service industries, and arts organizations in particular. The performing arts, for example, use a variety of means to open up the experience on offer to as many consumers as possible. Opera and dance companies take their work on the road, touring it to audiences nationally and internationally. Ticket agents make buying tickets easier for people living at a distance from a theatre, yet still requiring personal service. Amateur companies select certain venues over others because of the access they give to established audiences. These are all distribution decisions and they are a crucial element in marketing success.

In this chapter we will look at the following areas:

- the importance of distribution in the marketing mix
- the nature and function of marketing channels
- touring companies and venues
- physical access as a factor in marketing artistic experience
- ticket selling channels

Distribution in the marketing mix

Distribution addresses the issue of how to establish an appropriate relationship with the maximum number of relevant customers at the minimum cost to the organization. Attention to distribution can lead to coverage of a wider audience, accessing more customers and enabling existing customers to have a more satisfactory experience. Distribution deals with managing effective supply. Done successfully, it fulfils the opportunities that the rest of the marketing elements create in the market, establishing the all-important final link with the customer. Advertising and publicity can attract the customer, but the sales effort at the box office or the gallery counter is what seals the relationship. Reliable distribution is an absolute requirement of marketing success, whatever your art form.

Case 7.1 Transport of delight

English National Ballet is the UK's most popular ballet company, largely due to its extensive touring activities. Touring has always been a way of life for ENB – where a typical year on the road can involve 170 performances, in venues ranging from 250 to 5000 seats. Taking ballet to a wide audience has been part of the organization's brief since its foundation in the 1950s – when its programmes were designed to appeal to audiences outside London who would otherwise have been deprived of opportunities to see affordable, high-quality dance.

In the spirit of this tradition, the company devised an audience development scheme with funding from the Arts Council of England's New Audiences programme in 1999. In order to maximize access to its tour dates at Barrow-in-Furness's Forum 28 venue, it laid on a fleet of 17 buses to bring in audience members from the surrounding regions of Cumbria and North Lancashire. Barrow-in-Furness lies in the middle of a part of England famed for its beauty and remoteness. An uneven population distribution means that in many areas people are outnumbered by sheep. Poor public transport infrastructure contributes to this rural isolation.

The 'Ballet Bus' scheme addressed this problem by providing free transport to and from the theatre for people who otherwise could not have got to the performances. In order to publicize its availability, and to promote the performances more generally, the company employed five part-time local representatives to spread word-of-mouth publicity at grass-roots level. A useful side effect of their work was that people who had their own transport found out about the performances and were motivated to attend under their own steam.

Tickets cost up to £10 – a bargain for ballet whatever the transport situation. Bus travellers paid the standard ticket price, but received a package which included not only transport but also a number of other 'audience development' benefits – a copy of the company magazine, a complimentary CD and programme, and the attentions of a company representative on the bus who was able to give them background information on the performances and company. Over 500 people used the service. Many of them had never been to the ballet before, but vowed to return when the opportunity next presented itself. The company and venue benefited from the scheme as well. Largely as a result of 'Ballet Bus' all three dates at Forum 28 were sold out.

Source: Pulford, 2000.

Traditional definitions tend to connect distribution with moving goods or services from those who produce them to those that consume them. In the arts, as Case 7.1 suggests, it can also be about moving customers to the opportunity of consumption. But it should also be remembered that all organizations, whatever their size or role, are involved in purchasing as well as supplying demand. Our examination of distribution will emphasize how arts organizations can improve their position and effectiveness by reviewing their operations at both ends of the process: managing supply both as a customer and a supplier. Increasingly, managers are finding that their ability to satisfy their customers' needs more efficiently and effectively hangs on their relationships with their own suppliers.

Distribution patterns in all areas of marketing have been a major area of change driven by new technology and lifestyles. The out-of-town shopping centre, reflecting increased car ownership, is complemented by out-of-town leisure activities such as multiplex cinemas. The combination of credit cards with information and communications technology has fuelled the boom of 'direct' marketing. It has changed the way we buy and sell a number of goods and services, including tickets. Data capture at point of sale is becoming the norm at box offices, leading to more efficient and responsive customer care. These are just some facets of the distribution revolution that surrounds the arts marketer.

The fourth 'P'

'Place' is the fourth P – completing the set of product, price and promotion. It concentrates on where the product is available. In marketing tangible goods, the emphasis is on 'physical distribution' – getting the product to the customer in the right condition and at the right price and time. These activities take place in the human context of a 'marketing channel', which adds the functions of selling and transferring goods from manufacturers to consumers. The actions in such channels are performed by organizations and individuals known as 'channel intermediaries'. Each of these concepts is relevant to opening out the experience of the arts to customers, even though (apart from equipment and people) very few tangible elements are involved.

Distribution needs to work with, and complement, the other marketing mix elements. The kind of 'Product' you are dealing with has a fundamental influence on distribution decisions. Galleries and museums have to deal with issues of transport and security for their exhibits. Auction room prices have made the issue of insurance during transport particularly problematical, creating costs which either swallow up large amounts of subsidy or have to be passed on in admission prices. Touring opera and theatre companies, or visiting orchestras, have their own solutions to the physical distribution difficulties of getting from one performance venue to another with equipment and sets. Often the only way to facilitate international touring for a major orchestra is to negotiate sponsorship in kind with an airline.

For the individual artist, the cost of travel may be a barrier to market entry abroad, preventing attendance at exhibitions or meetings with international intermediaries such as galleries or dealers. Since 1991 the Irish Arts Council and Aer Lingus have co-operated on a scheme called Artflight which offers opportunities to people working in the creative arts to visit major cities in Europe and North America. The scheme has been highly successful in helping individual artists access the market potential that exists outside Ireland itself, with its relatively small population. An Chomhairle Ealaíon, the Irish Arts Council, assists in other ways with distribution – for example, promoting a presence for Irish artists at major international exhibitions such as the Venice Biennale.

Travel and transport activities represent a major investment in resources, and are therefore appropriate operations to keep under review from the point of view of savings or alternative strategies. They offer the closest analogy we can find in the arts industries with the physical distribution strategies covered in standard marketing textbooks – finding the most appropriate methods of transport and storage to ensure that the product is available in the optimum combination of quality and accessibility. Touring companies face the additional complexity of the human factor with performers. But the focus of this chapter will be on the aspect of distribution which all arts organizations have in common, whatever the art form. The marketing channel needs to place the customer at the centre of the process.

As well as Product, 'Price' is a very live issue in distribution. Traditional marketing analysis divides intermediaries into 'merchants' and 'agents'. Merchants take title to the goods (i.e. buy them outright) and thus fix their own resale prices. Agents, on the other hand, operate on a fee or commission basis, and will adhere to their clients' wishes in setting a price to the customer. Pricing decisions in touring drama or music, as we have seen in Chapter 5, need to take local considerations into account.

Specialist forms of distribution can be combined with special pricing in order to appeal to specific segments of the market without devaluing the product for other customers. Major opera companies, for example, approach music societies early on in their campaigns with discounts in order to secure early booking. And, as Case 7.2 suggests, discounts can also be used to 'dump' unsold tickets on casual ticket buyers without prejudicing full-price sales.

Case 7.2 Brisk business at the booth

Launched in 1980 the half-price ticket booth in London's Leicester Square has filled over 5 million empty seats in London theatres which would otherwise have gone unsold. The idea was borrowed from an American original (like many good marketing ruses): the joint distribution outlet created by the League of New York Theater to sell cut-price 'on the day only' tickets in the 1970s. In its twenty-first century incarnation the business is now run under the Tkts brand, and has spawned imitations not only in and around Leicester Square, but also in many North American cities.

In order to protect against the risk of cannibalizing existing full-price business, the ticket booths have stringent rules. They almost sound like de-marketing, but ensure that only a very specific market segment is addressed with the opportunity of stand-by tickets through this distribution outlet.

- Customers must pay cash or (at some outlets) by credit card.
- There is a booking fee, and sometimes the available discount is less than 50 per cent.
- There is a limit on the number of tickets that can be sold in any one transaction.
- Only unsold tickets for that day's performance are available.
- There is no choice as to where you sit – tickets are sold from the 'top of the pile' in a particular price range.
- Customers have to queue – sometimes in the rain. Tourist websites featuring the London booth advise prospective buyers to bring a book to pass the time!
- The only way to find out what is available is to turn up – there is no access via telephone or internet.

In terms of market segmentation (see Chapter 2) we could describe the booth's customers in the following terms:

- Demographic: younger, with less disposable income. To be prepared to queue that long they must be time-rich but income-poor.
- Geographic: 90 per cent are tourists visiting London from elsewhere, 50 per cent from overseas.
- Psychographic: informal, but bargain prone.
- Behavioural: the benefit sought is a night out – a taste of London theatre rather than a specific show.

If such ventures are to avoid channel conflict (i.e. upsetting standard ticket outlets), they need to be very clear about their segmentation and targeting.

Source: http://home.clara.net/cap/half, accessed 10 October 2002.

Then, 'Promotion' is an important element to reconcile with any distribution pattern. If channel intermediaries are required to play a role in communicating the benefits of what they are making available, this is known as a 'push' strategy. It concentrates promotional effort on each stage of the marketing channel to drive the offering towards the eventual end user. This is usually carried out in tandem with a 'pull' strategy which aims its promotion at the consumer in order to stimulate demand and 'pull' the offering through the chain. One of the main challenges facing arts marketers dealing with channel intermediaries such as touring venues or ticket agents is to ensure that they are properly resourced and motivated to promote effectively.

The nature and function of marketing channels

As we have seen, intermediaries (whether individuals like a literary agent or organizations like a theatre) connect the seller to the buyer. Viewed together in sequence, these intermediaries form distribution chains or marketing channels. In the performing arts, especially for the more commercial side of the market such as large-scale musicals or open-air festivals, ticket agents have become a very important intermediary to potential audiences. Like retailers, they offer a wide selection of different products in one place, saving the arts customer considerable inconvenience. Travel agents often piggyback ticket sales on their standard business, but there are also dedicated ticket agents, for example those operating kiosks at indoor shopping malls. The advantage of such outlets is the personal access they give to large numbers of shoppers. Just as online book and music sales are taking business away from high-street retailers, so online ticketing (discussed towards the end of this chapter) is threatening this traditional channel of availability. On the other hand, there is likely to be for some time yet a significant market segment of arts attenders who prefer the personal assurance offered by a physical channel, particularly one with local knowledge which can add value to a transaction by offering opinions and friendly advice.

The traditional form of remuneration for agencies is to work on a commission basis, whereby the venue remits them a proportion (usually 15 per cent) of the selling price. The price to the customer is the same as it would be at the theatre box office. More recently there has been a growth in the number of agencies who charge a booking fee direct to the customer, such as First Call which specializes in telephone booking. This reflects the commercial cost of distribution (for example, the agency may be providing box office facilities which would otherwise not exist for a one-off event). It appears to be something which customers are happy to pay in return for convenience and speed, although it has been noted that customers outside large cities are less tolerant of such premium pricing (Tomlinson, 2002).

Intermediaries like ticket agents provide an essential service in any distribution chain by reducing contact costs for suppliers in reaching their buyers. We can see this process at work in the way that literary agents place work on behalf of authors and playwrights, or gallery owners or exhibition curators provide a shop window to bring the artist or craftworker into contact with collectors. But intermediaries are also worth cultivating because of the entrepreneurial role they can play in presenting opportunities to individuals or organizations in the arts which would be unavailable otherwise.

Relationship marketing, which was mentioned in Chapter 1 as a marketing approach with which arts organizations could naturally identify, is as important in dealing with intermediaries such as ticket agents as it is in dealing with the final customer. Just as organizations need to segment their customer market and decide which parts of the market to prioritize in line with their mission, so a venue must decide on what kind of agent to work with. What expectations are there in terms of volume and service levels? If the outlet is only selling a minimal number of tickets, the time and resources spent dealing with it could be better used supporting an outlet offering greater actual or potential business. In this area of management, as in so many others, Pareto's law of 80 per cent of the results coming from 20 per cent of the effort applies. Increasing effective effort by not squandering scarce resources on sluggish agencies needs to be a priority for arts marketers.

On the positive side, relationship marketing approaches point the way to close regular contact with the more active agencies, sharing information and providing active promotional support. Almost without exception agencies sell tickets on behalf of a number of clients. This means that your tickets are effectively in competition with other forms of entertainment. You can boost them by making your organization distinctive in the agency's eyes. It is worth cultivating major agencies by invitations to first nights or previews, and making sure there is an adequate flow of promotional material. This is also the best way to capitalize on the distinctive advantage of a ticket agent – the personal conviction with which they can recommend a show or venue.

Channel conflict

Marketing channels, as we have seen, are made up of a number of intermediaries connecting organizations to their customers. While at first sight all the parties involved in a channel have a mutual interest in the success of the process, there are plenty of potential clashes. This is known as channel conflict (Figure 7.1). A venue's immediate priorities may differ from those of a visiting company, especially if the venue has in-house work to market as well as visiting work. Conflict between successive stages in the chain like this is called vertical conflict because it is caused by trouble down the channel (like a manufacturer in dispute with a retailer for not granting it enough shelf space). This kind of conflict can knock-on to all the other aspects of running a touring company as Liza Stevens, a former Administrative Director of Phoenix Dance Company, recalls (personal interview): 'We attempted longer-term planning of our season's work, in line with our artistic policy. But in the end we found ourselves at the mercy of the venues into which we toured. Their ability to plan ahead varied enormously.'

Conflicts can also arise between venues. An arts centre may be unhappy about the fact that a touring company is planning to visit a theatre bordering on its catchment area before it reaches the arts centre itself. This could spoil the potential audience for the later date. Or a professional repertory company can get the rights to a show like *Oliver* for a particular season, thus effectively

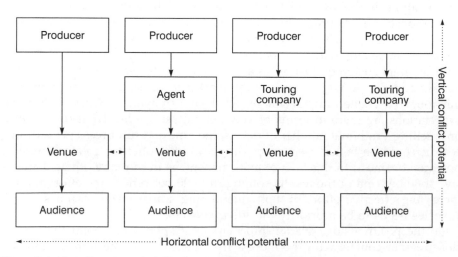

Figure 7.1 Marketing channels indicating possible conflict direction

preventing local amateurs from mounting it. This kind of conflict is across intermediaries at the same stage in two parallel channels, and is thus called horizontal conflict. An analogy here might be with two rival supermarkets trying to outdo each other on lowering the price of a particular special offer.

Both kinds of channel conflict can be minimized by negotiation and clear lines of communication. But the only sure way to stamp out the possibility of conflict is for one of the members of the chain to assume a dominant role. This can be in one of three ways:

- Through multiple ownership, such as a consortium of theatres which has considerable negotiating clout because of the number of major touring venues it operates. This is known as horizontal integration because it spreads ownership across the same stage in a number of marketing channels. A touring company playing at a member venue virtually has to accept the terms offered by the theatre or lose an outlet to a major part of its audience.
- Through buying out an intermediary at an earlier or later stage in the same channel. This is known as vertical integration because it involves ownership up and down the channel. Again, a major UK theatre consortium provides an example. At Christmas it effectively becomes a manufacturer as well as a retailer by assembling its own pantomime production team with television soap-star casts to create shows which play in its string of large-scale regional venues. This allows it complete control over an annual production the success of which is crucial to financial health throughout the rest of the year.
- Through one of the members of the chain establishing clear legal conditions governing the other members. This is known in marketing-speak as a contractual vertical marketing system as it governs relationships up and down the channel. Depending on the attractiveness of the show on offer, a touring management can take this role in its dealings with its venues. In the subsidized sector, funding bodies who are keen to see public money used effectively take on a similar role to prevent the duplication of provision between the organizations they support.

Tour heads are better than one

The manager of a major venue and a touring production company compare notes on how to make the relationship work:

Gary Iles (Swansea Grand Theatre): 'I am a great believer in building up good and trusting relationships between venues and the touring companies which deliver product to us. Things have changed greatly over the past ten years or so. Far more visiting companies these days have key marketing staff who develop a very good working relationship with their counterparts at the venue. Indeed, many now have PR and marketing companies working on their behalf, so we might be dealing with the same contact person for several different shows at the same time.

'The company's own marketing representative can start to build up a picture of the audience make-up of a particular theatre or geographic area, and they can then directly apply marketing ideas that have been successful in other towns and cities, to others on the tour.'

Chris Harper (Pola Jones): 'When we have a lot of shows taking place at the same time, I do use freelances, but I prefer to do as much of the work as possible in-house. I believe that loyalty should be direct to the producer and, from the venue's point of view, it is important that they have regular contact with the same person or team. They need to know they can trust us to do what we say we will do.

'When we do have a problem with the theatre or sales, I will try anything. I have in the past moved into that city for a length of time, jumped up and down, screamed – and as a last resort, cried! . . . I find it very frustrating that venues set themselves very low targets – sell-out is my only aim!'

Source: Iles and Harper, 1998. Reproduced by kind permission.

Channel length and control

Distribution chains are deemed long or short depending on how many intermediaries are involved. While there is no golden rule about the length of a chain, the shorter the chain, the more control a manufacturer has over the presentation of the final product. Building-based repertory theatre companies thus have complete control over their product and its presentation, compared to the vagaries and conflicting priorities faced by touring companies. The disadvantage of such a short channel is that the repertory theatre bears complete responsibility for all the costs and operations involved. At the other end of the scale, the individual craftworker is dependent on galleries and event organizers to reach customers. While this allows craftspeople to concentrate on their core activity, it also means that they are to some extent at the mercy of the intermediaries in terms of support and merchandising (display and sales effort). The writer seeking a market for his or her work often faces marketing channels which seem more like obstacle courses, but determination pays off. Playwright Maureen Lawrence comments (personal interview): 'If you delve enough and get the right information, it's not difficult to get a play staged . . . there are not enough good plays, it ought to be pointed out in careers advice.'

Case 7.3 Nosing ahead

The artist's studio has always been more than just a place in which to paint or sculpt quietly. Throughout history it has also been a place to socialize, gossip, show off, and market work to prospective buyers. The 'open studio' movement in the UK is a relatively recent development, but it is aimed at widening the market for original works of art. Open studio events bring together artists, crafts makers and the general public for an annual encounter in places as diverse as Sheffield, Cambridge and Deptford. Some events span a month, others are concentrated into weekends. The idea is not just to provide an extended gallery space in search of sales or new commissions for work, but also to promote and facilitate a wider discussion of the role and place of artwork and crafts in contemporary society.

Research commissioned by Yorkshire Arts (part of the national development organization for the arts in the UK) confirms the value, both social and financial, of the events. Twenty-three organizations who held open studios in 2001 contributed to the survey. They revealed a picture of over 240 000 visits by the public to events involving 2500 artists and makers. The resulting sales, excluding income from future commissions generated by the events, were in excess of £1 million. There may be lessons for other art forms from this enterprising approach to distribution. It's collaborative, it's developmental (not only for attenders but also for professionals who can network and learn from each other) and it creates a new form of contact between artists and the public.

A good example of a successful open studio event is provided by NOS&E – the Northamptonshire Open Studios and Exhibition, which has run annually since 1996. Funded through a combination of fees from participating artists, Lottery money, and backing from local authorities and advertisers, the event has grown into a series of studio openings around the region lasting a fortnight. As well as the general public, the event targets key audiences such as gallery owners, journalists, curators and potential sponsors. These are taken on specially arranged minibus tours to ensure they are exposed to the full range of work available. The organizers are hoping to develop a reach beyond Northamptonshire itself by strengthening links with regional tourist development initiatives from the county branded 'the Rose of the Shires'.

Promotion centres on print distribution around a wide area, culminating in a launch exhibition with a representative selection of participants' work at a local contemporary art gallery. This gives the local and regional media a focus for their reporting, as well as some excellent visual opportunities for photographs. Local newspapers receive enough material to run a series of articles focusing on different aspects of the events, as well as featuring art trails for readers to follow round the region. Local radio is an ideal medium for artist interviews, and even the regional television news has shown shots of selected work, backed by a short interview. Other publicity plans include taster exhibitions in libraries running up to the event itself, and the development of a friends organization to increase support and spread word-of-mouth.

Source: Armstrong, 2002; Hayman, 2002.

Distribution and innovation

As well as institutional or personal intermediaries, marketing channels can incorporate new ways of mediating artistic experience, either through innovative organization (as illustrated in Case 7.3) or new technology. Picture loan schemes, such as those run by many municipal art galleries, allow works of art to be enjoyed in subscribers' homes over a period of time instead of sampled fleetingly in gallery settings. In galleries and museums there is an increasing use of video and other electronic media to explain and interpret material for the visitor.

A good example is the Tate Modern's innovative use of wireless multimedia in its gallery tour, where visitors use a handheld computer to access information about the works on display. Audio descriptions are commonplace as a way of enhancing visitors' experience of museum objects, and several galleries in the USA have built on this by incorporating multimedia elements of still and moving pictures to complement the soundtrack on portable devices as the visitor tours the exhibits in a determined order. The Tate's system builds on this by being the first in the world to sense the visitor's exact position in the gallery at any time and feed the appropriate information to him or her. Because the information comes from a central server rather than having to be loaded, like an audio track, onto a particular device, the amount of content is potentially limitless and can be updated with ease. This distribution channel goes beyond the gallery itself. The visitor can use the handheld device to request further information about the work they have seen to be sent to them by e-mail after their visit, allowing the gallery to build and nurture its relationship with what might otherwise be a transient visitor.

Allowing or enabling?

Merely allowing the public to juxtapose themselves with an artwork, by letting them in to see a picture in a gallery for instance, is not genuine access. Granting someone this kind of access may amount to little more than *allowing* them to see it. Genuine access would work towards *enabling* them to see it.

Source: An Chomhairle Ealaíon, 1987.

Technology can also be used to broaden the potential audience for an artistic event. This can occasionally have uncomfortable public relations consequences, as Jeremy Isaacs discovered when he tried to open up Covent Garden's opera performances to national television audiences in the late 1980s. His struggles with the highly unionized workforce were operatic in themselves, but have led to a realization of the genuinely popularizing potential of the medium. Tony Hall, a later chief executive of the Royal Opera House who shares Isaacs' background in broadcasting, pointed out to a UK national newspaper that 'the first night of *Rigoletto* this season was seen by 2200 people in the house, 3000 in the Piazza and 900 000 on BBC2' (BBC News Online, 2002). Hall's visions for Covent Garden include extending the big-screen performances which have made such an impact in the Piazza outside the Opera House into other open-air venues, and even live relays via a nationwide chain of cinemas. 'We have to stand for excellence on the main stage and at the same time get that excellence to as many people as we can. I have spent a lot of time working on how we can improve on that. Partly it's about price, but it's also about developing our partnership with the BBC' (BBC News Online, 2002).

This aspiration underlines the way in which distribution is linked into the other marketing mix elements of product (excellence) and price.

Sound and vision

At the beginning of its 2002 season, Houston Grand Opera became the first opera company in the world to enhance views of the stage by the use of permanent cinema-style screen – a system it calls Opera Vision. The six plasma and projection screens are positioned in parts of the Grand Tier and Balcony areas of the Houston's Wortham Theatre. A combination of three cameras provide close up views of the action through what David Gockley, the Houston Opera general director, calls 'a communal set of opera glasses'.

Source: Driscoll, 2002.

Working with touring companies

The most traditional way of extending the availability of artistic experiences to wider audiences – whether dramatic, musical, or visual, is through touring. As we have seen earlier in this chapter, this requires mutual effort at building an effective relationship between the touring company supplying the product and the venue at which it is delivered to audiences. Arts marketers on either end of this particular distribution chain need to work together to construct a common understanding of their audience in order to adopt the most effective ways of reaching them.

It may help at the outset of this discussion to acknowledge the basic tension which exists between any touring management and a venue. In a classic example of channel conflict (a concept discussed earlier in the chapter), they are competing with each other for the income from ticket sales. Deciding how this is split may not be the direct responsibility of the marketing manager, but the outcome of the negotiation will affect the resources available and the amount of commitment which can be expected from either party to marketing the show. Raymond (1999) points to the relationship between a venue's business acumen and its financial health: 'The key reason that theatres do not achieve better margins lies in attitudes to deal-making.'

For a theatre the ideal would be to persuade a touring company to hire its venue at top rates, and some theatre chains are powerful enough to be able to get visiting companies to agree to a 'straight hire'. This places the entire responsibility on the touring management to sell tickets in order to cover this cost and make money. For a touring company the ideal would be to extract a very high fixed fee from the venue for its appearance. This would place the entire ticket-selling responsibility on the venue – and some starry touring productions can dictate terms like this. In real life, of course, the vast majority of deals involve either side taking a risk on ticket sales, but with one usually securing an advantage in terms of a safety margin. The factors at play are not limited to the power of a particular outlet or the allure of a particular production. Timing comes into it, as tour promoters need to fill their schedules and organize the logistics of getting the production around the country. Similarly, presenting venues may be desperate to fill a particular week in an otherwise full season with a suitable show which will complement the rest of what they have on offer. It may be that touring managements will be prepared to accept less attractive deals on the first outing for an unfamiliar orchestra or company, in the hope that next time they tour as a known quantity they will be able to negotiate better terms.

Here is a checklist of some common types of deals struck between touring managements and theatres which present their work:

- *Straight hire* – the visiting company keeps the ticket income (net of VAT) but has to pay the venue a high guaranteed sum in rental. If tickets do not sell, it is a recipe for company ruin.
- *Straight guarantee* – here the venue takes 100 per cent of the risk, but can keep all ticket income beyond the guarantee, which will be as high as the company can manage to push it. Again, potentially ruinous for the venue if sales are low.
- *First call* – this is like a guarantee, but has the advantage (if offered to a touring company by a venue) of meaning that if the predicted level of sales fails to materialize, it does not owe the visiting company the shortfall. Assuming it is reached, any income beyond it is kept or shared by the company and/or the venue depending on the terms of the negotiation. If it is not reached, one party ends up with nothing, of course.
- *Percentage split* – where the two parties negotiate to take a percentage each of ticket income. Deals can get complicated by the agreement of different percentages at different levels of total income, and by the combination of percentage splits with guarantees or first calls.
- *A guarantee against split* – this is a guaranteed fee to the company OR high percentage of ticket income, whichever is the greater. If the visiting company manages to negotiate a deal like this, the venue can be left in a no-win situation. If the show sells well, the company stands to pocket most of the money. If sales disappoint, the venue is committed to making up the shortfall.
- *A guaranteed fee to the company AND percentage of ticket income* – this is a more satisfactory deal from the point of view of the venue, if it can negotiate a healthy percentage split for itself beyond the guarantee.

It is important, then, that the negotiation on either side takes into account a number of possible options and their consequences at different levels of ticket sales. Spreadsheet software can help managers to conduct 'What if?' analyses and test a range of assumptions. It is essential that, whatever the detail of the negotiation, the venue aims to cover its weekly overheads as a minimum. Arrangements and responsibilities for marketing are part of the contract which is agreed. Some theatres just ask for a fixed financial allowance to cover marketing and publicity expenses. Others charge for some or all of the costs associated with print production, distribution, advertising and marketing staff to cover the incoming tour. Most contracts will include a stipulated allowance of printed publicity prepared at the expense of the touring company which can be overprinted with the venue's details and the dates of the visit.

While deal-making can affect the context of marketing for a particular tour-in, the essential ingredient for a successful campaign involving a touring company and a presenting venue is the direct relationship between the marketing functions of either party. Good touring companies pay close attention to marketing and working co-operatively with venues. The process should begin with a very early initial planning meeting at the venue to discuss promotional strategy, local needs and opportunities, and the detailed allocation of responsibilities between the company marketing department and the venue. For London-based production companies, it makes sense for national media to be handled by a company publicist, while the venues work with local and regional media. Print details and quantities are finalized, so that the company can originate the material. The company marketing officer ideally should make sure he or she establishes personal contact with key members of the administration and box office team at the venue as well as the marketing department. In a venue which may be dealing with a number of different touring managements, this personal touch can make a great deal of difference to the commitment of the staff. In particular, box office staff should be invited to see a performance of the show on tour before it reaches the venue (although clearly the feasibility of this will depend on timing and geography).

In the medium term the touring management will supply detailed briefings for the box office as well as pictures, programme copy and reviews to the marketing department. Many companies offer venues additional resources for particular audiences, such as teachers' packs, direct marketing letters and samples of show merchandise or music (Iles and Harper, 1998). Regular telephone and e-mail contact to update booking figures and compare them with previous visits (or performance elsewhere) is vital in order to diagnose early problems. Should a particular performance be selling slowly, this gives both venue and company time to take some kind of remedial action – such as extra mailings or telephone campaigns directed at particular segments.

Immediately before the visit the activities focus on arranging interviews with performers and helping brief local media. Touring shows are often built around starry 'names' – but if the artist in question is unpredictable, or unwilling, a lot of pressure can be put on the venue's marketing department. Here the political skills of the touring company marketer may come into play, as the performer may well feel a greater loyalty to the company than to the venue. Like the members of any distribution channel, touring companies and the venues which receive their productions are links in the same chain connecting to the final customer. While this gives them common cause, their perspectives on the process and their ways of operating may differ. Marketing staff have a pivotal role in ensuring the success of the relationship. This is recognized by the fact that a number of successful touring managements and receiving venues exchange marketing staff for extended periods as an element in their training and development policy.

Case 7.4 From Russia with love – but no money

In December 1999, the 80-strong National Philharmonic Orchestra of Russia finally decided to abandon their tour of the UK and return to their Siberian home town of Tomsk. Organized by a relatively inexperienced promoter, Mario Gutierrez, the tour had been dogged by disaster from the outset. It had begun with a five-day journey on the trans-Siberian express to Poland, followed by dates in Holland, Luxembourg and, finally, the UK. Playing to depressingly poor houses, staying in youth hostels (sometimes ten to a room), subsisting on a diet of junk food, and being subjected to an exhausting and illogical itinerary, the musicians ended up busking outside McDonald's in Swansea. This was, admittedly, a desperate publicity stunt to raise interest in that night's concert – but there was also the fact that the tour had run out of money and they needed to eat.

Earlier in the tour there had been something of a crisis in Aberdeen, when the musicians – at the end of their tether – had refused to play that evening's concert until the concert hall's management came across with money up-front (the princely sum of £800, working out at £10 per player). The venue refused – and things looked bleak until the promoter explained that, because of last-minute sponsorship from Global TeleSystems, a company whose sympathy had been aroused by news reports of the orchestra's plight, they would be paid their fee the following day. The venue did, however, provide soup and a roll for the exhausted players – after which they went on to give a spirited account of Tchaikovsky's *Fifth Symphony*.

The tour's musical director, Polish-born Boguslaw Dawidow, told a *Guardian* journalist that he was determined to see it through to the end – although he had signed his contract unaware that the musicians were to be paid from ticket sales alone, nor that the punishing schedule would entail 10-hour coach trips followed hard upon by performances. The promoter had budgeted on houses of 700–800 at each venue. In the event, attendances were much lower (except for the final few concerts where audiences came as a result of the media interest surrounding the ill-fated orchestra). The absence of a sponsor, until the intervention of Global TeleSystems, meant that there was no buffer against disappointing box office takings – and the deals Gutteriez had negotiated with each venue gave them first claim on what little income there was.

To some extent he was the victim of his own inexperience. Up to this point he had only promoted solo recitals by his wife in small venues in the Low Countries. Taking on a major tour of large-scale concert halls was possibly a step too far – although Gutteriez put on record his disappointment that the high quality of his posters, programme, orchestra and conductor had not attracted bigger crowds. He was particularly surprised at this, given that several of the venues had not been visited by a Russian orchestra for years. Why weren't the public more excited at the prospect?

The idea for the tour had come to him, he admitted in a newspaper interview, on a plane as he read a report in the *New York Times* about how Russian musicians were being forced to play on the Metro to earn enough to live. Spotting the opportunity to engage talented and well-trained players for a fraction of the sum he would have to pay Western musicians, he jumped at the chance of casting his wife in the role of soloist. He maintained that, even if the 1999 tour had been a financial failure, it represented an investment in getting the musicians, and their conductor, known to a wider audience, in anticipation of future visits. The musicians were unconvinced of the merits of this argument, however. The flurry of public interest in the tour as it reached its conclusion meant that suddenly they had just about enough money to go home – and home they went, leaving their soloist to complete the dates on her own.

Source: The Guardian (1999); Moss (1999).

Physical access

Stone barriers

The physical inaccessibility of a building can limit an organization's capacity to welcome disabled people and its level of commitment to audience development. Manchester poet Sue Napolitano made this point succinctly in her poem *Disabled Apartheid*.

The municipal might of Victorian architecture
No need for a sign saying
CRIPPLES KEEP OUT
When triumphal stone flights
Of stairs,
Lead the way to
The art gallery
The library
The committee meeting.

Not that it was deliberate you understand,
They were far too nice for that,
They simply forgot
To think that we might want to
Get in
Take our share
Play our part
Claim some space.
Perhaps they had in mind
That our place
Was outside
With begging bowl in hand.

Source: Napolitano, 1993. Reproduced with kind permission.

It is a salutary fact that attendance at arts events still presents an enormous amount of difficulty to many disabled patrons. Progress has been made in recent years due to the opportunities presented by Lottery capital funding for new buildings to be designed with access for wheelchair users in mind and to include the latest technologies to improve the arts experience for disabled customers. Signed performances for people with hearing difficulties and taped summaries for visually-impaired customers are becoming increasingly common as part of the service package offered by theatres, opera companies and even cinemas. Working in collaboration with specialist agencies will help an arts organization to meet the particular needs of its disabled customers effectively. Many galleries now provide Braille labels and audio guides for their exhibits, giving information about the artist and the object on display.

Access in more general terms is an important issue for arts marketers. Quite apart from what is on offer in the theatre or gallery, or the price of admission, ease of physical access can dictate whether customers come or stay away. But for many people, the simple issue of transport to and from the venue, and the problem of parking and security, is one of the most important factors in whether their experience is a satisfactory one or not. For those venues who have the advantage of proximate car parking or public transport services, this information needs to be given high priority in publicity leaflets. Venues in less fortunate circumstances (many city-centre theatres, for example) need to adopt creative strategies to address the problems this may cause for their patrons in terms of performance times, information, provision for late arrivals, and lobbying local authorities. Distribution is about customer convenience. The more comfortable your audience or attenders are, the richer their experience will be, and the greater the likelihood of a return visit.

The importance of the physical elements of the environment presented by the venue itself in mediating an arts experience should not be underestimated. Reviewing the research literature on museums, Goulding (2000) identified three main approaches which scholars have taken to understanding visitor behaviour: social, cognitive and spatial interaction. The social school of researchers look at visitor interactions with each other; the cognitive school look at their involvement with the material exhibited; and the spatial interaction school of research emphasizes the effect on visitors of the physical environment of the museum itself. Goulding's own research, conducted by observing visitors to the UK's Birmingham Museum and Art Gallery, confirmed the relevance of these factors, but pointed in particular to the importance of physical factors in mediating the service experience of a museum. Devices to route or map the way through an exhibition were seen to be vital to the visitors' psychological orientation, as were basic physical and environmental factors such as crowding, seating and noise levels. The conclusions from her research, which are applicable to any form of attended arts event, are that audiences like coherence and completeness, and that physical comfort matters. The implications for arts marketers are to keep the physical environment of their venues under constant review. What difference might clearer signage make to the audience's experience? What about heat, noise, and ventilation? Many of these atmospheric factors overlap with product considerations (as discussed in Chapter 4) but they offer marketers useful pointers towards improving the delivery of arts experience.

Families with younger children are targeted by most venues at specific times of the year (such as school holidays or the Christmas season). But facilities for pushchairs, baby changing and family areas are usually rudimentary if they exist at all. With increasing daytime use of arts venues, the opportunity presented by family audiences can only be realized by catering for their needs through the right kind of access environment. Often this will involve a trade-off with other audiences at particular times of the day or week, as a marketing mix which works for families can often be off-putting for adults (O'Sullivan, 1999). In this respect, arts organizations can learn from the policies of successful service industries. For example, the restaurant chain TGI Fridays actively encourages family parties early in the week and during daytime opening hours on Saturdays and Sundays, when they are encouraged to sit in certain areas in the restaurant. Weekend evenings are, by contrast, aimed at a more boisterous adult crowd, whose antics might strike a discordant note with families. Furthermore, adults are encouraged to congregate around the central bar area in the restaurant. Time and physical environment are manipulated in this way to form two distinct distribution patterns with appeal to two very different market segments.

Bottoming the problem

To get more bums on seats at the Sydney Opera House, the venue's 5000 seats themselves needed an overhaul. The original leather upholstery tended to get rather hot during performances, and squeaked – or worse – at tense moments. The Opera House called in Sydney microsurgeon Dr Earl Owen. For the new seats, reupholstered patriotically in Australian wool, Dr Owen designed a revolutionary three-layer system of foam padding, sandwiching layers of very soft, soft and firm to create a bowl-shaped structure for extra comfort and support. He then went on to design the chairs for Stadium Australia, one of the main venues for the highly successful 2000 Sydney Olympics.

Source: Company information.

Performance times and opening hours

Time is a crucial element in the delivery and consumption of the arts experience, yet it is remarkable how inconvenient arts attendance still manages to be from the point of view of time-utility. The most obvious aspect of this subject is performance starting times, or gallery opening hours, which can often result from precedent or inertia rather than conscious consideration of the options available with the customer in mind.

As suggested in Chapter 2, segmenting the audience of arts attenders may lead to fresh thinking on performance times or opening hours. Mid-week early afternoon performances can be much preferred by older patrons who may feel uncomfortable about the prospect of returning home in the dark. Matinées also cater for people living at some distance from the theatre who would prefer to travel during daylight hours. A number of galleries and museums have taken to shutting on Mondays in order to enable Sunday opening; and evening opening has become far more common in recent years, particularly in London where those who commute daily into the city can be tempted to visit after work. Another way of coping with problems created by the opening times of galleries is the introduction of booking in advance for attendance at exhibitions at a specific time. Lengthy queues used to be one of the characteristics of blockbuster exhibitions, and while these queues provided valuable public relations material in terms of talking points and photo opportunities, they were a source of some inconvenience to the exhibition-goer and were seen as a deterrent to attendance. The crush of people at very popular events can also mean that the art objects themselves are more difficult to enjoy because it is impossible to get near to them, or to appreciate them at one's own pace. The distribution solution of a booking system has the advantage of minimizing the waiting time for the customer, and maximizing the quality of the experience by limiting the crowds in the gallery at any particular time. Extending opening hours on special occasions can enrich the experience of attenders by offering them the opportunity to visit an exhibition at an unusual time. For example, the Oktoberfest in Munich – when the south German city gives itself over to a month-long festival of beer and funfair attractions – now also features what is called 'The Long Night of the Museums' when some 70 of Munich's museums and art galleries stay open all night by common consent.

Ticket selling channels

Ticket purchase itself is often fraught with difficulty for many arts attenders, particularly for theatregoers. Whether buying tickets in person or on the telephone, the process can be complicated and time-consuming. Well-trained box office staff can make a crucial difference to the experience of the customer either in person or on the telephone.

Helping box office staff to develop their skills in handling such encounters can make an enormous difference in the efficiency of this potentially circuitous and time-wasting procedure (Figure 7.2).

- Customers can save time, increasing their convenience.
- The organization can save time and resources.
- Future customers can be dealt with more speedily, compounding the benefits all round.

Box office training encourages staff to be more active in their response to customers by structuring their contact with customers and retaining the initiative throughout.

- A greeting begins the encounter. On the telephone it is particularly important here to identify the venue and, ideally, the member of staff personally.
- Then, having established a friendly but professional rapport with the customer, questions can be used to get specific answers enabling choices to be made quickly.

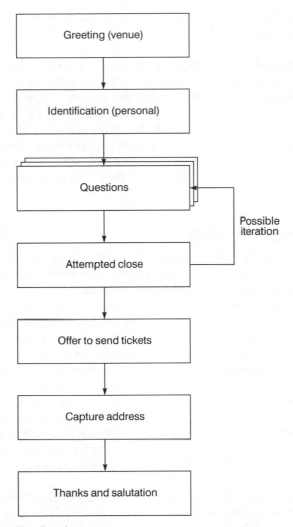

Figure 7.2 Ticket selling flowchart

- Even customers who appear to be enquiring for information are capable of being converted into purchasers – the customer is telephoning because he or she is interested enough in what the venue has to offer to want to know more. Purchase is just another step in fulfilling that interest.
- The key part of the encounter is to 'close the sale'. On the telephone this can be done by encouraging payment by credit card: 'Would you like to pay for those tickets now by credit card so I can send them to you immediately?' The offer to send the tickets on to the purchaser should be made.
- This guarantees an opportunity to collect the name and address of the customer, a valuable asset when used, with his or her permission, for marketing purposes. Posting tickets direct to a telephone purchaser saves the inconvenience of further visits to the box office or having to wait on the night to collect the ticket. Naturally this also frees the box office staff from

the time required by those further contacts, enabling them to serve all their customers more effectively.

It might be objected that a structured approach to selling, however gently, is uncomfortably close to manipulating the customer. After all, the first principles of marketing enjoin us to respect what the customer needs rather than the organization's desire to sell. However, such an objection misrepresents the nature of the procedure which aims to bring the standard of customer service up to a uniformly high level. By using a structured approach to answering the telephone, or dealing with a personal caller, box office staff can actually help their customers far more effectively than if they treat the encounter as informal or casual.

The changing box office

The box office is in many ways the public face of the organization. Unfortunately, in many venues, it has traditionally worn a far from welcoming expression. The historical nature of some arts buildings has left their box offices stuck in an earlier century – a small window at which ticket buyers queue uncomfortably to purchase or collect their tickets. Even the term 'box office' has a quaint air, with its connotations of confined spaces and excessive bureaucracy. Remodelling historical venues is controversial, and frequently impractical, but even when foyers cannot be extensively redesigned there is a case for creating a ticket sales point in an adjoining space. The Munich Opera House, for example, has created a light and airy space next to its imposing entrance foyer where ticket buyers can browse information and purchase tickets across open plan desks from knowledgeable and enthusiastic sales staff. The Royal Opera House in London's Covent Garden has solved the problem of cramped space by locating its ticket selling operation in a separate building across the road.

This is another area where the arts can steal good ideas from other service industries. Travel agents and banks now have tables and chairs where customers can sit while discussing their purchases with expert advisers. Plate glass screens, while occasionally necessary for security purposes, have given way to lower counters, open space and friendlier furniture. Multiplex cinemas and railway stations have made it easier to buy and collect tickets by installing kiosks and vending machines. Gradually the arts are picking up on these trends and adopting them. The original Leeds Playhouse which opened in the 1970s was notable for its open box office, which promoted an air of accessibility and friendliness that continues into its more recent incarnation as the West Yorkshire Playhouse. Clear signage, well-trained staff and customer-friendly technology can all contribute to the kind of relationship that arts organizations need to build with their customers.

One of the biggest marketing advances in recent years for both performing arts venues and museums and galleries has been the widespread adoption of computerized box office systems. This has transformed what might once have been seen as the simple business of selling tickets into a crucial source of information about customers and their needs. By capturing data at the point of sale, a picture builds up of the preferences and behaviour of individual customers. Over time this forms into an audience profile which can inform and guide marketing strategy. For example, by recognizing different attendance patterns across an audience as a whole, broad segments can be discerned and approached with appropriate marketing (as discussed in Chapters 2 and 3).

Data protection and the box office

Collecting data of any sort involves ethical issues of privacy. UK data protection legislation guarantees the rights of individuals to see data which is being kept about them and to correct mistakes in it. Crucially, it allows an individual to prevent the use of his or her personal data for the purposes of direct marketing. Data needs to be 'fairly processed' in the words of the UK legislation. That means that organizations collecting data need to be transparent about what they are doing. It is not only good manners to make sure you have the permission of your customers to collect and store data, it is the law. As a Data Controller (an organization or individual who collects, stores and manipulates data) you need to be registered with the Information Commissioner. A detailed discussion of the intricacies of the UK Data Protection Act (1998) and its implementation is beyond the scope of this chapter, but there is plenty of information about it online at www.dataprotection.gov.uk and Tomlinson (2000) has produced a guide specifically for managers in the arts and entertainment industries. Legislation based on similar principles either exists or is evolving in other countries as well, so this is a useful site for international arts marketers keen to establish good practice in this area.

The principles of data protection

Anyone processing personal data must comply with the eight enforceable principles of good practice. They say that data must be:

- fairly and lawfully processed
- processed for limited purposes
- adequate, relevant and not excessive
- accurate
- not kept longer than necessary
- processed in accordance with the data subject's rights
- secure
- not transferred to countries without adequate protection

Source: http://www.dataprotection.gov.uk, 15 August 2002.

It is important that the customer knows which organization is collecting the data and why. Clearly, identification of the organization is not a problem for inbound calls or personal visits to a box office, but any active attempt to solicit information (such as mailing list registration forms either in hard copy or online) needs to be clearly branded. For customers to feel comfortable about disclosing data such as their addresses or contact details they need to trust the organization and see a benefit from sharing this information. This underlines the need for immediate identification of both the organization and the member of box office staff in any encounter where information may be shared. Practical measures to ensure this happens include habitual identification of the caller and organization at the beginning of any call, and wearing a branded name badge (and possibly some kind of uniform) for face-to-face encounters.

Internet ticketing

While computers have increased the options available to marketers, the benefits to arts attenders have been less immediate. Clearly, receiving better-targeted publicity because of the careful use of box office data minimizes irritation and maximizes opportunities to derive satisfaction from events of genuine interest. On the other hand, gains in customer convenience have been less obvious. Telephone queuing systems have helped box offices avoid the off-putting 'always engaged' effect at peak times. And technologies such as re-routing calls to agencies when all a venue's lines are busy can help customers gain access to sought-after tickets for premium shows. However, many customers feel uncomfortable talking to computers – and some ticket agencies demand a booking fee. An area which promises genuine customer utility through the spread of information technology is internet ticketing. This is a development from which both venues and customers can benefit significantly.

After the dot.com euphoria of the 1990s, the growth of online retailing has been slower than expected. However, some products are better suited to internet distribution than others. CDs, books and software have been the most successful product lines so far. This is for a number of reasons. Books and CDs are relatively easy to mail to buyers, and software can be downloaded direct from the internet itself. The enormous range of titles which an online retailer like Amazon can offer gives it an immediate advantage over its high-street rivals. Of course, the demographic profile of early adopters of the internet as a purchasing medium, predominantly male and upmarket, provided a very good fit with the relevant market segments for such products and services.

Tickets, not only for budget airlines but for the performing arts, exhibitions, and other events, are poised to make an even bigger splash on the internet than these early successes. In many ways, tickets are the ideal internet product. They do not even need to be posted to the purchaser, but can be sent in digital format over the internet and printed out. The proliferation of mobile communications devices connected to the internet such as WAP (Wireless Application Protocol) phones and personal digital assistants opens up further payment and delivery possibilities. With mobile phones, the newly-emerging technology of 'm-ticketing' allows the ticket to appear in the phone window, and verification by venues that the phone in question is the one on which the tickets were booked. The traditional inconvenience of paying for tickets and then worrying about having to collect them, or paying to have them sent by what may be an unreliable postal service, disappears in such a scenario.

Furthermore, there is evidence that the online purchasing audience is growing. In a classic example of the diffusion of innovation (see Chapter 2), the turning point requires a critical mass of people adopting the idea for everyone else to follow suit. The main problem in the early years of e-commerce has been the reluctance of customers to divulge their credit card details on the internet. Yet the vast majority of such customers have no qualms about revealing the same information to a salesperson on the telephone or a waiter in a restaurant. Customers will have to make a trade-off between the immediacy and convenience of the internet as a purchasing channel and any qualms they might still have about its security. Branding, which is discussed in greater detail in Chapter 4, is one way to try to reassure them.

The internet presents arts organizations with a powerful new ticket selling channel. Through online sales they can reach customers anywhere in the world – a considerable advantage when, for example, targeting high-spending business travellers who may be browsing the Web to see what the entertainment options are in a city to which they will be on a trip in a week's time. By combining an informational presence on the Web with the opportunity to buy tickets there and then, such business can be secured. As with any fast-developing technology, however, online ticketing provides a potentially confusing range of choices. These need careful review before committing resources to a new or upgraded system.

Distribution decisions like these are the nearest the arts get to the kind of logistics management problems facing organizations in more product-based marketing situations. The options fall into three main categories – creating in-house solutions, using a ticket agent, or using an internet ticketing service. We will briefly review the advantages and disadvantages of each of these, but each organization's case will be different, and even the same organization will have needs and capabilities which change over time. It pays to keep this aspect of distribution, like any other, under constant review.

In-house solutions are bespoke internet ticketing systems developed by software designers, who link an organization's computerized box office system directly to its website so that online transactions can take place. This approach gives the organization maximum control over its ticketing processes and the presentation of its identity on the Web, which is a vital source of differentiation. There are no fees or commissions to pay to third parties, and the cash generated by all transactions goes immediately to the arts organization itself. The disadvantages of this route relate to costs, time and expertise. Initial costs, as well as maintenance and development costs, are likely to be extremely high for organizations going it alone, and it takes considerable time and expertise to develop an appropriate online presence. Furthermore, specially-written software can leave the organization stranded if industry standards move on.

One alternative is to sell tickets online through an external intermediary – an online ticket agent. This route gives an organization access to wide coverage and exposure on the Web, but with the proviso that its tickets are available alongside those of many other venues. The number of visitors per day to a ticket agent's site may be seen as an advantage, but unless these visitors are looking specifically for your venue, you are likely to go unnoticed. Those who are looking specifically to buy your tickets will be taken straight to the part of the site dealing with transactions, and will not be automatically exposed to any other promotional material on your website. Further disadvantages include the fact that you may not have automatic access to customer data, and the income from ticket sales is reduced by agency commission. You may also have to wait for anything up to 90 days for the cash from the transaction to be deposited in your bank account.

A third alternative, and one currently preferred by the highest proportion of UK arts organizations, is to 'rent' a ticket selling presence online by negotiating a hosted service with a specialist internet ticketing provider. These services are effectively online sales kiosks which can be attached to an existing box office system. They can be branded to match the look and feel of the organization's existing website, so that in some cases customers cannot tell when they buy tickets that the actual transaction is being conducted not by the organization itself but by a specialist third party. These services always make customer data available to the arts organization, and many permit additional marketing opportunities such as online questionnaires, text messaging and other promotional activities. On the other hand, like ticket agents they charge transaction fees, and on some systems the manual updating of box office records is still necessary to enable the box office computer to 'catch up' with actual sales online. This means they can lack the elegance of a well-designed in-house solution and can involve a significant amount of administrative time.

Summary

Arts marketing channel decisions have some points of similarity to the ways in which tangible products are distributed. Sometimes services rely on tangible products as part of their delivery (such as small-press magazines or exhibitions). Even performance-based arts are capable of being enhanced by ancillary products. But the essential element in opening up the experience of the arts to customers is interpersonal contact and a commitment by the venue to building relationships with customers and intermediaries.

In this chapter we have emphasized how appropriate forms of distribution combine strategically with the other elements of the marketing mix, product, price and promotion to maximize the number of arts customers reached in the optimum combination of cost and the achievement of organizational objectives.

The role of marketing channels in promotion is often vital in the arts, as they act as conduits of information to and from the customer. Intermediaries play a crucial part in this process. Just as retailers in commercial marketing perform functions which manufacturers could not execute unaided, so intermediaries like managements, venues and entrepreneurial agencies open up audiences and opportunities which would otherwise be unavailable to artists and performers. The members of a channel of distribution (such as a touring production company and a venue at which it performs) need to interact effectively to optimize the experience for the final customer.

The process of distributing the arts relies heavily on the aspects of space and time. Both of these are strategic issues, careful attention to which can improve an organization's position and effectiveness. The box office and other outlets have a crucial role to play as the retail element of the channel connecting arts organizations to their paying customers.

Technological developments have repositioned box offices as the information hub driving an arts organization's marketing systems, and the internet has opened up a powerful new ticket-selling channel. However, the human interaction at the heart of the arts encounter remains an indispensable element of successful distribution strategy.

Key concepts

access

box office

channel intermediary

data protection

database

deals

horizontal/vertical channel conflict

internet ticketing

marketing channels

presenting venue

retailer

ticket agents

touring company

vertical integration

vertical marketing system

Discussion questions

1 Illustrate the influence of the other elements of the marketing mix on distribution for: (a) the Royal Shakespeare Company touring *King Lear* to France, (b) a major retrospective exhibition of a living painter at a national contemporary art gallery, (c) a craft jeweller producing a new collection of work.

2 What is channel conflict? Give examples of potential channel conflict, both horizontal and vertical, in a tour of a production of a popular musical. How might such conflict be resolved or prevented?

3 Discuss the promotional role of marketing channels in the visual arts as opposed to the performing arts.

4 How might audience segmentation inform decisions about time as an element in distribution for the performing arts?

5 Use the box office selling flowchart (Figure 7.2) to prepare briefing notes for a website designer working on an online sales site for a venue with which you are familiar.

Case study: Musical journey

The mission statement of the Australian Chamber Orchestra (ACO) declares its purpose as to 'provide Australia with a world-class orchestra'. Touring is part of any orchestra's way of reaching audiences, but this commitment to 'world-class' status means that touring internationally is a core activity for the ACO. Such activity not only reaches a wider audience and (in spite of the financial risk involved) increases available income, it vouches for the ACO's credibility at this level. Selecting the right kind of programming, pitching fees at an appropriate level, creating a distinctive but high-quality image, and – crucially – working with reputable agents and venues, creates a marketing mix which embodies the orchestra's claim to international excellence.

Tim Walker, who managed the orchestra for ten years from the early 1990s, saw his key role as developing international touring to demonstrate and maintain quality. His strategy, like that of many an international marketer, began with research. A demanding schedule of personal visits to potential markets, combined with energetic networking with peers in other countries, led to an ambitious plan for the 1993 season, involving six overseas tours. This was a high-risk strategy. Walker had inherited a deficit, and his decision to spend time and resources on up to eight visits abroad a year, as well as the resulting touring activity, represented a major gamble. In the event it paid off, as the 1993 touring income cleared the deficit. It also proved useful experience, as it helped the ACO to establish a less frenetic pattern of touring activity, focusing on two tours a year. One is aimed at the summer festival circuit, the other at venues with winter international subscription series.

Walker's networking produced contacts with venues, agents and peers. Joining the International Society for the Performing Arts (ISPA) helped him get a feel for what other chamber orchestras were able to charge for performances, and to work out the best way to establish a presence on the international circuit. Because of the need to manage the orchestra's reputation for quality, the distribution channel used had to send out the right kind of messages.

While the orchestra organized some of its early dates direct with venues (for example, the Queen Elizabeth Hall on London's South Bank), Walker came to the conclusion that the best way to access the UK and European market was through an agent. Not only does such an arrangement reduce some of the operational pressures of touring, but it also gives the orchestra access to an 'insider' who understands the nuances of a market – for example, which venues are making the running with audiences and critics. At the same time, having a reputable agent prepared to take an orchestra on says something about the quality of the orchestra itself. This kind of third-party endorsement is clearly an advantage when striking deals with venues who might be wary of an unfamiliar band.

The ACO's programming for international tours proclaims their distinctiveness. The proportion of Australian music in their overseas concerts is higher than for their domestic tours, as a way of positioning the ensemble as unique in the eyes of promoters and the public. Variety is an important element in what the performing arts have to offer, but customers can be intolerant of what they see as unfamiliar or difficult repertoire. A platform of national identity is a relatively safe way to introduce new work to ticket buyers and promoters wary of contemporary music.

Australianness is an advantage in terms of product for the ACO, but can cause problems in terms of promotion in overseas markets. Country-of-origin perceptions are an important part of the image of any internationally-marketed product or service. This can work to the ACO's advantage in a market where there is some shared cultural heritage, as in the UK. But in Japan, in spite of its proximity to Australia, promoters and audiences tend to associate classical music with European ensembles, and are wary of an unknown quantity from Australia. The ACO's strategy has been to persevere with the Japanese market in spite of the difficulty of gaining a foothold in it. In spite of having only performed there three times in the 17 years leading up to its 1999 tour to Japan, the orchestra is determined to appeal to Japanese audiences through commissioning work from Japanese composers and employing Japanese musicians. It has also considered branding itself differently for its Japanese tours.

In order to suit local conditions in Europe, the ACO uses a multilingual London-based publicist to manage its promotion in Germany and the UK. The ACO's print image captures the orchestra's distinctive identity and quality appeal, but its promotional strategy in each overseas market is geared towards what works at a local level. Radio stations in the UK are an important vehicle for developing the reputation of particular ensembles and composers (particularly since the addition of a commercial classical music broadcaster to the list of national stations). The orchestra targets its recordings at them to coincide with touring, and mounts the occasional promotional performance. In Germany, the choice of venues has been crucial. Because the 1997 tour was the first by the orchestra there for 13 years, the local agent put together a seven-date circuit where only two venues were in major cities. This 'B-grade' tour was a conscious attempt to re-establish the ensemble's reputation on the circuit, and was followed two years later by a highly successful tour of premier venues in large German cities. Several of the concerts capitalized on the orchestra's identity by featuring internationally-renowned Australian guitarist John Williams as soloist.

The ACO's touring activity has occasionally presented examples of channel conflict. Sponsorship has been at the heart of two of them. Having fixed up two appearances at London's Wigmore Hall, a 550-seat venue which is an essential date on the premiere chamber music circuit, the ACO negotiated a sponsorship deal with an Australian company based in the UK. Unfortunately, the Wigmore Hall had already arranged sponsorship of the series of concerts it was promoting, and of which the ACO dates were only one part. The venue was unwilling to allow another sponsor access to the package of benefits around the concerts. The problem was resolved by a renegotiation of the orchestra's fee with the venue. This kind of difficulty is something that touring venues and producing companies often face, because of the difficulty of co-ordinating sponsorship negotiations with third parties. The second situation occurred in Germany during the 1997 tour. Here the problem arose because of German legislation over funding arrangements. The promoter's support from local funding bodies depended on the tour taking place on a non-commercial basis. The ACO needed to show that at least a third of its costs were being subsidized by the Australian government to comply with this, and as a result was not able to accept sponsorship for the relevant dates.

Source: Walker, 2002. www.fuel4arts.com, © Australia Council for the Arts, Commonwealth of Australia.

Questions

1 Country-of-origin associations are shown to be both an advantage and, potentially, a disadvantage in this case study. Analyse the country-of-origin associations of an arts organization with which you are familiar and demonstrate how they can be used in its targeting and promotion strategy.

2 Compare and contrast the approach of Tim Walker in this case study with the tour described on page 256 'From Russia with love – but no money'. What points of good

practice in organizing and marketing a tour can you summarize from the ACO's example?

3 Sponsorship was the cause of the channel conflict described in this case. List three other factors which might cause channel conflict between a touring management and a venue, and propose how you would deal with them and why.

References

An Chomhairle Ealaión (1987) *Art and the Ordinary*. The Arts Council of Ireland.

Armstrong, P. (2002) 'A growing event', *ArtsProfessional*, 14 January, 9.

BBC News Online (2002) 'Opera boss plans screens on greens', 1 March (available at: http://news.bbc.co.uk/1/hi/entertainment/arts/1817923.stm. Accessed 20 July 2002).

Driscoll, P.F. (2002) 'Opera watch', *Opera News*, Vol. 66, No. 9, March, 6.

Goulding, C. (2000) 'The museum environment and the visitor experience', *European Journal of Marketing*, Vol. 34, No. 3/4, 261–78.

The Guardian (1999) 'Russian orchestra goes home', 3 December (available at: http://www.guardian.co.uk/Archive/Article/0 4273 3937783 99.html. Accessed 17 July 2002).

Hayman, K. (2002) 'Opening up the arts', *ArtsProfessional*, 14 January, 8.

Iles, G. and Harper, C. (1998) 'Venue–company relationships: duel or dance?', *ArtsBusiness*, 20 July, 8–9.

Moss, S. (1999) 'Brassed off', *The Guardian*, 30 November (available at: http://www.guardian.co.uk/Archive/Article/0 4273 3936437 00.html).

O'Sullivan, T. (1999) 'Meet the family', *ArtsBusiness*, 13 September, 5–6.

Napolitano, S. (1993) 'Disabled apartheid', in *A Dangerous Woman*. Greater Manchester Coalition of Disabled People.

Pulford, D. (2000) 'All aboard the ballet bus', *ArtsBusiness*, 31 January, 9.

Raymond, C. (1999) *Essential Theatre: The successful management of theatres and venues which present the performing arts*. Arts Council of England.

Tomlinson, R. (2000) *Data Protection: A guide to the Data Protection Acts and their implications for managers in the arts and entertainment industry*. Arts Marketing Association.

Tomlinson, R. (2002) 'Long live the 21st century box office', *ArtsProfessional*, 11 February, 4–5.

Walker, T. (2002) 'Australian Chamber Orchestra Tour Europe, UK and Japan', Let's Tour Case Studies, Australian Council for the Arts (available at: http://www.fuel4arts.com/touring/case/europe/aco.htm. Accessed 20 July 2002).

8

Marketing planning

Introduction

The purpose of marketing planning is very simple. It aims to help managers identify a range of potential marketing activities, to choose the most effective ones and to work out what they will cost to implement. It is a systematic process which forces an organized approach to marketing decision-making, leading to greater effectiveness in meeting the needs of current and future audiences and greater efficiency in the use of resources in achieving this. While it is not a panacea for all the problems facing the organization, marketing planning can be an invaluable instrument for identifying and responding to emerging issues in uncertain environments and can be a catalyst for constructive and effective marketing activity. It cannot ensure success, but it does improve the chances of success and reduce the risks of failure.

A marketing plan is defined by McDonald (1999) as

> a clear and simple summary of key market trends, key target segments, the value required by each of them, how we intend to create superior value (to competitors), with a clear prioritization of marketing objectives and strategies, together with financial consequences.

He sees the process of marketing planning as being about applying marketing resources to achieve marketing objectives. This is a dynamic process, comprising a series of logical steps which help drive the organization forward by co-ordinating resources and channelling them towards the achievement of predetermined goals (see Table 8.1).

Table 8.1 A marketing plan checklist

- Is there a clear and unambiguous definition of the market you are interested in serving?

- Is it clearly mapped, showing product/service flows, volumes/values in total, your shares and critical conclusions for your organization?

- Are the segments clearly described and quantified? These must be groups of customers with the same or similar needs, *not* sectors.

- Are the real needs of these segments properly quantified with the relative importance of these needs clearly identified?

- Is there a clear and quantified analysis of how well your organization satisfies these needs compared to competitors?

- Are the opportunities and threats clearly identified by segment?

- Are all the segments classified according to their relative potential for growth in profits over the next three years, and according to your organization's relative competitive position in each?

- Are the objectives consistent with their position in the portfolio (volume, value, market share, profit)?

- Are the strategies (including products, services and solutions) consistent with the objectives?

- Are the measurement metrics proposed relevant to the objectives and strategies?

- Are the key issues for action for all departments clearly spelled out as key issues to be addressed?

- Do the objectives and strategies achieve the corporate goals of the organization?

- Does the budget follow on logically and clearly from all the above, or is it merely an add on?

Source: McDonald, 1999.

The aim of this chapter is to examine the key steps in the marketing planning process and to look at the role of the marketing plan itself, and how its implementation can be monitored. This includes sections on:

- mission statements and organizational objectives
- the marketing audit and SWOT analysis
- marketing objectives and strategies
- marketing tactics and budgets
- implementing the marketing plan
- monitoring and evaluation

The framework suggested for marketing planning should enable arts organizations to embark on marketing planning in a structured way and to reconcile the aims of their own organizations with the constraints of the environment and the needs and expectations of their markets.

The benefits of marketing planning

The benefits of marketing planning can be seen at both the organizational level and the individual level.

Marketing planning takes place within the context of the aims and objectives of the whole organization. It can even help to clarify them, reinforcing the artistic policy and providing a sense of direction and purpose to the activities in which arts organizations are engaged. When the organization is clear about what it is and where it is going audiences, too, will be more certain as to the organization's role and position, reducing the likelihood of disappointed expectations.

For the organization, the benefits of marketing planning stem from:

- better anticipation of change and less vulnerability to the unexpected
- a long-term perspective and proactive responses to environmental changes
- acceptance of the need for change and preparedness to meet change
- fewer bad decisions when taken by surprise
- greater inter-functional co-ordination
- better communication and less conflict between individuals
- minimum waste and duplication of resources
- the existence of a structure around which to manage

Individuals, too, benefit from the planning process, which can create a sense of belonging to and ownership of the organization and increase personal motivation by creating opportunities for achievements to be formally recognized.

Objections to marketing planning

As the benefits of marketing planning are so significant, it is quite surprising that resistance is often encountered by those who wish to introduce it into arts organizations. Planning is sometimes accepted as a necessary evil, on the basis that sponsors and funding bodies require it, and that budgets are needed to prevent over-spending, but it is often treated with suspicion:

> Planning is an unnatural process; it's much more fun to do something else. The nicest thing about not planning is that failure comes as a complete surprise, rather than being preceded by a period of worry and depression.
> *Sir John Harvey Jones*

Underlying the excuses often given for not planning may lie some quite understandable insecurities (Table 8.2). Some people dismiss planning as irrelevant because they do not really know what it is about or where to start, or they believe that it requires a special skill which they do not possess. Others fear that plans are hostages to fortune, and work on the basis that if they do not publish their intentions, no one can turn around and say that they failed to reach their goals. Another objection is that planning time is time that could be spent more productively 'getting on with the job', though it is likely that the time management of such people could be improved by having better direction and focus for their work.

Table 8.2 Why people don't plan, and what to say to them

Reason	Response
'things are changing too quickly'	'then it's easy to change with them'
'we're too small to need a plan'	'then your plan will be short and simple'
'I've got more important things to do'	'how do you know which is the best place to start?'
'what's the point of planning'	'you know which is the best place to start!'
'it's not my job'	'then whose is it?'
'no one will take any notice even if I *do* plan'	'they will if you involve them'
'I already know which direction we're going'	'but does everyone else?'

Underlying reasons!	
'I don't like planning'	'but you'll like the results of planning'
'maybe I can't achieve what I'd like to'	'at least you'll know before you start trying'
'where do I start?'	'read this chapter!'
'I'm not qualified'	'you will be when you've read this chapter'
'what happens if I don't achieve my plans?'	'you'll be able to give good reasons for it'
'I've never thought of planning before'	'there's no time like the present'
'I hate bureaucracy!'	'the best plans aren't bureaucratic!'

Source: Adapted from the Business Planning seminar pack, Arts Council Incentive Funding Scheme, 1988.

To overcome objections to planning it is important that the process is introduced with maximum communication and minimum mystique, in a constructive rather than critical atmosphere, and with appropriate support, including training, for those who are directly involved in the creation of the plans.

Berwick means business

The Maltings Theatre and Arts Centre in Berwick-upon-Tweed was built on the ashes of an old warehouse, destroyed by fire 12 years before. It was the dream of a small group of forward-thinkers who at the time wanted the town to find a place on the arts map. The region is not wealthy, and there were some objections at the time, 'Waste of money', 'What's the arts got to do with me?' but nevertheless it was built. What followed was a 10-year mixed history of underfunding, overspending, lack of financial controls, very little serious marketing and a lack of popular programming, leading to a deficit of over £100 000. Eventually, the local council – the Centre's core funders – decided to pull the plug; but a stubborn determination to confound the critics led to the drawing up of a radical 3-year business plan to change the entire thinking and development of the organization.

First and foremost, the Maltings needed money, so business thinking overrode the arts in the need to survive and managers set about defining the needs of its catchment area. Supporters of innovative theatre and arts programming were temporarily disappointed as tribute bands and 'end-of-the-pier' productions were staged in order to put bums on seats. But audiences who wanted challenging theatre were told the reasons for this and remained loyal through to year two, when consolidation and planning for growth was possible and a stronger and more varied artistic programme was financially viable.

Source: Benton, 2001.

Problems with marketing planning

Marketing planning does not always realize its potential benefits. This can be for a number of reasons, but arts organizations which are dissatisfied with the results of planning systems may find the following to be the most significant:

- *Weak support from top management:* While chief executives are usually in support of financial planning, they may perceive marketing planning to be in conflict with artistic policy. (Marketing is often taken to mean 'market-led' and 'giving people what they want', though in an arts environment a marketing plan should respond to, rather than lead, artistic policy, which forms part of the mission of the organization.)
- *Lack of information:* A marketing plan is dependent on information to enable sound analysis of markets and the environment. An inadequate commitment to marketing research (or inadequate resources for it) may leave the planner to make assumptions which may be inaccurate, thereby distorting the base on which the plan is constructed and leading to inappropriate objectives and unrealistic strategies.
- *Ambiguous purpose:* The marketing plan may be used to try to extract funding from sponsors and funding bodies. To accommodate this purpose, targets and objectives may be unrealistically optimistic and ultimately unattainable.
- *Complexity:* The plan does not exist as an end in itself. It needs to be communicated to the board for agreement and to the staff for action. While the analysis required in the planning process is intrinsically complex, the detailed presentation of these complexities in the marketing plan itself simply serves to confuse the readers. Planning terminology can sound like meaningless jargon and detracts from the impact of the report, sometimes

leading to otherwise sound plans being rejected by those who would be involved in their agreement or implementation.

- *Expectations of instant results:* Organizations which introduce marketing planning in response to a particular management crisis are often looking for quick solutions to pressing problems. In these situations, managers may hold unrealistic expectations as to the speed at which plans can be implemented and results observed. Plans may be dismissed as failures before the full process of monitoring and adjustment has been undertaken. It is important therefore to phrase objectives in terms which allow realistic timescales.

The implication of all this is that marketing planning may be rejected as being unhelpful or a waste of time. By being alert to the reasons why plans fail, arts marketers should be able to avoid the most common planning problems and reap the full benefits of a system which is designed to simplify the task of marketing management and improve its effectiveness.

The arts marketing planning process

The process of arts marketing planning involves four key stages: analysis; planning; communication, and action (Figure 8.1).

- *Analysis:* This begins by examining the *raison d'être* of the organization. This may be explicit in the form of a mission statement, a set of organizational objectives and a clearly articulated artistic policy, but it may simply be implicit in the activities that the organization is engaged with, the art forms that it produces and the audiences that it attempts to serve. This understanding serves to create the framework within which the marketing plan should be developed.

    After this, an evaluation takes place of the readiness of the organization to meet the demands of its changing environment. This evaluation takes the form of a marketing audit which examines the nature of its external environment (especially its existing and potential audiences) and the extent of changes in that environment. The capabilities and constraints of the organization are assessed within this context, and the audit should culminate in a statement of the organization's strengths and weaknesses in the face of the opportunities and threats arising in its environment.

- *Planning:* In possession of this knowledge about the organization's current position, the marketing planner can set objectives and design strategies to help the organization reach its target audiences more effectively and efficiently. Objectives are targets it wishes to reach (usually expressed numerically, perhaps in the form of seats booked or percentage capacity filled, but also in the form of financial goals) and strategies are the broad approaches to achieving these.

    Tactical plans can then be formulated. The term tactics refers to the ways in which the strategy will be implemented; there are usually several possible routes for achieving a goal and a route needs to be chosen which will fall within the organization's capabilities. For this reason, budgets are set to

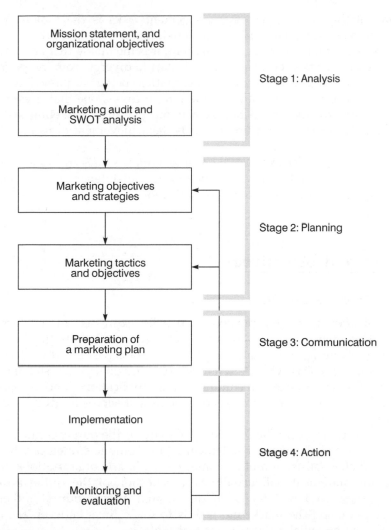

Figure 8.1 The arts marketing planning process

ensure that the planned tactics will not overstretch the financial resources of the organization.
- *Communication:* The marketing plan is the vehicle for communicating the planned marketing activity, mainly to those who are involved in its implementation, but also to other interested stakeholder groups, such as the board and funding bodies. It should reflect the outcome of analysis and clearly present the strategic and tactical marketing plans along with forecasts of their impact on the market and their implications for the organization.
- *Action:* The quality of a marketing plan will normally be judged by the results of its implementation, so the management of its implementation (which more often than not means the management of change) is fundamental to the outcome of the planning process.

One of the most important management tasks is the monitoring and evaluation of the plan as it is implemented. As the planning process is based on forecasts of an uncertain environment, it is inevitable that at some stage the outcomes of marketing activity will start to diverge from the projections put forward in the plan, with targets either being surpassed or underachieved. The monitoring and evaluation process is one that is essential to enable corrective action to be taken if the planned marketing activity is failing to lead the organization towards the achievement of its objectives.

The rest of this chapter explores these four critical stages in more detail and provides a blueprint for the introduction and maintenance of an effective marketing planning process in arts organizations.

Mission and objectives

The mission statement

An organization's primary purpose is usually expressed in the form of a mission statement. (As the mission statement is the starting point for marketing planning, organizations which do not have one should consider drawing one up.) This will stand as the organization's policy statement in a number of circumstances, including grant applications and sponsorship approaches, but from a marketing point of view it serves to give direction to marketing strategies.

In organizations where the overriding objective is the purely commercial one of making money, the mission statement will encourage strategies which lead to the profitable satisfaction of customer needs. In arts organizations, though, the mission statement will usually be a reflection of the ruling artistic or cultural policy, and will focus on the desired artistic output rather than audience demand. The marketing task is to make links between the artistic work and the potential audiences for that work.

A mission statement is likely to include some or all of the following elements:

- *A statement of purpose:* This should identify the organization's primary reason for existence. It is likely to describe the artistic or cultural policy and outline the main processes by which these are implemented (including the scope and range of artistic activity).
- *A description of target markets:* This will outline the types of audience that the organization wishes to attract, but may also recognize a responsibility to sponsors and funding bodies.
- *A statement of philosophy:* This will establish the values and beliefs that guide the policies and strategies of the organization. It may encompass values relating to audiences (particularly with respect to access policy), artists (perhaps in terms of quality of the artistic product and artistic freedom), and also employees (giving a commitment to staff development).

- *A statement of vision:* This will explain where the organization is going, and how it sees itself at some future point in time. Its aspirations may relate to both its purpose and its target markets, but may also refer to its assets and resources (for example, the extension of premises).

Better vision

In his research comparing commercial enterprises with the non-profit sector, Davidson (2002) found that non-profits held the stronger visions. 'Companies scored poorly on strong vision, because their visions were usually neither memorable nor motivating. Some died emotionally many years ago, although the people there still go through the motions, generating sales and profits. They are like the characters in Oscar Wilde's *The Eighth Day:* "She died when she was 32, and was buried at 87".'

Source: Davidson, 2002.

A few guidelines are useful in creating a mission statement. According to Piercey (1991) it should be:

- *Succinct:* comprise a few words and ideas, not pages that no one will ever read, let alone take any notice of.
- *Memorable:* so that those who are working within it can remember what it is.
- *Enduring:* though not a tablet of stone, it should not need changing on a frequent basis.
- *Believable:* it reflects the reality of the organization and its environment.
- *Roughly right:* giving general directions and core values rather than precise goals and actions.
- *Energizing to all:* it should be exciting and visionary.

Finally, a mission statement must be a statement to which all the stakeholders in the organization can subscribe, whether they be market stakeholders (audiences and potential audiences), funding stakeholders (sponsors, trusts and funding bodies) or internal stakeholders (employees and artists).

Mission impossible?

Arts organizations' missions are wide-ranging in style, but they attempt to sum up the essence of why the organization exists. For example:

The Maltings Art Centre

The Maltings Trust aims to be a vibrant part of the community of Berwick, bringing the arts to people throughout the Borough, in village halls, schools and community facilities as well as within The Maltings Arts Centre. It will present a broad programme of theatre, music, dance, film and visual arts, some familiar and popular, some challenging and innovative. As a home for local arts groups it will provide a base, friendly advice and technical guidance; for creative professionals it will provide training and business support. The Maltings will be a key feature in promotions to attract cultural tourists and inward investment.

Eastern Touring Agency

ETA is an innovative team of specialists, rooted in the East of England, which enables the development of best practice in the arts and provides frameworks for finding creative solutions to meet the needs of arts sector partners. ETA aspires to be respected nationally and renowned for effective delivery.

North West Arts Board

To invest in, advocate for and develop the arts and creativity so that they impact positively on the cultural, social and economic well-being of the north-west region of England.

Source: The Maltings Arts Centre, 2002; Eastern Touring Agency, 2002; North West Arts Board, 2001.

Organizational aims and objectives

The mission statement may be supported by a series of more specific organizational aims and objectives which link a statement of purpose with a statement of vision.

Aims will never finally be achieved as they will always persist. A gallery, for example, may state the following objectives:

- 'To broaden the audience base for contemporary fine art by presenting work in an accessible format.'
- 'To ensure that the gallery's work represents a balance across gender and tradition.'
- 'To provide the opportunity for local and regional artists to show their work in a national and international context.'

Objectives are measurable and give timescales within which a particular desired state should be achieved. For example:

- 'Within two years to create in the gallery a welcoming social space in which people from all backgrounds can meet to eat, drink and talk.'
- 'To mount two exhibitions each year which reflect the ethnic and cultural diversity of the region.'
- 'Each year to provide new facilities which improve access for disabled people.'

Both aims and objectives are useful in marketing planning as they give specific direction to marketing activity, though closed objectives also provide a useful yardstick against which achievements can be measured.

Aiming high

Cornerhouse is an international centre for contemporary arts, based in Manchester. It comprises three galleries, three cinemas, a visual arts book distribution service, two specialist bookshops, two cafés and a bar. Cornerhouse articulates its corporate aims as follows:

- To inspire and inform audiences by presenting a distinctive programme of diverse, challenging and innovative work.
- To be leaders in the development of audiences for the contemporary arts.
- To continue to play a major part in the cultural and social life of Greater Manchester.
- To work collaboratively with regional, national and international partners in extending cultural debate, access and distribution.
- To be a centre of excellence in the presentation of artists' work.
- To provide a high quality experience and service in a welcoming and stimulating environment.
- To explore the relationships between contemporary art and popular culture.
- To be a well-resourced, effective and efficiently-managed organization for the benefit of artists and audience.

Source: Cornerhouse Annual Review, 1999.

The marketing audit and SWOT analysis

A marketing audit is the process by which an arts organization gathers relevant information about its environment (an external audit) and itself (an internal audit). The purpose of the marketing audit is to help organizations to answer the question 'where are we now?' It should be a systematic, unbiased and critical review which leads to an evaluation of the organization's Strengths and Weaknesses in responding to the Opportunities and Threats in its environment. It is this SWOT analysis that helps the identification of appropriate marketing objectives and strategies (see Figure 8.2).

The external audit (environmental analysis)

This is concerned with the appraisal of those factors which affect the fortunes of the organization but over which it has limited, if any, control. The purpose of the external audit is to identify trends in the environment so that actions can be taken to exploit the positive trends and minimize the impact of the negative ones.

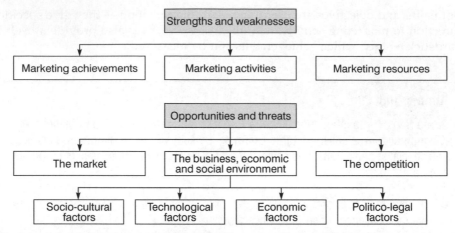

Figure 8.2 The components of a SWOT analysis

Three areas need to be considered – the business, economic and social environment (sometimes known as the macro environment), the market, and the competition.

Business, economic and social environment

Developments in the business, economic and social environment affect society as a whole, but certain of them will have specific relevance for arts organizations. The STEP factors (Socio-cultural, Technological, Economic and Politico-legal) touched on in Chapter 1's brief analysis of the arts marketing environment are a useful model for identifying the most important trends. For example:

Socio-cultural factors

- *The mobility of populations:* Increased racial integration and a boom in international tourism mean that ethnocentric arts programmes are becoming less relevant and efforts to expand the cultural diversity of work are required if the arts are to remain accessible to the wider community.
- *Increase in crime:* Venues sited in the inner cities may suffer from public fears of rising crime on the streets. This may be compounded by the reduction in public transport services which may restrict access to car owners and require that safe parking facilities close to the venue are available.
- *Leisure patterns:* An increase in the number of working women can reduce demand for arts events during the day, though a simultaneous increase in the retired population and non-working men may provide a target audience for arts activities at this time and alleviate the pressures on facilities at weekends.

Technological factors

- *Improved software:* Far better target marketing can be achieved using sophisticated database-driven box office systems, providing opportunities to reduce mailing costs while improving response rates.

- *Penetration of home computing facilities:* As more and more households have access to e-mail and the internet, the importance of maintaining effective well-maintained websites will increase, and the practice of online ticket booking will undoubtedly grow.
- *Advances in telecommunications:* Text messaging, currently in its infancy, looks as if it will become a valuable means of reaching some target audiences, especially young people.
- *Improved home entertainment:* As the arts are in competition with other forms of leisure activity, home entertainment technology such as digital television can potentially threaten attendances at live arts events.

Economic factors

- *Unemployment:* This may lead to increased demand for arts activities but a reduced ability to pay for them. Pricing structures may need to be redesigned in periods of high unemployment.
- *Rising interest rates:* House owners experience a reduction in their disposable income when mortgage rates increase. As leisure activities comprise a part of the discretionary expenditure of a household, they may be the first to be cut back in times of economic constraint, and arts organizations may notice that even their most loyal attenders are coming less frequently. Reduced price subscription schemes may be an appropriate measure for encouraging a commitment to attend in these circumstances.
- *Recession:* Businesses often reduce their expenditure on marketing in an attempt to survive a recession. Sponsorship is likely to be one of the first elements of a marketing budget to be cut as it is difficult to measure its results. Arts organizations are one group likely to suffer from reduced funding as a result.

Politico-legal factors

- *Arts funding policy:* This is likely to change according to the political persuasion of the ruling government. It can change very quickly, leaving arts organizations in the midst of the implementation of long-term plans but without the assurance of long-term income. Relatively fixed forms of financial support such as revenue grants have been to some extent replaced by project-based schemes such as the Lottery, where the funding income and patterns are far less certain. Marketing plans should anticipate and forecast policy change as far as possible, but be sufficiently flexible to react to unexpected developments.
- *Health and safety regulations:* Legal requirements with regard to visitors and audiences as well as employees may influence venue design and the provision of facilities. Marketing plans must be constructed within these constraints and the finance for any measures to achieve compliance must take priority over other marketing activity.
- *Data protection legislation:* As we have seen in Chapter 7, any arts organization which keeps a database of names and addresses of people who have attended its events is obliged to register under the Data Protection Act, and is constrained as to the ways in which it can use this data. The implementation of the act will change as case law develops, which may

mean that the practice of database marketing adopted by an arts organization will have to evolve to meet the requirements of the law.

These STEP factors are inevitably beyond the control of an arts organization. They will produce opportunities for the organization to respond to and threats which it must face up to, but they cannot be ignored. An assessment of the significance of changes in the STEP factors should therefore be the starting point for a marketing audit.

Of much more immediate relevance to an arts organization, though, are trends which are of specific interest to the arts sector, so the next stages of the audit require an assessment of trends among target markets and developments in competition. These give an organization a much clearer picture of the more immediate opportunities and threats that it faces. Continuous efforts to obtain current marketing research through both primary and secondary sources can produce the data on which such an assessment can be made (as discussed in Chapter 3).

The market

The audit needs to search for any changes and trends in the following aspects of the organization's target market (including actual and potential audiences):

- the geographic and demographic characteristics of the primary target market
- the characteristics of different market segments within the overall target market (e.g. regular attenders as opposed to irregular or infrequent attenders; day-time attenders as opposed to evening attenders; weekday attenders as opposed to weekend attenders; or attenders for different types of art form)
- the benefits sought by different market segments (e.g. facilities expected; types of programme or exhibition; or quality of artistic product)
- the price sensitivity of different segments
- purchasing patterns (e.g. popularity of subscription schemes or group bookings; sources of ticket purchase (agent or direct); or preferences for opening hours or performance timings)
- information sources used to find out about arts events

This type of knowledge and understanding of the market can enable arts organizations to identify opportunities such as emerging market segments or new means by which they can communicate with their target audiences. It can also help them prepare for eventualities such as increased demand for improved facilities or a decline in the popularity of certain art forms. Marketing research is the key to this (as explained in Chapter 3). Information can be pooled with other arts organizations to gain a more complete picture, or funding bodies may be able to provide an overview.

The competition

The audit also needs to recognize changes and trends in competition although, as we have seen in Chapter 5, this is a complicated area in the arts. Two important questions need to be answered in building up a picture of the ways in which competition of various sorts may be affecting attendance patterns:

1 What is the nature of the competition? Competition may come from a wide range of sources. An orchestra, for example, will need to recognize:
   – desire competitors (e.g. alternative ways of spending an evening, such as going to the pub or the bowling alley)
   – generic competitors (e.g. other forms of live entertainment, such as a play or a ballet)
   – form competitors (e.g. other types of live music, such as rock music, jazz or chamber music)
   – brand competitors (i.e. other orchestras)
2 How threatening are the different competitors? If audiences are simply deserting one venue for another in the locality, for example, then marketing strategies need to address the impact of a brand competitor, perhaps by identifying a niche in the market that the other venue is not well placed to serve. On the other hand, if audiences are deserting a particular art form, or even the arts per se, marketing communications may need to be enhanced in an attempt to change attitudes. This is likely to require a long-term commitment and more may be achieved by the lobbying of funding bodies and collective action by all the brand competitors than by unilateral strategies.

A perceptual map is a useful tool for evaluating the extent of brand competition (Figure 8.3). It is developed by identifying the most important criteria by which audiences judge different arts organizations on two axes and plotting the competitors within the framework. Qualitative market research is a useful tool for identifying both the criteria and audience perceptions of different organizations (see Chapter 3). If an organization is positioned well away from its competitors, audiences are likely to perceive the product offerings of the various organizations to be quite different, so the intensity of the competition will be relatively low. However, if a number of organizations fall into the same quartile on the grid, competition is likely to be more fierce, with audiences choosing between broadly similar offerings. (An analysis of the effects of competition on pricing strategy is discussed further in Chapter 5.)

An understanding of the nature and strength of competition usually leads arts organizations to one of two conclusions (and occasionally a combination of both):

● That marketing strategies must involve collaborating with competitors (for example, through the formation of arts marketing consortia; see Table 8.3).

This is a conclusion often reached in regions well served by arts organizations in the subsidized sector. If a number of different organizations are attempting to serve similar target markets, the extent of the competition may render them

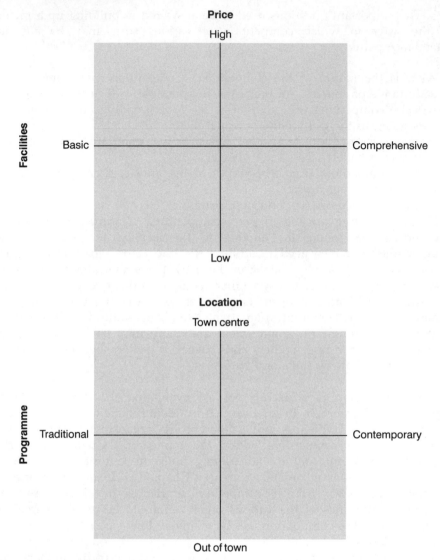

Figure 8.3 Examples of perceptual mapping grids for the assessment of competitive positioning

individually non-viable. Target audiences will become fragmented if they have to choose between different venues offering broadly similar programmes at the same time, and the cost of reaching these target audiences will be high due to the intensive promotion needed to encourage them to attend one venue rather than another. However, if the arts organizations work together, programme schedules can be designed so that different segments of the overall target market are attracted to different venues at different times. Joint promotional activity becomes possible, bringing economies of scale which reduce costs for each participating organization.

Table 8.3 Consortia: critical success factors

The following factors are likely to determine whether a consortium approach is likely to work or not:

- Common purpose – a grouping with enough in common to be able to work together.

- Ownership and motivation – a genuine willingness and commitment to co-operation: time, money, ideas, and involvement at a senior level.

- Strategy – a clear and agreed collective vision, realistic aims and objectives, achievable operational programme based on need and opportunity.

- Viability – enough resources to employ staff to lead, plan, and implement the desired outputs.

- Agreement – a shared understanding of its role on the part of all the stakeholders.

- Impact assessment and accountability – a commitment to monitoring and evaluation so that costs and benefits can be quantified.

Source: Hadley, 2000.

Case 8.1 Hampshire's houses of horror

'andco' is a consortium of six Hampshire arts centres, involving the Ashcroft Arts Centre, Fareham; Fairfields Arts Centre, Basingstoke; Forest Arts Centre, New Milton; Havant Arts Active; The Tower, Winchester; and The West End Centre, Aldershot, together with Hampshire's County Arts Office. The consortium has at its heart the aim to improve the quality, quantity and range of programming at its centres and to encourage new audiences to attend. By working collaboratively, it has the clout to book tours that would otherwise be outside members' reach. One of andco's most unusual and successful ventures saw the arrival from Paris of La Compagnie du Carnage and their Grand Guignol theatre of horrors. Grand Guignol is a type of French theatre not seen in the UK for many years, the last French company to have performed it coming over in 1908. In Paris the 'tranches des morts' as they were known, attracted a wide audience, including such illustrious patrons as the Kings of Greece and Romania, the Sultan of Morocco's children and Ho Chi Min, at the time a noodle chef at a local Chinese restaurant. Fainting in the audience (particularly the men, who would not avert their eyes) was commonplace. Andco booked a tour during Hallowe'en week 1999, with the production visiting all six centres. It garnered acclaim and controversy in both local and national media: and audiences loved it. Commenting on why Grand Guignol was chosen, andco's James Barry said, 'We wanted something out of the ordinary that would draw new audiences and would not have been available to any other arts centre in the country. It was something we could market to young people and that would provide us with a legacy of new contacts for the future. We hope all the "goths", horror fans and people who attended out of sheer curiosity will come again to enjoy a wider range of productions.'

Source: Johnson, 2000.

- That marketing strategies must involve proactive competition (attempting to defend oneself against competitors while simultaneously trying to attract their audiences).

In the commercial arts, this has always been and will no doubt remain the overriding attitude towards competition. 'Angels' will only invest in West-End musicals if they can anticipate a financial return, so the objective of the show is to make as much money as possible. In a finite market, this means not only persuading potential audiences to spend money on theatre instead of an evening in the pub or a trip to the cinema, but also persuading them to attend a particular production, rather than any of the others available within a short walking distance of the theatre. The impact of this competitive orientation must not be ignored by the subsidized sector. These commercial competitors are looking for audiences for live entertainment which are very likely to overlap to a large extent with the segments being targeted by the arts organizations with non-commercial objectives.

The internal audit

The purpose of the internal audit is to indicate how prepared the organization is to meet the demands of the changing environment identified in the external audit. The internal audit should evaluate three broad areas:

- marketing achievements
- marketing activities
- marketing resources

Marketing achievements

Marketing achievements (usually over the past 12 months) are evaluated by looking at the extent to which the organization has met its objectives. These objectives can vary widely. They may relate to new audiences generated; to customer loyalty; to membership levels; but for many arts marketers, they relate primarily to the nature and sources of income generated, particularly box office income and other earned income from catering, programmes, sales and advertising space etc. Organizations with computerized box offices are in a position to obtain more information about the success of different marketing policies with different market segments, by looking at:

- income for different types of show or exhibition
- types of tickets sold (subscription, members, party, corporate, single tickets, concessionary groups – young, OAP, unemployed etc.)
- price paid and method of payment
- day and time of attendance
- seasonal variations
- time booked (in advance or on the door)
- sales channel (box office or agencies, personal, postal or telephone)

This information is particularly helpful if it is collected over many years so that trends can be identified and conclusions drawn as to the effectiveness of previous marketing strategies.

Marketing activities

An organization's marketing mix comprises those activities which are undertaken with a view to generating the visitor traffic and income streams described above. As explained earlier, these comprise product- (or service-) related activities, pricing, promotional activity and any distribution activity (aimed at making the arts experience accessible). The impact of these elements should be evaluated.

The product evaluation may include an assessment of the effectiveness of programming policy; the range of productions (or exhibitions); the quality of artistic work being presented, indicating the proportions of amateur, professional, national or international events; and the nature of venue(s), including location, amenities, ambience etc.

An evaluation of pricing could involve a consideration of general price levels; price structures (including concessions); differentials used to influence demand (e.g. lower prices for matinées, higher prices at weekends); incentives to promote frequency (including subscription schemes); and incentives to attract parties and groups.

A review of the impact of promotional activity will look at advertising, including the relative success of different media; print and its distribution; posters; PR; and direct marketing, including, for example, the size and composition of any mailing, e-mailing and text messaging lists.

Finally, an assessment of distribution may look at the impact of box office opening hours and staffing levels; levels of internet booking; other selling points, including ticket agencies; and the range of venues and locations being used (for touring productions or exhibitions).

Marketing resources

The marketing resources committed to the generation of income and the development of audiences must also be considered. Not only do they indicate the efficiency with which the marketing function operates, but they also create the constraints within which the marketing function is performed. Four key resources should be examined:

- staff (including job responsibilities, organizational structure, staff experience and support from higher levels of management)
- budgets (including box office systems and opportunities for increasing revenues)
- information technology (including box office systems)
- other help (for example, from public bodies such as local authorities or universities; board members; volunteers; funding bodies; venues – for touring productions and exhibitions – and marketing consortia)

SWOT analysis

The most useful way of drawing conclusions from a marketing audit is by conducting a SWOT analysis. From the list of issues identified in the external environment, the specific opportunities and threats facing the organization can be drawn out. The strengths and weaknesses of the marketing function in meeting the opportunities and counteracting the threats can then be developed from the evidence in the internal audit. Although this is a largely subjective process, it is a useful way of summarizing the marketing audit.

Not all of the strengths and weaknesses of the organization should be listed; neither should all of the opportunities and threats. An arts organization only has a strength if it is perceived as being good at something in the eyes of its customers and relative to its competitors. For example, a brand new state-of-the-art building is a strength if customers find it an enjoyable place to experience the arts, but new is not necessarily better, and the new building could be a weakness if the ambience of the auditorium and foyer is perceived to have been lost in the renovation process.

The SWOT analysis should draw out the major opportunities and threats facing the organization, together with those strengths and weaknesses which affect the way in which the opportunities can be seized and the threats avoided. In doing this, it creates a framework for the formulation of objectives and strategies, helping the organization to decide 'where do we want to go'.

Objectives and strategies

As explained earlier in this chapter, an objective is 'what' you want to achieve, and should be a specific target which can be demonstrably attained. A strategy is 'how' you plan to achieve your objectives. It is a general statement which gives direction to the activities (or tactics) that must be undertaken to achieve the objectives. For the purposes of a marketing plan, these objectives and strategies relate to the arts provision, the related facilities and the audience (or sponsor).

Marketing objectives

Marketing objectives have two very specific dimensions, as illustrated in Table 8.4: customers (audiences, visitors or participants) and products (the arts experience offered to those audiences).

Consequently, there are three possible generic marketing objectives:

- *Loyalty building:* aim to attract those who are currently attending your artistic experience to do so more consistently.

Table 8.4 Generic marketing objectives

	Existing audiences	New audiences
Products		
Current artistic experience	Loyalty building	Audience development
New artistic experience	Audience development	Diversification

- *Audience development:* either aim to attract new customers for the artistic experience you currently offer or aim to attract your current attenders to new types of artistic work.
- *Diversification:* develop new types of artistic work and aim to attract people who do not normally attend.

Currying favour with white audiences

Theatre venues often labour under the impression that Asian plays will appeal only to Asian audiences, and are timid about marketing non-traditional work to their 'regular' attenders. But some Asian theatre companies believe their work can be effectively targeted at a much wider audience base. Tamasha Theatre Company toured *Balti Kings*, a pungent comedy set in the kitchen of a Birmingham curry house, to places where there were hardly any Asians. At Liverpool's Everyman Theatre it played to 75 per cent capacity audiences, and at Plymouth's Theatre Royal, the figure was 77 per cent.

Source: Bhuchar, 2001.

Depending on the strengths, weaknesses, opportunities and threats identified in the marketing audit, any or all of these generic objectives may be appropriate and will need to be further developed into specific statements of planned achievement. These statements need to be written very carefully in the form of SMART objectives, as they are the driving force behind the future marketing activity of the organization. SMART objectives are:

- Specific (make it quite clear as to what the target is)
- Measurable (be capable of evaluation of progress)
- Agreed (supported by all who are involved in achieving them)
- Realistic (not unattainable dreams)
- Time-constrained (to be achieved by a specific deadline)

Examples of specific marketing objectives relating to each of the generic areas might be:

- 'To increase the sale of subscription schemes by 10 per cent next season' (loyalty building).
- 'To double the number of first-time attenders during the autumn season' (audience development).
- 'To increase audiences for new work by 30 per cent over the next 12 months' (audience development).
- 'To regularly fill 20 places in a new after-school workshop by 1st September' (audience development, or possibly diversification).
- 'To generate £20 000 by the end of the year from the hire of facilities for business conferences' (diversification).

Marketing strategies

Marketing strategies outline the way in which the organization's skills and resources should be used to achieve its marketing objectives. They are inevitably wide in scope, and describe overall 'routes' to achieving objectives rather than giving details of specific activities that must be undertaken.

Marketing strategies are broadly concerned with the four main elements of the marketing mix, and should provide general policy in each area.

- *Product:* The general policy for the scope of arts activity and facilities to be provided.

  Proposed marketing strategies may indicate the advisability of either a wider or narrower range of arts activities; this is a controversial area, and often one which causes conflict between the artistic director and the marketing department, though compromises can normally be found. Other product-related strategies may relate to non-core arts activities, such as the role of the catering or retail outlets, perhaps the provision of a crèche, or the improvement of facilities for sponsors.

- *Price:* The general pricing policies to be followed for different audience segments.

  Pricing strategy determines the way in which revenue is generated. For example, in recent years 'pay what you can' strategies have grown in popularity as the conditions under which public funding is granted include the requirement of being accessible to all. Other pricing strategies may relate to the introduction of concessionary discounts; price banding for seats with different quality sightlines; or differential pricing for different nights of the week.

- *Promotion:* The general policies for communicating with a range of target audiences.

  The objectives may suggest that a change in the balance between the use of advertising and direct marketing is appropriate, so a strategy related to this could involve the commissioning of a new database. Alternatively, if the objectives are to reposition the organization to attract different types of audiences, the strategic emphasis may be on PR and advertising, and lead to the appointment of agencies. While the details of a promotional campaign should not be raised at this stage, an account should be given of the promotional tools that will be used.

- *Distribution:* The general venue policy (especially for touring organizations) and/or ticket distribution systems.

  Ticket distribution strategies will indicate the best ways of making tickets available to target audiences. A change in the role of ticket agencies may be suggested, or perhaps increased distribution through schools and clubs. The use of telephone selling may be proposed, and touring organizations may advocate a change in the proportion of performances or exhibitions held in rural venues.

These are just a few examples of marketing strategies. These will set the boundaries for the design of more specific tactical marketing plans.

Case 8.2 The incidental visitor

When Liverpool's Tate Gallery started to collect data about the nature of its audiences, it discovered that its attenders were a far cry from the self-defining art lovers that the curators tended to believe formed the main core of visitors. Forty-five per cent were found to be first-time visitors, of whom two-thirds were incidental visitors who had just drifted into the building as part of a general day trip to visit the cafés, shops, and the Beatles museum. Fifty-five per cent were found to be repeat visitors, but even in this group nearly half were in the incidental attender category. In total, 41 per cent of attenders had very little or no knowledge of modern art.

	First timers %	Repeat visitors %
Intentional visit	15	30
Incidental visit	30	25

These different groups of visitors had different needs which formed a hierarchy starting with the needs of a visitor who was new to the building or new to modern art. The new or uninformed visitors needed help to find their way around the building and without drawing undue attention to themselves. Family groups, on the other hand, might have the need for a gallery assistant to talk about an exhibit or theme; but at the same time, confident visitors prefer the place not to be full of families so that they can have peace and quiet to reflect on the work.

For those new to the building, Tate identified that they needed to establish a relationship with the visitor as soon as they walked in, making them feel welcome. There was a need for easy access orientation plans, detailed floor-by-floor signage, free information written for people who have very little knowledge of modern art, and proactive assistants, rather than 'guards' of the artworks. For more confident visitors, audio and video guides, information rooms, detailed contextual information and well-informed assistants were needed. In their Lottery application for refurbishment, Tate Liverpool planned to stratify the gallery so that they could make plenty of guidance available on the ground floor. Paid exhibitions, which used to be on the ground floor, were moved to the top floor in recognition that it's mainly people with commitment who will get that far! Promotional strategy also had to change. Traditional promotional tactics, such as print and word-of-mouth, were fine for attracting first-time intentional attenders, and direct mail for repeat visitors, but for the first-time incidental attender, external signage was important. The building needed to be more transparent, and generic advertising around Albert Dock was required.

Source: Morris, 1999.

Marketing tactics and budgets

A set of overall marketing objectives and strategies should subsequently be translated into a detailed statement of planned marketing activities indicating exactly what actions need to be taken.

Marketing tactics

There has already been a lot of discussion in this book about tactical marketing activity. Chapters 4 to 7 explain the use of the marketing tools of product, price, promotion and place in an arts environment. For the purposes of planning this type of activity, a useful device is a tactical marketing planning grid, which takes each marketing objective and recommends a series of activities to lead to its achievement. Figure 8.4 gives schemes of a possible activity linked to an example of the objectives given in the previous section.

	Target audience			
	Current subscribers	Lapsed subscribers	Regular attenders	Friends and members
Marketing tactics				
Product				
Pre-show 'meet the cast' events	X	X	X	X
Seat upgrading facility	X	X	X	X
Priority booking arrangements				X
Price				
Discount for early subscriptions	X			
Refund for usage below stated levels		X	X	
Discount voucher for bookshop		X	X	
Promotion				
Direct mail	X	X	X	X
Updated subscription leaflet	X	X	X	X
Advertisement in programmes		X	X	
Place				
Telephone sales	X	X		
X - indicates the target audiences which the proposed marketing tactics are primarily designed to attract				

Figure 8.4 Tactical marketing planning grid: 'To increase the sale of subscription schemes by 10 per cent next season'

Cost and revenue forecasts should be generated for each of the activities on each of the grids, and the activities should be prioritized in the event of financial constraints curtailing some of the plans. These calculations can then be used to prepare a marketing budget. The timing of the activities should also be indicated and, if possible, the name of the person responsible for implementing the planned activity. Clear performance indicators should be put in place to measure success.

Case 8.3 E-mail beginnings

Sadler's Wells was one of the first arts organizations in the UK to embrace the use of e-mail and internet ticketing among its marketing tactics. The organization comprises three venues: Sadler's Wells Theatre (1500 seats) and the Lilian Baylis Theatre (200 seats) in London's Islington, and the Peacock Theatre (1100) seats) in Holborn, central London. It presents dance, opera and music theatre, attracting more than 400 000 visitors a year.

In the late 1990s, surveys had indicated that over 80 per cent of the audience had internet access, with nearly 70 per cent of these having access at work. Sixty five per cent said they would consider booking tickets online. With marketing objectives which aimed to increase the frequency of attendance of existing audiences, as well as engaging new audiences, Sadler's Wells was enticed by the potential for e-mail campaigns to increase the levels of communication with existing attenders at minimal cost. To begin with, 1000 e-mail addresses were collected manually; then, when online ticketing was launched in July 2000, the list quickly grew to 3000 as people registered.

For the first few months e-mail was used in much the same way as direct mail, with messages sent out to promote a single show. It was felt that there was no need to segment the list, as it cost no more to send the message to all than to just some of those who had registered. Messages were incentivized with last-minute offers, partly so that their effectiveness could be monitored. But in November 2000 this approach was modified, to avoid the danger of e-mail recipients feeling that the messages were seldom of relevance to them. A change of tactics saw the launch of a monthly e-mail bulletin instead, with occasional e-flyers for specific shows.

The content of the e-mail bulletins is created with care. Rather than replicate information that recipients might have read in print elsewhere, the information is presented as being 'hot off the press', a reason why people would read it rather than delete it. Other features included value-added offers such as meal deals, and links to the website where video trailers of future shows could be downloaded and competitions entered. Because of the cheapness of sending e-mail, other aspects of the Sadler's Wells 'product' could also be promoted, such as pre-performance talks, the work of the artist in residence, and the sale of bottled water from its very own well!

In the first nine months of the e-mail bulletin's life, online booking rose by 18 per cent and the average number of visits made rose from 2.3 a month to 3.5. Overall visits doubled from 15 000 to 30 000 a month. Of the people who had booked online, 12 000 opted to receive the e-mail and a further 3000 had given their e-mail addresses through offline methods such as audience surveys.

Source: De Kretser, 2001.

The marketing budget

A marketing budget details the planned expenditure on marketing activity to take place in the time period of the plan. It summarizes the expenditures associated with specific activities on each of the tactical marketing planning grids, and sometimes will include projected marketing overheads, such as staff costs, photography and telephone.

It has a very important role to play in convincing the management and board of the organization that the marketing plans are sufficiently stretching without being overambitious, that the expenditure required is within the constraints of the organization and that the risks involved are calculated risks. (The whole issue of budgeting is developed further in Chapter 9.) Marketing budgets are usually submitted to financial managers to be considered in conjunction with other budgets from different departments. Their job is to ensure that the organization as a whole will be able to meet its financial commitments.

Writing the marketing plan

The next stage in the marketing planning process is to communicate the plan to all those who will have an interest in its implementation. It is easy to underestimate the importance of this stage. Having done all the hard work of analysis, objective setting and designing tactical solutions, it is tempting to cut corners when it comes to simply writing it all down. The best approach, therefore, is to think first about the people who will want to read your plan and the influence they have. For reasons of commercial sensitivity, external bodies may receive an edited version of the plan. The detailed marketing plan is likely to have a restricted readership.

Target readership for all or part of the plan will include:

- *Staff in the marketing department:* responsible for the tasks involved in implementing the plan.
- *Top management:* with the power to veto, postpone or curtail any part of the plan of whose effectiveness they are not fully convinced.
- *Other departments:* whose co-operation is vital if 'customer focus' is to permeate the organization.
- *The board:* looking for evidence that the plan will enhance and build on the mission of the organization.
- *Funding bodies:* evaluating the proposals alongside those from other arts organizations.
- *Sponsors:* seeking reassurance that links with the organization will enhance their reputations and offer good value for money.
- *Advertising and marketing research agencies:* needing firm direction to help them create appropriate campaigns.

The clarity with which the marketing plan is written and presented is likely to have a major impact on the willingness of these diverse parties to embrace it and help to make it work.

The structure of a marketing plan

It is likely that the marketing plan will be a subsection of a strategic plan, so its structure may be dictated by those conventions. Normally though, the marketing plan should basically consist of a document which gives a summary of the findings from stages 1 and 2 of the planning process, given in Figure 8.1. That is:

- A brief statement of the organization's mission and objectives.
- The key findings of the marketing audit, summarized at the end in the form of a SWOT analysis.
- A statement of marketing objectives and related strategies.
- A set of tactical marketing plans and their related costs and projected benefits.
- A marketing budget, indicating the allocation of expenditure.

There are three golden rules for writing the plan:

1 Start with a summary of the main conclusions and recommendations (for those who find the details either uninteresting or unnecessary).
2 Tell the readers what they need to know, not everything that you know (your main findings and conclusions are relevant, but the statistical details of how they were obtained are not).
3 Write in English, not in marketing-speak! (Note the very diverse backgrounds of your readers, whose understanding of marketing theory is likely to range from a considerable amount to none at all. If the readers do not understand what you are talking about, they are more likely to reject the plan altogether!)

Implementing the marketing plan

There is no point designing clever marketing strategies and detailed plans if they cannot be implemented to enable the organization to reach its objectives. Marketing implementation, therefore, is ultimately far more important than the plan itself, and the central role of the marketing department is to apply its marketing skills to the organization's resources to execute the tactical marketing plans.

Implementation can prove difficult for a number of reasons, and can be considered to have failed if nothing happens as a result of the marketing plan. If this occurs, it is generally for one of three reasons:

1 The plans are incomplete, incoherent or unrealistic

Some plans are never implemented because they are either so vague or so optimistic that they give no real guidance as to what should be done. In the absence of clear and realistic guidelines, marketing staff will, with some justification, ignore the plan altogether and rely on their own experience and judgement when making marketing decisions.

- Lesson: if plans are not crystal clear they will be ignored!

2 The marketing resources are inadequate

Unless adequate resources are available for the implementation of the plans, lip-service may be paid to them but no real progress can be made in their implementation. This may be due to financial priorities, but in under-resourced arts organizations it is often due to a lack of staff – and those who are available may be inadequately qualified or experienced to tackle the implementation issues that arise.

- Lesson: fight for your budgets and get your staff trained!

3 The organization resists the proposed change

As suggested in Chapter 1, this can be a greater problem in arts organizations than in commerce or industry, due to the suspicion with which marketing is sometimes viewed by artistic directors. If influential members of an organization, particularly those in top management and board positions, are concerned about the potential impact of the plans, they may use counter-implementation tactics, ranging from delaying decisions (in the hope that the deadlines for implementation will pass) to destroying the credibility of the plans and their writers or diverting essential resources to other parts of the organization (Piercey, 1991).

- Lesson: gain the commitment of colleagues early in the planning process to encourage them to feel ownership of the final plan.

If the marketing plan is designed with its implementation in mind, then constraints and resistance can be anticipated and avoided, and barriers to implementation should be minimal.

Monitoring the marketing plan

Assuming that the plans are implemented, it is important to ensure that they are achieving their objectives and that nothing is going drastically wrong. This is best achieved by 'comparing actual results against the desired results given in the plans, and taking appropriate corrective measures to ensure that the desired results are achieved' (Greenley, 1986). This is known as controlling (or monitoring) the marketing plan. Effective control requires that mechanisms are put in place before the plan is implemented to enable performance to be monitored, measured, evaluated, and corrective action taken if necessary (Figure 8.5). In this way, marketing successes and failures can be identified at an early stage and actions taken to cash in on successes and make good any failures.

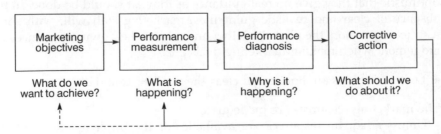

Figure 8.5 The monitoring process

The monitoring process offers a wide range of benefits (Shaw, 1993).

- It assists decision-making.
- It gives staff and the board the opportunity to learn by experience and improve their performance.
- It provides an opportunity to acknowledge the results achieved in a given period of time.
- It provides a framework for training.
- It motivates staff and encourages co-operation between them.
- It provides a structure within which to report on progress to the funding bodies.
- It facilitates the early detection of problem areas and provides a chance to avert disaster.

Monitoring techniques are dealt with in more detail in Chapter 9. What is of critical importance to the marketing function is the way in which the findings from the process will affect the marketing plans.

Assessing success

Meyrick and Sinkler described evaluation as 'an assessment of whether or not you have achieved what you set out to do'. For them, assessing success involves collecting and analysing data and coming to some conclusions about what is working and what needs attention. They identified five evaluation stages:

- setting aims and objectives on local needs assessment
- identifying indicators of success
- monitoring indicators
- assessing progress towards aims and objectives
- dissemination and action

Source: Meyrick and Sinkler, 1998.

Corrective action

There are a range of conclusions which can be drawn if it is found that the planned marketing activity is not meeting the marketing objectives, and these will determine the type of corrective action that is needed. These conclusions will fall into one of three broad categories:

1 The marketing objectives and strategies are inappropriate

The objectives set may have been too ambitious considering the organization's environment, or the environment may have changed unexpectedly and made the objectives unrealistic (for example, if a new and very popular competitor emerged). Alternatively, the organization's resources may have been insufficient to enable such objectives to be met (particularly if there has been an unexpected reduction in income, say from funding sources). It may be impossible, under new financial constraints, for the planned level of marketing activity to be sustained.

2 The marketing tactics are inappropriate

The planned marketing mix may not have the desired impact on its target audiences. It may be that the pricing levels set were too high and deterred attendance, or the message of an advertising campaign may have been wrongly perceived, and the wrong audience profile was attracted. Perhaps audiences had difficulties getting hold of tickets or sponsors were unimpressed with the levels of corporate hospitality available.

3 The marketing budget is insufficient

A plan should be budgeted at the outset and tied in to resource availability. If this is not done carefully, cash constraints may arise to hinder the success of the marketing tactics. This could reduce the impact of advertising, for example, if corners have to be cut in the creative process.

Before corrective action can be taken, the cause of the discrepancy between planned results and actual results must be identified. Only then can new proposals be put forward with confidence.

Summary

Marketing planning is a process which can lead an arts organization to the most effective and efficient use of its limited marketing resources, helping to direct it towards its artistic goals as well as its financial and market objectives. This structured and rational approach to marketing planning is more likely to gain the support of others in the organization than an ad-hoc, piecemeal approach as it clearly demonstrates the logic behind the marketing recommendations through its thorough analysis, its specific objectives and its explanations of marketing solutions.

The plan itself should not be thought of as a tablet of stone, but as a living document which communicates intentions, guides and moulds marketing decision-making, and gives direction and support to the day-to-day marketing activities, as well as the more fundamental and underlying strategic issues. The purpose of marketing planning is to maintain a match between what we can offer and what our audiences want and, at the end of the day, it is their satisfaction that will be the judge of our efforts.

Key concepts

competition
consortium
external audit
environmental analysis
internal audit
marketing audit
marketing budget
marketing objectives

marketing strategy
marketing tactics
mission statement
perceptual map
organizational objectives
STEP factors
SWOT analysis

Discussion questions

1 In what ways is the marketing planning process likely to differ in a commercial theatre from a subsidized repertory theatre?

2 What is the nature of competition facing contemporary visual art galleries? How might an understanding of this lead to marketing decisions related to gallery opening hours?

3 Explain the difference between marketing objectives, marketing strategies and marketing tactics, giving examples from an arts organization of your choice.

4 In which aspects of the marketing planning process do you feel it is important to involve the board, and why?

5 'Marketing planning is a barrier to imaginative marketing.' Discuss.

Case study: Hull Truck Theatre

Hull Truck Theatre Company is a relatively small organization, but one with a big reputation. Based at its own 300-seat venue but with an extensive UK small- and medium-scale touring programme, it is led by the high profile playwright and Artistic Director John Godber, whose work forms the majority of its repertoire.

Development plans

A series of internal and external issues arose in the late 1990s which caused Hull Truck to rethink its entire future, and redefine its mission as follows:

- to present popular and imaginative programmes of activity from a wide range of performing arts, including drama, dance and music, which have a broad appeal to all people in the Humber region
- to pursue excellence in the production of popular and accessible theatre
- to develop new writing for the theatre by new and established playwrights
- to develop and retain new audiences
- to produce a community and education programme which supports the work of the theatre by actively engaging with as wide a range of people as possible through appropriate forms of activity

At the same time, proposals were prepared to restructure the organization and rehouse it in a new building. As part of a feasibility study for this, the organization undertook a programme of quantitative and qualitative marketing research to enable an assessment to be made of the market implications of moving the theatre from its location in one of the less desirable areas of the city to a new site much closer to the city centre. Focus groups were conducted to help identify the key issues, and a street survey of 500 theatre attenders living in the Hull area was undertaken to reveal the structure and composition of current and potential audiences for Hull Truck Theatre.

The Hull Truck audience

The research found that only just over half of Hull's theatregoing population had been to Hull Truck Theatre in the past two years, compared with nine out of ten who had been to the Hull New Theatre, a much larger mixed programme venue in the centre of Hull. Over a quarter of the people who went to the theatre three times a year or more had never been to Hull Truck, and neither had a third of those who claimed to attend contemporary drama, which was the most popular of the 'high' art forms in Hull: over half of theatre attenders said they attended contemporary drama.

Current Hull Truck audiences (defined as people who had attended Hull Truck Theatre in the previous two years) were found, in general, to be theatre enthusiasts, going to the theatre quite regularly and attending a range of different theatres. They tended to see the theatre as a good place to go for a night out and associated a trip to the theatre with eating out. They liked to go to shows they knew they would enjoy, as well as trying things that are new and different, but they would be put off if they did not like the description of a production in the theatre's publicity material or the media. These people tried to keep well informed about what is on at the theatre, as they tended to be consumers of various art forms, including ballet, classical drama, contemporary drama, contemporary music, rock concerts and jazz. Almost universally, they read the *Hull Daily Mail*, and in terms of demographics they were quite similar to national drama audiences, being predominantly ABC1, female and broadsheet-readers. They were, however, mainly aged 25–44.

In comparison, potential new audiences (people who attend theatre but not Hull Truck) were in general found not to be real theatre enthusiasts. They tended to stick to what they liked rather than experiment with something new and different, and went to the theatre if they liked the look of what was on, or were influenced by friends or relatives. Fear of the unknown put them off plays or playwrights they had not heard of, and they tended to be more attracted by performances which were relatively safe, unchallenging and popular. The current location of Hull Truck Theatre tended to put them off going there.

Influences on attending

The research respondents identified a number of factors that would make going to Hull Truck a more popular choice. Almost half of all theatregoers in Hull said that a new building in the city centre would make them more likely to attend Hull Truck Theatre and only a tiny proportion felt that the proposed new location would be a drawback. The enthusiasm for the new location was partly due to its proximity to the centre of town, and partly because it was perceived to be in an area that was less threatening to personal safety. The most important improvement to be incorporated in a new building would be improved parking, which was particularly important to older theatregoers.

Current attenders stated that improved foyer and bar areas would make the theatregoing experience a more attractive one at Hull Truck, and the prospect of a more comfortable auditorium appealed to younger audiences. There was also demand for a wider range of art forms, and an extension of the programme at Hull Truck would be welcomed. A core of current attenders were clearly fans of the Artistic Director John Godber, and welcomed the thought of more John Godber productions. However, the majority of both current and potential attenders said they would go to Hull Truck more often if the programme was more varied. Musicals, stand-up comedy and plays by companies other than Hull Truck would be the most popular additions to the programme.

Marketing issues

Hull Truck's marketing communications were found to be failing to reach a high proportion of the potential market. Whereas Hull Truck enthusiasts were aware of what was on from the theatre's mailings, less frequent attenders (including those who had attended but not booked themselves) found it more difficult to access information. The majority of theatregoers used the local newspaper (the *Hull Daily Mail*) for information about local entertainment, yet Hull Truck had a very low profile in this paper. Young people tended to look for information about the theatre in the city itself, including posters and leaflets, but they also used the internet and the Hull Truck website appeared to be serving a dual purpose, providing information at the superficial mechanistic level (e.g. what's on, the location of the theatre etc.) as well as in-depth comment for Hull Truck enthusiasts.

Questions

1 Propose a series of marketing objectives that Hull Truck should work towards in order to realize its mission.
2 Develop a series of strategies to achieve those objectives, and prepare a tactical marketing plan for the implementation of these strategies in year one.
3 List the information you would like to have had to help you prepare these plans. If you were the marketing manager for Hull Truck Theatre, do you think this information would be readily available?

Source: Whitehead, 2000. Reproduced with kind permission.

References

Arts Council Incentive Funding Scheme (1988) *Business Planning Seminar Participants Pack*. Arts Council of Great Britain.

Benton, F. (2001) 'Fishermen's tales: the rebirth of the Maltings', *ArtsProfessional*, Issue 9, 10 September.

Bhuchar, S. (2001) 'Case study 4', *Journal of Arts Marketing*, Issue 03, October.

Davidson, H. (2002) 'What companies can learn from arts organisations', *ArtsProfessional*, Issue 25, 8–9.

De Kretser, H. (2001) 'Case study 3', *Journal of Arts Marketing*, Issue 02, July.

Greenley, Gordon E. (1986) *The Strategic and Operational Planning of Marketing*. McGraw Hill.

Hadley, R. (2000) 'Getting it together: the development of the marketing consortium', *ArtsBusiness*, Issue 48, 10 April.

Johnson, M. (2000) 'andco tours theatre of horrors', *ArtsBusiness*, Issue 48, 10 April.

McDonald, M. (1999) 'The role of world class marketing in the arts', Healthy, Wealthy and Wise: Arts Marketing Association Conference, Cardiff, July.

Meyrick, J. and Sinkler, P. (1998) *A Guide to Evaluation for Healthy Living Centres*. HEA.

Morris, G. (1999) 'Getting Engaged at the Tate: Keeping and Developing our Visitors', *Revolving Doors: Arts Marketing Association Awayday*, Warwick.

Piercy, Nigel (1991) *Market-led Strategic Change*. Thorsons.

Shaw, P. (1993) *Board Member Manual*. The Arts Council of Great Britain.

Whitehead, B. (2000) *Hull Truck Theatre Audience Development and Marketing Plan 2000–2009*. Arts Intelligence Ltd, for Hull Truck Theatre.

9

Managing the marketing function

Marketing in an arts organization involves managing scarce resources effectively. Because you and your staff are your most important resource, this book ends with a chapter that looks at general management principles in the context of arts organizations. It concentrates on some basic ideas about what management is, the nature of organizations and teams, internal marketing and effective communication. Because marketing is one of the biggest spending functions in an arts organization we begin with some thoughts addressed to managers tasked with controlling budgets. Being an effective manager has much in common with marketing orientation. The more credible you are to those inside and outside your organization, the more likely it is that your colleagues (even those who have reservations about marketing) will facilitate rather than block the adoption of marketing orientation. The chapter will be relevant not only to those who manage a department with several or more members of staff, but also to people who work with a variety of organizations, alone, or in a community or amateur environment. The sections included in this chapter are:

- Financial resource management
  - budget setting and monitoring
- Human resource management
  - organizational structures
  - team building and management
  - working with creative people

- Communications
  - making presentations
  - negotiation
  - internal communication
  - internal marketing
- Managing yourself

Room at the top

In 2001 the Chief Executive of London's National Gallery moved to a parallel job at the British Museum. At the time, a number of national UK arts institutions were having difficulty filling their top jobs, in recruitment exercises that resembled the reshuffling of a small pack of senior arts administrators. As a result, the Clore Duffield Foundation, a charitable trust, instituted a consultation process to examine the problem of this seeming shortage of leaders in the arts and heritage sector. Among its findings were the following:

- Changes in the definition and role of arts organizations have made the job of leaders more difficult and less attractive. For example, museums 50 years ago were simply places where objects were conserved and displayed. Now they have to accept a complex of roles in the community, spanning education, commercial enterprise, entertainment and social amenity.
- In spite of the fact that the role of arts organizations has become less well defined, funders are imposing highly-detailed performance targets on institutions in keeping with short-term policy objectives. This is difficult to reconcile with visionary leadership.
- Recent developments in UK arts funding, namely the National Lottery, had in effect distracted a number of experienced managers of arts organizations into being inexperienced managers of building projects. Some had been successful, others less so – with the consequent cost in morale and self-confidence.
- While there were plenty of training and development opportunities available for arts managers (though not on the same scale as in the USA) the provision lacked co-ordination, and practising managers felt they could spare neither the time nor the resources to take advantage of it.
- Career development opportunities, recruitment processes and pay levels, as well as an acknowledged under-representation of women and minorities in senior positions, all came under fire in the feedback gathered by the exercise

Source: Holden, 2002.

Overview of the management function

There are many definitions of management. The common-sense view is that it is the process of making things actually happen, to a plan and on time. There are a number of different resources that can be called upon to assist this process. The two most important resources are money and people. Much of the attention of management research and development is therefore focused on finance and human resource management.

Other resources to be harnessed include yourself – the facilitator and leader of the marketing function; the resources of modern technology; volunteers; suppliers and external contractors; and physical resources such as offices, vehicles and equipment.

Good management begins with good planning. Marketing planning is discussed fully in Chapter 8. The principles of good planning discussed there, including monitoring and evaluation, apply equally to all management planning. In looking at resource management, it is important to make plans as solid and specific as possible, e.g. to set deadlines, to quantify expected outcomes and to define the measures by which you will gauge whether or not the plan is being achieved.

Financial resource management

Probably more anxiety is expressed about financial resource management than any other aspect of management. This is surprising, as money is far easier to manage than people. Part of the reason for the anxiety is probably the seeming mystique of accountancy language, replete with jargon such as balance sheets, cash-flow statements and working capital.

It is unlikely that the marketing team in any arts organization will have to worry about the precise meaning of these terms. However your organization is structured, there will be accountants (either internally or externally) to turn the financial transactions for the year into financial statements that can be audited as the 'true and fair' view of what happened within your organization in financial terms in the last 12 months. This is important to the organization, because it represents an account of good or bad stewardship of the resources you received from either the public purse or shareholders. As such, financial statements offer a great marketing opportunity to celebrate good financial results, or plead for greater resources on the back of your organization's excellent management.

The reason why the accountancy profession has developed very structured ways of reporting financial data is because of a need for accuracy in this information. Financial data is used to inform many important decisions, including lending money and employing staff, so it is important that the meaning of figures is precise and credible.

The best way for a marketing manager to understand financial resource planning is to work closely with the person who manages the overall finances of the institution. Both have a strong common interest – the box office receipts are a key measure of both the financial and the marketing success of the organization. In addition, the head of finance will have a vested interest in helping the marketing team stay within budget. Neither party will wish to cope with an overspend.

Depending on the size of the organization, at some point there is likely to be a dialogue between finance and marketing about the financial resource needed to manage the marketing effort. This is the process called 'budgeting'. This may be a more or less formal process, depending on the complexity of the organization, and whether or not the budget is for a specific project or an annual spend.

Budget setting

The process of setting the budget is an integral part of strategic planning.

> A budget is a plan, usually expressed in monetary terms and usually for one future year. Almost all organizations have a budget. If the organization has a formal long-range plan, the budget is prepared within its constraints. Budget preparation essentially consists of fine-tuning the first year of the long-range plan. (Anthony, 1988)

This is represented diagrammatically in Figure 9.1.

The notion of 'fine-tuning' the strategic plan is a useful way to look at the budgeting process. The manager demonstrates a commitment to the overall plan, and looks at the practical obstacles to achieving that plan, by considering the detailed financial implications of actually putting it into practice.

A budget normally consists of revenue expenditure. By that is meant recurrent spending of the type that is normal for that department. A decision to buy, for example, a new computer system for the department would

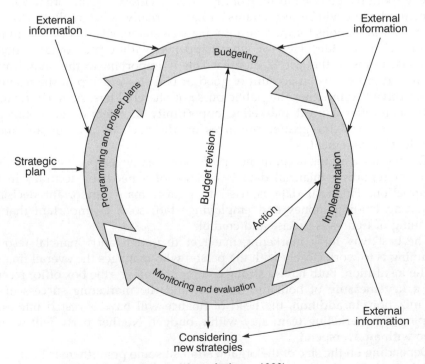

Figure 9.1 Controlling a budget (adapted from Anthony, 1988)

normally be treated separately, as a 'capital' project. The costs of such a project would include not only the cost of the equipment, but also staff costs for training, inputting all the initial data and developing software such as document templates or database systems. These costs would be distinct from the normal day-to-day activity of the department, and thus would not be included as part of the 'revenue' or 'recurrent' budget.

Some budgets may include income as well as expenditure. Income from the attendances generated by marketing activity will, of course, go into central funds. However, income from the sale of programmes, advertising, merchandise, mailing-list rental or other activity relating very directly to the marketing effort will probably be included in the budget for that department. A checklist of items to consider is included in Table 9.1.

Some general principles in preparing a budget:

- Be conservative. If in doubt, understate your income and overstate your expenditure – to avoid nasty surprises.
- Use historical data. Last year's actual spending is a useful starting point, but remember the differences. If the venue had six exhibitions last year, and intends to have nine in the next year, the budget will have to be adjusted accordingly.
- Remember to include inflation, but check price rises with key suppliers – they may be increasing at a different rate from the general trend.
- Match the income and expenditure to the financial year to which it relates – for example, the autumn season brochure will probably come out of next year's budget even though the work starts this year. However, make sure you are not just transferring a financial problem from one year to the next.
- Phase the budget as best you can over time – i.e. work out how much you will be spending each month or quarter. This will help with budget monitoring, but also can add some leeway for changes in the course of the year.
- Be consistent. If you are assuming 5 per cent inflation in setting the new price of merchandise, you will need to assume the same figure in the cost to you of purchasing the materials for sale. You should also be consistent from year to year, unless you have made changes in your activity that are impacting on the budget.

It is rare for a budget to balance (i.e. for the planned expenditure to equal the available money) right at the start. There are a number of techniques available for dealing with this. First, all assumptions underlying the budget should be looked at critically, to ensure they are sound. It is possible that there is a mismatch between income and expenditure, e.g. an extra member of staff has been recruited to do sponsorship and development work but no extra income has been projected. However, care should be taken to ensure that unrealistic changes are not made in an attempt to balance the budget.

The next possibility is to reduce planned expenditure. It is preferable to cut something out entirely than to reduce the budget for a given head of expenditure. For example, a theatre's publicity photography budget may have

Table 9.1 Checklist for budget preparation: what to include

Income	
Programmes	Multiply the number of copies you expect to sell by the sales price, e.g. 20 performances with average expected attendance of 60%, with 50% attending to buy programmes
Advertising space	One full page advertisement; two half pages and four boxes at £x each. Consider reviewing the arrangement if space is sold on your behalf by the printers or another agency who retain the profit
Expenditure	
Salaries	The annual gross pay of each employee (not what they take home) plus National Insurance (check current rates with finance staff or DSS) plus any benefits like pension or performance related pay. Remember to include annual pay rises, if appropriate. Don't forget overtime, or sickness and holiday cover if appropriate
Staff related costs	This includes mileage allowance, training, cost of recruitment (e.g. the press advertisement)
Publicity design	Usually a set fee agreed in advance, but check implications of corrections and delays
Printing	Seek at least three quotes and look at differences in price involving changes in paper or in number of colours
Print distribution	Number to be mailed plus cost of envelopes and postage, and envelope stuffers (if not in-house or volunteers)
Photography	Set fee, by number of events
Press nights	An amount, by number of events
Cost of programmes	Cost of all programmes purchased from the printer – not just all those sold to the audience. It will usually be better to have some left than run out – but waste is a cost
Advertising	This is very expensive. It may pay you to use an external media buyer. The cost of advertising needs to be compared with direct marketing
Miscellaneous	This includes everything else, e.g. flowers, subscriptions
Contingency	A wise precaution – to allow for overspends and new opportunities (e.g. a cheap promotion jointly with another venue). Try using a fixed percentage of the entire budget

been calculated on the basis of six events in the year, and some photographs of the facilities for a conference leaflet. It might be possible to produce the conference leaflet with a diagram of the spaces rather than a photograph and use existing event photographs for visual interest. That is a real saving, because the planned expenditure will now not happen. Savings that depend on reducing the fee with an external supplier may not happen in practice. To keep the contract the photographer may well offer a 'deal', but travelling and other incidental expenses may go up in proportion. Combining pieces of print, reducing the size or frequency of advertisements, increasing programme prices (having gauged elasticity of demand, as outlined in Chapter 5) or delaying the appointment of a member of staff are all ways of bridging the shortfall in the budget.

The final thing to do is to talk to other people. If the cost of marketing has increased because of increased activity in the overall organization, there may be further resources available for the department. There may be the opportunity to combine forces with other local organizations to share the costs of promotion or distribution, as illustrated in Case 6.1. Most importantly, if the marketing manager believes it is not possible to carry out the strategic marketing plan within the available resources, this needs to be communicated to the rest of the management team. According to Lisa Burger, Financial Director of the Royal National Theatre, financial literacy in arts organizations has improved (personal interviews):

> I have worked for over 17 years in the arts – at Welsh National Opera, Covent Garden, the National Gallery and now the RNT. Over that time I have been amazed at the increased financial awareness of non-financial managers. An understanding of cost constraints is now found at all levels in creative teams.

At the end of the budgeting process, a sensible plan for the year's marketing activity will have emerged, expressed in the form of monetary targets.

The wisdom of Oz

Australian arts marketing web site Fuel4arts.com offers the following tips on marketing budgets:

- you need to budget time and people as well as dollars
- for free events, 20 per cent of the production cost is a reasonable guideline
- for ticketed events, try 20 per cent of the anticipated revenue
- larger organizations with regular performance patterns have annual marketing budgets representing 10–15 per cent of their total costs, and up to 28 per cent of revenue
- most galleries and museums have monthly promotional allocations, but the decision on how to spend them will be driven by the needs of the programme as a whole

Source: James, 2001. www.fuel4arts.com © Australia Council for the Arts, Commonwealth of Australia.

Monitoring the budget

As with all plans, it is an essential part of the planning process that the financial plan is monitored as it is implemented and corrective action is taken where necessary. The exact way that the budget is monitored depends on the type of organization concerned. The prevalent use of computers makes it likely that most people will have access to some sort of computerized financial information, and may even have some responsibility for generating it.

As money is actually spent within an organization, a chain of evidence is produced about the financial transactions that are taking place. An order is raised for goods to be supplied, which will later result in an invoice being sent and finally paid. Staff are paid direct into their bank accounts and given pay slips. Cash is received from the sale of tickets and banked. Grants from local funding bodies will probably be paid monthly directly into the bank. This data is then sorted and processed; and a report is produced for the benefit of the marketing department to show their share of income and expenditure. It is common practice for this information to be produced in the form of a monthly management report, which compares the 'actual' performance for the period against the 'budget' that was originally set. There may be all sorts of reasons for what are usually called 'variances' from the original budget.

- *Timing differences.* These can occur when, for example, goods have been received into the building but the invoice has not yet arrived. These sorts of differences can be adjusted in the management reports.
- *Accounting treatment.* You will need to discuss this in more detail in your own organization, but it might include such things as the treatment of VAT or the grossing-up of income and expenditure (e.g. you have budgeted for the profit on the sale of programmes, but the reports show the income and expenditure separately).
- *Planned variations.* In the course of the year, all sorts of changes will happen in the day-to-day running of the organization, and the budget may be adjusted accordingly. For example, a local company may sponsor a particular piece of publicity on an ad-hoc basis, so the income and expenditure budgets both change. Some organizations prefer to leave the original budget presentation unchanged, but explain the seeming 'actual' overspend in terms of planned, and therefore legitimized, variations.
- *Over/underspends.* These are the important things for the operational manager to consider, as they represent unplanned changes to the budget. Examples of these may include underachievement on income (e.g. a dip in programme sales attributed to the poor box office because of bad weather) or an overspend (e.g. the reprinting of a leaflet because the incorrect dates were supplied). The first step is to identify the variance, and the reason for it. This may not be as straightforward as it seems. In the above example, for instance, it may turn out that, despite the weather, the box office target was met. One can only surmise that perhaps patrons, arriving late for the performance because of the weather, may not have had time to buy the programme. Perhaps the box office target was met because of a large block booking to a local company, and programmes were included free as part of the package.

Having identified the reason for the variance from budget, corrective action should be taken to ensure the overall budget remains balanced. An under-spend in one area may compensate for an overspend elsewhere. Another department may be able to help – front-of-house staff hours may be underspent as a result of the poor box office. It may be possible to cut some planned activity later in the year. Finally, this may be the point at which the budget manager remembers with relief the contingency set aside within the overall budget.

In addition to monitoring the budget for the current period, the process of planning next year's budget is already beginning as the marketing staff evaluate the success with which the financial resource is being used.

The concept of 'value for money' is of importance here. Value for money (VFM) strategies seek to deliver the most efficient and effective outcomes, in the most economical way. For example, the effectiveness of the marketing strategy might be measured in the number of attenders at a given event. In efficiency terms, the most straightforward way to promote that event might seem to be to place a large advertisement in the local paper – quickly reaching a large number of readers at a relatively low cost per reader (although the absolute cost of such an advertisement may be very high). Setting up a database of attenders for a direct marketing campaign may cost more first time, but will allow greater development and further campaigns in the future. Direct marketing may thus deliver better value for money than advertising.

Other areas to consider include:

- use of own staff versus sub-contract labour
- using volunteers for certain tasks (bearing in mind their need for management and support)
- staff productivity
- the relative costs and visibility of different advertising media
- promotions such as 'two for one' offers or early booking discounts

It can be difficult to quantify the value of many marketing activities as the long-term payback of some initiatives may not be visible immediately. However, the more that the marketing department can develop their own performance indicators, the better they can develop effective strategies for future years.

Financial performance will always be one of the key indicators for evaluation. Marketing teams generally tend to be viewed as high spenders in their organizations, and this charge can best be countered in value-for-money terms. For example, an advertising campaign may seem expensive at £25 000 but if it can be tied to extra ticket sales of £250 000 it represents excellent value for money. The evidence for such claims would need to be capable of convincing sceptics at all levels in the establishment. This is a good argument for routine and rigorous evaluation of marketing expenditure. Other perform-ance indicators would be attendance figures, against budgets and against previous years; customer perception surveys; and audience development data, such as party bookings or subscribers. The practical effect of this sort of evaluation will be seen in the next cycle of planning and budgeting, as well as in the appreciation of the contribution of marketing throughout the organization.

One other practical aspect to monitoring the financial resource available to the marketing department concerns cash-flow management. This means ensuring that money comes into the organization before it has to go out. For the marketing team, promoting ticket sales in advance of the performance represents an important contribution to the overall cash flow. Interest can be earned on the money, if it is in the bank. Conversely, expenditure should be incurred as late as possible and the maximum credit period negotiated. This is a factor to take into account in agreeing fees with designers or photographers, for example, who may require payment in advance.

Some of these concepts may seem foreign or daunting when approached for the first time. However, as with all management, the best way to approach having responsibility for a budget for the first time is to learn by doing it. The principles are the same as managing domestic finances, and there will be others in the organization to help you with explanations or advice.

Courage and financial control

Michael Kaiser, President of the John F. Kennedy Centre for the Performing Arts, reflects on the need for courage in hard times for arts organizations (particularly in the wake of the tragic events of 11 September 2001) in this excerpt from an address to the National Council on the Arts, 2 November 2001:

'Having spent the better part of my career working with troubled arts organizations, I have observed that the actions taken by most boards and staffs to address financial challenges tend to make matters worse rather than better and initiate a vicious cycle that is powerful and difficult to escape.

'Most arts organizations that face fiscal shortfalls react to these crises by cutting back on expenditures. This makes sense. But the costs they most commonly cut are two discretionary expenditures – artistic initiatives and marketing. These cuts tend to create the least short-term disruption and do not require firing anyone.

'Yet it is these two very activities that encourage income flow to the arts. Donors and ticket buyers are attracted to exciting artistic ventures and the marketing that explains these new initiatives.

'Organizations that cut back on these two areas typically see revenue shrink further. This leads to more cutbacks and worse fiscal results.

'This downward spiral affects arts organizations throughout the world. I have been involved in turnarounds at the Kansas City Ballet, the Alvin Ailey American Dance Theater, American Ballet Theater and the Royal Opera House. In each case, the day I arrived I was faced with huge revenue shortfalls resulting from cutbacks in art and marketing . . .

'As I observe the initial reactions to September 11th and the impact on ticket sales, fund-raising and especially endowments, I am unhappy to see so many boards and staffs reacting, predictably, in this dangerous manner.

'In fear of reduced earnings, new projects are shelved and marketing initiatives reduced. But instead of one or two or three organizations in danger of initiating this vicious spiral, I now see an entire arts world in danger. Taken to its extreme, arts organizations across America could risk losing the tremendous momentum established in the 1990s and a serious diminution of activity and fiscal stability could result.

'Of course some accommodations must be made for the realistic potential for reduced income. But what should they be?

'In working with troubled organizations, I have always found the cure to be saving on administrative expenditures: saving on all non-performance and non-marketing areas and putting as much money on the stage as possible. While ABT [American Ballet Theatre] was at its sickest, we announced the first full-length new ballet to a commissioned score in the company's history – our production of *Othello* brought in far more money than it cost and helped revitalize our fortunes. We also created a high profile educational program in Harlem, added a series of master classes featuring important dancers from the company's past and set up a series of summer Institutes across America.

'At the same time, marketing has to be bolstered and the public has to be enticed. Most arts organizations do not understand the importance and methods for creating strong institutional identity . . .

'Creating a strong marketing profile is particularly challenging now as so many organizations fear that they will be viewed as frivolous and that the activities of the arts must take a lower profile as we face life-and-death terrorist issues.

'I could not disagree more.'

Source: National Endowment for the Arts, 2001. Reproduced with kind permission.

Human resource management

Marketing people tend to be outgoing and articulate. They may thus approach the people management side of their role with greater confidence than the money side, only to find a year or two into the job that they have underestimated the diversity and sometimes sheer perversity of the human factor. The marketing team, be it one person or a unit, will be a smaller part of the larger whole. It is necessary therefore to examine organizational structures and cultures, before focusing in more detail on the management of the marketing team itself. The role of the marketing manager as team leader will be considered in this section, together with some aspects of personal development and management. Managing oneself is a necessary stage in managing others, and at the end of this chapter we have included a section on personal development and management. As arts organizations adopt the marketing concept more wholeheartedly, the scope of a typical marketing manager's human resource responsibilities is likely to widen to include staff responsible for customer contact, sales and fund-raising.

As well as the people with whom the manager has a line relationship, there will be a number of other people that relate closely to the marketing department. These relationships will also need to be managed. In the arts industry, there may be particular issues to address concerning, for example, liaison between the venue and a touring company; or working with creative artists. These are therefore considered in more detail below.

Organizations and organizational culture

The huge field of organizational behaviour has attracted many eminent writers. One of the most accessible is Professor Charles Handy, who explains why it is so difficult to generalize about organizational behaviour (see Figure 9.2), listing over 60 variables which can differ from organization to organization (Handy, 1993).

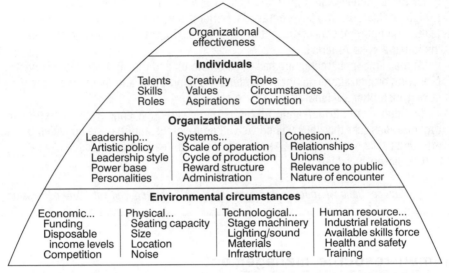

Figure 9.2 Factors affecting organizational behaviour in arts organizations (adapted from Handy, 1993)

While such influences vary from organization to organization, it is nevertheless valuable to spend time considering some of the following aspects of the individual organization in which you work:

- *Organizational structure.* What is the structure in which you work? Is it an autocracy or a co-operative? Who takes decisions? How are decisions taken?
- *Politics.* How is the power divided in your institution? Who are the people with influence, and from where is that influence derived?
- *Groups.* How do you and your team fit into the wider structure? How are you regarded?

An understanding of the structure and organizational culture of your institution will enable you to plan and implement marketing more effectively, and help you to work with, rather than at cross-purposes with, your colleagues.

Structure

There are many different possible organizational structures, each with its advantages and disadvantages. It is common in the arts, for example, for a dynamic and visionary artist to gather a company of disciples and supporters around himself or herself to further a specific vision or art form. Many companies make a virtue of this by naming themselves after a particular figure. It is equally common to find highly successful companies with a structure akin to a private sector organization, headed up with someone called a chief executive. At the other end of the scale, so to speak, arts organizations also offer plenty of examples of co-operatives or democratic groups of paid and unpaid workers, where all have an equal voice on policy. The scale and mission of the organization will have an impact on its ideal structure and, as the organization changes and develops, its structure may need revisiting.

In the creative sector, where the values of spontaneity and flexibility are to the fore, the concept of a formal organizational structure may seem alien. However, structures are essential, and inevitable, for some very good reasons:

- they provide a framework for people to work together in a way which allows responsibility and accountability (for example, how can an arts organization promote an equal opportunities policy without a formal framework?)
- they establish the organization's identity (for example, for a funding body to support, or for customers to have relationships with)
- they ensure continuity in changing circumstances – preventing wasted effort in 'reinventing the wheel' every time a new situation presents itself

As we have discussed in earlier chapters, the arts industry flourishes in the context of the wider economy. The changes that impact other sectors offer opportunities and challenges to the arts, as a dynamic environment suits some kinds of organizational structures better than others. Burns and Stalker (1961) differentiate between what they call mechanistic and organic structures. Mechanistic structures are highly bureaucratic, and cope superbly well with a stable environment. Organic ones are continually adjusting themselves to changing circumstances. Rapid change in the environment forces mechanistic organizations to break down, allowing smaller and more flexible ones to move in.

The role of arts organizations in economic regeneration (as discussed in Chapter 1) provides plenty of examples of this as organically-structured firms in the cultural industries replace disappearing manufacturing jobs in declining mechanistic organizations in many parts of Europe. It is those organizations who are able to work in new ways who will continue to develop. Of course, the mission of arts organizations goes well beyond economic regeneration in their communities. Many aim to rebuild pride, and confidence, in groups who have been disenfranchised or marginalized.

Harvard academic Rosabeth Moss Kanter (1989) advocates opening up organizations to new types of manager, including positive strategies for women; moving to flatter organizational structures, with less hierarchy;

challenging established practice; and placing great importance on shared values. Her vision of a flexible and empowered workforce, which can adapt to rapid change, has had enormous influence on the development of corporate cultures in large industrial companies. Her ideas translate particularly well to the arts environment, where adaptability for survival and individual empowerment are a feature of many organizations.

Dancing the changes

Phoenix, as a small-scale company, was very much dancer-led. Growth caused change, and though some of the changes were welcomed by the dancers, like the opportunities offered by external choreographers and so on, nonetheless growth is painful. All sorts of issues surfaced. Talking in a neutral environment, and taking enough time, and using external people, showed us that we all believed in, wanted, the same things.

Source: Liza Stevens, formerly Administrative Director, Phoenix Dance, personal interview.

Power

An understanding of organizational structure can help an individual manager implement marketing plans or drive through changes to make an organization more customer-centred. It certainly helps to have the clear lines of communication and accountability and defined spheres of influence which a formal structure provides. However, such definitions are not always explicit, and effective managers need to take account of informal as well as formal power structures in their organization. Power, in this context, means the people with authority to take decisions and make things happen.

Handy (1993) describes a number of different types of power:

- *resource power* – influence derived from the control of key resources
- *position power* – also sometimes called 'legitimate' power, that derived by virtue of being, for example, chief executive
- *expert power* – this might well be 'artistic' or 'creative' power in an arts organization
- *personal power* – or 'charisma', although this is often more tied to position than the powerful individual would wish to admit
- *negative power* – the power to delay or prevent things from happening, which can often be wielded by quite junior people in the organization

In the complex ways organizations function, many people will derive their authority for action from a number of these sources, and may use them both to further and to impede organizational progress. Group dynamics may affect the way individuals use their power, through the formation of alliances or factions. Understanding the sources of influence within your organization and cultivating the right contacts are essential to getting 'buy-in' to your marketing ideas and their possibly unpopular consequences.

Culture

Structure and power are components of the wider issue called 'corporate culture'. Much of current thinking on culture in the workplace started with Edgar Schein, who describes the sorts of assumptions about an organization's values and practices which are commonly held by its members (Schein, 1985). Difficult as the culture is to pin down and describe, it is what makes one company different from another, and makes one employee fit in one place and not in another. A useful, if rather formal definition, of culture in this sense is 'the collection of traditions, values, policies, beliefs and attitudes that constitute a pervasive context for everything we do and think in an organization' (McLean and Marshall, 1993).

In a small museum, for example, the culture would embrace such diverse issues – implicit or explicit – as the mission; the goals; the dress codes and office layout; the values and perceptions of the nature of history, contemporary culture and local society; the organizational ethic, which might include frequent references to the museum's founder and the original collection; and underlying assumptions, concerning behaviour in the workplace, the expected visitors, and strategies for coping when things go wrong.

The organizational leader has an important role in managing the corporate culture, but does not set it, may not understand it and may not be able to change it in time to learn a new culture for new circumstances. The marketing department is likely to have its own culture, which may or may not be at odds with the wider organizational culture. However, understanding the wider corporate culture will be a key to the success of internal marketing, which is discussed in more detail later in this section.

Managing the marketing team

For most arts organizations, good practice in employment is centred on an equal opportunities policy developed in consultation with the governing board. Many such policies provide what seem like exhaustive lists of those individuals or groups that must not suffer discrimination, but the key to equal opportunities is having a positive action plan to develop individuals to their full potential and address disadvantage. There is a direct link here to the marketing mission of an organization – especially when audience development is driven by the principle of social inclusion, as discussed in Chapter 1. As well as governing management and employment practices, an equal opportunities policy will extend naturally to all other aspects of an arts organization's operations – programming decisions, access, customer care, catering and other facilities are just some of the areas likely to be affected.

The extent to which equal opportunities policies are fully integrated into the staff development practice of any individual institution depends on the degree of understanding and ownership of the real meaning of human resource development. Many organizations lack the funding to implement their genuine commitment to the principles of developing individual potential. Others pay lip-service to trendy policies while continuing to restrict employment opportunities to a limited range of people who are essentially just like themselves: 'A greater degree of organizational participation by itself is no guarantee that equal treatment of women and minorities, for example, will automatically follow. "Participation" alone will not wipe out sexism and racism' (Kanter, 1983).

Implementing a staff equal opportunities policy will help the organization foster a wider empathy with the audiences it is hoping to develop. This is particularly true of staff involved in marketing and customer contact, who provide the organization's public face. Effective marketing to external audiences stems from your understanding and knowledge of your own staff to play to their strengths and overcome weaknesses in order to develop their full potential, and your ability to manage them as a team which balances individual skills to produce something greater than the sum of the individual parts. This is one of the aspects of the management role which inexperienced marketing managers find most challenging, as it takes them away from the kind of marketing job they are used to doing. However, viewed strategically, it is an essential stage in the journey towards customer-orientation.

Able and willing

Actor Mat Fraser, at the launch of the Independent Theatre Council's 'Disability – Policy into Practice' initiative: 'I insist that unless all British mainstream producing theatres, especially those that have received relatively recent access funding, start to use some of the many available professional disabled actors in a good percentage of their main house productions, that they must accept the following charge: that they are narrow minded, exclusive, elitist, right wing, cowardly, unimaginative, harbingers of artistic apartheid. They're a large part of the problem, and unless they can become part of an inclusive solution, they should go.'

Source: Jones, 2001. Reproduced by kind permission.

Recruitment and selection

In an area where there is often rapid turnover of staff, recruitment and selection skills should be a priority for arts marketers. If the cost of a member of staff over three years, including National Insurance and any allowances, is calculated, it can be seen that the appointment of any individual staff member represents a significant investment of the company resources over that period. For that reason alone, it is worth putting considerable effort into making the right appointment. Marketing departments in arts organizations often have high staff turnover rates. This is inevitable to some extent because of the need to move jobs in order to progress, and the relatively junior status of many of the posts involved. But it does mean that recruitment is a regular task for most arts marketing managers.

Over and above the financial cost, the management time needed to sort out problems, and the lost opportunities that result from underperformance, make the selection of the right candidate a key skill of any manager. In the arts, as in all service organizations, it is the attitude of the people that make the difference to the quality offered to customers.

The recruitment process should be planned in advance, and should accord with any personnel policies on appointments that have been developed within the organization.

A job description should be drawn up that identifies the key areas of the role, rather than one that seeks to include every possible task that the new employee might be asked to perform. At this point, a list of desired characteristics in the applicants should be identified. It is vital to be as specific as possible at this stage in order to stop applicants with inappropriate skills or experience from applying (thus saving them, and you, a great deal of wasted time and effort). However, great care must be taken to ensure that what you are asking for is relevant and will not preclude certain candidates from applying. For example, an insistence on formal qualifications may deter women or minorities from applying, as there is evidence to suggest that such groups have less access to formal education than some others.

Getting this part of the process right is of great importance, as employers may be taken to an Industrial Tribunal for sex or race discrimination, if their employment practices can be held to exclude certain sections of the community. If there is no personnel expert within the organization, as is likely in most smaller organizations, it is well worth seeking specialist advice on good recruitment practice. This can be obtained from ACAS, the UK's Advisory, Conciliation and Arbitration Service, which is a government organization with a number of regional offices, whose purpose is to provide advice to employers and employees. Its website (http://www.acas.org.uk) is a mine of useful resources on staffing issues.

At this point, the advertisement can be placed in relevant media – newspapers and journals have the advantage of being targetable, and the organization's website offers the opportunity to maximize the availability of information in advance of applications. It is good practice to include a closing date, telephone number and e-mail address in job advertisements. Inclusive organizations will also make application packs available in alternative formats (such as large print, audio and Braille). The job description and employee specification will normally be sent to candidates, with other supporting material as appropriate. A checklist of these is included in Table 9.2.

The next stage is to design the selection procedure. The normal process is an interview. However, increasingly, employers are extending the process to include a number of different interviews, a practical test, or psychometric testing of some kind. The latter test can take a number of forms, but aims to get candidates to produce a self-evaluation against a number of criteria. Most tests can identify those candidates who select the answer that they think is required, rather than give an honest assessment. People tend to have strong views about these tests, but research demonstrates that they result in about the same level of good appointments as do interviews – which is not very high! The best appointment procedures include a range of different inputs into the final choice (and these, of course, include the letter of application and references). Whatever the advantages of psychometric testing, the cost of it may well preclude smaller organizations from selecting it as an interview tool except for their most senior appointments.

Table 9.2 Appointments checklist

Job description	Include post title, main responsibilities, to whom the employee reports, for whom the employee is responsible, salary
Employee specification	Often split into 'essential' and 'desirable' characteristics
Application form	A good way of ensuring that the same information is sought from, and sent by, all candidates
Equal opportunities policy	No point in having one if you don't tell people that you do
Background material	This might contain information on the history of the organization, some examples of your work, something about the department, and a map – anything to help candidates make an intelligent application
Advertisement	Ensure as wide a readership as can be afforded
Interview	Do not disadvantage candidates by the constitution of the interviewing panel, room choice or layout, or timing. Prepare questions based around the job description and ask them of all candidates
Other exercises	Practical tests might include writing a press release, preparing a brief for a designer or working out a marketing plan for the next subscription series. Identify desired outcomes in advance. Consider asking candidates to give a formal presentation
Selection	Consider all the candidates equally on the basis of application and supporting letter, interviews, presentation, references. Be able to evidence reasons for choice
On appointment	Offer the position formally in writing. Prepare contract and induction programme. Contact unsuccessful candidates and offer a de-brief

An interview, or interviews, is likely to remain the main selection method for most appointments. Decisions need to be taken about the constitution of the panel (which might include someone from another department or, for a senior marketing appointment, a member of the board); the questions to be asked; the location of the room (will it set candidates at ease?); and the duration of the interview. Pre-set questions relating to the job description, which are asked of all candidates, are a fundamental feature of equal opportunities recruitment practice. This does not preclude different follow-up questions to ensure all candidates have an opportunity to shine. It is also acceptable to reassure candidates who cannot evidence experience or competence in a certain area, that you expect that the person you appoint may lack experience in some aspect of the job and that training can be offered to compensate for this, if appropriate. However, it is worth remembering that you may be called upon to justify why one person was appointed, and another was not, so you need yourself to be clear about what you want in the candidate. The individual appointed should have the necessary skills to contribute to the marketing function and should complement the others in the marketing team. Having designed in advance the interview process, a shortlist can be drawn up, matching individual applications to the job description and employee specification. Candidates may be informed in advance of the format that the selection process will take.

After the interview, and any other exercise that the candidates may undergo, the panel should meet to assess each applicant against the same criteria. A job offer should be made and a formal acceptance sought, which confirms salary and start date. A written contract will need to be issued subsequently. It is important to keep up to date with current legislation on employment contracts, as this is an area that does change frequently. Unsuccessful candidates may be offered a debrief on their interview. It is important to look for positive outcomes for all participants, as recruitment itself is a way of marketing the organization not only to candidates but to anyone else who might see the advertisements or hear about the process.

On the morning the new employee starts it is good practice to offer an induction. This can be as formal or informal as the organization wishes, but represents the welcome of the employer to a new member of the team. It can also include a short tour of the premises, introduction to other staff, explanations of how to get a cup of coffee or where the photocopier is, and a copy of all relevant employment policies. Above all, it offers the manager the opportunity to sell the organization solidly to the now successful candidate. It is important that they are made to feel that they have made the right decision in taking the job; and that they are a highly valued member of the team.

Team building

A marketing team, like any other, will not come together without effort. A systematic effort must be made to harmonize the individual's own objectives and goals, which are based around their career development, with the requirements of the organization. The better this harmonization, the greater the eventual contribution of the individual. Team building goes beyond this, as it seeks to create a unit to support and encourage each member, so that together their achievements amount to more than the work of each member in isolation. Marketing involves a great deal of teamwork in any context, but especially in the arts. Successful marketing teams, of whatever size, begin with the recognition that they have more in common than a shared office or line manager; they have a common purpose which needs the efforts of each individual member to achieve fulfilment.

Figure 9.3 represents the stages in team development.

According to a classic piece of research by Tuckman (1965) a team learns to work together by going through a number of stages: clarifying underlying assumptions and values; listening to one another; challenging compromises; supporting and reinforcing each other's work; sharing information and developing consensus decision-making. All members of the team should contribute. In a team situation, it is best to leave decisions until all can agree – a majority vote does not represent the optimum outcome, as it splits the team.

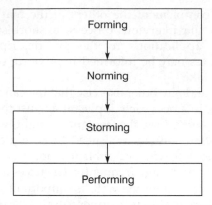

Figure 9.3 Stages in team development (adapted from Tuckman, 1965)

Volunteers as part of the team

Although unpaid, the principles of working well with volunteers are akin to those of managing employees. Points to bear in mind are:

- They will not be with you for ever – two years is a reasonable commitment to expect.
- As with Friends organizations (from which many of them will come) clear communication should reinforce their value to you – keep in touch by regular newsletter or with press releases.
- The 'motivators' and 'hygiene' factors discussed later in the chapter (Table 9.3) need to be right. Refund reasonable expenses. Offer tickets, invitations to previews, include them in first night parties.
- Include volunteers as part of the marketing team. Make sure they understand why they are doing things, and how their actions contribute to the wider marketing effort.
- Give them work to do which is within their abilities, and with which they feel comfortable.
- Make sure someone is looking after them, and ask a senior member of staff outside the department to thank them for their efforts from time to time.

Leadership

The team leader is one of the team, but with a special role. Professor John Adair argues that whereas managers focus on administration and control, leaders need to communicate and inspire others. Indeed, he sees leadership as a vocation rather than just a job, a perspective which may appeal to marketers motivated by their enthusiasm for an art form or cause (Adair, 2000). His most famous contribution to leadership literature is the idea of 'action-centred leadership', which holds in balance the task, the team, and the needs of individuals (Thomas, 1998). As shown in Figure 9.4, although these are separate there are areas of overlap – and a failure in any one area impacts on them all. Managing the marketing effort means paying attention to individuals, getting the job done, and developing the team – all at the same time.

Figure 9.4 The motivation and management of an arts marketing department (adapted from Adair, 1973)

There are many styles of leadership, and a good leader will adopt different styles in different situations and with different people. Among other definitions, the following types of leadership style can be identified within arts organizations:

- *Authoritarian:* statement rather than confrontation is the preferred mode of operation; opposition is disabled or ignored. Might be the original founder of department, or organization.
- *Managerial:* operates systems and has documented policies and procedures. Leader works with senior management team, or through line structure. Has meetings and committees.
- *Interpersonal:* high visibility and mobility; consultative and empathetic; avoids formal situations; may have problems taking decisions.
- *Adversarial:* encourages and participates in debate; believes in 'creative conflict'; uses public arena to get messages across, persuade and gain commitment.

All of these styles have advantages and disadvantages, and all managers will tend to adopt a mixture of approaches. Handy (1993) suggests that the best leadership style is the one that best fits the leader's own preference, the preferred styles of the subordinates, the particular task and the environment in which all are operating.

The leader needs to possess an impressive list of attributes, ranging from consistency to flexibility, the ability to take decisions and the ability to delegate to staff empowered to take them, the ability to provide inspirational vision and the ability to operate invisibly so that the team are self-motivating, and, perhaps, most importantly, resilience and bags of energy.

One tried-and-tested way of developing leadership skills is to adopt as a 'mentor' an older person, preferably from another department or organization, whose own leadership style and experience can be an example of good practice. This sort of mentorship can also be extended downwards, to develop the leadership skills of the rest of the team.

Case 9.1 Womentoring

Arts Training NSW, the state arts training body for New South Wales, ran a pilot mentor programme in which ten women in lower- to middle-rank management roles in Australian arts organizations were offered career development towards more senior positions. Each was fixed up with a mentor – a more senior 'friend' to act as a sounding board and advisor. One of the aims of the exercise was to develop networks across art forms and institutions, in order to create a wider framework of professional contacts for participants.

Examples of the pairings included Edwina d'Apice, manager of the Wagga Wagga City Art Gallery, who was mentored by the deputy director of Sydney's Australian Museum, and Kerri McIlvenny, executive officer of the Community Arts Association, NSW. Her mentor was the director of Carnivale – the multicultural arts organization which stages Australia's biggest annual arts festival (now over 25 years old).

Both mentees had specific objectives. D'Apice wanted ideas and skills about raising the profile of her gallery, and working more effectively with exhibition designers. McIlvenny, an Aboriginal woman herself, focused on intellectual property issues emerging from her work with Aboriginal communities seeking to become more self-sufficient. Both had mentors with specific and relevant expertise – the resources and know-how of a major national arts institution on the one hand, and an individual with wide-ranging contacts and knowledge of cultural development on the other.

Women and ethnic minorities are under-represented in senior management positions in general, and the arts are no exception. Mentoring schemes such as the Women in the Arts Mentorship Programme offer a positive framework for releasing this untapped talent into arts organizations, as well as offering both mentor and mentee a new perspective on their careers.

Source: Arts Training NSW, 2000b.

Motivation, training and staff development

Motivation in the workplace was analysed by Frederick Herzberg (1966) as comprising two different sorts of factors (see Table 9.3). His much misunderstood theory does not say that it does not matter how much or how little a member of staff is paid; but says that individuals are most motivated by growth and self-realization through their work. It is a necessary precondition of such self-realization that the environmental factors (the hygiene factors) surrounding the job should be satisfactory. This sort of thinking can be

Table 9.3 Factors affecting staff motivation

Motivating factors	Hygiene factors
Achievement	Company policy
Recognition	Working conditions
Satisfaction in the work	Salary
Responsibility	Status
Progress	Job security
Personal growth	

Source: Herzberg, 1966.

paralleled by Maslow's hierarchy of needs, which is discussed in Chapter 4. Herzberg thus advocates 'job enrichment' which might consist of additional responsibility or new projects – for which there is plenty of scope in most arts organizations!

The arts sector in general is not very good at facilitating individual self-development within the framework of a staff appraisal or review scheme, usually because of the size of the organizations in question and the resources of time and expertise available. There are, however, benefits to undergoing a formal process; it establishes that progression is something that competent staff have a right to expect, and it demonstrates the institutional commitment to developing staff to their full potential. It also means that the organization's customers are better served by more effective staff. As a marketing manager you should make it a priority to lobby for such a system if it does not already exist in your organization.

As well as formal internal development and review systems, there are many other forms of staff development other than expensive external courses.

- *Mentoring.* As mentioned above, an apprenticeship to a senior manager can be a very effective form of learning.
- *On-the-job training.* This used to be called 'sitting next to Nelly' but has since been formalized through National Vocational Qualifications at a number of levels according to various nationally-agreed industry standards.
- *Team training.* Various individuals can deliver a training session or practical workshop to their colleagues. Inputs might be sought from the press officer, the head of finance, the artistic director, heads of the different production departments or special collections etc. Anything that widens the team's appreciation of their organization, and their understanding of the inter-dependency of the different sectors, will help them in their role of promoting and marketing all aspects of the artistic work.
- *Shared training.* Arts organizations tend to be good at collaborative working. Developing opportunities for shared training is a good example of this.
- *Funding bodies.* Funding bodies may well be willing to support training activity, if the need is made clear. They often have the contacts to persuade other organizations to participate, or offer secondments.

Case 9.2 Great art well marketed

In 2001 Michael Kaiser left his post as Chief Executive of London's Royal Opera House after two years in post to take up the position of President of the Kennedy Center in Washington DC. His mission at the Royal Opera House had been to turn around an organization which (however undeservedly) represented everything the UK media love to hate about profligate arts organizations. The American Kaiser commented on his appointment that 'It does help to come from the outside, because my experience of troubled organizations is that when you are in the midst of all the problems, everyone is focused on the past. They point fingers at each other, the staff blames the board, the board blames the staff. And no one is saying, "Where do we go from here?" '

This forward-looking vision, focused on the needs of organizations as a whole rather than individual personalities or factions, is something which Kaiser's work at the Kennedy Center has continued. The Vilar Institute for Arts Management, named for its $40 million benefactor the philanthropist Alberto Vilar, was founded at the Center in 2001 to provide comprehensive management training for selected individuals who aspire to manage performing arts institutions and arts service organizations in both the public and private sector. The programme emphasizes excellence, creativity, economic problem-solving, internationalism and a commitment to new technologies. Core courses cover management, planning, technology, financial, and quantitative and communication skills within the context of arts and non-profit organizations

In its first year of operation, 150 candidates applied to the Institute from 30 countries. Twelve were selected as annual fellows, including Briton Fiona Richards, whose previous experience included seven years at London's Royal National Theatre. Her routine consists of an hour's class at the beginning of each day (in accounting, marketing, fund-raising and strategic planning) followed by work in a succession of three or four placements within the Kennedy Center itself through the year to give an insight into decision-making across the organization. The one compulsory placement is with fund-raising – demonstrating the importance placed on fund-raising for the arts in the twenty-first century. Richards comments: ' "Great art, well marketed" is a mantra I've heard from Michael Kaiser many times over the past six months. Thanks to being a product of his visionary ambition for an arts management training programme, I'm learning that those four deceptively simple words are the key to running a successful arts organization.'

Problems with staff

Inevitably there will come a time when even the best manager has to deal with a discipline issue. Failing to address difficult issues around staff is a recipe for disaster when customers are involved, so this is likely to be something a marketing manager needs to face more often than most. All organizations should have a disciplinary policy, and it is important to follow this exactly. Because a disciplinary matter may end in dismissal, it is important to be clear and to document all stages beyond the most informal preliminary ones. This will also satisfy the equal opportunities principle of offering people positive opportunities, and treating individuals equitably. More pragmatically, an arts organization with scarce resources does not want the unnecessary expense of a fine from an industrial tribunal.

Whatever the precise framework adopted by a particular institution, there are likely to be the following stages:

- Informal period of dissatisfaction, culminating in some sort of meeting to discuss the problem.
- First warning, which may be verbal but which should be recorded in written form as a safeguard. This should identify the problem and set clear targets for improvement, with a timescale. Training and support may be offered. The employer may wish to consider mitigating circumstances.
- Second warning/final warning – must be recorded in writing and be as clear as possible. The employee should be informed for how long the warning will remain on the personnel file. It should be clear what the implications of a failure to improve will be.
- Dismissal. It is likely that only a senior member of staff will have the authority to dismiss an employee. There may be a procedure for suspension, followed by an investigation and disciplinary hearing. There should be the right of representation at the hearing for the employee by a friend or trade union representative. There should be an appeals procedure, probably to the board (and the final appeal for employees with the relevant service is to an industrial tribunal, and the law courts).

For cases of serious or gross misconduct it is possible to start at any stage in the above procedure, although the majority of disciplinary cases will never get past the informal stage. That does not mean it is easy to sit down with a colleague and discuss their underachievement or unacceptable attitude. The employee should be made aware of the exact nature of the problem and what is expected in the way of improvement, but the tone of the interview needs to be positive and supportive. It can be helpful to talk over the intended interview with a trusted colleague in advance (a good example of a situation where a mentor can be invaluable). You can expect the process to be stressful – but nothing like as stressful as the consequences of not dealing with the issue.

Working with artistic and creative people

The marketing team in an arts organization will work with two different groups of creative workers – the practitioners of the art forms which are the product of their own organization, and designers and copywriters from external marketing services agencies. As the title of this book implies, marketing itself involves a considerable amount of creativity; but one of the problems of creativity is that it can largely be an unconscious process, and therefore resist deliberate management altogether. The eminent twentieth-century philosopher Bertrand Russell described his own experience of creativity as follows: 'Having, by a time of very intense concentration, planted the problem in my subconscious, it would germinate underground until, suddenly, the solution emerged with blinding clarity, so that it only remained to write down what had happened as if in a revelation' (Fletcher, 1988).

Research work carried out by psychologists and behavioural scientists, starting with Freud, has described some characteristics found in creative individuals. Like all generalizations, these are open to challenge in the case of any particular individual, but some common themes include:

- non-conformity: creativity is often associated with challenging received ideas and perceptions
- frustration: Freud argued that all creativity involves fantasy and 'a happy person never fantasizes, only an unsatisfied one'
- seeking appreciation: requiring admiration of their creative output
- sensitivity: to experience, but also to criticism
- visibility: more than most other workers, creative individuals are personally identified with their work, and its success or failure
- independence: a high degree of autonomy and identification with their peer group rather than their organization
- intelligent: although intelligent people may not be creative, creative people generally are intelligent
- the ability to work hard: driven by their standards of excellence
- poor timekeeping: meeting a deadline may be perceived as less important than getting things right

While being very wary of applying a stereotypical view of creativity to the artists with whom the marketing staff work, some understanding of their perspectives may help facilitate the relationship. For example, attending a photo call in some inconvenient location to attract publicity for a gallery's forthcoming season may not be high in the priorities of an artist currently finishing work to show there. Good communication skills – about what is required and how it is to be arranged; listening skills – about how that individual feels about what is being asked of him or her; and appreciation for what is being done, will minimize friction.

With the creative suppliers who work for the marketing team, the situation may appear more straightforward. This will not necessarily be so. Particularly at the start of the working relationship, their interpretation of a brief may be very different from yours, and they will inevitably bring their own ideas and inspiration to bear on it (or why would you employ them?). It may be necessary to be firm, as your responsibility is to have work appropriate for the house style of your organization, brilliant though you may feel the alternative to be. Problems at a later stage may be largely avoided if care is taken at the planning stage to be very clear about the brief, the deadlines and the design standards. Briefs should be in written form, and should contain accurate information about time, budgets and any other mandatory elements (such as corporate identity guidelines).

If a piece of creative work has to be rejected, and possible amendments have already been explored, then the rejection should be clear and definite. As far as possible, the explanation given should be rational, and not subjective ('I don't like it'). You will be aiming to retain the relationship in the longer term. It is also important to be honest about your own contribution to the lack of success of the project, and to pay accordingly.

Communications

As will be evident from the issues dealt with in this chapter so far, managing the marketing effort requires considerable powers of communication, both verbal and non-verbal. The most important of all of these is the skill of listening – as the saying goes, two ears to one mouth. Just as it is vital for marketing organizations to listen to their customers, so marketing managers need to listen to their organizations. Furthermore, marketers have to be adept at negotiation with external suppliers, and capable of effective internal marketing – of which two-way communication is a vital component. In this section we will explore the basics of some of these areas, starting with one of the most basic skills in communicating to groups and individuals.

Making presentations

The ability to stand up in front of an audience and speak persuasively is a great asset in arts marketing. Presentation skills are relevant in a number of areas covered in this book:

- Briefing journalists at a press conference.
- Market research debriefs to other managers or board members.
- Talking to groups about your organization with a view to encouraging their interest.
- Putting proposals to potential sponsors.
- Motivating and informing colleagues and staff.

Presentations are a personal way of communicating your organization's message. But an effortlessly assured performance does not just happen. It is the result of careful preparation and rehearsal.

Consider your audience
First of all, what do you know about the people in your audience?

- they will normally be well disposed to you, but will have high expectations
- they will listen more closely if you involve them by showing how your subject affects them
- the only access to their minds is through their senses
- seeing things helps them understand and remember them
- their concentration fades after 5 or 10 minutes
- being human they tend to remember patterns, structures and examples rather than abstract concepts
- they don't mind meaningful repetition – in fact they like to be reminded that they have understood

Presentations can fulfil a number of objectives. Is the purpose of the presentation to persuade someone of something (e.g. to sponsor your forthcoming exhibition) or is it to provide information (e.g. to announce a new season of opera)? Getting the basic purpose of the exercise clear is the best foundation for making the right decisions later on.

Deciding on content is the first of these:

- jot down all your ideas
- group them
- allocate priorities between essential details and support (rather like a press release)
- prune and select
- arrange in the best sequence for your audience's understanding

Next comes writing the script:

- this can be done in full, beforehand, but it is best to deliver from headings.
- an AIDA type structure can help (described in Chapter 6)
- use an introduction to command attention
- round off with a conclusion to review and consolidate content, with an action option

Deciding on the extent and function of visual aids is the next step. Will you need handouts, and what should their content and role be? Costing and arranging their preparation needs to be taken care of early.

The next stage is to do a 'run through' of the presentation, checking the following factors:

- appropriate visuals
- sequence
- balance
- coherence
- fulfilling objectives

After this it should be possible to amend the package to iron out ambiguities or awkwardness. It should also be possible to decide finally what materials will be necessary and prepare them accordingly. A dress rehearsal in front of a friendly colleague completes this step, and allows you to use feedback to prepare a final version.

At the end of this process you will be well prepared. It may seem an arduous exercise, but the sequence of suggested actions is meant to minimize the time spent going round in unnecessary circles. Some experienced speakers find it useful to time their presentations, which certainly helps avoid the common, but unforgivable, error of going on too long.

The presentation surroundings

Physical environment, the general importance of which to arts marketing is discussed in greater detail in Chapter 7, plays a crucial role in presentations.

Equipment needs to be checked. In an unfamiliar venue the kind of technology used may be different from what you are used to.

Furniture has its role to play. What kind of seating arrangement should apply? Is it necessary (or desirable) that the audience should have a strong sense of each other (as encouraged by a horse-shoe shaped arrangement), or should their attention be focused individually on you as speaker from serried ranks of chairs and desks? If there is a table, which side of it should you be?

Lighting is another important consideration. If you are planning to use a projector, it is necessary to achieve a good level of blackout in the presentation room. Sometimes this is not possible just by drawing the curtains, so it is necessary to do some advance investigation and establish a solution to the problem, if necessary.

Heating and ventilation are very important. Drowsiness and inattention, even nausea, are possible through a room being too stuffy. Other distractions might include extraneous noise or simply untidiness – other people's material hanging in your audience's field of view, for example. Finally, your own appearance is something which will communicate even before you open your mouth. Make sure it demonstrates respect and consideration to your audience.

Delivery

Now comes the moment of performance. It is important to maintain your audience's good opinion of you by making a good initial impression. A simple routine conquers butterflies. Here is a tried-and-tested formula:

- Introduce yourself.
- Say how delighted you are to have the opportunity of speaking to them today.
- Tell them what you are going to tell them.
- Tell them.
- Tell them what you have told them.

Eye contact is important. It will help your listeners concentrate and give you useful feedback. Smiling helps (if you can manage it). It puts both the presenter and the audience in a more relaxed and communicative state. As you continue, the contact needs to be maintained and developed. Looking at individuals, avoiding the temptation to talk to your slides or notes, keeping things simple and well structured, are all instrumental in this kind of care for your customers (in this case, your listeners). If things are going well in the presentation, you will find it flows with little effort. All the hard work has been done in the previous weeks. So, speak naturally, and use your notes as support rather than script. This will increase your chances of looking relaxed and comfortable, and help your audience's attention as well.

A little humour can enliven a presentation, but it can also be distracting, embarrassing or simply irritating. So it needs to be approached with care. The focus of the speaker needs to be on communicating first and foremost rather than being amusing or entertaining.

Visual aids

As ever in communication, simplicity, relevance and ease of comprehension make for good visual aids. When designing, or using them, the following points are worth bearing in mind:

- use space imaginatively
- ensure clear text
- diagrams can be helpful when sharing information or getting agreement
- build up gradually to complexity (if complexity is unavoidable)
- allow time for understanding
- do not leave visual aids up longer than you need or they become distractions in their own right

Negotiating with suppliers

Among the suppliers that marketing teams deal with frequently are designers, printers, media, consultants, photographers, and marketing services agencies. It is refreshing for a marketing manager to be in the position of customer, because it reinforces from the other side the principles of marketing – particularly the importance of price! As discussed throughout this book, marketing is about forging long-term relationships between suppliers and customers. Achieving such a relationship with your own suppliers can give you an insight into the advantages involved.

The negotiations between you and any supplier depend on your mutual needs being satisfied – you get the service you require at the price you can afford and they get the contract. Wherever possible, you need to strengthen your negotiating position by identifying precisely what it is that the other party values and needs. Money is, of course, a key consideration; but cash-strapped arts organizations can sometimes throw non-financial benefits into the pot such as publicity or corporate hospitality opportunities, workplace arts activity or training (the kind of extended product described in Chapter 4). In offering any sort of non-standard deal, it is important to negotiate with someone with sufficient standing to take non-standard decisions.

In other cases, the marketing manager may find himself or herself as the side with greater bargaining power; for example, in dealing with a freelance designer or photographer who is just setting up and is keen to build a portfolio of clients. It is important in these sorts of negotiations to maintain the same high standards in coming to an agreement, because a reputation for sharp practice can easily get round, and may be very destructive of other supplier relationships.

The principles of good negotiations include:

- *Preparation:* define your ideal outcome, your realistic target, and the minimum for which you would settle. Work out what you can offer, and what the other party's needs and expectations are.
- *Opening stance:* both parties reveal their negotiating stance. This is a time to listen carefully. It is important to close no doors, but at the same time make no concessions at this stage.

- *Hard bargaining:* identify the weakness in the other's position. Try to shift them nearer your own. Make conditional offers – 'I'll consider this if you are able to move on something else.' Try not to allow the other party to define the deal – you are negotiating the package you require.
- *Handshake:* judge whether there is scope for further negotiation. Agree trade-offs, and make sure both parties know exactly what has been agreed (confirm in writing). Settle practical details.

Whether or not an agreement is reached, it is good practice always to be courteous and appreciative. Although in this relationship you are the customer, you will get better service by being magnanimous in victory. It represents a failure in both parties when a customer–supplier relationship breaks down to the extent that the contract is invoked in court.

Internal communications

Handy (1993) suggests that 'poor communications are a reliable symptom of an underlying disorder in the organization or in the relationship between the people concerned'. If true this is a sobering thought, as many in arts organizations are highly critical about their internal communications. This may be compounded by the difficulties of communicating with visiting artists and companies, touring to unfamiliar venues and galleries, and the sheer multiplicity of projects and roles undertaken by workers. In addition, amateur arts companies may have to meet relatively infrequently, around the pressure of their other activities. This means that importance has to be given collectively to improving communications. All communications – written and verbal – imply dialogue: there is a sender and a receiver.

Handy identifies the following reasons for communication problems:

- perceptual bias by the receiver – ignoring unpalatable information
- omission or distortion by the sender – either consciously or unconsciously
- lack of trust – on either side
- mixed messages – contradictions between what is said, and the body language or tone which accompanies it
- overload – too much information
- distance – physical or hierarchical
- lack of clarity – jargon, woolliness, ambiguity and imprecise thinking

The marketing team has a role to play in facilitating both formal and informal communications. Rumours are less likely to take root where all staff feel involved, and have access to information. This contributes towards the quality of customer service by having a direct effect on improved morale.

Formal communications may include briefing sheets, a staff bulletin, staff meetings, focus groups, upward information such as the show reports, box office printouts, management reports. Informal communications include the famous meetings in corridors, the grapevine, gossip and rumour. Marketing departments in arts organizations need to be at the centre of the internal buzz – not only as a way of achieving 'buy-in' to marketing ideas throughout an organization, but also as a source of the kind of stories that interest the press (as discussed in Chapter 6).

The importance of such informal communication should never be under-estimated. One commentator on management practice, Henry Mintzberg, found that successful managers spend most of their time responding to external stimuli, and cherish 'soft' information, in the belief that today's gossip is tomorrow's fact (Mintzberg, 1989). Keeping an ear to the grapevine and analysing what is heard can help early identification of problems and issues that are surfacing both internally and externally. People operating daily in a particular environment know a lot about what is going on. Rumour, on the other hand, may be a symptom of unrest, fear or hostility that needs to be addressed, even if the actual rumour is without foundation.

Internal marketing

Organizations that treat their own employees as customers are practising internal marketing. It has been defined as the process of 'attracting, developing, motivating qualified employees through job-products that satisfy their needs' (Berry and Parasuraman, 1991). The idea of a 'job-product' aimed at satisfying the needs of an employee might sound a little strange, until you consider that the needs in question centre on what employees require in order to be able to satisfy their customers. So, alongside the kind of motivational and hygiene factors discussed earlier in this chapter, the 'job-products' available need to offer benefits to the employee such as information and understanding of the organization's products and services, skills and delegated authority to deal with their own customers effectively, and opportunities to take pride in their work. In practice, for an arts organization such as a theatre, this would involve clear communication of the theatre's mission and policy, regular updates (perhaps through departmental meetings) on developments and decisions, the opportunity to experience performances and other theatre offerings as a customer (either free or at a discount), adequate training and development (particularly for customer-facing staff) and the chance to share and contribute to the organization's vision.

Getting this 'marketing mix' right for staff who never meet external customers is every bit as important as getting it right for people who deal with the paying audience every day. This is because internal marketing emphasizes the links between everyone in an organization and its final customer. So even someone who has an office job in the finance department of a major museum or gallery can make a difference to the quality of experience of a gallery visitor in the long term by, for example, ensuring that the provision of financial information on which programming decisions are made is speedy and accurate. The idea is rather like the 'invisible organiza-tion' depicted in the Servuction model developed by Bateson and Hoffman (1999) and discussed in Chapter 4. The final customer cannot see the finance department, and might not even know it exists. But because of its effective-ness, the customer benefits through, let us say, a more ambitious exhibition programme brought about by the organization's confidence in the accuracy of its planning information.

Clearly, internal marketing has important links with human resource development and the senior management direction of an organization. It is, however, an essential point of leverage in transforming the orientation of an arts organization towards the customer. Marketing managers can take the lead in three simple ways:

- Make sure everyone in the organization, from the cleaner to the chief executive, gets regular briefing on its successes, its plans, and soundbite details ('Did you know we have exhibited more new developing world sculpture than any other UK gallery – we are a known centre of excellence, according to the British Council?'). Feeling proud of your organization, as we have seen above, is a powerful motivator, and can turn staff into knowledgeable and credible advocates in the local community.
- Never miss an opportunity to explain the importance of marketing to everybody in terms of the organization's ability to survive and develop its work. Practical ways of helping can be identified, from taking leaflets to distribution outlets near where an employee lives, to coming up with an exciting angle for a press story.
- Don't forget to explain the potential damage that can be done by inappropriate publicity or marketing, so that the whole organization is working with the marketing department to ensure consistency in approach.

Finally, in case of a major disaster, be open with all employees. If a potential scandal is lurking which could cause serious adverse publicity, share the facts with all staff and trust them to understand the necessity for a common approach to the crisis: 'A well-managed crisis develops a sense of togetherness among employees – in the spirit of "all for one, and one for all". This can be an enormous gain for the company, affecting the working climate long after the crisis has ended' (Ten Berge, 1990).

The board of governors

A key market segment of internal customers for any arts marketing manager is the board of governors, or management committee. These unpaid volunteers can act as superb ambassadors for the organization, as they are often pre-eminent in their own sphere, or can be a distraction or irrelevance if the relationship is not managed successfully.

Different boards manage their affairs differently, and may adopt a more or a less hands-on approach. In a sense, they represent the apex of the upside-down triangle in Figure 9.5. Their role therefore is to support the management in supporting the artists who create or perform for their various attenders and audiences. This support can best be exercised by the board confining their role to long-term policy-making, allowing the executive management of the organization to get on with the marketing planning and implementation.

> Trustees are the guardians and interpreters of the values and purposes of an organization. Their primary concern is to clarify principles, to develop insight, to maintain standards and chart a direction which will further the purpose of the organization. Trustees are distinguished not so much by what they do but by the way they see. (Spiegal and Turner, 1993)

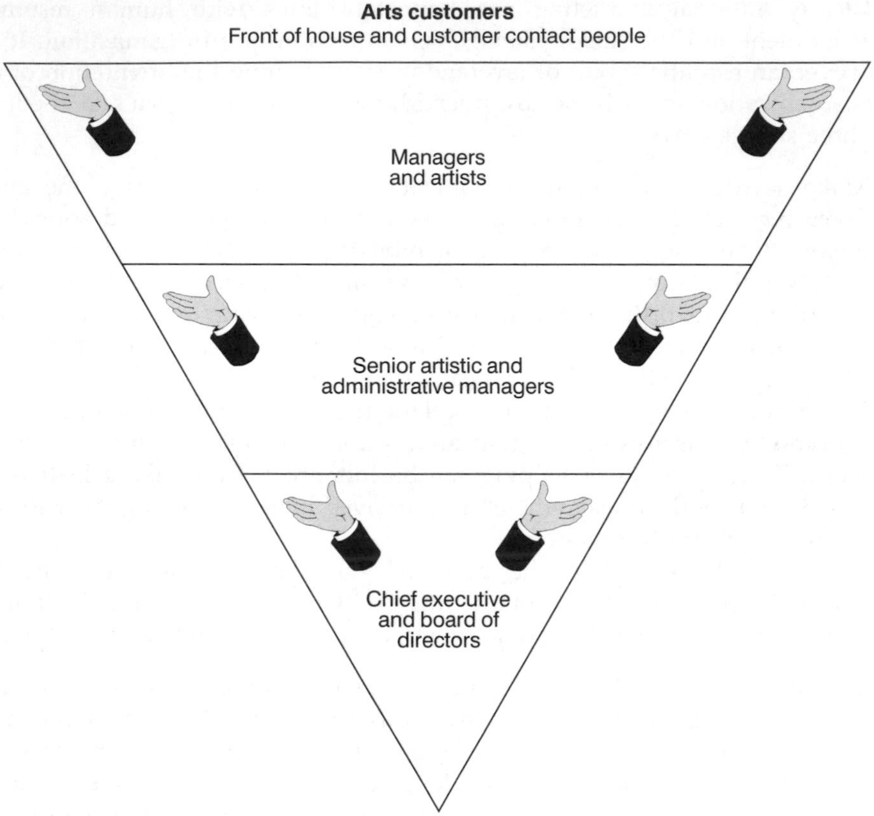

Arts customers
Front of house and customer contact people

Managers
and artists

Senior artistic and
administrative managers

Chief executive
and board of
directors

Figure 9.5 Supporting arts customers starts with the board (adapted from Nordstrom Organization Chart: Peters, 1988)

Good communications with the board will facilitate their thinking, and help them in their long-term planning. At the same time, a greater knowledge of the way the organization is run may help preclude helpfully-meant but inappropriate suggestions ('Your new leaflet must have cost a lot of money, surely you could get someone to sponsor it?'). Governors can be a great asset in publicity terms for the marketing team and, with a good brief, can be persuasive advocates with people of influence.

Managing yourself

Grappling with the challenges of the budget, the team, and communication, while attempting to apply the marketing mix: product, price, place and promotion, the beleaguered arts marketer might start to have serious doubts about his or her chosen career path. Better resourced companies probably have more staff carrying out the marketing function, and may well be able to offer greater training and support. Most people who work in the arts find compensations in the excitement and variety of the work they do, and the

Table 9.4 Ten principles of good management practice

---

1 Accept that you are the one person you can actually change.

2 If you haven't got enough time, blame yourself.

3 Respect other people's views – yours may be wrong.

4 Don't appoint people because they remind you of yourself.

5 Never assume they heard what you said, or understood what you meant.

6 Catch people doing things well – and tell them so.

7 Learn from mistakes and problems.

8 Persuade yourself, before you try to persuade others.

9 Make it easy for people to give you what you want.

10 Don't live in the past – it's gone, and was never really like that.

Source: Adapted from Nicholson, 1992.

satisfaction of being associated with a product that brings so much richness into people's lives: 'The importance of the customer is not how much they spend on the arts but how much they participate in the arts, and how much they benefit from art' (Pick, 1994).

However, the work can at times be highly pressured, and it is necessary to develop techniques for coping with this (see Table 9.4).

Time management

For those who, while competent in other spheres of management practice, have problems with time, it might help to reflect on the following (Drucker, 1999):

- time is a unique resource
- the supply of time is totally inelastic
- time is perishable and cannot be stored
- time is in short supply

Thinking about time in this way, as a valuable resource, can allow the same sorts of resource management techniques as have been described above for finance and human resources. Good planning is the key.

Most people use lists and diaries as the key planning tools. Lists can then be prioritized:

A   must be done today
B   should be done, if time
C   might be done, if time

It is important to use your analytical powers on this exercise, as it is necessary to distinguish between 'important' and 'urgent' tasks. Urgent tasks may need to be done first, but should only be allowed to take up time if they are also important – which may well not be the case.

Table 9.5 Avoid time-wasters

- Poor meetings
- Long telephone calls
- Unwanted visitors
- Crisis management
- Panic
- Background reading
- Other people's paperwork

If there are too many 'A' tasks to manage, other resources can be substituted – i.e. people or money. In other words, tasks can be delegated or farmed out to an external agency.

Learning to say 'no' is an important time-management technique, and this may mean saying no to yourself, for example not becoming involved in a fascinating project that is not your job (see Table 9.5).

A great deal of time can be saved by adopting structured techniques in common communication activities such as letters and e-mails or telephone calls. For example, when using the telephone it is a good idea to group outgoing calls in one particular period rather than making them intermittently throughout the day. Not only will this make you think in advance about the purpose and necessity of the call, it will mean you keep each as brief as possible in order to move on to the next.

You can structure written communication to maximum effect (in the minimum time) by applying the most basic of marketing principles – customer-orientation. Instead of focusing on what you want the recipient of the communication to know, think or do, why not consider the matter from their point of view? What are they likely to want to know when they receive your letter or see your e-mail in their inbox? The three most likely questions to cross their minds are:

- Why is this person writing to me?
- What's in it for me?
- What do I have to do?

This leads to three essential sections in a piece of written communication:

- *Purpose:* I am writing to invite you to a briefing meeting on 2 August . . .
- *Benefit:* We are hoping to place the design work with a local agency . . .
- *Follow-up:* Please can you reply to me by Tuesday on this?

This is a flexible model, but using it as a basic template for written communication can save a surprising amount of time (and paper).

Meetings

Everybody who attends a meeting, whether or not they are chairing it, needs to work at making the meeting effective. However, effective chairing is an enormously valuable service to participants. A great deal can be learned by observing other people doing it well. This includes:

- setting and circulating an agenda
- starting on time
- encouraging everybody who needs to contribute to do so
- keeping to the point
- not interrupting
- summing up
- not going round in circles
- being willing to defer a decision
- making sure that agreements are recorded

The co-operative style of working adopted by many arts organizations may make it harder to chair a meeting in a firm way, and there are, of course, different sorts of meetings. The best method of obtaining everybody's consent is to get their agreement in advance on the length of the meeting and the approximate time that should be devoted to each item. Everybody should then stick to this.

Management diary

A helpful way of maximizing the value of your experience towards your personal development is to keep a management diary (also known as a reflective journal) which allows you to analyse your performance in your working life. If you are doing any reading, you can relate your own experience to the theoretical material being suggested in the books. The real value of a management diary is that it allows you to reflect on your practice over time. This can help you both to see how you are developing, and to identify any particular issues or problems that surface again and again.

Entries need only be short, and occasional. They should be concerning things that immediately rise into your mind, because they are the issues that are really concerning you – a missed deadline, a meeting that went wrong, a wasted opportunity, or unexpected tribute.

All workers need to learn for themselves the difference between being 'efficient' and being 'effective'. Being efficient involves doing things right; being effective means doing the right thing. A management diary can help you to identify the difference between the two in your own work.

Summary

The focus of this chapter has been on the different management functions and processes which are aspects of working life as a marketing practitioner in an arts environment.

This book has emphasized marketing's role in the development of long-term relationships with customers, audiences, attenders, funders and a complex web of other people and organizations who interact with an arts practitioner or organization. An effective marketing professional will have this definition in mind when managing human and financial resources, and in dealing with internal and external customers and suppliers. The source of the energy and commitment which distinguishes a good marketer is fed by an ability to continue to learn, both from your own experience and from the good practice of others.

Key concepts

board of governors
budget
communications
equal opportunities
internal marketing
leadership
management
management diary
mentoring

motivation
negotiation
organizational culture
organizational structure
power
recruitment
team building
time management
training

Discussion questions

1 Imagine you are managing the marketing budget for an amateur production of the *The Pirates of Penzance*. How would you quantify the resources you need, and how would you ensure you operated within those resources?
2 It is six months into the financial year of your organization. How can you satisfy the administrative director that the marketing budget is being controlled effectively?
3 What advice would you give the newly-formed management committee of an arts project aimed at young offenders as they draw up plans to recruit a project manager?
4 As press officer of a national touring orchestra, how might you facilitate internal communications.
5 What are the most important characteristics of a good marketing manager in the arts? Can these be learnt?

Case study: Opera co-operation

The Sydney Opera House is one of the most instantly recognizable buildings in the world, with a reputation for being at the leading edge of architectural design. Under the four-year directorship of Chief Executive Michael Lynch, who left Sydney for the top job at London's South Bank Centre in 2002, it has established itself as an innovator in organizational development as well.

Lynch took over the running of the iconic Australian institution in 1998, after a career in theatre management culminating in his charismatic leadership of the Australia Council, the innovative national arts support body. His stewardship coincided with preparations for two of the biggest events in the House's history – New Year's Eve 1999 and the Sydney Olympics of 2000. Events like this can galvanize an organization into new ways of approaching its work, and Lynch took advantage of the opportunity to recreate the House in the image of a 'learning organization'.

This term, popularized by US management guru Peter Senge in his 1990 classic *The Fifth Discipline*, describes an organization pledged to testing, developing and sharing experience in a systematic way, in much the same way that individual human beings learn. Of course, the advantage of an organization is that the whole is greater than the individual parts – and so placing learning as a core activity can have a powerful effect on building and multiplying the organization's capacity. To put it another way, 'its members are continually focused on enhancing and expanding their collective awareness and capabilities' (Senge *et al.*, 1994). Gaining the commitment and participation of staff at all levels has been the key to the success of this process at the House. Lynch puts it thus: 'The approach we have adopted is to encourage our staff to take part in how the work of the House is done. The result is a workplace where staff members are empowered to make an individual contribution to the development of the organization. It is a workplace that encourages personal growth, where innovation, performance excellence and a "can do" attitude are recognized and rewarded.'

Central to the process was the formation of multi-disciplinary Project Teams involving colleagues of different levels of seniority and from different functional backgrounds. Their task was to prepare for the major events at the turn of the century as well as a series of related issues such as readying the organization for Y2K computer compliance and the introduction of a new Goods and Services Tax. Providing the context of necessary cultural change was the task of a central team, also drawn from different levels and departments in the organization. The Concept Team, as this was called, focused on the task of developing the institution itself and the individuals who work in it.

As a result, the Sydney Opera House is now a flagship institution, not only in Australia but internationally. The list of initiatives stemming from the learning organization development include:

- The implementation of ReaL – standing for Relationship, Empowerment and Leadership – an internal staff development programme aimed at broadening leadership and skills throughout the House.
- The accreditation of the institution as a Registered Training Organization, capable of delivering the full suite of industry-based qualifications in entertainment (the parallel of the UK's National Vocational Qualifications system).
- A new focus on developing opportunities for indigenous Australians in the performing arts and entertainments industries. Lynch told a conference at Arts Training New South Wales at the end of 2000 'It was appalling that this organization had one Aboriginal employee three years ago. It's just not good enough in terms of taking leadership positions to be in a situation on such a critical site that we do not have Aboriginal and Torres Strait Islanders' employees.' The House now offers a programme of traineeships targeted at these communities in the areas of Theatre Technical Services and Front of House, and regularly showcases the talents of contemporary indigenous Australian artists.

Lynch summed up the achievements and future potential of his learning organization to the same conference: 'We have huge knowledge advantages, huge intellectual capital sitting within this building, that we need to capitalize on, we need to be able to seize the advantage to use our people and our expertise, to tap those opportunities throughout Asia [where the first decade of the twenty-first century is seeing an unprecedented expansion in the number of Asian performing arts venues] and throughout the rest of the world. And we can do all sorts of interesting things in terms of online opportunities to provide these solutions.'

Sources: Arts Training NSW, 2000a; BBC News Online, 2002; http://www.sydneyoperahouse.com/h/m_story_fs2.html, accessed 18 January 2003; Senge, 1990; Senge et al., 1994.

Questions

1 Thinking of an arts organization with which you are familiar, what are the main obstacles to becoming a learning organization, and how might internal marketing help overcome them?
2 Michael Lynch mentions online opportunities to provide solutions. In what ways can technology be harnessed to extend the benefits of organizational learning outside its boundaries?
3 Major external events such as the Sydney Olympics led to radical organizational change at the Sydney Opera House. What effects would you expect such change to have on its attitude to and practice of marketing and audience development?

References

Adair, J. (1973) *Action Centred Leadership*. McGraw Hill.

Adair, J. (2000) *How to Find your Vocation: A guide to discovering the work you love*. SCM Press

Anthony, R.N. (1988) *The Management Control Function*. Harvard Business School Press.

Arts Training NSW (2000a) 'Forum Speech: Michael Lynch addresses the Arts Futures Forum: Investing in the Arts' (available at: http://www.arts-trainingnsw.com.au/resources/Michael_Lynch.html. Accessed 20 August 2002).

Arts Training NSW (2000b) 'Research Project: Project 3 – Women in the arts mentorship programme' (available at: http://www.artstrainingnsw.com.au/about_arts_training/research_project_3.html. Accessed 20 August 2002).

BBC News Online (2002) 'Sydney boss comes to South Bank', Entertainment/Arts section, 22 May (available at: http://news.bbc.co.uk/I/hi/entertainment/arts/2001949.htm. Accessed 20 August 2002).

Bateson, John and Hoffman, Douglas (1999) *Managing Services Marketing: Text and readings.* The Dryden Press Series in Marketing, Thomson Learning.

Ten Berge, D. (1990) *The First 24 Hours.* Basil Blackwell.

Berry, L.L. and Parasuraman, A. (1991) *Marketing Services: Competing through quality.* Free Press.

Burns, T. and Stalker, G.M. (1961) *The Management of Innovation.* Tavistock Press.

Drucker, P.F. (1999) *The Effective Executive*, Butterworth-Heinemann.

Fletcher, W. (1988) *Creative People.* Hutchinson Business Books.

Freud, S. (1959) *Creative Writers and Daydreaming.* Hogarth Press.

Handy, C. (1993) *Understanding Organisations*, 4th ed. Penguin Books.

Herzberg, F. (1966) *Work and the Nature of Man.* World Publishing.

Holden, J. (2002) 'Why are there not currently more successful leaders of arts organisations and museums, and why are there not more suitable candidates for these posts?', Discussion Paper prepared for the Clore Duffield Foundation, January 2002 (available at: http://www.cloreduffield.org.uk. Accessed 2 August 2002).

James, J. (2001) 'Campaign Strategy', Sauce: Hot Tips for Effective Arts Promotion, Australia Council for the Arts (available at: http://www.fuel 4arts.com/sauce/staging/04_campaign_strategy/tips/expenditure.htm. Accessed 20 August 2002).

Jones, C. (2001) 'Discrimination in the arts workplace', *ArtsProfessional*, 17 December, 5–6.

Kanter, R.M. (1983) *The Change Masters.* Allen & Unwin.

Kanter, R.M. (1989) *When Giants Learn to Dance.* Simon & Schuster.

Lebrecht, N. (2000) *Covent Garden.* Simon & Schuster.

McLean, A. and Marshall, J. (1993) 'Intervening in cultures', Working Paper, University of Bath.

Mintzberg, H. (1989) *Mintzberg on Management.* Collier Macmillan.

National Endowment for the Arts (2001) Michael Kaiser Keynote Address to National Council on the Arts, 144th Meeting, 2 November (available at: http://arts.endow.gov/explore/Council11–01/Kaiser.html. Accessed 20 August 2002).

Nicholson, J. (1992) *How Do You Manage?* Business Matters Management Guides, BBC Consumer Publishing.

Peters, T. (1988) *Thriving on Chaos.* Macmillan.

Pick, J. (1994) 'A pick up the arts: arts and economics . . .', *Mailout*, June/July, 5.

Richards, F. (2002) 'Hands-on management training', *ArtsProfessional*, 25 March, 9.

Schein, E.H. (1985) *Organisational Culture and Leadership.* Jossey-Bass.

Senge, P. (1990) *The Fifth Discipline.* Currency Doubleday.

Senge, P., Kleiner, A., Roberts, C., Ross, R.B. and Smith, B.J. (1994) *The Fifth Discipline Fieldbook: Strategies and tools for building a learning organisation.* Nicholas Brealey Publishing.

Spiegal, B. and Turner, P. (1993) 'Common knowledge, common ground', *Mailout*, June/July, 19–21.

Thomas, N. (ed.) (1998) *The John Adair Handbook of Management and Leadership*. Thorogood.

Tuckman, B.W. (1965) 'Developmental sequences in small groups', *Psychological Bulletin*, Vol. 63, No. 6, 384–99.

Further reading

Anyone interested in further reading around the subjects raised in this book will find the following a useful starting point:

Magazines and journals

ArtsProfessional: a fortnightly magazine for arts managers published by Arts Intelligence Ltd (www.artsprofessional.co.uk).

ArtsReach: a monthly magazine of arts case studies and debate, published in California (www.artsreach.com).

Arts Research Digest: a summary of recently published arts research and other reports, published three times a year (www.arts-research-digest.com).

International Arts Manager: a monthly round-up of news and features published by Arts Publishing International (www.api.co.uk).

International Journal of Arts Management: an academic journal published three times a year by the University of Montreal in collaboration with the International Association for Arts and Cultural Management (www.hec.ca/ ijam).

Journal of Arts Management, Law and Society: American scholarly commentary mapping cultural, social and legal issues. Published quarterly by Helderf Publications (www.helderf.org/html/body_jamls.html).

Journal of Arts Marketing: the professional journal of the Arts Marketing Association (www.a-m-a.co.uk).

Mailout: a bi-monthly magazine for people involved in the community arts (www.e-mailout.org).

Museums Journal: the monthly magazine of the Museums Association (www.museumsassociation.org).

Prompt: the magazine of the Theatrical Management Association (www.tmauk.org).

Also, see the website at www.fuel4arts.com

Books

Abbott, S. and Webb, B. (1996) *Fine Art Publicity.* Allworth Press.

Colbert, F., Nantel, J., Bilodeau, S. and Poole, W. (2001) *Marketing Culture and the Arts,* 2nd ed. HEC.

Cowen, T. (1998) *In Praise of Commercial Culture.* Harvard University Press.

Diggle, K. (1994) *Arts Marketing.* Rhinegold.

Kotler, N.G. and Kotler, P. (1998) *Museums Strategy and Marketing.* Jossey-Bass.

Kotler, P. and Andreasen, A.R. (1996) *Strategic Marketing for Non-Profit Organizations,* 5th ed. Prentice-Hall.

Kotler, P. and Scheff, J. (1997) *Standing Room Only.* Harvard Business School Press.

Lavender, P. (ed.) (1995) *Market the Arts! An anthology of effective research, planning, implementation and follow up,* revised ed. Arts Action Issues.

Maclean, F. (1997) *Marketing the Museum.* Routledge.

Maitland, H. (2000) *The Marketing Manual.* Arts Marketing Association.

Melillo, J.V. (ed.) (1983) *Market the Arts!* Foundation for the Extension and Development of the American Professional Theater.

Morison, B.G. and Dalgleish, J.G. (1987) *Waiting in the Wings: A larger audience for the arts and how to develop it.* American Council for the Arts.

Newman, D. (1981) *Subscribe Now! Building arts audiences through dynamic subscription promotion.* Theater Communications Group.

Raymond, C. (1999) *Essential Theatre: The successful management of theatres and venues which present the performing arts.* Arts Council of England.

Reiss, A. (1995) *Don't Just Applaud – Send Money! The most successful strategies for funding and marketing the arts.* Theater Communications Group.

Rentschler, R. (2000) *Innovative Arts Marketing.* Allen & Unwin.

Shagan, R. (1995) *Booking and Tour Management for the Performing Arts.* Allworth Press.

Tomlinson, R. (1993) *Boxing Clever.* Arts Council of Great Britain.

Booklets, reports and guides

Arts & Business (2001) *The Sponsorship Manual.* Arts & Business.

Baker, T. (2000) *Stop Re-inventing the Wheel.* Association of British Orchestras.

Durie, J., Watson, N. and Pham, A. (1998) *Marketing Your Film Around the World: A guide for independent film makers.* Silman-James Press.

Forrester, S. (1999) *Arts Funding Guide,* 5th ed. DSC.

Galvin, A. (2000) *How Much?* Sheffield Theatres Trust.

Hadley, D. (2001) *Boost Your Performance: Writing your marketing action plan*. Scottish Arts Council.

Hill, E. (2000) *Commissioning Market Research*. Arts Marketing Association.

Hill, E. (ed.) (2001) *Targeting the Now Generation: A case study on marketing the arts to 15–19 year olds*. Arts Marketing Association.

Hilton, J. (1997) *The Arts Promoter's Pack: A guide to putting on an arts event for small-scale venues and promoters*. East Midlands Arts.

Hodge, S., James, J. and Lawson, A. (1998) *Miles Ahead: Arts marketing that works in regional Australia*. Australia Council.

Ings, R. (2001) *Funky on Your Flyer: A guide to reaching younger audiences*. Arts Council of England.

Lathrop, T. and Pettigrew, J. (1999) *This Business of Music Marketing and Promotion*. Watson-Guptill.

Lawrie, A. (2001) *The Complete Guide to Business and Strategic Planning for Voluntary Organisations*, 2nd ed. DSC.

Maitland, H. (1998) *The Golden Guide: Marketing for touring companies*. Arts Council of England.

Maitland, H. (2000) *A Guide to Audience Development*, 2nd ed. Arts Council of England.

Maitland, H. (2000) *Is It Time for Plan B?* Arts Marketing Association.

Millman, A. (1999) *Prove It! A practical guide to market research for museums and visitor attractions*. McCann Mathews Millman.

Rawlings-Jackson, V. (1996) *Where Now? Theatre subscription selling in the 90s*. Arts Council of England.

Rawlings-Jackson, V. and Shaw, P. (eds) (1994) *Paying Attention: A guide to customer care in the arts*. Arts Council of England.

Rogers, R. (1998) *Audience Development: Collaborations between education and marketing*. Arts Council of England.

Tomlinson, R. (1998) *Box Office Marketing Guides*. Arts Council of England.

Tomlinson, R. (1999) *Data Protection: A guide to the Data Protection Acts*. Arts Marketing Association.

Verwey, P. (1998) *Market Planning: Guidance on the planning process for marketing strategies and campaigns*. Arts Council of England.

Voluntary Arts Network (2001) *Mapping the Future: A guide to business planning for small arts organisations*. Voluntary Arts Network.

Author index

Index

Marketing titles from Butterworth-Heinemann

Student List

Creating Powerful Brands (second edition), Leslie de Chernatony and Malcolm McDonald

Customer Relationship Management, Simon Knox, Stan Maklan, Adrian Payne, Joe Peppard and Lynette Ryals

Direct Marketing in Practice, Brian Thomas and Matthew Housden

eMarketing eXcellence, P. R. Smith and Dave Chaffey

Essential Law for Marketers, Ardi Kolah

Fashion Marketing, Margaret Bruce and Tony Hines

Innovation in Marketing, Peter Doyle and Susan Bridgewater

Internal Marketing, Pervaiz Ahmed and Mohammed Rafiq

International Marketing (third edition), Stanley J. Paliwoda and Michael J. Thomas

Integrated Marketing Communications, Tony Yeshin

Key Customers, Malcolm McDonald, Beth Rogers and Diana Woodburn

Marketing Briefs, Sally Dibb and Lyndon Simkin

Marketing in Travel and Tourism (third edition), Victor T. C. Middleton with Jackie R. Clarke

Marketing Plans (fifth edition), Malcolm McDonald

Marketing: the One Semester Introduction, Geoff Lancaster and Paul Reynolds

Market-Led Strategic Change (third edition), Nigel F. Piercy

Relationship Marketing for Competitive Advantage, Adrian Payne, Martin Christopher, Moira Clark and Helen Peck

The Fundamentals and Practice of Marketing (fourth edition), John Wilmshurst and Adrian Mackay

The New Marketing, Malcolm McDonald and Hugh Wilson

Relationship Marketing: Strategy & Implementation, Helen Peck, Adrian Payne, Martin Christopher and Moira Clark

Strategic Marketing Management (second edition), Richard M. S. Wilson and Colin Gilligan

Strategic Marketing: Planning and Control (second edition), Graeme Drummond and John Ensor

Successful Marketing Communications, Cathy Ace

Tales from the Market Place, Nigel F. Piercy

The CIM Handbook of Export Marketing, Chris Noonan

The Fundamentals of Advertising (second edition), John Wilmshurst and Adrian Mackay

The Marketing Book (fifth edition), Michael J. Baker (ed.)

Total Relationship Marketing (second edition), Evert Gummesson

Professional list

Advalue, Leslie Butterfield (ed.)

Brand New Justice: the upside of global branding, Simon Anholt

Cause Related Marketing, Sue Adkins

Creating Value, Shiv S. Mathur and Alfred Kenyon

Customer Relationship Management, Simon Knox, Stan Maklan, Adrian Payne, Joe Peppard and Lynette Ryals

Cybermarketing (second edition), Pauline Bickerton and Matthew Bickerton
Cyberstrategy, Pauline Bickerton, Matthew Bickerton and Kate Simpson-Holley
Direct Marketing in Practice, Brian Thomas and Matthew Housden
e-Business, J. A. Matthewson
Effective Promotional Practice for eBusiness, Cathy Ace
Essential Law for Marketers, Ardi Kolah
Excellence in Advertising (second edition), Leslie Butterfield (ed.)
Fashion Marketing, Margaret Bruce and Tony Hines
Financial Services and the Multimedia Revolution, Paul Lucas, Rachel Kinniburgh and
    Donna Terp
From Brand Vision to Brand Evaluation, Leslie de Chernatony
Go-to-Market Strategy, Lawrence Friedman
Internal Marketing, Pervaiz Ahmed and Mohammed Rafiq
Marketing Made Simple, Geoff Lancaster and Paul Reynolds
Marketing Professional Services, Michael Roe
Marketing Strategy (second edition), Paul Fifield
Market-Led Strategic Change (third edition), Nigel F. Piercy
Relationship Marketing (second edition), Martin Christopher, Adrian Payne and
    David Ballantyne
The New Marketing, Malcolm McDonald and Hugh Wilson
The Channel Advantage, Lawrence Friedman and Tim Furey
The CIM Handbook of Export Marketing, Chris Noonan
The Committed Enterprise, Hugh Davidson
The Fundamentals of Corporate Communications, Richard Dolphin
The Marketing Plan in Colour, Malcolm McDonald and Peter Morris
Total Email Marketing, Dave Chaffey

Forthcoming
Creating Powerful Brands (third edition), Leslie de Chernatony and Malcolm
    McDonald
Creative Arts Marketing (second edition), Liz Hill, Terry O'Sullivan and Catherine
    O'Sullivan
Customer Relationship Management, Francis Buttle
Hospitality Marketing, David Bowie and Francis Buttle
International Retail Marketing, Margaret Bruce and Christopher Moore
Marketing Finance, Keith Ward
Marketing Graffiti, Mike Saren
Marketing Logistics (second edition), Martin Christopher and Helen Peck
Marketing Research for Managers (third edition), Sunny Crouch and Matthew Housden
Market Segmentation, Malcolm McDonald and Ian Dunbar
Marketing Strategy (third edition), Paul Fifield
Political Marketing, Phil Harris and Dominic Wring
Principles of Retailing, John Fernie, Suzanne Fernie and Christopher Moore
Public Relations: contemporary issues and techniques, Paul Baines, John Egan and Frank
    Jefkins
Retail Strategy, Christine Cuthbertson et al
Strategic Marketing Planning, Colin Gilligan and Richard M. S. Wilson

For more information on all these titles, as well as the ability to buy online, please
visit **www.bh.com/marketing**